Understanding
'race' and ethnicity

Also available in the series

Understanding the mixed economy of welfare (Second edition)
Edited by Martin Powell

"This book provides an up-to-date account of welfare pluralism that is both accessible to students and likely to revitalise an important debate within social policy.
A must-read for academics and students alike." Kirk Mann, Senior Lecturer in Social Policy, University of Leeds, about the first edition.
PB £21.99 (US$36.95) ISBN 978-1-4473-3322-7 **HB** £75.00 (US$115.00) **ISBN** 978-1-4473-3321-0
250 pages January 2019
INSPECTION COPY AVAILABLE

Understanding social security (Third edition)
Edited by Jane Millar and Roy Sainsbury

"An indispensable, up-to-date guide to the UK social security system written by the country's leading experts in a clear and engaging style." Karen Rowlingson, University of Birmingham
PB £28.99 (US$49.50) **ISBN** 978-1-4473-3947-2
280 pages April 2018
INSPECTION COPY AVAILABLE

Understanding the cost of welfare (Third edition)
Howard Glennerster

"Understanding the costs and financing of welfare has rarely been so lively, engaging and real. Howard Glennerster has produced a text of outstanding scholarship, essential for undergraduate and postgraduate courses right across the social sciences."
Chris Deeming, Reviews Editor for the *Journal of Social Policy* and Chancellor's Fellow and Senior Lecturer, University of Strathclyde
PB £26.99 (US$45.95) **ISBN** 978-1-4473-3404-0 **HB** £70.00 (US$110.00) **ISBN** 978-1-4473-3403-3
288 pages May 2017
INSPECTION COPY AVAILABLE

Understanding health and social care (Third edition)
Jon Glasby

"This welcome third edition updates a most useful textbook for UK social science and social policy students. Its policy analysis is also particularly relevant to professional readers seeking to know how we arrived at the state we're in." Jill Manthorpe, Director of the Social Care Workforce Research Unit, King's College London
PB £21.99 (US$36.95) **ISBN** 978-1-4473-3121-6 **HB** £75.00 (US$110.00) **ISBN** 978-1-4473-3120-9
232 pages January 2017
INSPECTION COPY AVAILABLE

For a full listing of all titles in the series visit www.policypress.co.uk

www.policypress.co.uk

INSPECTION COPIES AND ORDERS AVAILABLE FROM
Marston Book Services • PO BOX 269 • Abingdon • Oxon OX14 4YN UK
INSPECTION COPIES
Tel: +44 (0) 1235 465500 • Fax: +44 (0) 1235 465556 • Email: inspections@marston.co.uk
ORDERS
Tel: +44 (0) 1235 465500 • Fax: +44 (0) 1235 465556 • Email: direct.orders@marston.co.uk

Understanding
'race' and ethnicity

Theory, history, policy and practice

Second edition

Edited by Sangeeta Chattoo, Karl Atkin, Gary Craig
and Ronny Flynn

First edition published in 2012, Second edition published in Great Britain in 2019 by

Policy Press
University of Bristol
1-9 Old Park Hill
Bristol
BS2 8BB
UK
t: +44 (0)117 954 5940
pp-info@bristol.ac.uk
www.policypress.co.uk

North America office:
Policy Press
c/o The University of Chicago Press
1427 East 60th Street
Chicago, IL 60637, USA
t: +1 773 702 7700
f: +1 773-702-9756
sales@press.uchicago.edu
www.press.uchicago.edu

British Library Cataloguing in Publication Data
A catalogue record for this book is available from the British Library

Library of Congress Cataloging-in-Publication Data
A catalog record for this book has been requested

ISBN 978-1-4473-3965-6 hardcover
ISBN 978-1-4473-3966-3 paperback
ISBN 978-1-4473-3967-0 ePub
ISBN 978-1-4473-3968-7 Mobi
ISBN 978-1-4473-3969-4 ePdf

The right of Sangeeta Chattoo, Karl Atkin, Gary Craig and Ronny Flynn to be identified as editors of this work has been asserted by them in accordance with the Copyright, Designs and Patents Act 1988.

The statements and opinions contained within this publication are solely those of the editors and contributors and not of the University of Bristol, Policy Press or the Social Policy Association. The University of Bristol, Policy Press and the Social Policy Association disclaim responsibility for any injury to persons or property resulting from any material published in this publication.

Policy Press works to counter discrimination on grounds of gender, race, disability, age and sexuality.

Cover design by Qube Design Associates, Bristol
Front cover image: www.alamy.com
Printed and bound in Great Britain by CMP, Poole
Policy Press uses environmentally responsible print partners

Contents

Detailed contents

List of tables, figures, boxes and case studies

Tables

Figures

Boxes

Case studies

Acknowledgements

We dedicate this book to all those individuals and organisations engaged in the struggle against racism in all its forms, past and present. Sadly, despite a history (albeit brief in the *longue durée*) of self-critique and resistance to ideas of 'race', this fight must continue. Europe's political leaders have little to say on the subject of the continuing racism that affects minority populations in most aspects of their lives, across national boundaries. Indeed, in some cases, they seem to be encouraging racism and intolerance.

We offer this book as a small contribution to that larger cause. The editors thank all the authors who delivered drafts of their chapters on time and with good humour, despite our persistent queries. We hope that they will agree that the changes were well worth the effort. We are also grateful to the staff at Policy Press who supported the book through stages of peer review and revision, with patience and perseverance. Karen Ramsden provided invaluable support in preparing the manuscript for publication.

Notes on contributors

Karl Atkin holds a personal research chair in the Department of Health Sciences at the University of York, where he is also Head of Department. He is a medical sociologist with a particular interest in qualitative research in multidisciplinary settings. His research interests include the experience of family carers; young people and identity; disability and chronic illness; and ethnicity and social disadvantage.

Laia Bécares is a Lecturer in Social Statistics at the University of Manchester. Her research interests are in studying the determinants of ethnic inequalities in health, with a focus on life course and neighbourhood effects. She is particularly interested in understanding the pathways by which the racialisation of people and places lead to social and health inequalities. This work has mostly focused on examining the association between racism and health, and looking at neighbourhood effects to examine how people, and the areas where they live, are racialised differently across minority ethnic groups (within and across countries).

Harris Beider is Professor in the Faculty of Business, Environment and Society at Coventry University and Visiting Professor in the School of International and Public Affairs at Columbia University, New York City, where he teaches graduate courses on 'race', urban policy and migration. In 2015 he completed a project on grassroots alliances between different low-income communities in London for Open Society Foundations. His new publications include *White working class voices: Multiculturalism, community-building and change* (Policy Press/University of Chicago Press, 2015). Previously, he was Executive Director of the Federation of Black Housing Organisations.

Maria Berghs is a VC2020 Lecturer in Health and Wellbeing in Society at De Montfort University. She is an anthropologist with a PhD in Sociology and Social Policy. She works in the field of medical anthropology and sociology, specialising in disability studies. Her research interests include disability, global health (sickle cell), humanitarianism, ethics, gender and West Africa (Sierra Leone). She is the author of *War and embodied memory: Becoming disabled in Sierra Leone* (Routledge, 2016).

Sangeeta Chattoo is Associate Professor/Senior Research Fellow at the Department of Sociology, University of York. Her areas of interest and expertise include: 'race', ethnicity and inequalities in health and health policy; genetics, genomics and global health governance; chronic illness, kinship and caring; ethnographic and biographical methods. She is currently carrying out fieldwork on the experiential and policy dimensions of inherited blood disorders in India.

Bankole Cole is Reader in Criminology and Human Rights at the Helena Kennedy Centre for International Justice in the Department of Law and Criminology, Sheffield Hallam University. His areas of expertise include human rights and social justice issues in relation to children, children in conflict and post-conflict countries, Africa, counter-terrorism and 'radicalisation' and young people.

Gary Craig is Visiting Professor at the School of Law, University of Newcastle upon Tyne, and Honorary Professor at the University of York. He has written widely about 'race' and ethnicity, and his other major current research interest lies in the field of contemporary slavery, where he co-convenes the Modern Slavery Research Consortium. He is currently working on books about social justice, organising against racism and contemporary slavery in the UK.

Simon Dyson is Professor of Applied Sociology and Director of the Unit for the Social Study of Thalassaemia and Sickle Cell at De Montfort University. His research interests include all social aspects of sickle cell and thalassaemia. His previous books include *Ethnicity and screening for sickle cell and thalassaemia* (Elsevier, 2005, with Gwyneth Boswell); *Sickle cell and deaths in custody* (Whiting and Birch, 2009), and *Genetics and global public health: Sickle cell and thalassaemia* (Routledge, 2012, with Karl Atkin).

Ronny Flynn is a retired academic and charity manager, currently living life as a grey nomad. From 2006 to 2010 she worked as Director of Health and Housing at the Race Equality Foundation in London, and was commissioning editor for their series of Better Health and Better Housing briefing papers. Prior to this, she worked at The Open University.

Saffron Karlsen is a Senior Lecturer in Social Research in the Centre for the Study of Ethnicity and Citizenship at the University of Bristol. Her work explores the different ways in which ethnicity has meaning and relevance in people's lives, both as a form of potential group affiliation and as a driver of health and other inequalities. It engages particularly with the negative impact of racism on these processes.

Frank Keating is a Professor in Health and Social Care in the Department of Social Work at Royal Holloway, University of London. His main research interests are ethnicity, gender, ageing and mental health, particularly focusing on African and Caribbean communities. Frank has recently co-edited a textbook with Tony Evans, *Policy and social work practice* (Sage, 2016). He is a strong advocate for racial equality in mental health services through his writing, teaching and public speaking.

Ian Law is Professor of Racism and Ethnicity Studies at the University of Leeds. His recent books include, with Nikolay Zakharov, *Post-Soviet racisms* (Palgrave Macmillan, 2017), with Martin Kovats, *Rethinking Roma* (Palgrave Macmillan, 2017), with Shirley Anne Tate, *Caribbean racisms* (Palgrave Macmillan, 2015) and *Mediterranean racisms* (Palgrave Macmillan, 2014).

Samara Linton is a junior doctor and co-Editor (with Rianna Walcott) of *The colour of madness: Exploring BAME mental health in the UK* (Skiddaw Books, 2018). She has published research on mental health stigma and frequently writes about gender, race and health for various online publications. In 2016, she was awarded Best New Journalist at the Ending Violence Against Women Media Awards.

Uvanney Maylor is Professor of Education at the University of Bedfordshire. Uvanney's research focuses on issues of 'race', ethnicity, racism and culture and includes studies of schools, further and higher education, and initial teacher education. By bringing greater scrutiny to educational policy, educator practice and student experience, her work seeks to positively impact on educational outcomes for Black and minority ethnic groups and inform anti-racist practice.

Gina Netto is a Reader in Migration at The Urban Institute, Heriot-Watt University. She has longstanding research interests in ethnicity, housing and employment, and has published widely on these issues. Her theoretical and empirical work focuses on deepening understanding of the ways in which ethnicity interacts with other aspects of identity and is shaped by both social relationships and socioeconomic inequalities. She has recently edited (with Gary Craig) a themed section for *Social Policy and Society* on migration and differential labour market participation.

Kate Pickett is Professor of Epidemiology in the Department of Health Sciences at the University of York, and the University's Champion for Research on Justice and Equality; she is a Fellow of the RSA and of the UK Faculty of Public Health. Kate's research focuses on the social determinants of health and health inequalities, with a particular interest in child development. Kate is co-author, with Richard Wilkinson, of the bestselling books *The spirit level* (2009) and *The inner level* (2018). Kate is also a co-founder and trustee of The Equality Trust and a global Ambassador for the Wellbeing Economy Alliance. She tweets at: @ProfKEPickett

Marilyn Roth is a Senior Research Associate at Bunker Hill Community College in Boston, Massachusetts, USA. In the past, her work has focused on the intersections of immigration, ethnicity and culture impact inequalities in health. Presently, her work uses predictive analytics, combined with targeted interventions, to reduce achievement gaps among first-generation, low-income and minority students in higher education.

Baljinder Virk is currently employed to carry out reviews of policy implementation across various social policies for a parliamentary watchdog. She has worked on a number of studies related to employment, skills and training. She has a PhD in Policy Studies from the University of Bristol and a BA from Coventry University. Her thesis, entitled 'Combating labour market disadvantage among ethnic minority groups', evaluated positive action training and government training programmes. She is a member of the Government Social Research and Social Research Association. She has extensive experience in labour market research, and has worked in an academic environment as a policy officer in the third sector and as a freelance consultant.

Katy Wright is an experienced researcher and teacher in social policy, with particular expertise in critical approaches to understanding community, localism and the dynamics of local participation and engagement. Much of her work has focused on analysing experiences of living in disadvantaged neighbourhoods and situating the trajectories of localities within the broader socioeconomic context. Most recently, this has involved case study research in Swansea exploring the concept of community resilience and how patterns of risk and resilience are distributed across different groups. She is also currently developing a project on older minority ethnic people and housing options.

Benjamin Zephaniah For information on Benjamin, see https://benjaminzephaniah.com/?doing_wp_cron=1540992740.71906805038452148 43750

Preface

The British

Benjamin Zephaniah

Take some Picts, Celts and Silures
And let them settle,
Then overrun them with Roman conquerors.

Remove the Romans after approximately 400 years
Add lots of Norman French to some
Angles, Saxons, Jutes and Vikings, then stir vigorously.

Mix some hot Chileans, cool Jamaicans, Dominicans,
Trinidadians and Bajans with some Ethiopians, Chinese,
Vietnamese and Sudanese.

Then take a blend of Somalians, Sri Lankans, Nigerians
And Pakistanis,
Combine with some Guyanese
And turn up the heat.

Sprinkle some fresh Indians, Malaysians, Bosnians,
Iraqis and Bangladeshis together with some
Afghans, Spanish, Turkish, Kurdish, Japanese
And Palestinians
Then add to the melting pot.

Leave the ingredients to simmer.

As they mix and blend allow their languages to flourish
Binding them together with English.

Allow time to be cool.

Add some unity, understanding and respect for the future,
Serve with justice
And enjoy.

Note: All the ingredients are equally important. Treating one ingredient better than another will leave a bitter, unpleasant taste.

Warning: An unequal spread of justice will damage the people and cause pain. Give justice and equality to all.

Source: 'The British', from *Wicked World!* by Benjamin Zephaniah (Puffin, 2000). Copyright © Benjamin Zephaniah, 2000. Reproduced by permission of Penguin Random House UK. With thanks to the author and publishers for permission to reproduce this.

Foreword

Kate Pickett

It is 53 long years since Martin Luther King made his 'I have a dream' speech on the steps of the Lincoln Memorial in Washington, DC. Writing in the summer of 2016, on the anniversary of that August day in 1963, America's foremost civil rights organisation, the NAACP (National Association for the Advancement of Colored People), felt compelled to 'call attention to the weighty work left to do and to the tragic continuities in our oppressions: economic inequality, police brutality, voter suppression, and segregated schooling' (Wright, 2016). Protests erupted on both sides of the Atlantic that summer and a movement emerged, Black Lives Matter, in response to police shootings of too many Black people.

Despite this, the US presidential election was won by an unrepentant bigot calling for a wall to be built to prevent the immigration to the USA of Mexicans, a population labelled collectively and indiscriminately by Donald Trump as rapists, drug users and criminals. The summer of 2016 also saw a sharp rise in hate crimes, including murder, against minority ethnic groups in England, Wales and Northern Ireland (Scotland seems thankfully immune) following the UK referendum vote to leave the European Union. And Europe continues to suffer an unprecedented crisis of migration as asylum-seekers, refugees from conflicts across the globe and economic migrants seek subsistence, security and sanctuary. Thousands have lost their lives as they are smuggled and trafficked with impunity in appalling conditions.

Not all migrants are equal, of course. I spent 16 years living as a 'resident alien' in the USA, a beneficiary of many Americans' Anglophilia, and it was never suggested that I should go back to where I came from. Because I am White, because I speak English, because I don't pray to the wrong deity, I attracted neither prejudice nor discrimination.

Ethnicity is at the heart of people's identity, culture and relationships. Ethnicity is often what brings us together, creates community and enriches our lives in uncountable positive ways. But 'race' and ethnicity, and their markers – language, religion, costume and custom – lie at the dark heart of much of the prejudice and discrimination that pollute our modern societies.

Minority ethnic status too often defines who is oppressed, who is excluded or segregated, who is denied access – to healthcare, education, citizenship and power – and who is enslaved. Economic inequality presses down most heavily on those who suffer the inequalities associated with belonging to stigmatised minorities, whether defined by ethnicity, gender, disability or other characteristics. When austerity bites, it is those same minorities who are hardest bitten.

Although the last few years have been marred by the growth of right-wing populism, nationalism, increasing securitisation and a harsh public discourse that labels minorities as terrorists, shirkers, skivers and criminals, perhaps the tide is starting to turn. In France, the Netherlands and Austria, far-right political parties ultimately failed in their attempts to gain power. The 2017 UK General Election saw an impressive proportion of the population voting for a radically progressive Labour Party manifesto and the demolition of the far-right UKIP. Donald Trump's election has galvanised protest and opposition in the USA. My optimism for the future is boosted by the fact that young people are overwhelmingly progressive and accepting of diversity – the future may well be safe in their hands.

In these complex and rapidly changing times, it is as important as ever to understand how 'race' and ethnicity shape people's lives and public policy. We need research that embraces the complexity of ethnic identity as well as the complexity of individual, political and policy responses to ethnic diversity. Much of the public discourse on ethnicity, migration, inequality, austerity and other great social challenges of our time is ill informed and simplistic; we need scholars who can offer a countervailing voice and perspective.

Whatever your discipline, your methods or your research questions, this book will enlarge the breadth and depth of your understanding. I hope it supports you in the learning and the research you undertake to understand and change our world.

Reference

Wright, J. (2016) 'NAACP Statement on the 53rd Anniversary of the March on Washington', *Englewood News*, 2 September (www.englewoodnjnews.com/naacp-statement-on-the-53rd-anniversary-of-the-march-on-washington).

1

Introduction

Gary Craig, Sangeeta Chattoo, Karl Atkin and Ronny Flynn

Policy Press approached us in late 2016, to commission a second edition of this book, reiterating the centrality of 'race' and ethnicity to social policy and related disciplinary areas informing practice. We are pleased to bring together the revised and updated chapters, and would like to thank all the authors, including those who contributed to the first edition and those who have taken their place in this second edition, for their valuable contributions. We are especially grateful to Kate Pickett for writing the Foreword and Samara Linton for sharing her blog which appears as the Postscript.

As we noted in the first edition, 'race' is a highly contested area and one where many people, including key politicians, feel that the 'race' agenda has now largely been addressed. Indeed, John Denham, the outgoing Secretary of State for Communities and Local Government in 2010, argued that 'it is time to move on from "race"', and one of Theresa May's first comments, on becoming Home Secretary that same year, was that 'equality [including race equality] is a dirty word'. This view was given additional impetus by George Osborne's (Chancellor of the Exchequer from 2010 to 2016) association of the Equality Act with needless red tape that was restricting the growth of enterprise, a view that belied any commitment to hard-fought social justice as we understand it or to a concern with equality, respect, recognition, fairness and democracy (see 'The Red Tape Challenge' at www.redtapechallenge.cabinetoffice.gov.uk/equalities). In the last few years, as one of us has argued elsewhere (Craig, 2013), there appears to have been a more or less systematic attempt to erase or 'invisibilise' a discussion on 'race' and ethnicity from public policy. Current debates on policy, especially debates around Brexit and its impacts on the UK population, have led to a substantial increase in 'race' hate crime in the UK (Burnett, 2017).

Our aspiration, that the first edition of the book might lead to a foregrounding of the dimension of 'race' and ethnicity in a positive way, has certainly not materialised, particularly given the current international political climate. The impacts of a series of UK government policies have substantially disadvantaged many members of minority ethnic groups who were already poorly served by existing policy frameworks, as our first edition of this book showed quite clearly. Indeed, the recent furore over the obliteration of the so-called Windrush Generation's rights to live in the UK demonstrates that successive governments have been operating racist policies by commission and by omission, both overtly and covertly. In trying to capture this deteriorating scenario, we identified three important policy foci, which we asked our authors to incorporate within their analysis and commentary: immigration, austerity and securitisation.

Immigration, where a series of Acts of Parliament, culminating (to date) in the Immigration Act 2016, have borne down hard on minorities of all kinds (whether those born here, economic migrants or refugees). These policies vary from introducing more demanding tests (including proof of sufficient income) as a means to legitimise claims to citizenship, to more limited access to a range of services, asking service providers, including staff in higher education institutions, to collude with immigration officials by acting as their 'spies' (see, for example, Bulman, 2017; see also www.jcwi.org.uk/saying-no-to-roll-out-of-rent-to-right-scheme). The impact of seven years of austerity has been felt most harshly among those of low and very low incomes (Oxfam, 2013). We use the term 'securitisation' to mean the rhetoric and techniques of governance through which the State transforms particular subjects into 'matters of security' (see Bigo, 2002). In the context of the so-called war on terror or perceived threats to national security, people most often under surveillance tend to be migrants, minorities and other 'outsiders'. Particular programmes such as Prevent further tend to focus on specific religious/ethnic groups such as 'Muslims' (see Chapter 12, this volume; see also Farny, 2016). All of our present authors have engaged, albeit differently, with these key concepts, although clearly the impacts of these three key policy trends have been uneven across differing welfare areas. Together, we argue, these three areas have constituted a significant further undermining of the position of minority ethnic groups in the UK since the publication of the first edition of the book a mere seven years ago.

Aims of the book

Apart from this preamble, which summarises key changes in the policy and political context since the first edition, the intention of this Introduction remains to foreground the theoretical, historical and empirical changes explored in the chapters to follow.

Discussion of ethnicity remains peripheral to social policy's more mainstream engagement with citizenship and welfare. The genesis of this book could be said to have started life in a keynote speech given by one of us to the Annual Conference of the Social Policy Association (SPA) in Nottingham in July 2006, observing that:

> It is important to acknowledge that neglect of the issue of 'race' is not confined to social policy as *political practice*; it is shared by the *academic discipline* of social policy. It is still not uncommon for mainstream social

policy texts to treat debates on 'race' and racism as marginal. This is striking considering that the social policy discipline is concerned centrally with issues of citizenship rights, welfare, equality, poverty alleviation and social engineering.… This failure of the social policy community also extends to social policy teaching and to the high-profile social policy journals. (reproduced in Craig, 2007)

We argued in the first edition that little had changed in the intervening years, despite the increasing media, political and policy interest in certain aspects of 'race', namely, immigration, community cohesion and multiculturalism. Since 2011, academic interest has grown slightly, judging by the number of journals and journal articles and by the emergence of several new research centres in the UK. While 'race' remains marginal to teaching within social policy, the introduction of a BA (Hons) in Black Studies at Birmingham City University might herald a positive shift (see www.bcu.ac.uk/courses/black-studies-ba-hons-2017-18). At the same time, the ability of the relatively few committed academics and researchers to engage in evidence-based teaching has generally been swamped by what has become intense and often virulently hostile and inaccurate media reportage (echoed by some politicians, a few of whom still feel empowered to disseminate racist comments under the guise of parliamentary privilege), culminating in the debates leading up to and following the European Union (EU) referendum in 2016. It is not an exaggeration to suggest that racism was one of the two or three single most significant factors contributing to the call for – and the result of – the EU referendum (see Chapters 2 and 3, this volume).

However, it is important to bear in mind that the UK remains an ethnically and culturally diverse – some would say a 'super-diverse' – society, within which shifts in social policy and practice are played out. While the picture has slightly improved since 2011, it continues to be poorly reflected within the literature in social policy. We noted that the Social Policy and Social Work subpanel of the 2013 Higher Education Funding Council for England (HEFCE) Research Excellence Framework (REF), as originally constituted, comprised an entirely White group of academics, only one of whom regarded 'race' as in any way central to their research interests. This issue was addressed to some degree by HEFCE later on, but we wait with interest to see if this is indicative of a permanent shift in this field.

We hope that this second edition, which combines empirical insights with theoretical debates, will once again offer a sound introduction to citizenship, equality and welfare within the wider context of dilemmas posed by addressing difference and diversity. These dilemmas are multifaceted, reflecting the complexity of current understandings and approaches to welfare provision. For example, a lack of clarity in defining ethnicity – and inconsistency in categorising and recording data – contributes to analytic confusion across different sectors of policy and in implementing guidelines into practice. Hence, even though the 2011 UK Census recognises 18 ethnic categories, some government departments still use simplified and even binary categories – 'White British' and 'Other' covering all (White and non-White) minorities (see www.ethnicity-facts-figures.service. gov.uk/ethnicity-in-the-uk). 'White' ethnicities are still silent yet dominant (see Bowler, 2017), defining the norms and values underpinning policy and practice, while minority ethnicities are treated as somehow deviant, representing the 'other' and even the 'exotic' (see Chapter 2, this volume). Such wilful political neglect, in conjunction with more explicit racist formulations, reflects a dilemma for most Western, liberal democratic states struggling to provide accessible and appropriate welfare provision for culturally and linguistically diverse populations. Offering a critical assessment of current understandings as a means to improve outcomes for ethnically marginalised populations is at the core of this book.

While most of the chapters reflect empirical material and histories of particular policy areas specific to the UK, the theoretical and social implications apply to most countries in the global North. Hence, the well-documented processes of disadvantage and discrimination can delude some of us familiar with the complexity of current debates into thinking that there is little else to do. Further cuts in funding to both the government's Equality Office and the Equality and Human Rights Commission (EHRC) signal a much-weakened regulatory system. Perhaps it is worth reminding ourselves of the most significant critique of institutional racism by Sir William Macpherson in his report into the death of Stephen Lawrence. This is not only because it is a definition to which many of the authors in this collection return, but because it remains an area whose relevance many policy-makers have continually failed to comprehend or uphold in their own practice:

> The collective failure of an organisation to provide an appropriate and professional service to people because of their colour, culture and ethnic background. It can be seen or detected in processes, attitudes and behaviour which amount to discrimination through unwitting prejudice, ignorance, thoughtless and racist stereotyping which disadvantages minority ethnic people. (Macpherson, 1999, para 6.34)

Some – notably the Metropolitan Police – now reject the charge of institutional racism, although the disproportionate use of 'stop and search' against young Black people continues to undermine this stance (see Chapter 12, this volume). Other organisations, such as the National Health Service (NHS), may, and increasingly do, argue that greater understanding and better use of evidence in the light of some high-profile scandals such as the death of Black mental health patients means sufficient change has already taken place (see Chapter 11, this volume). However, our experience – and that of the authors represented in this book –

is that, despite a growing body of evidence which should impact on practice, practice remains slow to change. The overall impact of austerity also means that the possibilities for change have narrowed down further, especially hampering the effective widening of service provision for migrants, given the current political climate of hostility and intolerance towards 'outsiders'.

The extensive range of legislation seeking to challenge racism and discrimination has often reinforced a sense of political complacency. Chapter 4 reflects this, and by tracing the development of such legislation, illustrates how each new Act points to the failure of its predecessors. Similarly, our growing awareness has not always equated with a more responsive welfare provision, and positive policy responses that do exist remain unevenly distributed across the UK. Indeed, our inability to act on evidence and replicate good practice – with the facts often being lost amidst political and public hostility and prejudice – remains a fundamental barrier in facilitating equality.

Broadly, the sensitivity and effectiveness of such responses correlate with the length of time that minorities have settled in particular parts of the UK. Recent migrants face similar prejudice and discrimination as both migrants who arrived 60 years ago and settled minorities living in more rural areas. Outside the main metropolitan areas, progress towards effective responses to diversity has been slow. Rural areas in particular still have a lot of catching up to do, particularly as the rate of growth of minority populations in those areas has become much faster than in urban localities (see Chapter 3, this volume). Long-established minorities, however, face continued discrimination and disadvantage, as shown by the recent programme of research on ethnicity and poverty funded by the Joseph Rowntree Foundation. The direct racism 'they' experience competes with the more subtle, ever-changing, indirect and systemic discrimination of minorities as the 'other' (see Hirst and Rinne, 2014).

Conceptualising the 'other' and the persisting threat of racialisation

The UK offers several examples highlighting the dangers and implications of racialising minority ethnic cultures, which, in turn, reflect a more general failure to transform understandings of citizenship, diversity and equality into effective policy and practice. Highlighting and learning from these longstanding examples is one key aim of our book. Empirical research within social sciences, for example, has long discredited the dangers of essentialised stereotypes of minority ethnic families. These ideas, sadly, continue to surface in the responses of many practitioners. For instance, the stereotype of fatalism characterising South Asian cultures persists in nursing and medical literature, and is often used to explain poor outcomes for chronic health conditions, such as diabetes and heart failure. There is little recognition that fatalistic attitudes (invoking God's will, or luck) do not preclude active engagement with a chronic condition or its treatment, and are certainly not unique to South Asian culture(s) (Chapter 2, this volume). Further, such a focus on culture implicitly locates the problem within individual practices and behaviours rather than reflecting the failure of collective welfare provision to engage with difference, a tension reflected in many of our chapters (see Chapters 8 and 9, this volume).

Despite the emphasis of policy-makers and funding bodies on multidisciplinary research, mainstream research within social policy, healthcare and welfare seem sadly not willing to engage with wider debates on the complex notions of 'race', ethnicity, culture and religion, ethnic identity and citizenship (see Chapter 2). This book is an attempt at bridging this serious gap, and reflects our continuing commitment to ensuring that critical engagement becomes central to debates within mainstream social policy, rather than a convenient add-on that further reinforces the marginalisation of these disadvantaged groups. As this book will demonstrate, there is much to be said for seeing ethnicity as part of a broader engagement with inequality and citizenship. We hope that it will stimulate a much healthier and more widespread discussion within academic teaching, research and publication arenas.

Hence, one of our primary concerns in revisiting this book is not to offer neat, prescriptive cultural descriptions or solutions purporting to explain and manage ethnicity. Instead, we want to offer a more self-critical discussion that contextualises diversity and difference, without recourse to simplistic explanations and naive solutions which, paradoxically, can perpetuate disadvantage and discrimination. As we argued in the previous edition, the production of a book such as this represents a contradiction, and one familiar to those working in this field. We are trying to address the marginalisation of 'race' and ethnicity in social policy, but find ourselves writing a book in which this process of marginalisation is highlighted rather than displaced. In the first edition we said that we 'hoped books such as ours would no longer be necessary in, say, five years' time'. This hope has been far from realised and, indeed, we all feel that the position of minorities is less promising in policy, political and practice terms than it was in 2011. Race hate crimes, to take just one indicator, are on the increase numerically, along with casual use of racist language. This is not just, we would argue, because people find it easier to report such incidents (a claim from the police that does not stand up to close scrutiny, as the number of racist-inspired murders in the UK continues to rise).

We are equally aware of how much our ideas about ethnicity have changed over time, in response to both theoretical understanding and the changing landscape of the ethnic composition of those living in the UK. There is now considerable diversity both within and between minority ethnic populations living in the UK. Policy, practice and research have been painfully slow to engage with this diversity. There are, for example, established minority ethnic populations, from

South Asia and the Caribbean, who settled in the UK between the 1940s and 1970s, 70% of whom are British citizens, spanning three or four generations (see Chapter 3). Further, half of all people of minority ethnic background now living in the UK have been born there. Then there are the more recently arrived, possibly short-term, migrants from Central and Eastern Europe, and refugees and those seeking asylum, largely from Africa, the Middle East – most recently Syria – and Afghanistan, who have come in substantial numbers since the mid-1990s. There remain neglected populations, such as Chinese populations (of which there are at least four main groups: mainland Chinese, Hong Kong Chinese, Taiwanese, and Malayan Chinese), Gypsies, Travellers and Roma and other 'invisible' White minorities: those of Irish, Polish, Turkish and Greek background, for example, who have a long history of settlement in the UK. Finally, the UK is beginning to see a steady increase in people who regard themselves as mixed heritage, the most rapidly expanding ethnic category according to the 2011 Census. This category, most poignantly, challenges the bureaucratic assumptions of mutually exclusive and distinct ethnic groups.

Engaging with the complexity of diversity is an important feature of this book, although a lack of empirical material in certain areas means such reflection must be theoretical. As the reader will see, the chapters use a range of definitions of ethnicity in relation to 'race'. Indeed, it would not be possible to impose fixed and consistent definitions of 'race' and ethnicity for theoretical reasons explained in Chapter 2. Ethnicity is notoriously difficult to define and has come to embody a broad range of ideas, such as language, religion, faith, culture, nationality and a shared heritage. It therefore applies to all of us, even though we often tend not to think of majority or white populations in terms of their ethnicity. Within the British context, this largely reflects the derogatory and exclusionary mode in which ethnicity is only attributed to minority, immigrant origin as a surrogate term for 'race'. However, it also signals strategic ways in which ethnicity is increasingly used as a political symbol of pride and belonging, a mobilising resource used to legitimise claims to citizenship. Equally, within particular contexts, rather than ethnicity *per se*, socioeconomic position, age, sexual orientation or disability might be more significant factors in explaining the discrimination faced by people of minority ethnic populations (see Chapter 9). Current research and policy debates, however, struggle to engage with this intersection between ethnicity and these other markers of differentiation, whose outcome can obscure fundamental similarities as well as differences within and between majority and minority ethnic populations.

Recent discussion on the remit of devolved parliaments and broader debates about the relationship between the different parts of the Union offer another, more localised, reminder of the importance of the themes being outlined here. Is an idea of an all-encompassing 'British' identity sustainable across Scotland, Wales and Ireland? And to what extent can the national identity of these countries embrace ethnic and cultural diversity? As a more practical expression of their growing autonomy, these nations may adapt different policies, whose outcomes may have different consequences for minority ethnic populations living within them. Personalisation, although not without meaning in other parts of the Union, is very much an 'English' policy (see Chapter 9). While acknowledging such changes and the need to understand them, we would argue that core ideas such as discrimination and racism, alongside the difficulties of defining and explaining ethnicity, assume relevance, regardless of the specific national context.

The UK is, of course, not alone in trying to come to term with these issues, and many of the themes outlined in this book will have a wider relevance to high-income, post-industrial Western societies, which have – generally, for historical reasons connected with their imperialist pasts – populations characterised by similar diversity (see Craig, 2017).

Outline of the book

In bringing this book together, we were concerned to offer a careful and thoughtful review of the literature and research, to confront many of the mistaken assumptions about minorities that still inform research, policy and practice, while simultaneously trying to make sense of the struggles faced by the State and the broader society, in engaging with cultural, ethnic and religious diversity. There are few social policy or social welfare books that address the issue of 'race' and ethnicity with a wider focus on a range of welfare issues (Ian Law's *'Race', ethnicity and social policy* being one obvious exception), and we have deliberately chosen, apart from the three in-depth contextual essays, to go for breadth rather than depth. There is a reasonably good 'race'-related literature within specific areas of social welfare (such as health and housing). In other areas, however, there is a paucity of good literature, and we have tried, throughout the book, to signpost the reader to different sources, where these exist. Those readers wishing to look at specific areas in more depth can turn to these sources, listed under 'Further reading' or 'Online resources'.

If the general literature is poor at engaging with broad issues of 'race', it is even worse at addressing recent changes in the demography of the UK. These include the growth of refugees and those seeking asylum, economic and other migrants from Eastern and Central Europe, and other communities with a relatively short history of settlement in the UK, such as Somali, Eritrean, Syrian and Afghani minorities. The book addresses the situation of these groups as far as possible, although for many more recent groups (and indeed, for some historically ignored groups such as Gypsies, Roma and Travellers), there remains a lack of useful data, a situation noted in the last moments of the outgoing Labour government in 2010 (Hills et al, 2010). This is an issue that ought to be addressed as a matter of extreme urgency. We also know little about the experience of longstanding minority ethnic populations living in Scotland, Wales and Ireland, a lacuna that continuing debates about devolution has brought into sharp focus.

Despite our commitment to breadth and depth, omissions inevitably remain. Some of these were a result of this volume originally being part of a book series that included texts on *Immigration and refugee policy*, *Social citizenship* and *Equal opportunities and diversity*. Limitation of space has meant that we have also had to make some difficult choices, which we will return to. Leaving all this aside and following this general Introduction, Part One contains three extended essays offering an introduction and core foundation on which to make sense of ethnicity and 'race'. Chapter 2, by reflecting on concepts, theories and discourses, focuses on some of the theoretical limitations of 'ethnicity' and its use as a framework for conceptualising the needs and experiences of people from minority ethnic communities. It argues that, given the historical roots and semantic underpinnings, which see ethnicity as a euphemism for racism in general and cultural racism in particular, the field of ethnicity, health and social care has remained highly specialised and marginal to mainstream academic, policy and practice discourses. This, ironically, has led to reinforcing the marginalisation of people from minority ethnic communities, who become peripheral to debates on politics and citizenship, despite wider shifts within policy and practice towards a more inclusive society. This has led to a conflation between the ascription of ethnicity as an essential defining characteristic of (only) immigrant communities – reconstituting these as *minority ethnic communities* – and inscribing the immutable stigmata of difference through a combination of the three terms. The chapter thus provides an overarching self-critique of the field, and sets out to offer a conceptual link between the two parts and the chapters of the book, while providing a reference point for subsequent chapters in Part Two.

Chapter 3 reviews the history and pattern of settlement of minorities in the UK. Every local authority area in the UK now has a settled minority ethnic population. Some have had a recent substantial increase of migrant workers (often in areas, notably rural areas, that previously had been largely mono-cultural). Others have received substantial numbers of refugees and those seeking asylum. Many parts of the UK, particularly within specific urban areas, receiving migrants from hitherto unfamiliar parts of the world are becoming super-diverse, with 50 or, in some cases many more, different languages commonly spoken. These patterns of settlement raise significant issues for policy development and service delivery for local government, health bodies and the third sector, although the responses of these agencies have largely been, at best, uneven and, at worst, plainly hostile. By laying out the historical origins of minority ethnic settlement in the UK, long before the UK became a United Kingdom, the chapter questions assumptions that suggest diversity is a recent phenomenon. Black faces have at least a 2,000-year history in the UK. The chapter then goes on to review the historical, economic, social, political and cultural factors that have shaped current patterns of settlement, including internal migration, of the UK's minority ethnic communities. In doing so, it points to a range of policy and service issues that need to be addressed, as well as the impact that settlement has had historically on local policies and services.

The final chapter in this contextual section, Chapter 4, provides a historical review of the development of policy, politics and practice. It follows on from Chapter 3, acknowledging the contribution that immigrants – especially the early cohorts soon after the Second World War – made to the establishment of public services such as the NHS and London Transport, and key industries such as the heavy and light textile, hosiery and footwear industries. This connects with the eight welfare sector-specific chapters in Part Two, by providing a political and policy context central to government policy. Chapter 4 documents how policy, particularly since the 1950s, has existed in a state of tension between continuity and change. On the one hand, there has been increasingly repressive and restrictive immigration policy supported by a vociferously xenophobic media and, initially at the margins, but more recently much less so, increasingly fascist political parties. On the other hand, there has been a series of more 'liberal' domestic policies, attempting to manage internal diversity, from, initially, assimilation policies, through 'race' relations, community relations and multiculturalism, to, most recently, community cohesion and then integration. The last of these have legitimised – both implicitly and explicitly – a return to the language of assimilation, arguing – falsely, we and others would claim – that minority communities are turning inwards on themselves and, in the process, providing a refuge for those driven by extremist views (see Rattansi, 2013). Chapter 4 ends with a reflection on how conceptualisation of the 'race' problem' is changing, by examining the practical meanings of concepts such as overt discrimination, multiculturalism, institutional racism and essentialism.

Part Two presents eight chapters, each focusing on one specific welfare sector. The authors have revised and updated their chapters (or, in a few cases, provided new chapters to the template provided by the publishers for the series as a whole), providing lists of 'Further reading' where appropriate and key 'Online resources', in addition to boxed examples of particular issues, key illustrative case studies and questions for discussion. We hope the book thus offers both a key theoretical and a teaching contribution to the subject.

The collection of chapters in Part Two cannot provide an exhaustive account of every potential relevant topic. There are also differences in the depth to which authors are able to develop their analysis. This reflects the nature of the specific sector, and the level of theoretical insights that have developed in relation to it; the particular expertise and interests of the authors; and, most of all, the existing state of knowledge and research. Some areas are relatively well researched, with much material to draw on; in others, the extent of our knowledge is still shamefully limited, and a description of the territory has yet to be more thoroughly theorised.

Despite covering many welfare sectors – housing, health, social care, education, the labour market, income maintenance, mental health and criminal justice – there are other areas not covered that we would like to have included. Old age, an increasing feature of the more established minority populations, although mentioned in several chapters (see Chapters 8 and 9), is perhaps now even more worthy of a more detailed discussion, given the obvious implications for policy and practice of an ageing population. There is also no chapter on the role and experience of the third sector (also known as the voluntary and community sector), facing systematic underfunding and marginalisation (see Craig, 2011). Nor were we able to address the role of minorities in the private welfare sector in an era of unprecedented cuts to public expenditure. Evidence suggests that the private sector largely pays little attention to the issues of 'race' and diversity; this is hardly surprising since trades unions, which now pay greater attention to issues of discrimination than it did historically, are substantially underrepresented within private sector companies (where union density is now only 17%) compared with the public sector, where it is 60%. This discrepancy is particularly apparent in the most exploited parts of the private sector, where most of the estimated 600,000+ irregular workers are located (Wilkinson et al, 2010: Waite et al, 2015).

The chapter on education (Chapter 11) largely covers the period of full-time schooling and does not deal in so much detail with higher education, because of the limitations of space. The latter, again, would be worthy of a separate chapter, particularly given continuing revelations about the failure of widening participation strategies to facilitate access for Black and minority ethnic students to the self-styled 'best' universities (Boliver, 2013). We reported in the first edition that in 2009, despite financial incentives from government and protestations from senior management at the university itself, the University of Oxford accepted only one Black Caribbean student for a place on an undergraduate course. More recent data show that the Universities of Oxford and of Cambridge have not done much to address this serious failing, despite their evident wealth, and many other self-proclaimed elite universities such as Durham are notable for the continuing whiteness of their student bodies (Weekes–Bernard, 2010).

In terms of specifics and changing demographic contexts, longstanding chronic illness and disability is equally important and although, again, touched on in several of the chapters, are likely to be an important feature of future work in the area of 'race' and welfare policy (see Chapters 8, 9 and 10). To what extent does the experience of chronic and longstanding disabilities differ between diverse ethnic groups? How well might self-management work within such contexts? What is it like to age with a longstanding condition while living in more socioeconomically deprived areas?

Political participation and engagement with civil society equally reflect broader concerns, worthy of further and more intensive investigation (see Chapter 7). Ethnic density, for example, is emerging as of potential analytical value in explaining a whole range of experiences and behaviours, as it reflects a creative tension combining resilience, participation and social exclusion (Bécares et al, 2012). Related to this, we have not been able to draw together separate evidence on the experience of minorities in areas where ethnic density is very low, particularly in small towns and in rural and remote areas (see Chapter 6).

A note on terminology

The word 'race' is used throughout in quote marks to indicate that it is a social construct with particular historical connotations and has no objective meaning. The editorial team were not completely agreed on whether the word 'ethnicity' should also be placed within such quote marks. A decision was made not to do so, just to signal the historical specificity and sensitivity of 'race', even though both the terms are constructs of language. The reader should assume that this is a debate that is still continuing! As one of the opening chapters (Chapter 2) indicates, terminology in this area is politically sensitive, and whether to refer to racialised minorities as Black and minority ethnic groups, as Black and minority groups or simply as minorities and so on remains contested. For some of the authors (and other academics), these phrases remain interchangeable, and we have chosen not to impose a particular term to be used across the book. This is to respect the diversity of backgrounds and areas of welfare represented by the authors who have, however, explained their usage of the terms within individual chapters. Similarly, some authors have found intersectionality a more appropriate framework than critical race theory and, again, we have not tried to nudge them in one direction or another. Multiculturalism within the British context refers to a political policy that is to be distinguished from multiculturalism or ethnic diversity as an empirical/descriptive term, although the two might overlap within certain contexts.

We also wanted to avoid the danger inherent in separate chapters on differing divisions of welfare of overlooking the cumulative effect of different aspects of disadvantage. Cross-reference between chapters occurs as frequently as possible. For example, a lack of access to healthcare and poverty means 'a child born to a mother born in the Caribbean is twice as likely to die before the age of five, than a child born to a UK-born mother' (Rutter, 2011, p 9; and see Chapter 5). And, of course, the growing interest in intersectionality means that ethnicity is now often seen as part of a cumulative process of disadvantage that might also include such dimensions as gender or disability. However, individual authors might have felt closer to critical race theory rather than to intersectionality (see Chapters 10 and 11), depending on their own theoretical leanings on the centrality of 'race' and racism in analysing the structural underpinnings of both access to and outcomes of welfare provision on the whole. As can be seen, institutional racism informs many of the chapters (see Chapters 6 and 7). We did not, however, want to impose a restrictive editorial policy on what we perceive as the author's prerogative.

The book has been a collaborative effort as far as possible. Our intent has been to stimulate debate in what is a contested area. We hope that, in making such debates accessible, social policy incorporates ethnicity and 'race' as part of its mainstream concerns, rather than relegating it to the margins of specialist interest. This is why our book is broadly aimed at students, academics and researchers, policy-makers, those delivering services and politicians, all of whom have an important role to play in improving the way we respond to diversity, both now and in the future. While our primary audience is those teaching the subject of social policy, the book is in every sense also a contribution to the research enterprise, bringing together, as it does, a unique collection of material often located in relatively inaccessible sources. We hope that we can make a significant contribution to incorporating the dimension of 'race' and ethnicity as an integral feature of both teaching and research that impacts on social welfare policy and practice.

References

Bécares, L., Shaw, R., Nazroo, J., Stafford, M., Albor, C., Atkin, K., et al (2012) 'Ethnic density effects on physical morbidity, mortality, and health behaviors: A systematic review of the literature', *American Journal of Public Health*, 102(12), e33-66.

Bigo, D. (2002) 'Security and immigration: Toward a critique of the governmentality of unease', *Alternatives*, Special Issue, 27, 63-92.

Boliver, V. (2013) 'How fair is access to the more prestigious UK universities?', *British Journal of Sociology*, 64(2), 344-64.

Bowler, R. (2017) 'Critical youth and community work and its struggle with white standards', in G. Craig (ed), *Community organising against racism*, Bristol: Policy Press, 41-60.

Bulman, M. (2017) 'Thousands of asylum seekers and migrants wrongly denied NHS healthcare', *Independent*, 16 April (www.independent.co.uk/news/uk/home-news/asylum-seekers-migrants-wrongly-denied-nhs-healthcare-cancer-doctors-phil-murwill-a7672686.html).

Burnett, J. (2017) 'Racial violence and the Brexit State', *Race & Class*, 58(4), 85-97.

Craig, G. (2007) 'Cunning, unprincipled, loathsome: The racist tail wags the welfare dog', *Journal of Social Policy*, 36(4), 605-23.

Craig, G. (2011) 'Forward to the past: Can the UK Black and minority ethnic sector survive?', *Voluntary Sector Review*, 2(3), 367-89.

Craig, G. (2013) 'The invisibilisation of "race" in public policy', *Critical Social Policy*, November, 712-20.

Craig, G. (ed) (2017) *Community organising against racism*, Bristol: Policy Press.

Farny, E. (2016) 'Implications of the securitisation of migration', E-International Students Relations, 29 January (www.e-ir.info/2016/01/29/implications-of-the-securitisation-of-migration).

Hills, J., Lister, R., Lupton, R., Machin, S., Mills, C., Modood, T., et al (2010) *The anatomy of economic inequality in the UK*, London: National Equalities Office.

Hirst, A. and Rinne, S. (2014) *Initial evaluation of the JRF Poverty and Ethnicity programme*, York: Joseph Rowntree Foundation (www.jrf.org.uk/report/initial-evaluation-jrf-poverty-and-ethnicity-programme).

Macpherson, W. (1999) *The Stephen Lawrence inquiry: Report of an inquiry by Sir William Macpherson of Cluny*, CM4262-I, London: The Stationery Office.

Oxfam (2013) *The true cost of austerity and inequality: UK case study*, September (www.oxfam.org/sites/www.oxfam.org/files/cs-true-cost-austerity-inequality-uk-120913-en.pdf).

Rattansi, A. (2013) *Multiculturalism: A very short introduction*, Oxford: Oxford University Press.

Rutter, J. (2011) 'The impact of poverty on the educational experiences of migrant children', *Poverty*, Spring, 15-17.

Waite, L., Craig, G., Lewis, H. and Skrivankova, K. (eds) (2015) *Vulnerability, exploitation and migration*, Basingstoke: Palgrave Macmillan.

Weekes-Bernard, D. (ed) (2010) *Widening participation and 'race' equality*, London: Runnymede Trust.

Wilkinson, M., Craig, G. and Gaus, A. (2010) *Forced labour in the UK and the Gangmasters' Licensing Authority*, Oxford: Oxfam.

Part One

Theoretical, historical and policy contexts

2

'Race', ethnicity and social policy: concepts and limitations of current approaches to welfare

Sangeeta Chattoo and Karl Atkin

'I speak of these developments ... to show how race has become a palimpsest, a parchment written upon by successive generations where nothing is ever *entirely* erased ...we keep tracing the same contours with different pens.'

KWAME ANTHONY APPIAH, 2016, BBC REITH LECTURES

Overview

This chapter, by providing a critical overview of ethnicity and its close association with 'race' and nationality, offers an overall theoretical framework for subsequent chapters. Exploring key concepts and theories underpinning contemporary debates, it highlights the limitations of the current approaches that inform policy and practice, and suggests alternative ways of thinking about ethnicity in addressing the challenges facing the UK as an increasingly diverse society. The chapter:

- explores the links between the concepts of 'race', ethnicity and nationality;
- examines the limitations of current understandings of ethnicity when discussing health and social welfare;
- provides empirical examples to illustrate the implications of diversity when considering access to welfare provision; and
- challenges the reader to think about dilemmas and contradictions underpinning health and welfare provision in a diverse society.

Key concepts
ethnicity; 'race'; securitisation; welfare; citizenship

Introduction

This chapter deconstructs the theoretical underpinnings of ethnicity and traces its relationship with 'race' and nationality, by turning to empirical examples from both our past and our present. The elections of Donald Trump as the President of the USA and of Sadiq Khan as the Mayor of London (the first person of an Asian/Muslim heritage to be elected as the mayor of a major European capital), in the context of the larger global landscape of terrorist violence and perceptions of national security, remind us of the enduring nature of these debates. While the chapter largely draws on the UK context, there are parallels with broader, contemporary debates on multiculturalism, austerity and securitisation within a global context.

It is argued in this chapter that, given the historical roots of ethnicity as a euphemism for racism in general and cultural racism in particular (through focusing on cultural and religious difference rather than the physical characteristics of 'race' *per se*), the field of ethnicity has remained highly specialised and marginal to mainstream academic, policy and practice discourses in the UK. While highlighting policies and practices that sustain disadvantage and discrimination, which have slowly prompted an (albeit) uneven shift towards a more inclusive society, a focus on ethnicity has also ironically reinforced the marginalisation of people from minority ethnic communities, often making them ('special' and) peripheral to broader debates about politics and citizenship. The field is thus marked by continuities and discontinuities, prompting us to recognise various contradictions at different levels. The conceptual and pragmatic tensions within policies related to immigration and particular 'immigrant' groups will be explained in greater historical detail in Chapters 3 and 4, and through specific case studies of particular policy areas outlined later, in Part Two. Here, we examine these contradictions and provide an alternative conceptual framework, better suited for understanding what is, despite political denials, a multi-ethnic society.

Contrary to its wider usage within social sciences, the language of state-sanctioned policy and practice and state-sponsored research on health and social welfare often treat 'ethnicity' as an essential defining characteristic of only immigrant, *minority ethnic communities*. A combination of these three seemingly inseparable terms often results in cumulative disadvantage in access to appropriate support. Hence, bureaucratic institutions representing the State, for both practical and ideological reasons, treat people of minority ethnic background as more or less undifferentiated collectives of less or more deserving or undeserving 'immigrants' (Lo and Stacey, 2008). Consequently, individuals and families may be denied basic welfare support, in breach of domestic and international laws. For example, unaccompanied children seeking asylum are legally protected and entitled to the same welfare provisions as British children under the Children Act 2004 and the United Nations (UN) Convention on the Rights of the Child

1990 (see www.ohchr.org). Yet ignorance, prejudice and the lumping of all asylum-seekers together has led to cases of children being unlawfully deported or denied foster care in the UK (Guentner et al, 2016, pp 403-5). This was brought into sharp relief when the then Home Secretary, Theresa May, launched the 'Go Home' vans in 2013, which were strategically placed to be visible in 'high-risk' neighbourhoods, nudging 'illegal immigrants' to self-deport themselves (see Figure 2.1). (For a detailed study of how people within the local communities perceived and experienced the state campaign for 'voluntary deportation', see Jones et al, 2017.)

As reflected in policy and public debate on 'austerity', the recent horrific terror attacks, cuts to immigration and the unprecedented Brexit referendum, a focus on national security (for example, the renewal of trident nuclear weapons) has been central to notions of nationalism. In the 2016 European Union (EU) referendum, those wanting to leave the EU, especially the United Kingdom Independence Party (UKIP), campaigned (often in an explicitly racist manner) on the basis of reclaiming jobs, securing borders and regaining British sovereignty. As in the Trump campaign in the USA, we saw ethnically racialised, negative images of immigrants and asylum-seekers, whether from Eastern Europe or elsewhere, projected as morally undeserving and threatening, thus creating new categories of 'non-citizens' (Guentner et al, 2016, p 393). In a gruesome attack during this campaign in June 2016, Thomas Mair, a right-wing extremist, who shot and stabbed to death Jo Cox, a Leeds and Spen Labour MP, was heard by eyewitnesses saying: "This is for Britain", "Keep Britain independent" and "Britain first" (quoted in Cobain and Taylor, 2016).

Figure 2.1: Operation Vaken campaign material

In the UK illegally?

Home Office

106 ARRESTS LAST WEEK IN YOUR AREA*

GO HOME OR FACE ARREST
Text HOME to 78070
for free advice, and help with travel documents

*30 June – 6 July 2013 covering Barking and Dagenham, Redbridge, Barnet, Brent, Ealing and Hounslow. We can help you to return home voluntarily without fear of arrest or detention

Source: Home Office (2013)

Migration is being increasingly linked to a security risk, even though most of the terror attacks, including the one on Jo Cox, were carried out by British nationals. Bigo (2002, p 65) defines securitisation as being part of the structure of a risk society:

> My hypothesis is that the securitisation of immigration is not only an effect of, even if it contributes to, the propaganda of the far right political parties, the rise of racism, a new and more efficient rhetoric convincing the population of a danger, or successful "speech acts" performed by actors.... Securitisation of the immigrant as a risk is based on our conception of the state as a body or a container for the polity. It is anchored in the fears of politicians about losing their symbolic control over the territorial boundaries.

In contrast to state and populist discourses on immigration and threats to national security and cultural values, social scientists highlight the increasing ethnic, religious and linguistic diversity both across and within immigrant and minority ethnic groups, reflecting a complex interplay of country of origin, migration history, legal status, access to human capital and the response of local authorities and service provision, among other factors. Sociologists, following Vertovec (2007, 2011), use 'super-diversity' as a descriptive and normative term to capture this phenomenon (see also Chapter 3). However, the concept has been criticised for prioritising a romantic notion of pluralism at the cost of inherent, stratified inequalities and conflict of values as well as state regimes of cohesion and integration. For instance, despite being the ideal type of a super-diverse city inhabited by people of around 180 nationalities, neighbourhoods and schools, London still largely remains segregated by ethnicity and class. Periodically, in response to significant acts of violence and terror, such as those witnessed in London and Manchester during April and June 2017, the (super-)diversity of our cities is simultaneously challenged and affirmed. The split vote in favour of Brexit reflected the underlying divisions across the frontlines of class, ethnicity, religion and nationalism (see Box 2.1). Not surprisingly, during the run-up to and immediately after the EU referendum, we witnessed a sharp escalation in incidents of racist hate crime, Islamophobia (BBC News, 2017a) and anti-Semitism (see BBC News, 2017b), alongside a populist, assimilationist narrative trying to reassert the importance of British values and history, as local communities came together in acts of solidarity and relief.

Box 2.1: Brexit and 'resentful nationalism'

In their book *Nation, class and resentment: The politics of national identity in England, Scotland and Wales* (2017a), published just before the EU referendum, Mann and Fenton talked about a 'resentful nationalism', which was simmering specifically within the working-class population in England, playing a new role in British politics. The authors conducted a survey of 10,000 people across England, Scotland and Wales, after the vote. Their results showed an association between a strong sense of English identity and voting to leave. In Scotland, by contrast, those with a strong sense of Scottish identity were more likely to vote to remain. However, there seemed no correlation between a weaker/stronger sense of Welshness and voting to leave or remain within the EU. The intersectionality between ethnicity and class within the context of Brexit is thus more complex than meets the eye (Mann and Fenton, 2017a, b).

Consequently, minority communities are persistently defined through stereotypes of culture, religion and tradition, rather than as citizens in their own right, negotiating their multiple identities differently within specific social and political contexts (Bhabha, 1994; Werbner, 1997). Such a focus on culture often deflects attention away from structural issues of socioeconomic inequality and forms of institutional cultures and racisms that sustain forms of disadvantage and discrimination (see Gunaratnam, 1997).

Further, as highlighted by Black and post-colonial feminist writers, it is important to understand the role of *intersectionality* between race, ethnicity, gender, age and class in shaping women's experiences of disadvantage and partial citizenship rights (Anthias and Yuval-Davis, 1992, pp 96-131; Mirza, 2009a, b; Phoenix, 2009; see also Chapter 4, this volume). These intersections are not cumulative or fixed but contingent on different subject positions and histories of migration. As a result, we find heterogeneity in experiences of social disadvantage for women of Black, White, Chinese or other minority ethnic groups (Yuval-Davis, 2006). A sole focus on structural disadvantage (class or gender) or a homogenised notion of a 'racialised community' can, therefore, underplay the significance of plural and creative modes of engaging with various aspects of race, ethnicity, culture, gender and citizenship at individual and collective levels (see Werbner and Modood, 1997; Silverstein, 2005).

Notwithstanding the intellectual debates, *dominant* discourses of self-identity within a group can, at strategic moments, also use simplified notions of culture, portraying an idealised, timeless vision of 'tradition' and a cohesive community, to set themselves apart from others (see Anderson, 1991). This meaning of culture, as a static, tangible set of shared normative values and rules passed from one generation to the next, is thereby mobilised for political and economic purposes, enabling communities to assert solidarity of interests premised on shared values. Policy discourses often reinforce these perceptions and generalisations about other cultures in search for simple workable solutions to what are increasingly complex problems.

This approach contrasts with culture as an analytical concept used in sociology. Here, culture refers to a dynamic process of interpretation and negotiation of shared values, dissent and change marked by gender and generation, as well as the material and political circumstances of individuals and communities. As suggested by Baumann (1997, p 219), in conjunction with a *dominant* discourse projecting a cohesive community we often find a *demotic* (common, everyday) discourse that reflects communities within community and cultures within community. Far from being a unity, community is a dialogic site of constant moral debate and conflict between right and wrong ways of doing things. Bureaucratic norms underpinning welfare, however, often reflect the cultural values of a majority, glossing over internal differences related to ethnicity and gender as well as socioeconomic position (see Lo and Stacey, 2008; Chattoo, 2014).

This chapter reiterates the need for critical reflection on how 'ethnicity' is used in popular discourses on health and social welfare. For instance, recent estimates suggest that nearly 60% of people classified as being of minority ethnic origin currently living in the UK have been born here (see Chapter 3). This has important implications for how we define 'immigrants' and citizenship, while addressing ethnic diversity in light of both the historical persistence of the racialisation of other cultures on the one hand, and the contemporary political scenarios of securitisation and redrawing of state boundaries, as signalled in the 2016 EU referendum, on the other. As we have mentioned, this chapter provides a 'social landscape' and a conceptual backdrop for the themes running throughout the book. We are, however, aware of the dangers of predefining these theoretical terms which have slightly different – and at times contested – connotations within the specific contexts of subsequent chapters. Given this proviso, the aim is to provide the reader with tools to critically engage with the idea of 'race' and ethnicity, whatever the context and location, and to use this understanding to better inform more finely grained social policies.

Linking ethnicity, 'race' and nationality

Ethnicity refers to a process of self–identity and a form of social stratification, and is 'as much the product of internal arguments of identity and contestation as of external objectification' (Werbner, 1997, p 18). Ethnicity is best defined as a field of enquiry that helps us locate the political and material context within which ethnic identities, premised on notions of shared descent, heritage and culture (encompassing religion and language), are constantly redefined and contested by different social groups. We do not have a unitary theory of ethnicity or a concept with a predefined content. As explained by Fenton:

ethnicity refers to the *social construction* of descent and culture, the social mobilisation of descent and culture, and the meanings and implications of the classification systems built around them. People or peoples do not just possess cultures or share ancestry; *they elaborate these into the idea of a community founded upon these attributes.* (Fenton, 2003, p 3; original emphasis)

A particular social group might redefine itself (or be redefined by others) over time as a national, religious or racial group, using either an 'idiom of race' or an 'idiom of ethnicity' (see Banton, 2000). Attempts by the regional parliament to declare Catalonia an independent Republic in October 2017, and the response of the Spanish government, are a recent example. We saw how historical claims to a separate ethnic/linguistic identity and contested boundaries of state and nation were relayed within a wider context of economic recession across Europe, while the central government of Spain denied legitimacy to the very idea of a referendum (Mortimer, 2017). As Anthias observes, the transformation of such claims is '... linked to political projects and may be the outcome of State and other discourses in interplay with economic and other cultural resources or aims of the group themselves or others' (Anthias and Yuval-Davies, 1992, p 25).

Hence, it is important to remember that ethnicity, culture and community are not fixed or essential characteristics that people 'have', but rather are dynamic processes of self-identity and differentiation involving negotiation of boundaries of inclusion and exclusion between groups. These boundaries shift according to the context of social interaction and struggles over power and resources over time (Hall, 1996). One major feature of this process of self-identification and differentiation is that a sense of shared culture (within a group) is reproduced in everyday interactions between members of different ethnic groups (Barth, 1969), often resulting in the codification of culture as coterminous with difference. Further, within the post-colonial context of the history of immigration patterns in the West and especially in the UK, 'ethnicity' is used to designate immigrant, minority cultures/groups. Hence, it acts as a source of social stratification, perpetuating forms of disadvantage and discrimination through what is now perceived as 'cultural racism' rather than racism based on biological difference *per se* (see Modood, 2008, p 155; for 'race' and other forms of racism, see below). This reminds us of the affinity between concepts of 'ethnic group', 'race' and nation that share an emphasis on a notion of common descent and culture (Bloch et al, 2013).

The word 'ethnic' has its root in the ancient Greek word *ethnos*, broadly referring to people living together, as a tribe, nation or caste, while also being used to exclude groups, for example, non-Athenians and non-Jews. The word in its adjectival form *ethnikos* had two meanings, denoting 'national' and 'foreign'. The earliest written English-language citation implies 'heathen and foreign'.

The meaning shifted towards a generalised notion of 'race' and common racial or cultural character during the 19th century, until 'race' was replaced by 'ethnic' during the 1930s, to designate minority cultural groups or those who were not Christians or Jews (see Fenton, 2003, pp 14-16).

'Race', racism and cultural racism

The notion of biologically distinct 'races', invoking relatedness through common genealogy or blood, first deployed in the 19th century, was closely associated with a fascination with biology and anthropology for the non-European (African, Asian, native American and Australasian) peoples, often perceived as the 'savage other'. Interestingly, earlier 18th-century meanings of 'race', despite being Eurocentric, reflected a concern with what made us similar rather than different (see Wootton, 2016). Indeed, political thinkers such as Jeremy Bentham and Adam Smith questioned the morality of subjugating other nations, by evoking John Locke's notion of toleration (which contributed to the abolition of slavery). By the 19th century, however, anthropometric recordings of physical characteristics (such as height, skin and eye colour, and weight of skull as a parameter for intelligence) and cultural descriptions of 'natives' as the 'distant other' formed the core legitimising strategy. This sat alongside the need to exploit natural resources, labour and markets (Tharoor, 2017), and the Christian values of salvation used by missionaries to colonise indigenous peoples perceived as intellectually, morally and culturally inferior to the Europeans (see Said, 2003). Even Wilberforce, despite his instrumental role in ending the British slave trade (see Chapter 3), advocated sending missionaries to India, and declared that Hindu deities were 'absolute monsters of lust, injustice, wickedness and cruelty' (cited in Keay, 2004, p 429).

Pseudo-scientific theories and methods of classifying racial types reached their logical conclusion in the mass extermination of the Jews, other so-called 'racial' minorities (such as Roma) and people with disabilities in Europe during the 1930s and 1940s. This belies the supposed respectable origins of such theories, which culminated in the growth of eugenics in the latter half of the 19th century (Mazower, 1998). As an ideology and a social movement, social Darwinism or eugenics (Greek for 'good birth') grew out of a corrupt adaptation of Darwin's ideas of 'natural selection', inspired by the Malthusian theory of overpopulation (see Burleigh, 2005). One of the key proponents of this theory, the statistician Francis Galton, who was also Darwin's cousin, propagated the idea of having a 'national breeding policy' for improving the 'national stock' during the 1860s (see Kuper, 2002, p 183).

The horrors of the Holocaust have sometimes obscured the enthusiasm for and respectable popularity of eugenic thinking among social and political thinkers at both ends of the political spectrum, including the Webbs, Keynes, Beveridge and Barnardo. In 1931, for example, Lord D'Abernon, Chair of the Medical

Research Council, argued that public policy had a responsibility to 'root out (the) weak-minded, inefficient and less capable' (quoted in Gardiner, 2010, p 211). Consequently, for much of the late 19th and early 20th centuries, eugenics was a perfectly acceptable idea, popular across much of Europe and North America, and seen as a way of bettering the lot of ordinary people by improving the racial health of the nation (Morabia, 2011).

Deterministic views on 'race' underpinning the UK eugenics movement were intertwined with notions of class, gender and disability and with wider concerns about social 'deviants' who were perceived as a threat to the moral or physical well-being of the nation. Hence, racial/immigrant groups (including White minorities such as the Irish, who have an ambivalent position in the UK), single mothers, unemployed people, as well as those with physical, mental or learning disabilities, were deemed socially and politically unfit to be granted full, substantial citizenship rights (Brendon, 2002).

The controversial policy of the forced sterilisation of people with mental disabilities across the UK and many countries of the world in the first half of the 20th century sought to prevent the reproduction of people considered to have 'faulty genes'; the theory, albeit with a more liberal emphasis on informed choice, laid the foundation for modern genetics (Kerr and Cunningham-Burley, 2000). The National Socialists' infamous Law for the Prevention of Hereditarily Diseased Offspring came into force in Germany in 1933 (see Evans, 2005). By default, the legislation included those with epilepsy or alcoholism, as well as people of mixed racial origin and the so-called 'Rhineland bastards' (children whose fathers were 'colonial' French troops, stationed there during the occupation of the 1920s and 1930s). The seeds of the policy were to be found in the 'social improvement' practices initiated during the liberal democratic Weimar Republic (Lifton, 2000), and in the first eugenic Sterilisation Act enacted in the USA (Indiana) in 1907 (and followed by other states), resulting in 15,000 Americans being sterilised by 1930 (Porter, 1999, p 640). Sterilisation programmes reached a peak during the 1970s. The Federal government supported a Medicaid-funded sterilisation programme which, although seen to be 'voluntary', largely targeted poor and Black, African-American people and Native American people, who were provided with little information about the procedures involved (see Johansen, 1998). Even though forced sterilisation has since been defined as a violation of human rights in Europe and in much of the Western world, Czechoslovakia followed a policy of sterilising Roma women until 1973, and in the state of Oregon in the USA, as late as 1981, the policy had wider reverberations for the poor and for women with disabilities (see Box 2.2).

Box 2.2: Sterilisation of the 'unfit'

Women incarcerated after having been convicted of drug use during pregnancy or of child abuse were, in several states, given the option to take Norplant (a contraceptive) to avoid or reduce the length of incarceration. Norplant has also been suggested as a 'cure for poverty' ... coercing poor women to take this medication for substantial periods. Illinois appellate court denied an attempt to have a woman with a mental disability sterilised against her will. This echoes the 1927 *Buck v Bell* decision that saw the US Supreme Court uphold a ruling that made it legal to sterilise those who were considered socially unfit; among the undesirables were numerous women with disabilities. In his decision at the time, Justice Holmes stated:

> It is better ... if instead of waiting to execute degenerate offspring for crime, or let them starve for their imbecility, society can prevent those ... manifestly unfit from continuing their kind. Three generations of imbeciles is enough.

Source: Martin (2010)

Martin (2010) suggests that debating the right to reproduce of the poor or of women with neurological conditions reflects a persistence of deep-seated social Darwinism in politics (visit the Eugenics Archive for a history and images of the American Eugenics Society, at www.eugenicsarchive.org/eugenics/list3.pl). These views are not restricted to politicians alone; periodically, we find vocal proponents of the idea within established academia in the UK and elsewhere.

The rise and persistence of social Darwinism since the Second World War has to be analysed alongside a severe critique of the theory and concept of biologically distinct races. Especially within the British context, this has led to the substitution of 'race' with 'ethnicity' which, nevertheless, continues to invoke features of race in terms of 'essential' difference related to descent. Consequently, 'race' and 'ethnicity' are often used interchangeably, leading to some confusion. 'Race' also continues to have a contested legal status in the UK (see Chapter 3), while some authors, taking their lead from the USA, continue to use 'race' in quote marks to emphasise its political meaning. The term 'ethnicity', however, has tended to assume increasing significance in the UK policy literature. Within a changing landscape of ethnic diversity and the intersectionality of identities and forms of discrimination, Modood (among others) has called for plural politics and 'coalitional anti-racism' to replace older, hegemonic forms of anti-discrimination based largely on colour (Modood, 2008, p 170).

How far are 'race' and ethnicity different concepts?

Historically, within the social sciences, 'race' and ethnicity were treated as different analytical concepts, 'race' implying nature or relatedness through genealogy or blood, while 'ethnicity' suggested relatedness through common history and culture. This corresponded with notions of citizenship by *jus sanguinis* (genealogical link) and *jus soli* (place of birth or soil). The two categories, of course, imply each other and cannot be treated as mutually exclusive. Just as 'ethnicity' evokes a sense of common heritage, kinship and descent, 'race' and racism are not only descriptive terms for physical difference but also involve potent cultural metaphors and value judgements justifying negative/discriminatory attitudes (for example, the term 'Paki' used for South Asians in general). This is reflected in many modern States recognising both types of claims to citizenship (Wade, 2007), although the two notions of citizenship are still problematic to reconcile in countries such as France and Germany.

Further, the theory of distinct biological races that can be hierarchically arranged and used to predict intellectual, moral and social qualities was extensively challenged during the 1940s and 1950s in the aftermath of the Holocaust. It is now widely recognised that there are huge variations in physical characteristics within as well as between racial groups, and that the boundaries of racial groups are fluid due to constant movements and intermingling of people from different geographical parts of the world, which were earlier associated with particular racial 'types'. The idea of biologically distinct racial groups has therefore become unsustainable (see Cavalli-Sforza et al, 1994), even though racism remains a pervasive theme of our social and political domains, leaning on racial categories and, at times, emphasising a form of cultural imperialism/superiority.

The term 'racism' has been part of the British lexicon since the 1930s. Its meaning and political significance has shifted over time. For many decades, racism was associated with an *ideology* structuring power, privilege and economic opportunities in favour of the dominant/majority ethnic group(s). The overt political context has gradually been replaced by a new focus resulting in what has been termed *cultural racism* or *racalisation of culture* in the UK (Banton, 1987; Gilroy, 1987). The latter assumes essentialised, immutable cultural and religious differences of immigrant minority communities, which are seen to be in conflict with traditional 'British values' and a 'British way of life' and to threaten the idea of a British nation as a cohesive, self-defined homogeneous unity in the imaginary past (see Chapter 4, including the section discussing the rise of 'community cohesion', p 68).

People of immigrant origin (irrespective of the length of their settlement), who may be different in terms of their culture (that is, religion, language, dress, gender and kinship relationships), are perceived as a threat to national identity and to dominant (White) cultural values, and are therefore pushed to the political periphery (see Modood, 2008, pp 164-8). The animated political debate on the practice of consanguineous marriage between Muslims of South Asian origin, who suffer higher incidences of birth disorders and certain genetically inherited conditions such as thalassaemia, reminds us of how the boundaries of liberal multiculturalism are defined around default/dominant White cultural values. Cultural amnesia about the practice of 'cousin marriage' in (White) Britain in the past, which is well documented in literature (see Kuper, 2002; Bittles, 2015; Shaw, 2015), serves to redefine such practices as alien and exotic. At the same time, a focus on culture and tradition draws our attention away from the disproportionate levels of poverty, unemployment, discrimination and lack of social capital faced by some people within these communities, resulting in poor communication, lack of access to appropriate health and social care services and hence poorer health outcomes (see Bradford and District Infant Mortality Commission, 2006; see also Chapters 6 and 7, this volume). These social factors can impinge on outcomes of childhood disability and chronic illness in more significant ways than a cultural preference for marrying a cousin *per se*.

Defining the cultural values or practices of minority communities as deviant and looking for 'acculturation' as the solution to their social and healthcare needs serves the same ideological purpose as policies of assimilation did in the past (also see Chapter 4). Recent policies aiming at the repatriation of the Roma in France, and the highly controversial and divisive Prevent strategy in the UK (discussed in Chapters 4 and 10; see also Halliday, 2017), remind us about the boundaries of the notion of a liberal democratic state (see Kumar, 2008; Modood, 2008). Importantly, and rather ironically, cultural protectionism can result in perpetuating discrimination and violence against certain groups, especially women and children, within minority communities, since challenging traditional cultural or religious practices runs the risk of being perceived as a form of cultural racism. In the UK, for example, the legal sanction against female genital mutilation (FGM) did not have much of an impact on curtailing the practice now widely condemned by a number of international and national organisations as a basic human rights violation (see www.equalitynow.org/issues/end-female-genital-mutilation; www.forwarduk.org.uk/wp-content/uploads/2014/12/CHANGE-Responding-to-FGM-A-Guide-for-Key-Professionals.pdf; the UN Universal Declaration of Human Rights, especially Article 4; and the UN Convention on the Rights of the Child, especially Articles 16, 19, 29 and 34).

'Race', nation and nationality

The word 'nation' is said to have found its way into the English lexicon through the French language, and has retained its Latin root (*natio/nasci*), which is associated with birth, tribe or common descent. Earlier definitions assumed the aggregate to be coterminous with a 'race'/ethnic group, sharing a common language, history and heritage and usually occupying a state or political territory. More recent definitions, however, concede the idea that a nation can incorporate people of one or more cultures and descents, forming a single state (such as Australia), or an aggregate of people sharing a common descent, language and history but not constituting a state (such as the French Canadian nation) (see Kymlicka, 2001; this also applies to the concept of First Nations in Canada, Australia, the USA, New Zealand, Scandinavia and Botswana). The idea of a deterritorialised nation and multiple nationalities seems to clash with constant struggles between ethnic groups over the redrawing of territorial boundaries of state and nationhood along ethnic/religious lines, as we have seen across Russia and much of Eastern and South-Eastern Europe (see Davies, 2012). Hence, the ideas of ethnic groups, 'race' and nation are socially constructed, intersecting in different ways within particular political contexts and changing over time. The declaration of the Republic of Kosovo as an independent state in 2008, recognised by some UN member states, is a good example of the constructed nature of ethnic identity (Beaumont, 2010).

Such debates have a particular salience for the UK. As mentioned above, almost 60% of people of minority ethnic origin living in the UK were born in the UK and may be of the second, third or fourth generation of families who moved and settled here in the past. This points to the dilemmas of diasporic identities involving plural claims to ethnicity, nationality and citizenship within a global context (see Koshy and Radhakrishnan, 2008). As outlined in other chapters, different minority ethnic groups may have particular histories of settlement and sociodemographic profiles that are linked closely to their post-colonial past. We know that certain ethnic groups (for example, those of Bangladeshi, Pakistani, African and Caribbean origins) face higher levels of unemployment and socioeconomic disadvantage than White majority and other (non-White) minority ethnic groups (see Chapters 9 and 10). The cumulative sociodemographic changes due to recent migration, and the presence of ethnic groups from the EU and war-ravaged societies from across Iraq, Syria, Afghanistan and parts of Africa, remain to be analysed in light of the economic and legal ramifications of the forthcoming Brexit negotiations (see Chapters 3 and 4).

It is important to remember, however, that these collective histories and profiles do not necessarily pre-empt the negotiation of individual identity and significance of ethnic origin/heritage, 'race' (often defined as 'colour of my skin'), nationality or indeed socioeconomic position. The following excerpt (see Case study 2.1) from research conducted with young people of Pakistani origin (between 2000-03) in Northern England provides an example highlighting the complex interplay between these three terms, and why we need to engage with the social and biographical context within which concepts of ethnicity and nationality must be operationalised (Atkin and Chattoo, 2006).

Case study 2.1: Dress as cultural identity

Yasmin is 15 years old. She was born and grew up in an inner-city neighbourhood in England, in a Muslim family originating from Pakistan. She goes to a 'rough' comprehensive school. Her White schoolmates pick on girls like her for wearing a hijab, as this is seen to symbolise a lack of choice and freedom at home. Wearing a hijjab is, however, central to Yasmin's religious and ethnic identity. At the same time, her resistance to the racist attitudes (to religious difference and immigrant origin) of her White schoolmates translates her ethnic origin into an inalienable part of herself (see Chapter 11 on the perceptions of Black men being 'mad and bad'). It is indeed likely that, had we conducted the research more recently, Yasmin might have had a very different response to wearing a hijab within the current pervasive mood of Islamophobia.

Yasmin: 'It's our decision really if you want to wear it [hijab] or not ... Yeah, I think it's important for us because that's like the, our, you know, we're known as Pakistanis, and that's like, you know ...'

Interviewer: 'Where you came from?'

Yasmin: 'Yeah, that's it, even though, you know, you say you're British, you are British, but then again, you know, in some people's eyes, you're Asian British, not like *British* British.' [her emphasis]

Interviewer: 'But do you feel that that's where you came from, although you were born here?'

Yasmin: 'But then again, if you go back on the parents, you know, if the parents were not here, obviously you would be a Pakistani. Then again, you know, it's the way you feel. So I sometime do say, "Yeah, I am British", but then again, sometimes they can discriminate, you know, then you feel as if, "Fine, okay, I'm not a British, but at least I'm a *Pakistani*"!' [her emphasis]

Yasmin's case study illustrates how ethnicity is a dynamic process involving negotiation of self-identity in relation to significant others within a particular context, rather than a fixed attribute of groups *per se*. However, dominant voices within ethnic groups as a collective (such as self-styled 'community leaders' or those adhering to particular versions of religious doctrine) can project a cohesive image of their culture, religion and family/kin relationships. It is therefore essential that we differentiate between these idealised self-descriptions of community and our analytical framework for making sense of (operationalising) ethnicity and 'race', as suggested by Baumann (1997) and discussed earlier. This is an important step in addressing the goal of a culturally sensitive health and welfare provision, without recourse to broad generalisations and stereotypes.

Why focus on operationalising ethnicity?

Despite the fact that people from a majority (White) background also share an ethnic background, ethnicity is often treated as an exotic feature of minority communities, designating their immigrant origins (also see above). Explanations for the health and social care needs of people from the majority White community are premised on a notion of individuals making autonomous choices, while those of people from minority ethnic backgrounds are located within culture, tradition, religion and extended family values. For example, South Asian communities, despite internal diversity related to ethnic origin, religion, language and socioeconomic position, are treated as a conglomerate of well-defined cultures. 'Asians' are still perceived to be living in patriarchal, extended family structures where young people and women, in particular, have no choice, and where families 'take care of their own'.

In our research on cancer-(treatment-)related threats to fertility, we found old stereotypes of fatalism, gender and extended family structure persisting in the attitudes of some professionals working within the fields of cancer and reproductive medicine. This occurs despite decades of research evidence illustrating the complex patterns of diversity and difference within and similarities across ethnic groups. Case study 2.2 provides an example of how similar responses of people from White and South Asian backgrounds to infertility and treatment were interpreted by professionals in different frameworks (see Chattoo, 2015).

Case study 2.2: Culture and fertility

The project explored the long-term social and emotional impact of cancer on adults (aged 18-40) whose fertility was threatened by their treatment. Apart from a sample of patients, 33 health and social care practitioners representing different disciplines and services took part in the research to provide a context of the clinical settings within which care is provided (Atkin et al, 2014). The findings from the professional interviews and focus group discussions suggested that 'Asians', without qualification, are believed to follow the tradition of 'arranged marriages', excluding notions of individual choice and romantic love. Following the same logic, any strain or breakdown of conjugal relationships due to the infertility of a partner is attributed to a 'pro-natalist' culture and to men who, due to family pressures, are perceived as being less supportive of women having trouble in conceiving. However, examples of White partners breaking off relationships in a similar situation are attributed to interpersonal strain and choice. For example, one of the professionals mentioned the case of a White man whose fertility was affected by treatment related to cancer. He broke off a long-term relationship with his partner, who was keen on having a child using donor insemination. Neither her desire to have a child nor his inability to 'get his head round' donor insemination was attributed to 'culture' or a wider set of shared values. In contrast, an 'Asian' man's refusal to let his wife use preserved embryos from a previous relationship was attributed to both personal and cultural reasons. Similarly, sharing information about fertility treatment selectively with family and friends, much respected as a matter of *privacy* in a White family, is construed as *secrecy* within South Asian families who, it is assumed, will not tell anyone about a child's donor conception. This attitude disregards evidence about the secrecy surrounding donor conception in the wider White culture. A relatively recent shift in legislation enabling adult donor-conceived children to find out the identity of their biological parent/s still does not make it obligatory for parents to disclose the information.

Personal views of professionals about minority religious or cultural values and professional judgements about conjugal/gender or intergenerational relationships can have implications for the treatment options and quality of information and support offered to individuals. Equally importantly, in focusing on cultural difference, people of immigrant origin are treated as partial citizens, somehow 'less civilized', who need to be brought into the fold of (taught) core liberal values of the 'host society'. It is assumed that, with time, they will assimilate and integrate into the 'British way of life' (see Chapter 4).

Further, bureaucratic policies, procedures and language reinforce the status and feelings of partial citizenship experienced by people of immigrant origin. The British Home Office document to help people undertaking the Citizenship Test, introduced in 2005, is a good reflection of the tensions underpinning the process of inclusion and membership for new citizens. Apart from knowledge of an idealised and imagined version of British history and 'way of life', they also have to pledge allegiance to the Queen, an act that others (non-immigrant citizens who regard themselves as Republicans) might interpret as a matter of personal choice (see Byrne, 2017; and www.lifeintheuktest.gov.uk/; see also Chapter 3). Further, cultural and historical differences between English, Scottish, Welsh and Irish citizens (and indeed Northern Irish citizens – see recent debates about abortion) are easily overlooked within this construction of a British identity.

Conclusion

To conclude, what relevance does the above discussion have to the broader issues of social policy and welfare raised within this book? Going back to our earlier point about cultural competence, as social scientists we need to be critical about what constitutes 'evidence', who is producing it and how professionals are being certified as 'competent'. On the surface, the basic components of different models of cultural competency cover the three areas of *cultural sensitivity, cultural knowledge* and *cultural skills* (Kim-Godwin et al, 2001). It is assumed that a combination of such skills, knowledge and sensitivity enables health and social care professionals to address issues of difference and diversity. However, each component assumes a static notion of culture as a set of shared system of beliefs and values that can be described and 'known' in order to be incorporated into short training courses for health and social care professionals. Gunaratnam, following Giddens' notion of an 'abstract system' (that helps define boundaries and responses to the uncertain), suggests that such attempts at regulating practice and responses to caring can:

> undermine equity and erode responsibility for emotional and moral thinking through their attempts to simplify and control the threat of the unfamiliar. (Gunaratnam, 2008, p 25)

However, she also shows how individual healthcare professionals challenge such attempts at the codification of responses in their negotiations of the emotional complexities of the lives of individuals they are caring for, highlighting uncertainties and dilemmas posed by caring within the context of old age and death. This serves as a reminder that the collective values underpinning professional codes and practices are interpreted and negotiated differently in practice by different individuals. Further, any understanding and responses to diversity and pluralism have to be part of the larger process of living, being educated in and feeling part of a plural or diverse society.

The current framework of ethnicity underpinning health and social welfare provision serves to reinforce perceptions of 'settlers' as partial citizens or 'permanent minorities' (Koshy and Radhakrishnan, 2008). We need to destabilise the dualism between majority and minority, immigrant and host, and traditional and Western cultures, reiterating the view of culture as a dynamic process marked by social divisions of gender, generation and socioeconomic position. This requires an anti-essentialist, conceptual shift in recognising difference as part of self rather than as a defining feature of the other as exterior to self. (The chapters in Part Two of this book highlight the analytical value of such an approach.) As suggested by Hall (1996), we need to disentangle ethnicity from its anti-racist paradigm and use it in a positive context of identities (and culture) that are both specific and responsive to dialogue and transformation (for an analytical review, see Papastergiadis, 1997). Such a move can help us to challenge historically specific discrimination against men and women of minoritised cultures, focusing on intersectionality between ethnicity, gender and socioeconomic position, and to grant equal citizenship rights to those who may, at different points of time in history, be considered settlers or immigrants. Recent debates on immigration and Brexit reiterate the enduring significance of ethnicity/'race' as the, 'parchment written upon ... where nothing is ever entirely erased', so poignantly highlighted by Kwame Anthony Appiah in his Reith Lectures, quoted at the beginning of this chapter.

Questions for discussion

- Why do we need to critically evaluate the use of 'ethnicity' as a social construct? How is it related to ideas of 'race' and nation?
- A couple in Berkshire were denied an application for adoption on the basis of their heritage 'race' (see BBC News, 2017c). Discuss the case in view of the change in adoption guidelines making the 'race'/ethnicity of adopting parents irrelevant to the process of adoption.
- Look up 'What does the 2011 Census tell us about inter-ethnic relationships?' (ONS, 2014). Discuss the implications for children growing up in such families. For example, how do you think these children might be treated at school and in the playground? How do we think of racial or ethnic boundaries between groups, especially where a parent and a child or siblings have different 'skin colour'?

Online resources

www.bbc.co.uk/programmes/b080t63w
  A recording of Kwame Anthony Appiah's Reith Lecture (3) 'Mistaken identities', BBC Radio 4.

www.migrationobservatory.ox.ac.uk
  The Migration Observatory (part of COMPAS – Centre on Migration, Policy and Society, University of Oxford) conducts research and analysis on the potential impact of Brexit, alongside other migration-related issues.

www.gov.uk/government/publications/operation-vaken-evaluation-report
  Operation Vaken: Evaluation report.

References

Anderson, B. (1991) *Imagined communities*, London: Verso.

Anthias, F. and Yuval-Davis, N. (1992) *Racialised boundaries: Race, nation, gender, colour and class and anti-racist struggle*, London and New York: Routledge.

Atkin, K. and Chattoo, S. (2006) 'Approaches to conducting qualitative research in ethnically diverse populations', in J. Nazroo (ed) *Methodological issues in research relating to Black and minority ethnic groups: Publishing the evidence*, London: Taylor & Francis, 95–115.

Atkin, K., Chattoo, S. and Crawshaw, M. (2014) 'Clinical encounters and culturally competent practice: The challenges of providing cancer and infertility care', *Policy & Politics*, 42(4), 581-97 (http://dx.doi.org/10.1332/030557312X655675).

Banton, M. (1987) *Racial theories*, Cambridge: Cambridge University Press.

Banton, M. (2000) 'Ethnic conflict', *Sociology*, 34, 481-98.

Barth, F. (1969) *The social organisation of cultural difference*, London: Allen & Unwin.

Baumann, G. (1997) 'Dominant and demotic discourses of culture: Their relevance to multi-ethnic alliances', in P. Werbner and T. Modood (eds) *Debating cultural hybridity: Multi-cultural identities and the politics of anti-racism*, London: Zed Books, 209-25.

BBC News (2017a) 'Is Islamophobia on the rise?', 20 June (www.bbc.co.uk/news/av/uk-40350292/is-islamophobia-on-the-rise).

BBC News (2017b) 'Anti-Semitic incidents "at record level in UK"', 27 July (www.bbc.co.uk/news/uk-40735634).

BBC News (2017c) 'Couple blocked from adopting "due to cultural heritage"', 27 June (www.bbc.co.uk/news/uk-england-berkshire-40416237).

Beaumont, P. (2010) 'Kosovo breakaway from Serbia was legal, world court rules', *The Guardian*, 22 July (www.guardian.co.uk/world/2010/jul/22/kosovo-breakaway-serbia-legal-world-court).

Bhabha, H. (1994) *The location of culture*, London: Routledge.

Bigo, D. (2002) 'Security and immigration: Toward a critique of the governmentality of unease', *Alternatives*, Special Issue, 27, 63-92.

Bittles, A. (2015) 'Prevalence and outcomes of consanguineous marriage in contemporary societies', in A. Shaw and A. Raz (eds) *Cousin marriages: Between tradition, genetic risk and cultural change*, New York and Oxford: Berghahn Books, Chapter 1.

Bloch, A., Neal, S. and Solomos, J. (2013) *Race, multiculture and social policy*, Basingstoke and New York: Palgrave Macmillan.

Bradford and District Infant Mortality Commission (2006) *Final report*, Bradford: Bradford Vision (www.bradford.gov.uk/media/1881/infant_mortality_report.pdf).

Brendon, R. (2002) *The dark valley: A panorama of the 1930s*, New York: Vintage Books.

Burleigh, M. (2002) *Germany turns eastwards*, London: Pan.

Byrne, B. (2017) 'Testing times: The place of the Citizenship Test in the UK immigration regime and the new citizens' responses to it', *Sociology*, 51(2), 323-38.

Cavalli-Sforza, L., Menozzi, P. and Piazza, A. (1994) *The history and geography of human genes*, Princeton, NJ: Princeton University Press.

Chattoo. S. (2014) '"Listening to voices": Immigrants, settlers and citizens at the ethnic margins of the state', in R. Chatterji (ed) *Wording the word: Veena Das and the scenes of inheritance*, New York: Fordham University Press, 211-35.

Chattoo, S. (2015) 'Reproductive technologies and ethnic minorities: Beyond a marginalising discourse on the marginalised communities', in K. Hampshire and R. Simpson (eds) *Assisted reproductive technologies in the third phase: Global encounters and emerging moral worlds*, Fertility, Reproduction and Sexuality Series, New York and Oxford: Berghahn Books, Chapter 10 (www.berghahnbooks. com/title.php?rowtag=HampshireAssisted).

Cobain, I. and Taylor, M. (2016) 'Far-right terrorist Thomas Mair jailed for life for Jo Cox murder', *The Guardian*, 23 November (www.theguardian.com/uk-news/2016/nov/23/thomas-mair-found-guilty-of-jo-cox-murder).

Davies, N. (2012) *Vanished kingdoms: The history of half-forgotten Europe*, London: Penguin.

Evans, R.J. (2005) *The Third Reich in power*, London: Allen Lane.

Fenton, S. (2003) *Ethnicity*, Cambridge: Polity Press.

Gardiner, J. (2010) *The Thirties: An intimate history*, London: HarperPress.

Gilroy, P. (1987) *There ain't no Black in the Union Jack: The cultural politics of race and nation*, London: Hutchinson.

Guentner, S., Lukes, Stanton, R., Vollmer, B.A. and Wilding, J. (2016) 'Bordering practices in the UK welfare system', *Critical Social Policy*, 36(3), 391–411.

Gunaratnam, Y. (1997) 'Culture is not enough: A critique of multiculturalism in palliative care', in D. Field, J. Hockey and N. Small (eds) *Death, gender and ethnicity*, London: Routledge, 166–86.

Gunaratnam, Y. (2008) 'From competence of vulnerability: Care, ethics and elders from racialized minorities', *Mortality*, 13(1), 24–41.

Hall, S. (1996) 'Introduction: Who needs identity?', in S. Hall and P. du Gay (eds) *Questions of cultural identity*, London: Sage, 1-7.

Halliday, J. (2017) 'Andy Burnham pledges to replace Prevent strategy in Manchester', *The Guardian*, 22 June (www.theguardian.com/uk-news/2017/jun/22/prevent-andy-burnham-greater-manchester-muslim-communities).

Home Office (2013) *Operation Vaken: Evaluation report*, Annexe A, 31 October (www.gov.uk/government/publications/operation-vaken-evaluation-report).

Johansen, B.E. (1998) 'Reprise/forced sterilizations: Sterilization of Native American women' (www.ratical.org/ratville/sterilize.html).

Jones, H., Gunaratnam, Y., Bhattacharyya, G., Davies, W., Dhaliwal, S., Forkert, K., et al (eds) (2017) *Go home! The politics of immigration controversies*, Manchester: Manchester University Press.

Jones, O. (2017) 'Have no pity for May. Don't forgive, and never forget why she must go', *The Guardian*, 14 June (www.theguardian.com/commentisfree/2017/jun/14/theresa-may-must-go-election-campaign).

Keay, J. (2004) *India: A history*, London: HarperCollins.

Kerr, A. and Cunningham-Burley, S. (2000) 'On ambivalence and risk: Reflexive modernity and the new human genetics', *Sociology*, 34(2), 283-304.

Kim-Godwin, Y.S., Clarke, P.N. and Barton, L. (2001) 'A model for the delivery of culturally competent community care', *Journal of Advanced Nursing*, 35(6), 918-25.

Koshy, S. and Radhakrishnan, R. (eds) (2008) *Transnational South Asians: The making of a neo-diaspora*, Delhi, India: Oxford University Press.

Kumar, K. (2008) 'Core ethnicities and the problem of multiculturalism: The British case', in J. Eade, M. Barrett, C. Flood and R. Race (eds) *Advancing multiculturalism, post 7/7*, Newcastle: Cambridge Scholars Publishing, 116-34.

Kuper, A. (2002) 'Incest, cousin marriage and the origin of human sciences in nineteenth century England', *Past & Present*, 174, 158-83.

Kymlicka, W. (2001) *Politics in the vernacular: Nationalism, multiculturalism and citizenship*, Oxford: Oxford University Press.

Lifton, R.J. (2000) *The Nazi doctors: Medical killing and the psychology of genocide*, New York: Basic Books.

Lo, M.M. and Stacey, C.L. (2008) 'Beyond cultural competence: Bourdieu, patients and clinical encounters', *Sociology of Health and Illness*, 30(5), 741-55.

Mann, R. and Fenton, S. (2017a) *Nation, class and resentment: The politics of national identity in England, Scotland and Wales*, London, New York and Melbourne: Palgrave Macmillan.

Mann, R. and Fenton, S. (2017b) 'English national identity, resentment and the Leave vote', *Discover Society*, 6 June (http://discoversociety.org/2017/06/06/english-national-identity-resentment-and-the-leave-vote).

Martin, R. (2010) 'Forced sterilisation: A Western issue too', *The Guardian*, 4 May (www.guardian.co.uk/commentisfree/libertycentral/2010/may/04/forced-sterilisation-women-motherhood).

Mazower, M. (1998) *Dark continent: Europe's twentieth century*, London: Penguin.

Mirza, H. (2009a) 'Plotting history: Black and post-colonial feminisms in "new times"', *Race Ethnicity and Education*, 12(1), 1-10.

Mirza, H. (2009b) *Race, gender and educational desire: Why black women succeed and fail*, London: Routledge.

Modood, T. (2008) 'South Asian assertiveness in Britain', in S. Koshy and R. Radhakrishnan (eds) *Transnational South Asians: The making of a neo-diaspora*, Delhi, India: Oxford University Press, 124-45.

Morabia, A. (2011) *Enigmas of health and disease*, New York: Columbia University Press.

Mortimer, C. (2017) 'Catalan crisis: Why does Catalonia want independence? Do the majority really support it?', *The Independent*, 29 October (www.independent.co.uk/news/world/europe/catalan-crisis-why-does-catalonia-want-independence-do-people-really-support-it-spain-latest-a8025836.html).

ONS (Office for National Statistics) (2014) '2011 Census analysis: What does the 2011 Census tell us about inter-ethnic relationships', 3 July (www.ons.gov.uk/peoplepopulationandcommunity/birthsdeathsandmarriages/marriagecohabitationandcivilpartnerships/datasets/2011censusanalysiswhatdoesthe2011censustellusaboutinterethnicrelationships).

Papastergiadis, N. (1997) 'Tracing hybridity in theory', in P. Werbner and T. Modood (eds) *Debating cultural hybridity: Multi-cultural identities and the politics of anti-racism*, London and Atlantic Highlands, NJ: Zed Books, 257–81.

Phoenix, A. (2009) 'De-colonising practices: Negotiating narratives from racialised and gendered experiences of education', *Race Ethnicity and Education*, 12(1), 101–14.

Porter, R. (1999) *The greatest benefit to mankind: A medical history of humanity from antiquity to present*, London: Fontana.

Said, E. (2003) *Orientalism*, London: Penguin.

Shaw, A. (2015) 'British Pakistani cousin marriages and the negotiation of reproductive risk', in A. Shaw and A. Raz (eds) *Cousin marriages: Between tradition, genetic risk and cultural change*, New York and Oxford: Berghahn Books, 113–29.

Silverstein, P.A. (2005) 'Immigrant racialisation and the new savage slot: Race, migration, and immigration in the New Europe', *Annual Review of Anthropology*, 34, 363–84.

Tharoor, S (2017) *Inglorious Empire: What the British did to India*, London: Hurst.

Vertovec, S. (2007) 'Super-diversity and its implications', *Ethnic and Racial Studies*, 29(6), 1024–54.

Vertovec, S. (2011) 'The cultural politics of nation and migration', *Annual Review of Anthropology*, 40, 241–56.

Wade, P. (2007) 'Race, ethnicity and nation: Perspectives from kinship and genetics', in P. Wade (ed) *Race, ethnicity and nation: Perspectives from kinship and genetics*, New York and Oxford: Berghahn Books, 1–32.

Werbner, P. (1997) 'Introduction: The dialectics of cultural hybridity', in P. Werbner and T. Modood (eds) *Debating cultural hybridity: Multicultural identities and the politics of anti-racism*, London and Atlantic Highlands, NJ: Zed Books, 1–28.

Werbner, P. and Modood, T. (eds) (1997) *Debating cultural hybridity: Multicultural identities and the politics of anti-racism*, London and Atlantic Highlands, NJ: Zed Books.

Wootton, D. (2016) *The invention of science: A new history of scientific revolution*, London: Penguin.

Yuval-Davis, N. (2006) 'Inter-sectionality and feminist politics', *European Journal of Women's Studies*, 13(3), 193–219.

3

Migration(s): the history and pattern of settlement of the UK's Black and minority ethnic population

Gary Craig

'... go back to your own f—g country!'
A GROUP OF IRISHMEN ATTACKING A CARIBBEAN MAN, LONDON, 1954,
PERSONAL ACCOUNT FROM AUTHOR'S GRANDFATHER

Overview

This chapter traces the history of minority migration to and settlement in the UK. Migration has been driven by invasion, persecution, compulsion (that is, slavery), economic migration, family reunion or the desire to achieve 'a better life'. In the past 70 years, patterns of settlement have reflected natural growth and the distribution of a settled minority presence; now, around 50% of the UK's so-called minority ethnic population were born in the UK. Some migration has been temporary, but most migrants come intending to stay.

The most significant migration occurred after the Second World War, stimulated by the settlement of refugees and post-war reconstruction. This was almost immediately limited by restrictive legislation, which continues to the present. In the late 20th century, immigration reflected family reunion and the impact of war and political upheaval, which led to a substantial number of refugees. Throughout the second half of the 20th century, a driver for minority population growth was natural growth among the settled population. In the early part of the 21st century, the most significant migrant flow to the UK was economic migrants from new European Union (EU) member states. Many of these may not settle permanently, particularly since the 2016 referendum result on the UK's EU membership.

Certain themes recur throughout history, such as the categorisation of immigrants as 'other', which – underpinned by racist ideologies – led to discrimination and difficulties for minorities trying to pursue lives as equal citizens in the UK. The present demographic mix in the UK is not the product of recent migrations but of change over 2,000 years; virtually all the UK population has genes and cultures reflecting migration from both within and outside the British Isles. This challenges ideas of a homogeneous British 'race' and identity and of 'Britishness', with its set of values relating solely to White UK-born residents.

The numbers, types and origins of migrants were originally determined by the UK's historical links and its international and national political and policy frameworks, but have been shaped by wider and more contemporary economic and political factors (IPPR, 2007; Khan, 2015). This has led to changing patterns of settlement in which categories of minority ethnic, majority, immigrant and settler have also been fluid, challenging the perception of a unitary, coherent British identity. Khan's report (2015) demonstrates how far Britain's Black and minority ethnic (BME) population still has to go to achieve real equality within the UK polity (see also EHRC, 2015).

The UK's population is now 'super-diverse', with settled minorities in every UK local authority area. These area populations vary in terms of the mix of settled BME populations, asylum-seekers and refugees, migrant workers and new migrant communities, with varying – but complex – implications for policy. Ideas of what ethnicity is and the meaning of diversity are changing in ways yet to be grasped effectively by public and private agencies. Previous ways of classifying and debating the issue are outdated, and require increasingly sophisticated responses.

Key concepts
complexity; continuity and change; diversity and difference; history of migration; 'other'; outsider; racism; super-diversity

Early minority settlement[1]

Migration to the UK did not start, as many believe, in 1948, nor is racism a recent phenomenon. Although the post-Second World War was a period of substantial migration, minorities have lived in the UK for over 2,000 years, and have experienced racism in many forms. Key events in the early part of the Common Era (CE) period are listed below, but see Olusoga (2016) for a full account:

- A succession of European invasions involving Romans (Italians), Vikings (Scandinavians), Saxons (Germans) and Normans (French). The Roman army brought with it Black Sudanese slaves.
- Black people settled in Britain soon after, whose remains have been found in archaeological digs.
- The first recorded institutionally sponsored racism was against Jews in the 12th century, many of whom had arrived in the previous century. Jewish families were persecuted and killed. King Edward I (1239-1307) forcibly expelled the Jews in 1290; most were not readmitted until Cromwell's time, in the 17th century.
- The first Muslims came to Britain in the 12th century; Queen Elizabeth I later offered to form an alliance against Spain with a Moroccan Islamic leader.
- People from Wales, Scotland and Ireland also migrated to England – forming 'Celtic minorities' – for a variety of reasons, including intermarriage.
- Millions of native Irish migrated to the UK and elsewhere, escaping poverty and famine, and now form one of the largest minorities within the UK. They were recognised in the 2001 Census, which introduced the category of 'White Irish'. Gypsies were first recorded in the British Isles in the early 15th century, labelled as such due to their perceived resemblance to 'Egyptians'.
- Substantial Black settlement started with the history of slavery. Most slaves captured in coastal African regions were trans-shipped directly to the Americas, and some were brought to the UK, where they were confined to domestic labour (for example, as footmen and nursemaids). Most lived in and around London and in ports such as Bristol and Liverpool, although a few lived in rural areas, who have been identified by gravestones in village churchyards. Some were freed, became residents, thus technically English citizens, but edicts continued to be issued against them.
- The Privy Council in 1596 ordered that all 'negroes and blackamoors' be deported; and again, in 1601 (just before the Poor Law), declared that 'the Queen's own natural subjects were greatly distressed in these hard times of dearth' (quoted in Olusoga, 2016), meaning that the settled English population resented others settling.
- By 1713, slavery provided a substantial income to Britain, when Spain granted England the right to supply British and Spanish American colonies with hundreds of thousands of African slaves. Consequently, by 1772, the UK Black population had increased rapidly.

Box 3.1: Slaves as citizens or 'other'?

The status of Black people was legally tested during the 18th century, through the Somerset case, where it was argued by Granville Sharp that toleration of slavery was toleration of inhumanity; and a famous – if reluctant – legal ruling was given that slaves could not lawfully be deported against their will and that all people in Britain were subject to its laws. This meant that (Black) slaves could not technically exist in Britain (a ruling later overturned). Despite the Somerset ruling, many 'freed' slaves in Britain continued to be kidnapped and returned to the Caribbean as slaves.

Box 3.2: Migration and links to seafaring

Most early African immigrants arrived in the UK as slaves, some jumping ship when they arrived. A few came as free seafarers, while others were freed by owners as a reward for years of service. London, Liverpool, Glasgow and Bristol became centres for slave trading, the economic growth of the last two being largely founded on it; cities with docks serving international trade became home to Britain's first concentrated minority populations, including many Muslims. These and other cities (Cardiff and Tyneside) later witnessed the arrival of thousands of seafarers from countries with significant maritime histories that provided unskilled labour (notably Chinese and Yemenis) to work below decks in mercantile shipping. These minorities remain there today.

- Some migrants arrived by strange routes. For example, 200 Black slaves from Dutch plantations accompanied William of Orange when he arrived in 1688 to become King of England. By 1772, there were approximately 14,000 'minority' people in Britain, mostly Black with some from Asia, out of a population of 8 million, that is, less than one quarter of 1%. Among them were Muslims who were either ex-slaves or traders. The flow of Muslims, particularly from South Asia, increased with Britain's imperial reach, reflecting wider movements of indentured labour from South Asia.

After the slave trade

The liberal myth is that the British slave trade was abolished in 1807 because of the campaigning of William Wilberforce and others (Equiano, 2007). Certainly, the parliamentary campaign was effective in raising consciousness of slavery's horrors, and slavery began to wither away by the end of the 18th century, although it was not formally abolished until the Slavery Abolition Act 1833. Black resistance and self-organisation were significant in making slavery uneconomic: slaves increasingly challenged their masters' authority and left their households. Partly in response to the vagaries of the law and to help gather support for slaves, Black organisations formed and campaigned, and Black prisoners were supported by their communities. Some worked as craftspeople and on the land, others as seamstresses and nurses. Freed slaves such as Equiano (1789 [2007]), who had learned to read and write – fed by revolutions in France and the USA and the writings of Thomas Paine – began to agitate about the conditions of slaves. Prejudice against Black people, however, remained embedded.

Racism took new forms, prompted by government example. Black American slaves fighting for Britain in the American War of Independence, whether technically citizens or not, and fleeing at the end of the war to British Canada, were resettled on poor farming land in Nova Scotia. They were then transported back to the disease-ridden, impoverished coast of Sierra Leone – where slavery was still active – under the illusion of forming the first Black colony. Those who came to the 'motherland' faced a life of poverty, an experience repeated in the 20th century. Black ex-slaves were denied levels of relief given to White ex-soldiers.

One continuing thread throughout the history of Black and minority settlement has been how racism has legitimised discriminatory treatment of the 'other' within private and public domains. Historically, this has not been solely about White racism against those of a different skin colour. As the UK emerged, Scots, Irish and Welsh citizens were incorporated into a unitary nation. Even after the Act of Union, these Celts were minorities within a White Protestant English nation state, discriminated against and subject to racist violence on the basis of geography, culture and, in Scots and Irish instances, their religion. This relationship only began to reverse following the recent partial devolution of Scotland, Wales and Northern Ireland with, ironically, reports of racism against English citizens residing in Wales and Scotland.

From the 16th century, Britain nevertheless developed a reputation as a refuge. Some minority arrivals – such as Jewish people, Protestant Huguenots from the 16th century onwards or Turkish refugees in the early 19th century – sought asylum from political or religious persecution – another irony since, from the early 20th century, the UK has increasingly become obsessed with controlling refugee flows, and now has one of the world's harshest immigration regimes.

The rise of the 'other'

The construction of British identity, begun in English society during the 18th century, required a conception of the 'other'. This not only operated in relation to Jewish populations and Black slaves, but also became associated with other minorities who were seen as not sharing White Protestant Britishness (usually equated with Englishness). Violent anti-popery was commonplace; Methodists were 'cockshires', and Scots- and Irish-baiting were 'national sports'. European neighbours, especially the French, were also targeted. Indeed, as this sense of national identity became more confidently asserted, anyone who was different or perceived as threatening British ideals, ambitions and way of life was classified as inferior and, in some cases, as an enemy. Britain was not alone in this, but chauvinistic suspicion of the 'other' became ingrained in national discourse, the consequences of which are still felt today. In Scotland, notwithstanding the strong Scottish presence in many British colonies, successive waves of migrants – the Irish, Jews, Indians, Italians, Lithuanians and, most recently, English and Polish people – have been characterised as 'other', and as an economic and social threat.

Box 3.3: Early justifications for racism

By the end of the 18th century, racism was being justified on pseudo-scientific grounds, the first major openly racist tract being produced by Edward Long in his 1774 *History of Jamaica*. Long campaigned for the recognition of Black people as sub-human. The notion of Black and Blackness had negative associations, with mourning, death, illness, evil, sin and danger. To this portrayal were added sexual depravity and being monkey-like, ugly and abnormal. This view, drawing on 'scientific' myths, was not far from declaring that people could be graded hierarchically in terms of the colour of their skin, with Black at the bottom. The established church suggest that Noah's son Ham, cursed by God for killing his brother Shem, was Black. Intermarriage was argued against as it would corrupt the 'purity' of English character.

This racism developed through the late 18th/early 19th centuries, seemingly supported by the writings of Carl Linnaeus, who provided an apparently scientific set of national characteristics, shaped by racism. The British Irish population, growing to meet the demand for labour to drive the Industrial Revolution, were similarly labelled and popularly portrayed as violent, drunk, fecund and stupid. The additional barrier of religion was emphasised to underline obstacles to intermarriage. The Scots and Welsh had long been regarded as inferior to the English, and hostility to Catholics overlaid this. Relative toleration of local customs and cultures, characteristic of British commercial engagement in India during the late 18th and early 19th centuries, became replaced by political hostility and condescension.

India became associated with filth and disease and was blamed for cholera outbreaks, which gave rise to an association between ethnicity and (ill) health, as minority ethnic populations became portrayed as carriers of disease. Present-day examples include the links between AIDS and Africa, and associations between tuberculosis and recent migrants to the UK, alongside the renewed call (a feature of 1960s debates) for all migrants to be subject to health checks before being allowed to enter the UK.

In the cases of Ireland and African countries, the sub-humanity attributed to them was used as an argument against self-government. Nineteenth-century racism was not, however, confined to a handful of cranks: most British scientists, politicians, religious leaders and intellectuals took it for granted that only people with white skin were capable of thinking and governing, a view that prevailed well into the 20th century. As one MP put it during a parliamentary debate in the 1920s, 'inferior races were unfitted for advanced British institutions such as representative democracy' (Fryer, 1984). This view, rarely expressed overtly, continues to be held by some politicians; for example, a Tory MP in a 1990s House of Commons debate referred to African governments as 'Bongo Bongo land'.

Increasingly, social and economic class intersected with 'race' and difference. Although Britain's trade often depended on negotiating with rulers in faraway places, most migrants to Britain until the late 19th century were from lower classes. Reflecting a trend that continues to the present, migrants were portrayed as a threat to the indigenous working class rather than as 'workers in common'; frequently, trades unions regressively opposed immigration. Indian migrants who came as servants tended to be Muslims, some later becoming destitute. However, by the mid-19th century, upper- and middle-class Indians were coming to the UK to study law and medicine.

As the Labour movement became more organised, ruling class attitudes towards 'labour agitators' – portrayed as troublemakers unable to govern – widened to cover its stance towards 'natives', illustrating how race and class were increasingly intertwined in political discourse, yet were accorded little attention (Fenton, 1999). Black and Irish peoples were both regarded as impecunious, undercutting English working conditions, and there was agitation against them. As in Africa, the problems of the Irish – of poverty, ill health and poor housing – were created by conditions imposed in their countries by the UK, the colonising power. The Irish made a substantial contribution – only latterly recognised – to the Industrial Revolution, through building urban and transport infrastructure. The contributions of other minorities were also significant, although less prominent.

Within Britain, minorities remained hidden from view, although a hostile focus was constructed by the state. Minorities were, however, organising more formally, attracted by the writings of radical thinkers like Thomas Paine; consequently, they were an easy target for repression and, in some cases, execution. Many were internationalists, joining trades unions and the Chartist movement in the early

19th century. However, it was the activities of their White male counterparts that dominated British historical accounts. For example, (Black) Mary Seacole was as active in promoting the health and welfare of soldiers as was (White) Florence Nightingale in the Crimean war (1853–56), but remained in obscurity until recently; Mary Prince was the first Black slave to have a biographical narrative, but it is far less well known than that of Olaudah Equiano. Similarly, in culture, the music of (Black) Samuel Coleridge-Taylor, 'the English Mahler' (see Elford, 2008), was regarded as highly as that of his European contemporaries, such as Grieg, but was largely written out of history.

By the end of the 19th century, political activism among the UK's minorities had grown, linked to demands for national liberation. The Indian Home Rule Society and the Pan-African Association were connected to political agitation in their 'home' countries by those within the UK and the colonies. Prominent leaders such as Gandhi spent time in London. These movements were encouraged by the Independent Labour Party, support from left-wing politicians such as Henry Hyndman, and growing European revolutionary fervour. Challenges to empire emerged strongly in this period.

Black political activism took more formal turns. The first Black person to hold local government office in Britain became a Battersea councillor in 1906; the first 'minority' MP was Dada Naroji, of Indian origin, elected in Finsbury in 1892. By the turn of the 20th century, new groups were migrating to the UK including Chinese people drawn into trading relationships or working in the merchant navy. Many Jewish people arrived at the end of the 19th century, fleeing pogroms in Russia and Poland. Racism against them was acute, stirred up by the British Brothers League, the forerunner to the National Front, and their arrival led to the first UK anti-immigration legislation, the Aliens Act 1905. More than 2 million people from Scandinavia, Central Europe and Russia – 60% of those migrating to and through the UK at this time – passed through Hull in the 80 years to 1914, transported in highly insanitary conditions and abused virulently by the local population.

The early 20th century

Migration to the UK in the 20th century was a direct consequence of British colonisation. Early on, most Black people were not activists, nor were their exploits on public record: they were poor labourers, 'below-decks' seafarers and in other labouring jobs. White workers were as racist as their ruling class equivalents. Such attitudes continued into the First World War, where, despite the major contribution of Black soldiers (Olusoga, 2016), White soldiers still regarded them as inferior. The army hierarchy promoted a view earlier expressed in 1886 by an adjutant general that Black people, as 'lazy cowards', would undermine the British Army's power. He overlooked the courage of the Ashanti and Zulu nations, which had won military victories when faced with technologically far better-equipped Western armies. After the First World War, and during the Depression of the 1930s, White workers were encouraged by racist propaganda, right-wing trades unions and racist ideologues to regard Black labourers as an economic threat. Tensions again grew, with riots in port areas where sea-based workforces had settled; these 'riots' were often protests against poor housing and working conditions, then used as an excuse by White racists – who often suffered the same conditions – for acts of retaliation, including racist murders, against the 'other'.

By the early 1920s, the Pan-African Congress was campaigning for the liberation of African nations. Within Britain, responses were muted: the League of Coloured Peoples promoted the welfare of people 'in an alien land' (that is, the UK); this was not a radical campaigning organisation but a social club and employment and welfare agency. Other organisations developed with equally modest aims, such as the Coloured Men's Institute. In 1938, a UK branch of the Indian Workers' Association was established in Coventry with a more political intent. Black and Asian people resident in the UK during the 1930s gained the franchise, and many were politicised by African, Caribbean and Asian leaders such as Kwame Nkrumah, Jawaharlal Nehru, Jomo Kenyatta and Julius Nyerere, all studying within the UK and agitating for national independence during the 1930s and 1940s.

The experience of the Second World War mirrored that of the First. Black soldiers became officers for the duration of the war, but their contribution was overlooked in official war histories. By then, however, the notion of the Black person as 'unable to govern' was further challenged: the Labour leader Clement Attlee commented early on that 'we fight this war for all peoples…. I look for an ever-increasing measure of self-government in Africa.' Prior to and during the war, a quarter of a million refugees from Eastern and Central Europe arrived in the UK: Jews, Poles and others fleeing fascism. These Jews were more likely than their 20th-century predecessors to be middle class and economically independent, and had significant impacts on the economies of cities such as Leeds, Manchester and London. Trade unionists continued, however, to campaign against immigration, fearing for their jobs.

By 1955, however, the Trades Unions Congress (TUC) was condemning manifestations of racial discrimination, although with little impact. Racism remained prevalent. Only during the war was the 'colour bar' removed within industry, only to be replaced when it ended; otherwise, it existed across all sectors of life, in hotels, the armed forces and housing and labour markets. In areas such as Liverpool, where Black people had settled relatively peacefully during the inter-war period, racism again took violent forms; by 1948, there were 8,000 Black residents and the National Union of Seamen organised to stop them getting work. Race riots took place with police collusion but often led, ironically, to the development of formal and informal political responses among Black communities. The Constantine case, in which a prominent West Indian cricketer successfully sued a hotel for refusing him accommodation, showed that the law could be used to protect Black Britons' citizenship rights if the plaintiff had enough popular support. Gilroy's (2007, p 15) photographic history of migrants after the Second World War reflects 'glimpses of the struggle and everyday practices of Black Britons throughout the country's difficult process of becoming post-colonial' (see also *The Guardian* Special Supplement, 'Lives on film', 2007). For most BME people, however, the experience of trying to settle in Britain was oppressive, captured by the notorious boarding house notice 'No Irish, no dogs, no Blacks'.

However, other industrial sectors – textiles, heavy engineering, public transport and the health service – were seriously short of labour at the end of the war, and the increase in post-war immigration, stimulated by recruitment by employers and political exhortation by unlikely figures such as Enoch Powell (Minister of Health in 1953), occasioned different responses. The media talked of 'willing hands', underlining their contribution to the labour market and economic reconstruction, as the HMT *Empire Windrush* arrived from the Caribbean in 1948 (despite attempts by the British government to stop it; see Phillips and Phillips, 1998), increasing the numbers of minorities already resident in the UK. They joined Black Britons, South Asian Britons and East Europeans, who had been active in the war effort – such as Polish airmen based in Lincolnshire, or Indian seamen who had worked in Birmingham's industries and remained in Britain. Polish people formed a sizeable settlement in nearby Scunthorpe, employed in the steelworks.

Box 3.4: The *Empire Windrush*: an iconic moment

The *Empire Windrush* was a German passenger cruiser later used as a troop and hospital ship. The British Navy seized it in 1945, changed its name and converted it to a troop carrier. In 1948, en route from Australia, it docked in Jamaica. An advertisement in the local paper that month offered cheap transport to anyone wanting to work in the UK. When it left Jamaica it had almost 500 passengers, most ex-service personnel who had fought for the British and believed they had jobs. Half of the immigrants found work straightaway for the National Health Service (NHS) and London Transport, but most, despite British passports, found Britain far from welcoming. Many were initially housed in a former deep shelter in South London. Their first stop was the labour exchange in nearby Brixton, which thus contributed to the growth of the African Caribbean population there. The post-war experiences of Black Caribbeans and the dominant stance of racism is captured poignantly in Levy (2007).

Ironically, the emergence in early 2018 of the failure of the government to substantiate the claims of the Windrush Generation to UK citizenship has produced a second iconic moment in immigration history, this one ending with official apologies to all those affected, some of whom had already been wrongly deported, and to the resignation of the Home Secretary for misleading Parliament.

At the same time, post-war governments encouraged earlier immigrants to return to their countries. These included about 150,000 Polish servicemen and dependents, who fought from British bases, and Eastern European political dissidents, reluctant to return to hostile Stalinist governments. Meanwhile, tens of thousands of migrant workers were recruited from European labour camps to fill UK labour market gaps (Walvin, 2004).

As a result of this recruitment, the numbers of Black Caribbean and South Asian people grew steadily. By 1958, for example, 125,000 West Indians had arrived in Britain, a ten-fold increase in their population. London Transport recruited 4,000 as drivers and conductors, and thousands of nurses and ancillary health workers were recruited into the NHS. About 55,000 had also come from the Indian subcontinent, particularly India and, to a lesser extent, Pakistan, by 1958. These migrants also had British passports. As their numbers grew, calls increased to stop immigration virtually before it had started. The right to British citizenship for all members of the empire was one of the first casualties of such debates.

Post-war settlement patterns

Patterns of UK minority settlement were shaped initially by historical factors (such as the slave trade and the history of empire), and more recently by local economic and industrial profiles, and, at a micro level, both by cultural needs, for example, to build strong communities, and by the racism that distorted local housing and labour markets. For example, strong Caribbean settlement in Brixton resulted from the availability of large rooming houses, where significant numbers of migrants could live by paying super-exploitative rents. A similar pattern emerged in other cities, where large houses on the periphery of city centres, formerly occupied by merchants or the bourgeoisie, were sub-divided into small flats.

Large-scale post-war immigration from the Caribbean, Africa and South Asia was stimulated mostly by the demand for labour, but in the past 40 years, specific regional factors have played a role, such as forced exodus and, recently, a rapid growth in the number of refugees seeking asylum and in economic migration from many countries including, since 2004, Eastern and Central European EU accession states.

Migration growth since the late 1940s was rapid, but was then limited by alarmist political reaction, expressed through ever-tighter immigration legislation, which continues today. The picture of immigration throughout the 1960s and 1970s, following the Commonwealth Immigrants Act 1962, is one of panic surges in immigration ahead of further controls. The profile of numbers shows peaks, for example, in 1963 and 1973, as anxieties grew about the UK government closing previously open doors.

The major instrument for monitoring minority populations has been the decennial census. The nature of questions asked has changed over the past century, so precise comparisons cannot be made. The 1991 Census was the first to ask direct questions about ethnicity. Figures prior to that date were estimates, confused by definitions such as 'those born in the New Commonwealth and Pakistan' (which had withdrawn from the Commonwealth), including many 'White British' people returning to the UK after colonial independence.

Table 3.1 shows the number of individual minority groups in the UK in 1951 and 1961 drawn from Census and Labour Force Survey data and immigration statistics. Other estimates put total figures about 30% higher and the number of total 'aliens' (that is, including all people of non–British origin, regardless of whether they are citizens or not) at 415,700 in 1961.

The largest single group was what were then called 'West Indian' (incorporating many of what were to become independent states), whose growth was over 1,000%. Those of Indian origin increased by just under 200%, whereas those of Pakistani origin (including those who later became Bangladeshis as Pakistan split into two autonomous countries) by 400% from a very small number. The categories of Far Eastern and West African origin grouped together several different countries, many of them independent by 1961. In the 18 months around the 1961 Census, the rate of immigration accelerated markedly because of impending restrictions. In some areas, there were a few people of what is now 'mixed race' or 'mixed heritage', but this category (as with White Irish) was not separately counted until 2001. The picture of nationality, settlement and ethnicity had become increasingly complex, and hidden behind this broad picture was one

Table 3.1: Numbers of minorities in the UK in 1951 and 1961

	1951	1961
Indian	30,800	81,400
Pakistani	5,000	24,900
'West Indian'	15,300	171,800
'Far East'	12,000	29,600
West African	5,600	19,800
Total 'coloured'	74,500	336,600

Source: ONS, licensed under the Open Government Licence v.3.0

of micro change. For example, Britain's Chinese population was moving away from its connections with seafaring into, first, laundry work, and, from the 1960s, fast food provision (Craig et al, 2009).

Throughout the 1960s, Black faces became more common, but minorities continued to be 'ghettoised' because of racism in the housing market. Individual achievements were celebrated in the media as exotic events, as happened with Norwell Gumbs, the first Black police officer (1968) and the first Black traffic wardens (1966). The arrival of Black players in popular sports such as football did not prevent them from experiencing extensive racist abuse (and from within the Football Association itself). Ironically, England's Premier Football League now has a higher proportion of overseas, including many Black, players than any other national football league. South Africa's refusal to accept a mixed race player, Basil D'Oliviera, in the 1968 English cricket touring party, led to the tour's cancellation, more, it seems, because of hurt national pride than a principled anti-racist stance. Popular hostile attitudes to immigrants are well captured by Patterson (1965).

By 1971, the 'non-White' population (note, again, the racialised formulation) in Britain was 1.4 million, the largest single group again from the Caribbean. The size of the White New Commonwealth population was probably underestimated. This suggests that the growth of the BME population had been greater than officially noted. British minorities were already not the same thing as immigrants: more than one-third of that 1.4 million had been born in Britain. That proportion increased to 40% by 1976, by which time the 'non-White' population was about 1.85 million, 3.4% of the UK population. Thus, while immigration, despite legislative attempts to control it, continued to grow numerically, a significant element of minority growth now resulted from natural growth within the settled population, with people born in the UK and, consequently, British citizens. It is now appreciated that young people born and brought up in the UK have different experiences and expectations from their parents, who may still perceive of themselves as 'immigrants' (Ali, 2003). This creates potential distinctions between those born in the UK and those who were not.

The BME population continued to be concentrated within certain districts in a few urban centres. For example, the first Indian settlers only arrived in York, a medium-sized Northern city, in the late 1970s (Craig et al, 2009), reflecting a pattern whereby migration to places outside urban and seafaring centres as well as to Scotland, Northern Ireland and Wales lagged well behind that in major English cities. For rural dwellers, 'immigrants' have largely remained an exotic, often unwelcome, phenomenon.

The 1991 Census

The 1991 Census suggested that the minority population was about 3 million, 5.5% of the UK population. During the 1980s and 1990s, minority settlement was shaped by continuing immigration, despite frequent legislation designed to slow or even halt it, but also by natural growth and specific events (such as the expulsion of 31,000 'Ugandan Asians', mainly of Indian Gujarati descent, from Uganda). These place-specific phenomena continued into the 1990s, with the Vietnamese 'boat people', Hong Kong residents exiting what had become a Chinese province, and Bosnians and Kosovars fleeing genocide in Yugoslavia. These were, however, relatively small numbers in the context of overall refugee flows, which accelerated during the late 1990s. The rate of growth of different minority groups differed markedly. Bangladeshi people now appeared as a separate category following independence, and the vague category of 'Arab' remained.

There was a decline in the 'West Indian' population, which had been overtaken by those of Indian origin as the single largest non–White minority; a relatively rapid growth of Pakistani, Bangladeshi and African groups; and a rapid growth of minority populations as a whole. Natural growth differed between minorities, with Bangladeshis and Pakistanis having – despite higher infant mortality rates – substantially higher fertility rates than other groups (see Table 3.2). They also had substantially lower mortality rates, reflecting a younger age profile (Ahmad, 1993). Mortality rates moved slowly towards the norm, but, although 'West Indian' rates doubled between 1981 and 1991, they were still barely one–third of that of White populations by 1991. Fertility and mortality rates illustrate the changing age profile of differing minority populations. Thus, the ageing Caribbean population (some beginning to migrate back to the Caribbean) saw its fertility rate drop from 36% to 21% between 1981 and 1991 (and its mortality rate increasing from 2.1 to 4.1%), while the fertility and mortality rates of the UK Chinese population remained steady, at around 80% and 3% respectively (Williams, 1996).

In the 1970s and 1980s, there was substantial out-migration, particularly of UK-born White residents; net migration was of those leaving the UK until 1984. From the 1950s and 1960s, as the Yemenis had done, the UK Chinese population reinvented itself, becoming the most dispersed minority within the UK, present in every local authority including the most remote areas. This is illustrated in the map of the North East English Region (Figure 3.1).

Since 1991, it has been possible to map patterns of settlement to show, for example, differing regional concentrations of minorities or the relationship between ethnicity and religion (see Dorling, 1995).

In the 1991 Census, people identified themselves with one of the groups in Table 3.3. The 10 categories were those most used during the following years for policy purposes, but the longer list represents the categories used by respondents. Both 'West Indies' and 'Caribbean' were in use and the 'Arab' population had been disaggregated to identify those from Iran (early refugees). However, there was no overarching category in which the Polish (to become important by 2011) could be located. This, and other issues, were picked up in the 2001 Census which used the categories in Table 3.3, allowing people to specify a particular

Table 3.2: Population of Great Britain by ethnic group, 1981-91

Ethnic group	1981 (N)	Mean for 1989-91 (N)	% change
White	51,000	51,808	1
Minority ethnic groups (all)	**2,092**	**2,677**	**28**
West Indian	528	455	−14
African	80	150	88
Indian	727	792	9
Pakistani	284	485	71
Bangladeshi	52	127	144
Chinese	92	137	49
Arab	53	67	26
Mixed	217	309	42
Other	60	154	157
Not stated	608	495	113

Source: Population Trends, 67:1 and Labour Force Surveys 1990 and 1991, Series LFS No 9, Table 6.29

ethnic origin in their own words. The 1991 Census outputs have been analysed in detail (Peach, 1996). Between the 1991 and 2001 Censuses, the *Fourth National Survey of Ethnic Minorities* provided profiles of Britain's minority populations (see Modood et al, 1997).

From 2001 to the present

The 2001 Census outputs, although not directly comparable with those of 1991, demonstrate important trends (Table 3.4 illustrates the 2001 classifications).

The Black Caribbean population had reversed the previous decade's decline, growing slightly, but was being caught up by the Black African population; both were behind the Pakistani population and the largest minority, those of Indian origin (see Table 3.5).

The Chinese population had almost doubled, in part because of economic refugees leaving Hong Kong as well as political refugees from mainland China (also see Figure 3.1). The total White population was now 92% of the total UK population, including White Irish and White Other, with White Irish, at 1.2% of the total population, one of the largest single minority populations. This group included Gypsy/Travellers, although some categorised themselves in other ways. Because of their nomadic life and continuing persecution, they remain an 'invisibilised' group even within the UK's minorities, as are the Roma, who have been arriving since the late 1990s (Clark, 2006). The 'pathologising' of Gypsies and Travellers remains common. Local authorities, while technically responsible for supporting Gypsy and Traveller populations, have often resorted to harassment and surveillance.

Table 3.3: 1991 Census ethnic categories

Four-fold classification	Ten-fold classification	Full listing
White	White	White
		Irish
		Greek/Greek Cypriot
		Turkish/Turkish Cypriot
		Mixed White
Black	Black Caribbean	Black Caribbean
		Caribbean Island
		West Indies
		Guyana
	Black African	Black African
		Africa – South of Sahara
	Black Other	Black – Other
		Black British
		Black – Mixed Black/Other
(South) Asian	Indian	Indian
	Pakistani	Pakistani
	Bangladeshi	Bangladeshi
Chinese and others	Chinese	Chinese
	Other – Asian	East African Asian
		Indo-Caribbean
		Black – Indian subcontinent
		Black – other Asian
	Other – other	North Africa/Arab/Iranian
		Mixed Asian/White
		British ethnic minority (Other)
		British (no indication)
		Other mixed Black/White
		Other mixed Asian/White
		Other mixed – Other

Source: ONS licensed under the Open Government Licence v.3.0

The 'mixed' category had now grown to over 1.2%, the fastest growing category in the population, possibly partly explaining the decline in those identified as African Caribbean. Overall, the minority ethnic population had grown by 53% between 1991 and 2001, from 3 million to 4.6 million, while the UK population grew by 4% (about 2.2 million); 73% of this growth was due to the growth of BME groups. Kyambi (2005) has derived a visual mapping of patterns of settlement and origins of major minority groups.

Table 3.4: 2001 Census ethnic categories

White	British
	Irish
	Any other White background (please write in)
Mixed	White and Black Caribbean
	White and Black African
	White and Asian
	Any other mixed background (please write in)
Asian or Asian British	Indian
	Pakistani
	Bangladeshi
	Any other Asian background (please write in)
Black or Black British	Caribbean
	African
	Any other Black background (please write in)
Chinese or other ethnic group	Chinese
Any other, please write in	

Source: ONS licensed under the Open Government Licence v.3.0

Table 3.5: Population of the UK by ethnic group, 2001

	Total population numbers	%	% of non-White population
White	54,153,898	92.1	
Mixed	677,177	1.2	14.6
Indian	1,053,411	1.8	22.7
Pakistani	747,285	1.3	16.1
Bangladeshi	283,063	0.5	6.1
Other Asian	247,664	0.4	5.3
Black Caribbean	565,876	1.0	12.2
Black African	485,277	0.8	10.5
Black other	97,585	0.2	2.1
Chinese	247,403	0.4	5.3
Other	230,615	0.4	5.0
All minority ethnic populations	4,635,296	7.9	100.0
All population	58,789,194	100	

Source: ONS licensed under the Open Government Licence v.3.0

Figure 3.1: Chinese population by ward (North-East England)

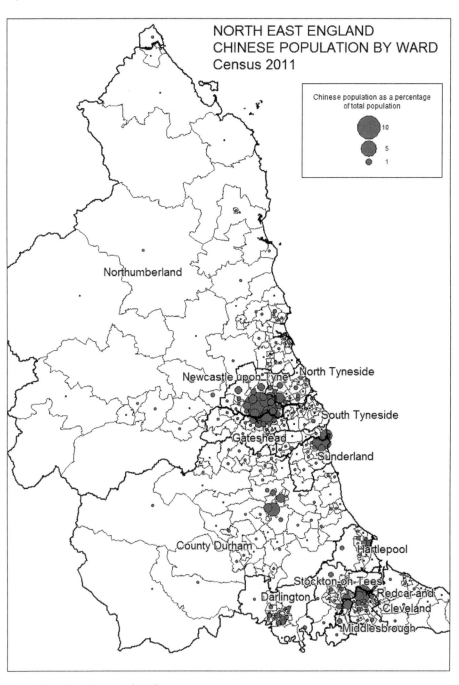

Source: Drawn from Tong et al (2014)

Britain's minorities were still far from evenly distributed: approximately 45% lived in London (representing 29% of London's population), which housed the largest concentrations of all major minority groups except for the Pakistani population, which were concentrated more highly in Bradford (where minorities constituted 22% of the population as a whole) and the North-West. Thus, 78% of all Black Africans and 61% of all Black Caribbean people lived in London. Roughly 13% of all minorities lived in the West Midlands, particularly in Birmingham (with a minority population of 39%), with no other region having 10% of its population coming from minorities. In Scotland and Wales, minority populations were about 3% and 2% respectively, with less than 1% in Northern Ireland: in these areas, virtually no minorities lived outside the major conurbations. In Northern Ireland, indeed, there has been little policy concern with minority ethnic groups until recently, as a consequence of the focus on religious divides and sectarianism. There was net emigration from Northern Ireland until 2003 (much later than on the UK mainland) but, as on the mainland, the arrival of refugees and migrant workers, and natural growth, have led to a relatively rapid increase in the BME population to about 5%.

Table 3.6 gives an overall picture of the growth of differing minority populations over the past 50 or so years.

Some large cities, such as Stoke-on-Trent and Hull, also had small minority populations until fairly recently when, in the latter case, dispersal of refugees, combined with 2004 A8 EU migration, led to a rapid increase. In most rural areas, minority populations remained small, at less than 2%, but growing more rapidly than the UK average. An analysis of the pattern of settlement of Britain's minorities by *The Independent* newspaper in 2006 (Alibhai-Brown, 2006) claimed that the least ethnically diverse community was Easington, County Durham; the chances of meeting someone from a different ethnic group were computed to be just 2%.

Contrasts between the settlement of longer-established minorities and more recent migrants are highlighted above (see Figure 3.1). Notable is the

Table 3.6: Growth of minority ethnic populations in Britain, 1951-2011

Ethnicity[a]	1951	1961	1971	1981	1991	2001	2011
West Indian or Caribbean	15,300	171,800	500,000	528,000	455,000	563,843	594,825
Indian	30,800	81,400	400,000	727,000	792,000	1,036,807	1,412,958
Pakistani	5,000	24,900	100,000	284,000	485,000	714,826	1,124,511
Bangladeshi	n/a	n/a	20,000	52,000	127,000	280,830	447,201
Black African	5,600	19,800	48,000	80,000	150,000	479,665	989,628

Note: [a] Changing definitions mean actual numbers are difficult to calculate.

Source: Adapted from data from the ONS licensed under the Open Government Licence v.3.0

complementary nature of settlement (whether settlement for migrant workers is permanent or temporary remains open). Migrant workers have largely gravitated – because of employment opportunities – to areas with historically small BME communities. This has shifted racist discourse – previously located in an urban context – to more rural contexts (NYBSB, 2006; Athwal et al, 2010). Additionally, because recent migrants have been working in more remote areas, labour market exploitation levels have increased substantially (Geddes et al, 2014).

Between urban populations, there were, however, marked variations (see Lupton and Power, 2004). In London in 2001, the boroughs of Brent and Newham had 'minority' populations of 55% and 61% respectively, whereas Havering and Bromley's minority shares were 5% and 8% respectively. London boroughs tended to be associated with particular minority ethnic groups, with 'Bangladeshis' concentrated in Tower Hamlets, 'Indians' in Ealing, 'Turkish' in Haringey and 'Black Africans' in Lambeth and Southwark. The same differentiation led the Chair of the Commission for Racial Equality to suggest that Britain was 'sleepwalking into segregation' (Phillips, 2005), a claim dismantled by statistical analyses (Finney and Simpson, 2009). As Smith (1989, p 37) had earlier observed, why should minorities pursue segregation 'in the more run-down segments of the housing stock, rather than in areas where they could secure the symbolic and economic benefits associated with suburban life'?

Analysis of migrant worker populations (Adamson et al, 2008) showed that the mix of national origins varied considerably between localities, even within regions (see Pollard et al, 2008). Although there is considerable churn, the Eastern and Central European migrant population has continued to grow. Local advice workers noted a shift a few years after the 2004 EU accessions in the nature of enquiries being made by migrant workers away from workplace exploitation to questions about family benefits and tax. Finney and Simpson's analysis (2009) also reminds us that, where spatial segregation occurred, it was often the consequence of racism in the labour and housing markets limiting choices (more than one-third of Pakistani and Bangladeshi owner-occupiers and renters were living in housing without one or more basic amenity), with many only able to access owner occupation, even in the worst housing, through collective purchases (Nazroo, 1997). This challenged several myths about minorities – that Britain was becoming a country of ghettoes, that minorities wanted to live in segregated neighbourhoods and that the growth of minority areas was caused by 'white flight'.

While it is true that Britain's minorities continue to remain concentrated in the most deprived areas, this is not equivalent to suggesting that they are segregated and, in particular, self-segregated. Overall, as well as being concentrated, Britain's minority population is youthful, with the proportions of Bangladeshis, Pakistanis and Black Africans under 16 about twice that of the UK White population (Owen, 2006) and continuing to grow relatively rapidly (Barnard and Turner, 2010; Hirst and Rinne, 2014), while remaining economically disadvantaged (Platt, 2007).

The 2011 Census results incorporated changes to questions about ethnicity and national identity, religion and place of birth, increasing our understanding of diversity. Different questions were being asked in different parts of the UK, with questions probing national identity not asked in Northern Ireland. The suggestion by the coalition government of 2010–15 of abandoning or narrowing the scope of the Census, given the problems faced by most agencies of recording and collecting data on ethnicity, could be a serious backward step in our understanding of diversity. This would make it more difficult to challenge continuing myths about migrants and Britain's settled BME population; for example, a 2002 MORI poll asked people what the proportion of 'immigrants' was. The general population believed the answer to be 23%; the real figure then was about 6%, including British-born minorities.

Current trends and patterns of migration show increasing numbers of countries of origin, with political asylum-seeking from countries with limited historical connection with Britain, such as Somalia, Afghanistan and the Democratic Republic of the Congo, and economic migration from recently acceding EU countries. The size and diversity of minorities has increased substantially since 2001, with the term 'super-diversity' now used (Phillimore, 2015; and see Chapter 2, this volume). ONS mid-censal estimates showed the White British population in 2006 to be about 84% of the total population; larger minority groups included Indian (2.0%), Pakistani (1.5%), Black African (1.3%) and Black Caribbean (1.1%), some of which are now large enough for detailed accounts of their own history and pattern of settlement to be published. Identities are now more complex than they used to be. Data on BME groups do not reflect refugees seeking asylum (most of whom were refused and disappeared from official data), nor the 600,000 to 800,000 irregular workers residing in the UK (Waite et al, 2015).

In the 20th century, the picture of ethnic diversity in the UK has been shaped by several major phenomena: these include a rapid growth in the number of economic migrants from Eastern and Central Europe; continuing downward pressure on the numbers of refugees seeking asylum whose applications were accepted (Carr, 2015, p 261); continued natural growth among minorities within the UK; increasing internal migration, including into rural areas, some of which now had minority populations in excess of 5%; and rapid growth in the 'mixed' ethnicity category, now exceeding 2% (see Figure 3.2).

This increasing diversity was reflected in the findings of the 2011 Census, key elements of which are summarised here:

- The BME population of England and Wales was now around 14%, more than double that of 1991.
- The White Irish group declined as a proportion of the UK population.

Figure 3.2: Minority ethnic groups, England and Wales, 2011

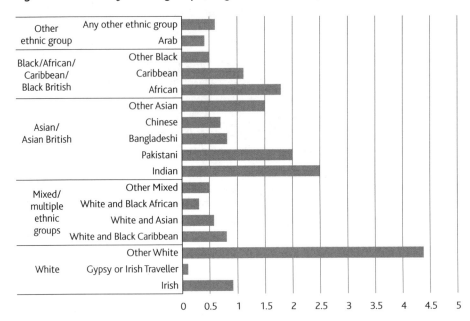

Source: Adapted from data from the ONS licensed under the Open Government Licence v.3.0

- The largest minority groups were Any Other White (4.4%) and Indian (2.5%). One-half of the 1.1 million increase in the former category was attributable to the growth in the Polish population, which increased ninefold between 2001 and 2011 to more than half a million. The number of people of Polish origin is now estimated to be greater than 700,000.
- The smallest separate minority category remained Gypsy/Traveller at 58,000, or 0.1% of the total England and Wales population.
- The two most diverse English regions were London, where White British constituted 60% of the city's total population, and the West Midlands, with a corresponding figure of 79%. The figure for Wales was 93% and for Scotland, 91%. Brent and Newham remained the most diverse boroughs in London, with White British populations of 16% and 17% respectively.

The local picture raises some interesting issues. Craig et al's update (2016) on their 2009 report on the ethnic demography of York found that, while diversity had continued to grow, albeit much more slowly – with almost 100 ethnic groups and languages identified locally – some minorities were moving out of the city because of the high cost of housing, difficulties in obtaining reasonably paid work and the continuing impact of racial discrimination.

Figure 3.1 above indicates this growing diversity and its distribution across the UK. An insight has been the extent to which 'new' migrants have used faith-based groups as an anchor as they negotiate new lives for themselves; this contrasts with the experience of immigrants of the 1950s and 1960s, who gravitated more towards trades unions (despite initial hostility from the unions) and the Labour Party (Wills et al, 2010; see also Dorling, 1995). The relationship between ethnicity and religion is a complex one, however, as is clear from the 2001 and 2011 Censuses (see Table 3.7), which show that we cannot simply read from a person's ethnic group their religious orientation, or vice versa. London alone has Muslims from over 50 ethnic backgrounds. The two censuses suggest a decline in some faiths, especially Christianity (the comparisons can only be taken as an order of magnitude, as some categories are not directly comparable).

One constant across the past 600 years has been the persecution of and discrimination and racism against the Gypsy/Roma/Traveller population, and their consequent high levels of deprivation, often obscured in official statistics, but now finally recognised in public accounts (Neale et al, 2009; Hills, 2010). Roma fled persecution in mainland Europe only to experience it in Britain (Craig, 2011, 2017).

Table 3.7: Ethnic group by religion, comparing data from the 2001 and 2011 Censuses

	Christian (%)		Hindu (%)		Muslim (%)	
	2001	2011	2001	2011	2001	2011
White	76	64	0.02	0.02	0.4	0.2
Other White	63	55	0.09	0.02	8.6	5.1
Mixed	52	46	0.9	0.8	9.7	7.9
Other Mixed	48	47	1.2	0.8	14.1	8.6
Asian or Asian British	4	6	23.5	20.7	50.1	53.4
Indian	5	9	45	44	12.7	14.1
Black or Black British	71	67	0.3	0.3	9.3	6.1
Chinese or Other	27	20	0.7	0.7	12.8	n/a

Source: ONS licensed under the Open Government Licence v.3

Conclusion

The history and patterns of UK minority settlement are, as this account shows, complex and changing, and to some degree specific to the UK. Much took place in the context of racism and hostility, well captured in the title of Winder's (2004) detailed account, *Bloody Foreigners*. This picture is again in flux. The June 2016 UK vote to leave the EU, coupled with an increasingly restrictive immigration policy, has raised serious questions about whether the intake of migrants will continue, and even whether EU nationals in the UK will be allowed to stay after the UK leaves the EU. Business interests have pointed out how their industries (ranging from food production to hospitality) are heavily dependent on migrant labour. The contradictions between this discourse and an increasingly racist one (illustrated by a substantial spike in racist hate crimes immediately after the Brexit vote; see Burnett, 2016) is contributing to a sharper focus on the role of minorities within the British economy, and in society as a whole.

Note

[1] Phrases such as 'the Jews', 'the Poles' etc have been used throughout as a shorthand for Jewish people, Polish origin people etc and are not intended to imply any disrespect.

Questions for discussion

- How were Black and Asian people seen by the UK population at the end of the Second World War?
- What were the key factors shaping migration to Britain in the 1950s and 1960s? Would the picture have been different in France and Germany, and if so, why?
- In what ways was the 2001 Census better – or worse – than previous ones in helping us understand changes in the UK minority population? Does the 2011 Census improve on this?

Online resources

www.statistics.gov.uk/hub
  The main source of data for understanding the pattern of settlement of minorities across the UK is the website of the Office for National Statistics (ONS). The link to population provides data relating, for example, to population change, estimates, migration, fertility rates, regional populations or populations by individual local authorities.

www.[anytown].gov.uk
  Most local authorities should have mapped their own minority populations as part of wider mappings of poverty and disadvantage.

www.gov.uk/government/collections/national-insurance-number-allocations-to-adult-overseas-nationals-entering-the-uk
  Data about migrant workers can be obtained either from the Department for Work and Pensions website (for National Insurance numbers data, mapped by place of residence), or through individual local authorities that had access to the Workers Registration Scheme data (mapping migrant workers by place of work, type of work, etc, until 2010).

References

Adamson, S., Craig, G. and Wilkinson, M. (2008) *Migrant workers in the Humber sub-region*, Hull: Humber Improvement Programme.

Ahmad, W. (ed) (1993) *'Race' and health in contemporary Britain*, Buckingham: Open University Press.

Ali, N. (2003) 'Diaspora and nation: Displacement and the politics of Kashmiri identity in Britain', *Contemporary South Asia*, 12(4), 471-80.

Alibhai-Brown, Y. (2006) 'Yasmin Alibhai-Brown: An eclectic country which retains its island mentality', *The Independent*, 6 October (www.independent.co.uk/voices/commentators/yasmin-alibhai-brown/yasmin-alibhai-brown-an-eclectic-country-which-retains-its-island-mentality-418883.html).

Athwal, H., Bourne, J. and Wood, R. (2010) *Racial violence: The buried issue*, London: Institute of Race Relations.

Barnard, H. and Turner, C. (2010) *Poverty and ethnicity: A review of the evidence*, York: Joseph Rowntree Foundation.

Burnett, J. (2016) *Racial violence and the Brexit state*, London: Institute of Race Relations.

Carr, M. (2015) *Fortress Europe*, London: Hurst & Co.

Clark, C. (2006) 'Defining ethnicity in a cultural and socio-legal context', *Scottish Affairs*, 54(1), 39-67.

Craig, G. (2011) *The Roma: A study of national policies* (www.york.ac.uk/inst/spru/research/pdf/EURoma.pdf)

Craig, G. (ed) (2017) *Community organising against racism*, Bristol: Policy Press.

Craig, G., Adamson, S., Ali, N. and Demsash, F. (2009) *Mapping rapidly changing ethnic minority populations*, York: Joseph Rowntree Foundation.

Craig, G., Boparai, H., Adamson, S., Demsash, F. and Martin, G. (2016) *A racial justice forum for York?*, York: York Workshops.

Dorling, D. (1995) *A new social atlas of Britain*, Chichester: Wiley.

EHRC (Equality and Human Rights Commission) (2015) *Is Britain fairer? Race in Britain*, Manchester: EHRC.

Elford, C. (2008) *Black Mahler, the Samuel Coleridge-Taylor Story*, London: Grosvenor House Publishing.

Equiano, O. (2007) *The interesting narrative of the life of Olaudah Equiano*, Harmondsworth: Penguin [first published in 1789].

Fenton, S. (1999) *Ethnicity: Racism, class and culture*, London: Rowman & Littlefield.

Finney, N. and Simpson, L. (2009) *'Sleepwalking to segregation?' Challenging myths about race and migration*, Bristol: Policy Press.

Fryer, P. (1984) *Staying power*, London: Pluto Press.

Geddes, A., Craig, G. and Scott, S. (2014) *Forced labour in the UK*, York: Joseph Rowntree Foundation.

Gilroy, P. (2007) *Black Britain: A photographic history*, London: Saqi Books.

Guardian, The (2007) 'Lives on film', 15 October, G2 Special Supplement.

Hills, J. (2010) *An anatomy of economic inequality in the UK*, London: National Equalities Office.

Hirst, A. and Rinne, S. (2014) *An initial evaluation of the JRF Poverty and Ethnicity programme*, York: Joseph Rowntree Foundation.

IPPR (Institute for Public Policy Research) (2007) *Britain's immigrants: An economic profile*, London: IPPR.

Khan, O. (ed) (2015) *How far have we come? Lessons from the 1965 Race Relations Act*, London: Runnymede Trust.

Kyambi, S. (2005) *Beyond Black and White*, London: Institute for Public Policy Research.

Levy, A. (2007) *Small island*, Harmondsworth: Penguin.

Lupton, R. and Power, A. (2004) *Ethnic minority groups in Britain*, CASE – Brookings Census Briefs, London: London School of Economics and Political Science.

Modood, T., Berthoud, R., Lakey, J., Nazroo, J., Smith, P., Virdee, S. and Beishon, S. (1997) *Fourth national survey of ethnic minorities*, London: Policy Studies Institute.

Nazroo, J. (1997) *The health of ethnic minorities*, London: Policy Studies Institute.

Neale, M., Craig, G. and Wilkinson, M. (2009) *Marginalised and excluded? York's traveller community*, York: York Travellers Trust.

NYBSB (North Yorkshire Black and Minority Ethnic Strategy Board) (2006) *Ethnic minorities in rural areas: A thinkpiece for Defra*, Easingwold: NYBSB.

Olusoga, D. (2016) *Black and British*, London: Macmillan.

Owen, D. (2006) 'Demographic profiles and social cohesion of minority ethnic communities in England and Wales', *Community, Work and Family*, 9(3), 251-72.

Patterson, S. (1965) *Dark strangers*, Harmondsworth: Pelican.

Peach, C. (ed) (1996) *Ethnicity in the 1991 Census*, Vol 2, London: HMSO.

Phillimore, J. (2015) *Migration and social policy*, Cheltenham: Edward Elgar.

Phillips, M. and Phillips, T. (1998) *Windrush*, London: HarperCollins.

Phillips, T. (2005) 'After 7/7: Sleepwalking to segregation', Speech to Manchester Council for Community Relations, 22 September.

Platt, L. (2007) *Ethnicity and poverty*, York: Joseph Rowntree Foundation.

Pollard, N., Latorre, M. and Sriskandarajah, D. (2008) *Floodgates or turnstiles?*, London: Institute for Public Policy Research.

Smith, S.J. (1989) *The politics of race and residence*, Cambridge: Polity Press.

Tong, Z., Craig, G. and O'Neill, M. (2014) *The Chinese population in North East England*, Durham: North East Regional Race, Crime and Justice Research Network.

Waite, L., Craig, G., Lewis, H. and Skrivankova, K. (eds) (2015) *Vulnerability, exploitation and migrants*, Basingstoke: Palgrave Macmillan.

Walvin, J. (1984) *Passage to Britain*, Harmondsworth: Pelican.

Williams, F. (1996) 'Race, welfare and community care, a historical perspective', in W.I.U. Ahmad and K. Atkin (eds) *'Race' and community care*, Buckingham: Open University Press, 15-28.

Wills, J., Datta, K., Evans, Y., Herbert, J., May, J. and McIlwaine, C. (2010) *Global cities at work*, London: Pluto Press.

Winder, R. (2004) *Bloody foreigners*, London: Little, Brown.

4

Policy, politics and practice: a historical review and its relevance to current debates

Ronny Flynn and Gary Craig

Overview

This chapter links immigration to the contributions made by Black and minority ethnic (BME) people to UK employment and economic growth.

- It highlights tensions between the search for migrant labour and the treatment of those recruited, and links with ideas on immigration and migration raised in Chapters 2 and 3.
- It examines domestic policies employed to 'manage' immigration and 'race' relations, and their contradictions and effects. Contradictions between restrictive immigration legislation and legislation to tackle disadvantage have featured in government policy since the 1950s.
- The move from an 'assimilation' policy through to multiculturalism, then back to a form of assimilation, in the guise of community cohesion, suggests that policy has come full circle. Current policy has substantially downgraded 'race' other than in the context of managing immigration and confronting terrorism.

Key concepts
anti-racism; assimilation; community cohesion; immigration; multiculturalism

Introduction

As we saw in the last chapter, migrants have entered the UK since Roman times. However, numbers were relatively small until the end of the Second World War. Since then, Britain has experienced increased levels of immigration, driven by the need for economic reconstruction and expanding public services. Levels accelerated during the 1960s, but a restrictive immigration policy and a slowdown in economic growth reduced numbers. Migrants have become more diverse, coming initially from former British colonies, but increasingly from countries less connected to the UK. By the beginning of the 21st century, some cities were hosting people from more than 100 ethnic or national origins. Diversity is now 'super-diversity' (Fanshawe and Sriskandarajah, 2010; Craig et al, 2016).

By the 1980s, as we saw in Chapter 3, a substantial proportion of the UK minority ethnic population was UK-born, and by 2011 around 50%. While political concern, fuelled by media panic and right-wing agitation, has led to punitive restrictions on immigration, governments have also sought to manage multiculturalism through policies known as 'race' relations, community relations and, in the early 21st century, community cohesion. Consequently, restricted immigration practices exist alongside policy (and legislative) commitment to tackle discrimination and racism, although this latter commitment has weakened in recent years. Community cohesion policy has also been weakened as 'race' has been afforded a lower profile.

Invited migrant labour and racism

During the first half of the 20th century, White Jewish, Polish and Irish immigrants and refugees were important sources of semi- and unskilled labour for the UK. However, these groups experienced racism, hostility and scapegoating, just as migrant workers do today (Brown, 1995).

The need for labour was followed by restrictions to immigration, a common trend in understanding immigration policies of the 20th and 21st centuries. The Aliens Acts of 1905 and 1919 restricted the employment of 'alien' workers in Britain and formed the basis of all Immigration Acts until 1971 (see Chapter 3). The 1905 Act refused entry if people could not support themselves. If migrants became homeless, lived in overcrowded conditions or needed poverty relief within 12 months of entry, they were deported (Williams, 1996). The 1919 Act, introduced in a climate of nationalist, anti-Semitic and anti-German feeling created by the First World War, strengthened the previous Act. Trades unions and a cross-section of parliamentary opinion supported both Acts (Brown, 1995).

Before and during the Second World War, Irish people filled many labour shortages. Afterwards, despite offering a home to some Eastern European workers, Britain looked towards former colonies and Commonwealth member states to boost the workforce. The emphasis was on rebuilding Britain and securing economic growth:

> In the early 1960s government ministers, as well as private employers, started to recruit directly in the West Indies. These included Enoch

Powell, who actively encouraged the migration of medical staff from India and the West Indies during his time as Minister for Health. The London Transport executive made an agreement with the Barbadian Immigration Liaison Service. Other employers, such as the British Hotel and Restaurant Association, made similar agreements. (Brown, 1995)

Nurses, like other employees, were actively recruited but, once here, were made to feel inferior. They were, for example, encouraged to take the State Enrolled Nurse (SEN) qualification rather than the State Registered Nurse (SRN), the latter being a passport to increased pay and promotion (Doyal et al, 1980, cited in Mama, 1984, p 27). Workers came from Pakistan to the jute mills of Dundee. London and Northern English industries such as textiles and steel actively recruited from India.

Not surprisingly, many migrants felt let down. British employers or trades unions did not recognise their qualifications. Indeed, unions were seen to be in league with managers to restrict opportunities for migrants (Hero, 1991), who, by the late 1970s, were protesting against their exclusion from better-paid, more comfortable jobs held by White workers, as demonstrated by the Grunwick dispute (Beckett, 2009). During the 1960s and 1970s minority ethnic people worked for less pay than their White counterparts, finding themselves in jobs for which they were overqualified (Blakemore, 1990), and this practice persists, for example, in the fruit-picking industry. In 1958, the first 'modern' British 'race riots' occurred in Nottingham and Notting Hill, West London, both initiated by White people but blamed on Black migrants. This blaming of BME people for the racism they experience continues to this day, as subsequent chapters illustrate. The police generally did not intervene, and evidence continues to emerge of the 'virulently racist attitudes of the police towards Blacks' (Muir, 2005). Copycat riots occurred in and outside London, and these tensions influenced policy (Kynaston, 2008). The initial belief in assimilation seemed naive and unsustainable (see below). Policy attention switched to the numbers of minority ethnic people living in the UK as the cause of the tensions between the majority population and the recently arrived migrants. Here lie the origins of the 'numbers game', which has come to dominate UK policy on 'race'.

Calls for immigration control grew throughout the 1950s and 1960s, despite evidence that it was not a 'Black' problem but a 'White' problem (Rex, 1969). Initially, the Labour Party adopted a more liberal view, but, once in government, it often competed with the Conservative Party to 'be tough' on immigration (Beckett, 2009). The Labour Party, however, remains the only party to introduce major legislation (in a series of five Acts in 1965, 1968, 1976, 2001 and 2010) to tackle racial discrimination and disadvantage. Shamefully, the recent coalition and current Conservative governments have wished to dismantle much of the legislative protection given to minorities of all kinds. Nonetheless, immigration control also became a feature of successive government policy, as part of managing a multicultural UK, interwoven with legislation to tackle racism and discrimination (Bhavnani et al, 2005). The first modern Immigration Act appeared in 1962; subsequently there has been a succession of Immigration Acts, which have been almost an annual feature of parliamentary timetables.

No longer welcome

As Hansen (199, p 816) has noted, 'a centuries-old tradition of free entry to the UK ended in 1962'. The Commonwealth Immigrants Act 1962 was introduced by a Conservative government, and:

> was the first legislation to introduce state regulation of Commonwealth immigration and … the first ever entry restrictions on British Commonwealth citizens, by making primary immigration dependent upon the possession of a work voucher … the intended targets of the Act were all black or Asian…. The 1962 Act enshrined in law for the first time the … notion that immigration equals black immigration, … upon which all successive immigration legislation has been built. (Brown, 1995)

Under the Act, employment vouchers were issued in three categories: those who had jobs to come to (A); those who had skills and qualifications 'likely to be useful in this country' (B); and unskilled workers (C), a category which had disappeared by 1964. A Commonwealth Immigrants Advisory Council (CIAC) was set up to advise the Home Secretary on immigrant welfare and integration, which, as Sivanandan writes, was 'as if to compensate for the discrimination now institutionalised' (1982, p 108). The Labour Party, hostile to the Act while in opposition, kept and strengthened it in government. The second category of 'useful' skills and qualifications firmly linked Commonwealth immigration to the requirements of the British economy, a linkage now replicated in Brexit debates. The increase in skilled workers that followed drained Commonwealth countries of valued personnel (Sivanandan, 1982), creating problems for the future. Many health professionals recruited in the 1960s have now retired from employment, prompting a panic about shortages in the NHS (Batty, 2003; Pati, 2003; Mason, 2011), particularly since many worked in areas of deprivation or rural areas where it was difficult to recruit skilled practitioners.

The Immigration Act 1962 was followed by others. These Acts changed the nature of immigration and the relationship of BME people to employment, the state and its other citizens. The 1968 Act specifically aimed to stop the immigration of Asian people with British passports, who had been driven out of Kenya (and later Uganda). A Labour government, responding to public pressure, rapidly passed the Act, thereby highlighting the racism, hypocrisy and U-turns common during the 1960s' and 1970s' political responses to 'race'. The 1968 Act meant that:

> A parliamentary Labour party that had claimed a profound commitment to the Commonwealth ideal of multi-racialism … effectively stripped British citizens, whose entry was controversial only because of their skin colour, of one of citizenship's basic rights. A Labour party that had passed a series of liberal measures … on hanging, divorce and abortion, and homosexuality – passed legislation that even its supporters admitted to be illiberal and 'racialist'. (Hansen, 1999, p 833)

Only in 2002, after over 30 years of campaigns, did the government give East African Asians, stateless since 1968, the right to live in the UK. The 30,000 or so Gujarati Ugandans expelled by Idi Amin in the early 1970s were reluctantly admitted as a special case.

Against this restrictive backdrop, on 8 November 1965, the Labour government passed the first 'balancing' 'race' relations legislation. The 1965 Act forbade racial discrimination in public places such as shops and restaurants. Private boarding houses, employment and social housing were not covered, and overt discrimination continued, but it demonstrated recognition of racism in the UK. The Race Relations Act 1968 strengthened the 1965 Act by making it illegal to refuse housing, employment or public services on grounds of colour, 'race', or ethnic or national origins. It also created the Community Relations Commission, aiming to promote harmonious community relations (see below). Both pieces of legislation, however, made discrimination a civil rather than a criminal offence, and placed the burden of proof on the prosecution to demonstrate intent. Table 4.1 illustrates the pattern of developing 'race' and community relations policies in tandem with restrictive immigration legislation.

The tensions between a commitment to equality and a perception that migration is a problem are evident, and the state response to the welfare needs of BME communities remained ambivalent throughout the 1960s and 1970s (Craig, 2007). There was restricted access to state welfare alongside specific funding to local authorities, for example, through Section 11 of the Local Government Act 1966, to help the 'integration' of minority communities. The 'twin-track' state response, aimed at improving integration while restricting immigration, had implications for BME populations (Solomos, 2003). Divided families were one consequence, with many men who had settled in the UK during the 1950s and 1960s unable to bring their families to join them (discussed below). Even citizens with a British passport and voting rights did not have equality of citizenship or access to state-funded social welfare. Expectations were that minority ethnic communities should prove their deservingness, both literally and symbolically

Table 4.1: Key immigration and race relations legislation in the UK since 1962

Year	Immigration legislation	Race relations legislation
1962	*Commonwealth Immigrants Act.* The first legislation to restrict the rights of Commonwealth citizens to reside in the UK.	
1965		*First Race Relations Act.* Racial incitement became a criminal offence, and some forms of direct racial discrimination a civil wrong; emphasis on settlement through local conciliation committees and the Race Relations Board. The Act was seen to have weak enforcement and to need to be extended.
1966		*Local Government Act* made provisions for the education and welfare of 'immigrants' through specific funding.
1968	*Commonwealth Immigrants Act* controlled the entry of Kenyan Asians with British passports.	*Race Relations Act* extended the existing Act to cover public and private employment and housing.
1971	*Immigration Act* introduced recourse to public funds. The notion of 'patriality', which favoured immigration from 'White' Commonwealth countries as a 'right of abode', was limited to those with prior links to the UK, eg, a parent or grandparent born here.	
1976		*Race Relations Act* extended previous Acts by identifying direct and indirect discrimination, providing for positive action in some circumstances and establishing the Commission for Racial Equality (CRE).
1981	*British Nationality Act* reclassified UK citizenship into three categories, one consequence being that children of 'British overseas citizens' of Asian background born in the UK could not automatically have citizenship.	
1993	*Asylum and Immigration (Appeals) Act* introduced fingerprinting and removed the rights to public sector housing.	
1996	*Asylum and Immigration Act* penalised employers employing those without appropriate documentation.	

(continued)

Year	Immigration legislation	Race relations legislation
1998		*Human Rights Act* gave further legal effect in the UK to the fundamental rights and freedoms contained in the European Convention on Human Rights.
1999	*Immigration and Asylum Act* introduced vouchers for support and devolved dispersal and accommodation to the National Asylum Support Service (NASS).	
2000		*Race Relations (Amendment) Act* introduced a statutory obligation on all public agencies to eliminate racial discrimination and promote good community relations.
2002	*Nationality, Immigration and Asylum Act* introduced new induction/accommodation/removal centres for asylum-seekers and withdrawal of support for individuals who are 'late', or unsuccessful applicants.	
2003		*Race Relations (Amendment) Act* introduced new definitions of indirect discrimination and harassment.
2004	*Asylum and Immigration (Treatment of Claimants) Act* withdrew support from families with children under 18 in selected areas of the country and leave limited rights of appeal.	
2006	*Immigration, Asylum and Nationality Act* introduced a new asylum model giving greater control over asylum-seekers.	*Racial and Religious Hatred Act* sought to stop people from intentionally using threatening words or behaviour to stir up hatred against someone because of their belief.
2007	*UK Borders Bill* gave immigration officers further powers, decreased rights and imposed further penalties.	
21st century	During the early part of the 21st century, almost annual *Immigration Acts* – the latest the *Immigration Act 2016* – made it more difficult to enter the UK for migrants (other than highly skilled migrants or EU residents) and made conditions for most migrants more difficult once in the UK. This last Act effectively equated 'illegal working' with criminality, although many of those found to be so were coping with the government's refusal to grant them asylum (Waite et al, 2015).	*2010 Equality Act* streamlined previous equalities legislation but was weakened by the coalition and Conservative governments, which have been reluctant to enforce compliance.

Source: Based on Solomos (2003, pp 57, 59) and Law (2010), with recent additions

(Ahmad and Husband, 1993). At the time of writing, the government's harsh immigration policy has meant that some families settled in the UK are again divided, with partners who have not achieved British nationality being deported. The Home Office's 2013 'Go Home' pilot campaign, which featured touring vans with threatening messages to illegal immigrants, is an example of this harsh policy (see Chapter 2; see also Jones et al, 2017).

The Immigration Act 1968 was passed before Enoch Powell made his 'Rivers of blood' speech, which resulted in his sacking from the Shadow Cabinet. Powell received massive support from the British population polled at the time (Hansen, 1999), suggesting that the Wilson government and the Act reflected the mood of large sections of society (although later research suggests this may not have been so). Supporters included trades union members such as dockworkers and meat porters (Sivanandan, 1982). The effect was that those who had the right to live and work in the UK were made even more unwelcome and reminded frequently of their 'otherness' (see Chapter 3). Rarely mentioned is that the emigration of White Britons during the 1950s and 1960s was, until the mid-1990s, regularly *more substantial numerically* than the numbers of immigrants (Brown, 1995). This has also been the case in recent years. Even in 2008, emigration from the UK was 427,000 and immigration 590,000, leaving 163,000 actual immigrants (ONS, 2009). These facts have rarely informed debates.

Further restrictions

During the 1980s, further restriction to immigration was introduced, following increasing fear of what Margaret Thatcher, while in opposition, described as being 'swamped' by people with a different culture (see Beckett, 2009). Following this, the British Nationality Act 1981 introduced a tiered system of citizenship. It gave citizens with UK-born grandparents (almost all White) the same right of abode in the UK as British citizens, while other British citizens (the majority Black) had none (Skellington and Morris, 1996).

From 1983, legislation continued to reduce numbers entering the UK, especially through marriage. The 'primary purpose rule' was introduced by the Conservative government to exclude young men from Bangladesh, India and Pakistan who wished to marry British women or women settled in the UK, and who were often of working age. Subsequent tightening of the 'rule' put the burden of proof on the applicant, and by 1990, the refusal rate was 60% (Parekh, 2000a). When the rule was found to discriminate in only deterring men from entry, it was extended to apply to women to ensure the even-handed nature of the British state. However, the rule was selectively applied to keep out women from the Philippines, but not from the USA or Australia (Parekh, 2000a). These Immigration Acts badly affected South Asian women, since the majority of their men had travelled to the UK alone, while men became isolated, unable to bring their families to the UK.

This was also the era of the infamous 'virgin tests', administered by immigration officers (see Ahmad, 1994). In 1997, the Labour government abolished this primary purpose rule, acknowledging that it was discriminatory.

During the 1990s, the debate moved from Commonwealth immigration to refugees and asylum-seekers. The 1971 Act had allowed the detention of 'illegal' immigrants. Two further Acts reinforced this. The Asylum and Immigration Appeals Act 1993 supported detentions and the Immigration and Asylum Act 1996 drastically affected the rights of those seeking asylum, and removed their benefits. The Immigration, Asylum and Nationality Act 1999 removed many of the rights of migrants to public resources. In response, several London hospitals insisted on seeing passports before beginning treatment, and many migrants were subject to dawn raids by immigration officers, which provoked national campaigns against deportation. This brutal legislation was challenged in the courts and in the European Court of Human Rights (Sales, 2007). It is a measure of the harshness of current legislation that the requirement to see passports before providing healthcare has now become normalised, and that the Department of Health had the confidence to run a poster campaign warning that NHS care was not free to all (Jones et al, 2017, p 44).

As Britain became more integrated within Europe, whether this would allow immigrants in 'by the back door' became a heated political issue, boiling over following the EU enlargements of 2004 and 2007. The idea of 'British jobs for British people', for example, was exploited by the major UK political parties (being voiced publicly by 2010 Labour leader Gordon Brown), and immigration became an important feature of the 2010 General Election for the first time since 1979 (as discussed previously; see Beckett, 2009). It remained the case in the 2015 and 2017 General Elections, and the 2016 EU referendum focused strongly on immigration control and the alleged negative impacts of migrant workers on jobs, skills and wages (for which there was scant evidence: see below). As noted in Chapter 2, the 2016 Brexit vote revealed high levels of racist hostility to migrants and immigration.

The 2010 election of members of the British National Party (BNP) to the European Parliament and the (albeit modest) electoral success of the United Kingdom Independence Party (UKIP), further reflected resentment towards immigration among sections of the British population, as did the Euroscepticism found among sections of the Conservatives and UKIP. With the changing membership of the EU, the 2000s saw workers from new member states coming to the UK. These migrants again worked in industries with labour shortages, made little demand on public resources and were useful to the economy. Research showed that EU migrants made a 'substantial net contribution to the UK fiscal system', paying 37% more in taxes than they received in welfare payments (Dustmann et al, 2009, p 18; Lemos and Portes, 2014; Netto and Craig, 2017). Researchers found that, on average, migrants were younger and better educated than the native population, as well as being 60% less likely to claim benefits and 58% less likely to live in social housing. Scotland, happily, has been noted for maintaining a more welcoming stance than other parts of the UK, and has been cited as the most welcoming place to live (Clifford, 2010), distancing itself from the Home Office 'Go Home' campaign of 2013 (Jones et al, 2017). It also challenged the coalition government clampdown on overseas student visas (Yousaf, 2010). Both the 2010 coalition and 2015 Conservative governments have counted students within migrant numbers, substantially inflating figures without recognising the vast annual income and other benefits they bring.

Becoming a UK citizen now requires taking a test, attending a ceremony and pledging allegiance to the Queen (discussed in Chapter 2, p 32). The point of such requirements was to create a sense of 'Britishness', the meaning of which has been contested (discussed below). The 2010 coalition government introduced English-language tests for those coming to the UK from non-EU countries to marry or join a partner (Home Office, 2010), despite severely reducing funding for English-language courses.

The Race Relations Act 1976 and subsequent amendments (2000)

Both the 1965 and 1968 Acts were repealed by the Race Relations Act 1976, which was broader in scope and covered discrimination on grounds of 'race', colour, nationality, ethnic and national origin in employment, provision of goods and services, education and public functions. It made prosecutions easier by removing intent and broadening what counted as discriminatory behaviour. The 1976 Act also established the Commission for Racial Equality (CRE), to ensure implementation of the Act and (allegedly) address the failures of the Community Relations Commission. It had a wider remit, covering private discrimination and indirect discrimination, but procedures were lengthy and complicated. Few successful cases went to completion. This continues to be a feature of equality legislation with important consequences, as much of what is permissible is determined by case law. Therefore, despite its sponsors' intentions, the 1976 Act struggled to have an impact. There were few investigations and fewer prosecutions, as was the case with previous legislation (Turner, 2008). The problems of enforcing legislation remained ongoing and affected subsequent attempts to act against racism.

In 2000, following the Macpherson Report into the death of Stephen Lawrence, the Labour government introduced amendments to the Race Relations Act 1976. A potentially powerful piece of legislation, this was premised on the idea that institutional racism was engrained in the fabric of British society, and charged public organisations with a statutory responsibility to promote equality and tackle discrimination (Atkin, 2009a). However, it has been criticised for its exclusions relating to gender, class and nation (Mirza, 2003). We return to this later and to its relationship with the Single Equality Act 2010.

'Managing' immigration and 'race'

So far, we have reflected on the changing legislative context influencing state policies on ethnic diversity. We now explore the social context and policy responses that emerged, as illustrated in Table 4.2.

As Craig and Lewis (2010; see also Lewis and Craig, 2014) note, the idea of community cohesion had faded by the time of the 2010 and 2015 General Elections, and 'race' issues became more focused on terrorism. Initial government thinking (that is, in the 1960s) on immigration did not plan for a multicultural society, assuming that minority ethnic populations would assimilate into a 'British way of life' and that cultural differences would disappear (Cashmore and Troyna, 1990; Gouldbourne, 1998). To facilitate this, for example, children from Asian families in Bradford and Southall were 'bused' to different schools to ensure that no school became associated with a minority population (Brah, 1996; McLoughlin, 2009; BBC News, 2017).

Assimilation policies were accompanied by 'blaming the victim', both implicitly and explicitly, for their 'deviant' cultural practices (Lawrence, 1982). Problems allegedly occurred because people did not speak English; married their first cousins; adopted unhealthy diets; had children without husbands; misunderstood the role of the welfare state; and so on. Such ideas informed policy in the 1980s and early 1990s, strongly influencing our current understanding of ethnic diversity (see Atkin and Chattoo, 2007; see also Chapter 2, this volume). The over-representation of Caribbean children in public care was a direct expression of beliefs that Black parenting was inferior and their children at risk of harm (ABSWAP, 1983; Pennie and Best, 1990).

In state education, African Caribbean children were labelled as 'educationally sub-normal' and segregated into 'special schools' and classes (Coard, 1971; Kowalczewski, 1982). Asian children were also labelled as 'backward' through their need to learn English (Bryan et al, 1985; Williams, 1996). Health services worked with similar assumptions. The majority population had rickets in the early 20th century, but had benefited from vitamin D supplements and additions

Table 4.2: The policy context for managing 'race' relations in the UK

Approach	Era	Policy issue	Rationale
Assimilation	1960s to late 1970s	Labour migration	'Race' riots
Multiculturalism	Late 1970s, 1980s, early 1990s	Managing diversity	Co-opting protest
Community cohesion	2000s	Asylum and terror	Security

Source: After Craig and Lewis (2010, p 11)

to flour and margarine. Consequently, rickets had been eradicated. However, for those of Asian background whose children had rickets in the 1970s, poor diet was blamed rather than using the strategies that had benefited the majority population (Bivins, 2007).

In 1966, Roy Jenkins, Home Secretary for the then Labour government, spoke out against assimilation in favour of integration:

> I define integration, therefore, not as a flattening process of assimilation but as equal opportunity, accompanied by cultural diversity, in an atmosphere of mutual tolerance. That is the goal. (quoted in Lester, 2009, p 4)

Brah (1996) has argued that such reasoning assumed a level playing field of equal opportunity from which to build 'race' equality, and that it put the emphasis on human characteristics such as tolerance as the key to success, while ignoring social, economic and structural aspects that contributed to inequality. Nonetheless, the seeds of multiculturalism, which flourished in the late 1970s and early 1980s, were sown. The failure to name and condemn racism, including its intersection with sexism, has been a theme of writings on this period (Carby, 1982; Troyna, 1984; Essed, 1994). This later became endorsed in the Macpherson inquiry which evidenced the institutional racism infecting state institutions.

Meanwhile, multiculturalism replaced assimilation as the basis of policy, peaking in the early 1980s (Modood, 2007). Addressing power inequalities and institutional racism was not prominent in a multicultural approach, as cultures were naively regarded as meeting on equal terms. The emphasis was on developing mutual understanding; once achieved, racism and discrimination would disappear (Atkin, 2009a). The problem with the focus on culture, however, meant that minority cultures became unfavourably judged in relation to the majority White culture (noted above). Minority ethnic family life was seen as 'other', and difference was emphasised at the expense of similarities and differences *between* and *within* ethnic groups. Elements of such assumptions persist today (see Chapter 2, this volume).

One unintended consequence of multiculturalism was that cultural diversity was used *against* minority ethnic populations (Karlsen, 2007). Healthcare problems became associated with their supposed 'deviant' cultural practices and lifestyles (Ahmad and Bradby, 2007; Atkin 2009b). Atkin and Chattoo (2007) note how in the 1980s, health and social care agencies explained the small number of minority ethnic people on their caseload, by saying 'they look after their own' (see also Craig, 2001). Further, it remains common in training material to see one-page static explanations of Muslim, Hindu and Sikh cultures, to which patients' beliefs are expected to correspond (Atkin and Chattoo, 2007). They also create the illusion of a solution to complex situations (Chattoo and Ahmad, 2004). During the 1980s, multiculturalism became challenged by anti-racism, which saw cultural explanations as forms of racism. Assimilation, integration and multiculturalism did not address power inequalities or the structures and systems that perpetuated racism. By now, Black feminist theory was making a substantial contribution to 'race' equality (Bhavnani et al, 2005). The Black perspective on immigration, summarised by the Runnymede Trust, evidences how Black voices were rarely heard in the increasingly toxic debates (Khan and Weekes-Bernard, 2015).

Anti-racism and 'the end of anti-racism': the rise of Black struggle

By the beginning of the 1980s, a groundswell was taking place. Women and men from minority ethnic groups had challenged unfair and racist practices in workplaces, and had written about them. Community struggles became more prevalent (Craig, 2018). There were now more Black academics, psychiatrists and teachers than in the 1960s. In addition, organisations had been set up locally and nationally, such as the Southall Black Sisters, Organisation of Women of African and Asian Descent (OWAAD) and the Association of Black Social Workers and Allied Professions (ABSWAP). These groups' messages were that racism was inherent in the systems and structures of British society (the institutional racism that was finally named and shamed by the Macpherson Report), and that without Black inclusion there could not be progress in addressing 'race' equality. Concerns were expressed about police racism and brutality, originally focused on the deaths of Blair Peach, a White teacher activist fatally assaulted by a police officer in Southall, and of Cherry Groce and Cynthia Jarrett, two Caribbean women who experienced police brutality during searches of their homes in London. These events fuelled the disturbances of 1981 and 1985, which were seen as a clear sign that Black people would not tolerate continued racism without fighting back. This issue remains live, with the continued deaths of Black people at the hands of the police, the disproportionate numbers of Black young people stopped and searched by the police and the continuing deaths of Black and Asian people as a result of racist attacks (now numbering substantially more than 100 since the death of Stephen Lawrence).

During the 1980s, the meaning of the category 'race' was questioned, and minorities were centrally involved as academics and practitioners in these critiques and questions. Plurality, multiple identities and intersectionality were highlighted and explored by Hall (1992), by Black feminists such as Bhavnani and Phoenix (1994) and by others (see Chapter 2, this volume). The 1980s led to a new multiculturalism, which recognised cultural difference alongside structural disadvantage and institutional racism. As Ballard (1989) observed, culture was not a problem *per se*; it was how cultural difference was perceived. Culturally capable practice (Dominelli, 2004; Papadopoulos et al, 2004) informed this 'new' multiculturalism. Tensions, however, remain, which are associated with the influences of previous debates. Essentialism, long discredited in academia, is re-emerging as mainstream policy and practice responds to super-diversity (Chattoo, 2008; and see Chapter 2). The new multiculturalism also attracted criticism associated with a concern to establish community cohesion.

Attacks on the 'new' multiculturalism

A major criticism of UK current multiculturalist policies has been that minorities are free to retain parts of their own culture, which undermines British values or 'a core of Britishness' (Cheong et al, 2007). Where these so-called 'British' values have been identified, such as freedom of speech and personal security, democracy, fairness and justice, research has shown (Rutter et al, 2007) that they are equally valued by new migrants and resident minorities as by the majority population (Jayaweera and Choudhury, 2008). Some, however, continue to argue that the failure of minorities to integrate has undermined policies of community cohesion and contributed to urban disturbances over the last 30 years, culminating in the 2005 and subsequent London bombings and other terrorist incidents.

As Parekh (2000b) reminds us, like it or not, multicultural societies are a fact of life and cannot be wished away – other than by ethnic cleansing. Those who now argue that multiculturalism has failed or is dangerous demonstrate little understanding of what a multiculturalist policy framework was/is trying to achieve. The then Prime Minister David Cameron's statement in 2011 pointing both to the end of multiculturalism and, disgracefully, to its supposed links with terrorism, is an extreme example of such utterances. Currently, debates in the UK (and elsewhere) are reverting to the assimilation policy mentioned earlier or even now, in parallel with the USA under Trump, to exclusion.

Those arguing for multiculturalist policy maintain that it is possible to respect difference and diversity within human rights and anti-discrimination legislation and practice as, for example, laid out in the United Nations (UN) Charter of Human Rights (see Craig, 2008). The failure lies with the British and other settled states and not with those minorities subjected to their policies.

Anti-racism, equality and diversity, and community cohesion

The *Fourth national survey of minority ethnic groups* (Modood et al, 1997) provided comprehensive evidence on inequality between minorities and the majority population. This survey identified different groups separately and highlighted inequalities to do with ethnic origin, social class, gender and religion and in specific services such as mental health, employment, housing and education. Coupled with the Human Rights Act 1998 and the election of the 1997 Labour government, the scene seemed set for progress. Devolution from 1999 also allowed the other UK countries to develop and implement their own policies, some of which have benefited 'race' equality.

The Macpherson Report precipitated a major shift in 'race' equality policy. The murder of Stephen Lawrence, a young Black man killed by four White men in London, and the subsequent inquiry, posed a challenge to public services that remains today. Institutional racism was named authoritatively (Macpherson, 1999, Recommendation 12 and para 6.34; see also Chapter 1, this volume). The definition allowed for changes to 'race' equality legislation in the UK. The Race Relations (Amendment) Act 2000 laid responsibility on public institutions to promote 'race' equality, monitor their services, and report and publish the results (see www.legislation.gov.uk/ukpga/2000/34). Any service in receipt of public money had a duty to develop a 'race' equality scheme (and action plan). The then Commission for Racial Equality had a watchdog brief.

However, rather than focusing on the continuing racism in British society profiled by the Act, leading politicians continued to attack multiculturalism (Johnston, 2007). Disturbances in several Northern English towns during the late 1990s and local and national enquiries (Cantle, 2001; Ouseley, 2001) led to a national policy on community cohesion (Home Office, 2001). The attack on multiculturalism that followed from the Macpherson Report, the 'Northern disturbances' and the new deracialised focus on community cohesion can be interpreted as an attempt by the state to divert attention away from racism into a channel, which (again) blamed minorities for many of the social and economic ills affecting the UK (Worley, 2005; Chouhan, 2009). Jones et al (2017) document the increasing hostility towards migrants from a speech given by Tony Blair in 2001, through the economic crash of 2008, to the present day.

Community cohesion

Despite the new 'race' equality legislation, change was slow, and communities continued to face deprivation and disadvantage (see later chapters in this volume). The government argued that their failure to 'integrate' and their desire to lead increasingly separate lives was at odds with the traditional values of White Britishness (discussed above). The fact that there was no consensus of the meaning of 'Britishness', even across the four UK countries, was overlooked. The dominant 'White' perspective of policy-making was also ignored (Craig, 2013; Bowler, 2017).

Community cohesion displaced '"race" relations' as the basis for policy-making (Worley, 2005; Flint and Robinson, 2008), creating a tension that remains unresolved. Both central and local government (LGA, 2002; Home Office, 2004) published guidance on what they understood to be the meaning of Britishness. For example, the Home Office acknowledged the continuing presence of racism and discrimination, and argued that 'to be British means that we respect the laws, the democratic political structures, and give our allegiance to the State' (Home Office, 2004, p 6). It also suggested, contradictorily, that 'to be British does not mean assimilation into a common culture so that original identities are lost' (Home Office, 2004, p 6). It concluded, also contradictorily, that respect for the law, fairness, tolerance and respect for difference were values shared by all Britons, of whatever ethnic origin (see also Forrest and Kearns, 2000), continuing the confusion over what Britishness really is. The domestic 'Northern disturbances' were followed by the attacks on the World Trade Center in New York City and the ensuing 'war on terror'; by bombings in Madrid, Bali, London and other Western cities; and by Western military intervention in Iraq, Afghanistan and Syria. Terrorist bombings, now associated with the work of extreme Islamist groups such as Isis/Daesh and Al Qaeda, have become more regular. These have been characterised as a struggle between two civilisations: the West and Islam (Huntington, 1996). The far right has argued that some of Britain's minorities lack commitment to integrating and should be 'encouraged' to return to their countries of origin, despite the fact that many are British-born. Cultural tensions have also been apparent in responses to government attempts to legislate against religious incitement (Jan-Khan, 2003). These tensions have grown downstream of the recent military interventions made by the UK in countries (such as Iraq and Afghanistan), and have arguably, as with other Western European states such as France, made the UK a target for terrorist retaliation.

Community cohesion appeared to be the acceptable government 'race' policy, and it shaped local responses (Lewis and Craig, 2014). For example, it compelled local government to take up the community cohesion theme with Public Service Agreement 9 requiring them to 'bring about a measurable improvement in 'race' and 'community cohesion' (see www.nao.org.uk/psa/publications), and also influenced the direction of third sector activity. Although the government published a community cohesion and 'race' equality strategy in 2004 (Home Office, 2004), later policy documents dropped 'race' equality. In 2008, the Commission for Racial Equality was abolished and its work incorporated into the Equality and Human Rights Commission (EHRC), which downgraded the work on 'race' relations for which the CRE acted as a focus. The government-established Commission on Integration and Cohesion (CIC) also argued that 'the national picture is a positive one: perceptions of cohesion are good in most areas – on average 79 per cent of people agreed that people of different backgrounds got on well in their local area' (CIC, 2007, p 8).

The strategy has been strongly criticised. First, although community cohesion appears to have replaced 'race' as the organising factor for work between local communities, it is clear that 'race' – or a particular racial or ethnic identity (being Muslim) – had become the prime concern of policy-makers and the police. Worley (2005, p 483) argued that 'talking about communities enables language to become deracialized while at the same time the language of community cohesion draws upon earlier discourses of assimilation…'. Second, the focus of the Prevent agenda (see www.justwestyorkshire.co.uk) has been criticised as narrowing down public understanding of extremist behaviour to the acts of a few radical Muslims. It is then generalised to Muslims as a whole rather than focusing equally, if not more strongly, on the far-right political parties, which have been behind racialised disturbances in cities over the past 50 years (JUST, 2009; Halliday and Dodd, 2015). Prevent also encouraged much wider surveillance of Muslim populations. Third, demographic analysis challenges the assumption that the UK's minority populations are becoming separated from one another and from the mainstream UK White population, and concentrated into areas in which extremists might ferment 'race' and religious hatred. Finney and Simpson (2009), for example, demonstrate that segregation, where it occurs, is shaped by racism in housing and labour markets, by poverty and housing unaffordability. A Scottish study carried out in Glasgow supported these findings (Hopkins, 2004).

If Britain's minorities are leading 'parallel lives', this is because racism continues to affect every aspect of those lives (Platt, 2003; Hopkins, 2004; Craig, 2007; Phillips, 2009; Barnard and Turner, 2010; Khan, 2015). Labour market participation is the key to integration (Rutter et al, 2008), but research demonstrates how racism affects minorities' access to decent work (Hughes, 2015), with women particularly disadvantaged (Mirza, 2003). Rutter et al's (2007, 2008) work also demonstrates that integration – and by implication, cohesion – is a long process, not to be driven by short-term political agendas. This presented a challenge to the typology developed by the Institute of Community Cohesion (ICoCo, 2009), for example, since Britain's minorities still do not have access to equal opportunity outcomes or rights enjoyed by the majority population for reasons external to the communities themselves (Craig, 2008). The suggestion that increasing diversity undermines social cohesion has also been challenged (Hickman et al, 2008).

The Department for Communities and Local Government (DCLG) published *Tackling race inequality: A statement on 'race'* (DCLG, 2010), summarising achievements since the Macpherson Report, outlining plans for 'race' equality and setting out a commitment to continue tackling 'race' inequality that was soon to be undermined, although John Denham, then Communities Secretary, denied that this was the case (Denham, 2010; Travis, 2010). However, at the same time, he argued it was time to 'move on' from 'race'. This policy was linked to £6 million of funding for the voluntary and community sector, to assist with the implementation of government objectives. The coalition government announced voluntary sector partners in early 2011: none were BME-led, and a review concluded that the BME voluntary sector, including quasi-statutory organisations such as the network of local Community Relations Councils, was under severe threat through steady withdrawal of funding. Even with widespread austerity and cuts in public services, the BME third sector was hit relatively hard (Craig, 2011; Tilki et al, 2015).

Equalities legislation was reviewed and streamlined. What emerged was an Equalities Bill and then an Act (2010), which included the existing 'race', gender and disability legislation and added religion (and non-religious belief), sexual orientation and age. When there was so much to be done to implement the Race Relations (Amendment) Act 2000, the fear of 'race' equality becoming less of a priority became reality in how some local authorities interpreted the CIC's recommendations on single group funding. They decided not to fund organisations that focused on just one of the equality strands, arguing that all equality strands needed promoting in order to achieve cohesion (Lewis and Craig, 2014). This led to Southall Black Sisters, a 'race' equality women-led organisation, losing its funding from Ealing Council. Subsequently, the organisation took the Council to the High Court and won their case. In a landmark decision, the Court ruled that there was no contradiction in funding specialist services for cohesion to be achieved (Southall Black Sisters, 2008).

The Single Equality Act 2010 was weakened by the coalition government prior to implementation (see www.equalities.gov.uk/equalitybill.aspx); some aspects – such as the requirement for public bodies to reduce inequalities based on class – were scrapped. The coalition government, led by Prime Minister David Cameron, took their lead from Denham's comment (above), and substantially downgraded work around 'race'. The Government Equalities Office (2010) lost staff, funding and legislative force. Soon after appointment, the Home Secretary Theresa May declared equality to be 'a dirty word'. The specific duties of public agencies have been similarly downgraded and the private sector remains free from these requirements. This weakening of local statutory commitments to 'race' equality was demonstrated in a report on agencies in York (Craig et al, 2016) which found, compared with 2009, a growing lack of interest in pursuing 'race' equality despite legal requirements (see Government Equalities Office, 2010). Clear messages were generated by the coalition and 2015 Conservative governments that race equality was no longer a policy priority (Craig, 2013). Indeed, the continuing high incidence of Black 'stop and search', and the emphasis within the Prevent programme on the surveillance of Muslims, suggests that the government is not listening to messages from research or the BME population. As Mayo (2015, p 21) notes, citing Hoque (2015), 'Prevent agendas tend to stigmatize ... evidence of transnational ties as potentially symptomatic of terrorist affiliations, [these alienate] precisely those whom the policies are intended to win over.' The distance travelled since race relations legislation was first enacted – and the distance yet to be travelled – has been summarised in two separate critical reviews (see EHRC, 2015; Khan, 2015). The EHRC, meanwhile, was itself subject to substantial cuts in funding, creating staff redundancies and undermining its own capacity to provide leadership on race equality.

Debates on 'race' within the UK have focused on the 'immigration' problem as a prominent subject for political discourse, especially around the time of elections.

On the political right, claims are made that the UK is 'full' and cannot accept further migration (although not when applied to White migrants or to those bringing high levels of skill – or capital – to the labour market). Immigration Acts have followed throughout the 2000s at, as noted, almost yearly intervals, each imposing more restrictions on potential migrants as they attempt to enter the UK and after they have attempted to establish themselves (Bloch et al, 2015; Carr, 2015). Links are made between immigration and security, with the latter dominating political concerns. The focus, during the mass migration from Syria, Libya, Afghanistan and Iraq, has been less on preventing the thousands of deaths by drowning in the Mediterranean or the number of unaccompanied children who have disappeared into the hands of traffickers than on limiting numbers reaching the UK. Particular concerns are that Isis/Daesh and other terrorists use migration as a cover to reach the UK and engage in guerrilla warfare, as happened in France and Belgium. At the same time, as evidenced by the response to the Brexit vote, the UK population, encouraged by a xenophobic tabloid press, takes a much more hostile approach to immigration. They have increasingly labelled as 'immigrants' the 50% or more of minorities born and raised within the UK, and this has been reflected in increasing levels of 'race' hate crime (Jones et al, 2017; see also Chapter 1, this volume).

Conclusion

'Race' policy and practice have moved from overt racism in the early 20th century, through Acts aimed at curbing racial discrimination and at promoting 'race' equality, while a parallel set of legislation has sought to curb Black immigration, thereby undermining progress and questioning government commitment and credibility. For a while, institutional racism had some attention, but services still struggle (as demonstrated in subsequent chapters) to redress inequalities and, within them, to share power and to engage with minority ethnic communities.

There is no consensus on how much has been achieved since the Macpherson Report of 1999 and the Race Relations (Amendment) Act 2000 came into force. 'Race' equality will be difficult to achieve while the ideology represented by current and past immigration legislation remains. The rise and fall of community cohesion adds to the uncertainty. Clearly the coalition government elected in 2010 and its 2015 successor Conservative government have backed away from a commitment to pursuing 'race' equality. At a time of financial austerity, this has encouraged public services to do the same, leaving the ability of the BME third sector to act as an advocate severely weakened. The political and policy focus on 'race' in recent years has shifted from a concern with integration towards imposing stricter limits on immigration and on confronting the terrorist threat, which has been implicitly associated with Muslim groups (Halliday and Dodd, 2015). At the same time, more recently formed grassroots campaigns and organisations such as Stand Up To Racism, Show Racism the Red Card, The People's Assembly, Black Lives Matter and the People's Momentum are holding the government to account and aiming to curb the excesses of racism in current policy and practice, by organising demonstrations, petitions and rallies, and engaging in political education for equality and justice. At the time of writing, the motivator of anger as a change agent, outlined by Jones et al (2017, pp 141, 148), seems badly needed.

Questions for discussion

- Identify and describe three policy approaches to managing 'race' and 'race' relations' since 1950, and give examples of these approaches in action in one or more public services.
- To what extent does legislation help tackle inequalities? To what extent are policy and practice being informed by the struggles of BME communities?
- To what extent did growing hostility to immigration shape the response to the 2016 EU referendum?

Online resources

http://migrationmatters.me
  Migration Matters aims to change the debate around migration through evidence-based information including short video courses.

http://migrationmuseum.org
  The Migration Museum Project plans to create the UK's first dedicated Migration Museum and to tell the story of movement into and out of the UK.

http://news.bbc.co.uk/hi/english/static/in_depth/uk/2002/race/
http://news.bbc.co.uk/hi/english/static/in_depth/uk/2002/race/short_history_of_immigration.stm
  The BBC websites have historical news items on 'race' and immigration.

Further reading

Bhavnani, R., Mirza, H.S. and Meetoo, V. (2005) *Tackling the roots of racism*, Bristol: Policy Press.

Jones, H., Gunaratnam, Y., Bhattacharyya, G., Davies, W., Dhaliwal, S., Forkert, K., et al (2017) *Go home! The politics of immigration controversies*, Manchester: Manchester University Press.

Solomos, J. (2003) *Race and racism in Britain* (3rd edn), Basingstoke: Palgrave Macmillan.

References

ABSWAP (Association of Black Social Workers and Allied Professions) (1983) *Black children in care: Evidence to the House of Commons Social Services Committee*, London: ABSWAP.

Ahmad, W.I.U. (1994) *'Race' and health*, Buckingham: Open University Press.

Ahmad, W.I.U. and Bradby, H. (2007) 'Locating ethnicity and health: Exploring concepts and contexts', *Sociology of Health and Illness*, 29(6), 793-811.

Ahmad, W.I.U. and Husband, C. (1993) 'Religious identity, citizenship and welfare', *American Journal of Islamic Social Sciences*, 10(2), 217-33.

Atkin, K. (2009a) 'Making sense of ethnic diversity, difference and disadvantage within the context of multicultural societies', in L. Culley, N. Hudson and F. van Rooij (eds) *Marginalised reproduction: Ethnicity, infertility and reproductive technologies*, London: Earthscan, 49-63.

Atkin, K. (2009b) 'Negotiating ethnic identities and health', in H. Graham (ed) *Understanding health inequalities* (2nd edn), Maidenhead: Open University Press, 125-40.

Atkin, K. and Chattoo, S. (2007) 'The dilemmas of providing welfare in an ethnically diverse state: Seeking reconciliation in the role of a "reflexive practitioner"', *Policy & Politics*, 35(3), 379-95.

Ballard, R. (1989) 'Social work with black people: What's the difference?', in C. Rojek, G. Peacock and S. Collins (eds) *The haunt of misery: Critical essays in caring and helping*, London: Tavistock, 123-47.

Barnard, H. and Turner, C. (2010) *Poverty and ethnicity: A review of the evidence*, York: Joseph Rowntree Foundation.

Batty, D. (2003) 'Britain's looming GP crisis', *The Guardian* (www.theguardian.com/society/2003/aug/27/primarycare.raceintheuk).

BBC News (2017) 'The child immigrants "bussed" out to school to aid integration', 30 January (www.bbc.co.uk/news/uk-england-leeds-38689839).

Beckett, A. (2009) *When the lights went out: Britain in the seventies*, London: Faber & Faber.

Bhavnani, K. and Phoenix, A. (eds) (1994) *Shifting identities shifting racisms: A feminism and psychology reader*, London: Sage.

Bhavnani, R., Mirza, H.S. and Meetoo V. (2005) *Tackling the roots of racism: Lessons for success*, Bristol: Policy Press.

Bivins, R. (2007) 'The "English disease" or "Asian rickets"? Medical responses to postcolonial immigration', *Bulletin of the History of Medicine*, 81(3), 533-68.

Blakemore, K. (1990) 'Does age matter? The case of old age in minority ethnic groups', in A. Bloch, L. Kumarappan and S. Mckay, 'Employer sanctions', *Critical Social Policy*, May, 132-51.

Bloch, A., Kumarappan, L. and McKay, S. (2015) 'Employer sanctions: The impact of workplace raids and fines on undocumented migrants and ethnic enclave employers', *Critical Social Policy*, 35(1), 132-51.

Bowler, R. (2017) 'Critical youth and community work and its struggle with white standards', in G. Craig (ed) *Community organising against racism*, Bristol: Policy Press, 41-60.

Brah, A. (1996) *Cartographies of diaspora: Contesting identities*, London: Routledge.

Brown, R. (1995) 'Racism and immigration in Britain', *International Socialism Journal* (http://pubs.socialistreviewindex.org.uk/isj68/brown.htm).

Bryan, B., Dadzie, S. and Scafe, S. (1985) *The heart of the race: Black women's lives in Britain*, London: Virago.

Cantle, T. (2001) *Community cohesion: A report of the Independent Review Team*, London: Home Office.

Carby, H. (1982) 'Schooling in Babylon', in Centre for Contemporary Cultural Studies (ed) *The Empire strikes back: Race and racism in 70s Britain*, London: Hutchinson, 83-211.

Carr, M. (2015) *Fortress Europe*, London: Hurst & Co.

Cashmore, E. and Troyna, B. (1990) *Introduction to race relations*, Basingstoke: Falmer Press.

Chattoo, S. (2008) 'The moral economy of selfhood and caring: Negotiating boundaries of personal care as embodied moral practice', *Sociology of Health and Illness*, 30, 550-64.

Chattoo, S. and Ahmad, W.I.U. (2004) 'The meaning of cancer: Illness, biography and social identity', in D. Kelleher and G. Leavey (eds) *Identity and health*, London: Routledge, 19-36.

Cheong, P., Edwards, R., Gouldbourne, H. and Solomos, J. (2007) 'Immigration, social cohesion and social capital', *Critical Social Policy*, 27(1), 27-49.

Chouhan, K. (2009) 'Cohesion creep', Paper presented to 'Rethinking Community Cohesion – Different Perspectives on Segregation and Community Relations' Conference, University of Birmingham, 14 October.

CIC (Commission on Integration and Cohesion) (2007) *Our shared future* (http://collections.europarchive.org/tna/20080726153624/http://www.integrationandcohesion.org.uk/~/media/assets/www.integrationandcohesion.org.uk/our_shared_future%20pdf.ashx).

Clifford, L. (2010) 'UK visa holders get biggest welcome in Scotland' (www.globalvisas.com/news/uk_visa_holders_get_biggest_welcome_in_scotland2302.html).

Coard, B. (1971) *How the West Indian child is made educationally sub-normal in the British school system: The scandal of the Black child in schools in Britain*, London: New Beacon Books.

Craig, G. (2001) *Taking power*, Huddersfield: Age Concern Kirklees.

Craig, G. (2007) 'Cunning, unprincipled, loathsome: The racist tail wags the welfare dog', *Journal of Social Policy*, 36(4), 605-23.

Craig, G. (2008) 'The limits of compromise', in G. Craig, T. Burchardt and D. Gordon (eds) *Social justice and public policy*, Bristol: Policy Press, 231-50.

Craig, G. (2011) 'Forward to the past: Can the UK Black and minority ethnic third sector survive?', *Voluntary Sector Review*, November, 367–89.

Craig, G. (2013) 'The invisibilisation of "race" in public policy', *Critical Social Policy*, November, 712–20.

Craig, G. (ed) (2018) *Community organising against racism*, Bristol: Policy Press.

Craig, G. and Lewis, H. (2010) 'Exclusion and assimilation: The lot of Britain's ethnic minorities', Paper presented to Symposium on International Multiculturalism, Deakin University, Melbourne, 25–26 November (mimeo).

Craig, G., Boparai, H., Adamson, S., Demsash, F. and Martin, G. (2016) *A racial justice forum for York?*, York: York Workshops.

DCLG (Department for Communities and Local Government) (2010) *Tackling race inequality: A statement on race*, London: DCLG.

Denham, J. (2010) 'Government is committed to tackling inequality and disadvantage wherever it exists' (https://webarchive.nationalarchives. gov.uk/20100202154705/http://www.communities.gov.uk/news/ communities/1432668).

Dominelli, L. (2004) *Social work: Theory and practice for a changing profession*, Cambridge: Polity Press.

Doyal, L., Hunt, G. and Mellor, J. (1980) *Migrant workers in the NHS*, London: Polytechnic of North London.

Dustmann, C., Frattini, T. and Halls, C. (2009) *Assessing the fiscal costs and benefits of A8 migration to the UK*, CReAM Discussion Paper 18/09, London: Centre for Research and Analysis of Migration.

EHRC (Equality and Human Rights Commission) (2015) *Is Britain fairer?*, Manchester: EHRC.

Essed, P. (1994) 'Making and breaking ethnic boundaries: Women's studies, diversity, and racism', *Women's Studies Quarterly*, 22(3/4), 232–49.

Fanshawe, S. and Sriskanarajah, D. (2010) *You can't put me in a box: Super-diversity and the end of identity politics in Britain*, London: Institute for Public Policy Research.

Finney, N. and Simpson, L. (2009) *'Sleepwalking to segregation'? Challenging myths about race and migration*, Bristol: Policy Press.

Flint, J. and Robinson, D. (eds) (2008) *Community cohesion in crisis? New dimensions of diversity and difference*, Bristol: Policy Press.

Forrest, R. and Kearns, A. (2000) 'Social cohesion, social capital and the neighbourhood', Paper presented to ESRC Cities Programme Neighbourhood Colloquium, Liverpool.

Gouldbourne, H. (1998) *Race relations in Britain since 1945*, London: Macmillan.

Government Equalities Office (2010) *Equality Act 2010* (www.equalities.gov. uk/equality_bill.aspx).

Hall, S. (1992) 'New ethnicities', in J. Donald and A. Rattansi (eds) *Race, culture and difference*, London: Sage, 252–9.

Halliday, J. and Dodd, V. (2015) 'UK Anti-radicalisation Prevent strategy a "toxic brand", *The Guardian*, 9 March (www.theguardian.com/uk-news/2015/mar/09/anti-radicalisation-prevent-strategy-a-toxic-brand).

Hansen, R. (1999) 'The Kenyan Asians, British politics, and the Commonwealth Immigrants Act, 1968', *The Historical Journal*, 42(3), 809-34.

Hero, D. (1991) *Black British, White British: A history of race relations in Britain*, London: Grafton.

Hickman, M., Crowley, H. and Mai, N. (2008) *Immigration and social cohesion in the UK*, York: Joseph Rowntree Foundation.

Home Office (2001) *Building cohesive communities*, London: Home Office.

Home Office (2004) *Strength in diversity: Towards a community cohesion and race equality strategy*, London: Home Office.

Home Office and The Rt Hon Theresa May MP (2010) 'Migrants marrying UK citizens must now learn English' (www.gov.uk/government/news/migrants-marrying-uk-citizens-must-now-learn-english).

Hopkins, P. (2004) 'Everyday racism in Scotland: A case study of East Pollockshields', *Scottish Affairs*, 49 (www.researchgate.net/publication/265245376_Everyday_Racism_in_Scotland_A_Case_Study_of_East_Pollockshields).

Hoque, A. (2015) *British-Islamic identity*, Stoke-on-Trent: Trentham Books.

Hughes, C. (2015) *Poverty, ethnicity and youth employment*, York: Joseph Rowntree Foundation.

Huntington, S. (1996) *The clash of civilisations and the remaking of world order*, New York: Simon & Schuster.

ICoCo (Institute of Community Cohesion) (2009) *Prospectus*, Coventry: ICoCo.

Jan-Khan, M. (2003) 'The right to riot?', *Community Development Journal*, 38, 32-42.

Jayaweera, H. and Choudhury, T. (2008) *Immigration, faith and cohesion*, York: Joseph Rowntree Foundation.

Johnston, P. (2007) 'Brown's manifesto for Britishness', *The Telegraph*, 13 January (www.telegraph.co.uk/news/uknews/1539367/We-need-a-United-Kingdom.html).

Jones, H., Gunaratnam, Y., Bhattacharyya, G., Davies, W., Dhaliwal, S., Forkert, K., et al (2017) *Go home? The politics of immigration controversies*, Manchester: Manchester University Press.

JUST (2009) *Evidence to the Home Office Select Committee on the Preventing Extremism Agenda*, Bradford: JUST West Yorkshire.

Karlsen, S. (2007) *Ethnic inequalities in health: The impact of racism*, Better Health Briefing Paper No 3, London: Race Equality Foundation.

Khan, O. (ed) (2015) *How far have we come?*, London: Runnymede Trust.

Khan, O. and Weekes-Bernard, D. (2015) *This is still about us*, London: Runnymede Trust.

Kowalczewski, P.S. (1982) 'Race and education: Racism, diversity and inequality, implications for multicultural education', *Oxford Review of Education*, 8(2), 145-61.

Kynaston, D. (2008) *Austerity Britain, 1945-1951: Tales of a New Jerusalem*, London: Bloomsbury.

Law, I. (2010) 'Migration, ethnicity and racism: Frameworks and formations', in I. Law (ed) *Racism and ethnicity: Global debates, dilemmas, directions*, London: Pearson, 121-5.

Lawrence, E. (1982) 'In the abundance of water the fool is thirsty: Sociology and black "pathology"', in Centre for Contemporary Cultural Studies (ed) *The Empire strikes back: Race and racism in 70s Britain*, London, Hutchinson, 95-142.

Lemos, S. and Portes, J. (2014) 'New Labour? The impact of migration from Central and Eastern European Countries on the UK Labour Market', *BE Journal of Economic Policy*, February.

Lester, A. (2009) 'Multiculturalism and free speech', Speech at De Montfort University, 10 June (www.blackstonechambers.com/news/publications/multiculturalism.html).

Lewis, H. and Craig, G. (2014) **'Multiculturalism is never talked about: Community cohesion and local policy contradictions in England'**, *Policy & Politics*, 41(2).

LGA (Local Government Association) (2002) *Guidance on community cohesion*, London: LGA.

Macpherson, W. (1999) *The Stephen Lawrence inquiry: Report of an inquiry by Sir William Macpherson of Cluny*, CM4262-I, London: The Stationery Office.

Mama, A. (1984) 'Black women, the economic crisis and the British State', *Feminist Review*, 17, 21-35.

McLoughlin, S. (2009) 'From diasporas to multi-locality: Writing British Asian cities' (www.leeds.ac.uk/brasian/assets/papers/WBAC003.pdf).

Mason, R. (2011) 'Shortage of family doctors leaves health care in crisis', *The Telegraph*, 26 December (www.telegraph.co.uk/news/health/news/8978509/Shortage-of-family-doctors-leaves-health-care-in-crisis.html).

Mayo, M. (2015) 'Looking backwards, looking forwards', *Community Development Journal*, 51(1), 8-22.

Mirza, H.S. (2003) '"All the women are White, all the Blacks are men – but some of us are brave": Mapping the consequences of invisibility for black and minority ethnic women in Britain', in D. Mason (ed) *Explaining ethnic differences: Changing patterns of disadvantage in Britain*, Bristol: Policy Press, 121-38.

Modood, T. (2007) *Multiculturalism*, Cambridge: Polity Press.

Modood, T., Berthoud, R., Lakey, J., Nazroo, J., Smith, P., Virdee, S. and Beishon, S. (1997) *Ethnic minorities in Britain: Diversity and disadvantage*, London: Policy Studies Institute.

Muir, H. (2005) 'Files show police hostility to Windrush generation: Racism from the top down in 1950s reports by Met officers', *The Guardian*, 16 February (www.guardian.co.uk/uk/2005/feb/16/race.world).

Netto, G. and Craig, G. (2017) 'Introduction: Migration and differential labour market participation', *Social Policy and Society*, September, 607–11.

ONS (Office for National Statistics) (2009) 'Emigration reaches record high in 2008', Press release, 26 November.

Ouseley, H. (2001) *Community pride not prejudice*, Bradford: Bradford Vision.

Papadopoulos, I., Tilkim, M. and Lees, S. (2004) 'Promoting cultural competence in health care through a research-based intervention in the UK', *Diversity in Health and Social Care*, 1(2), 107–16.

Parekh, B. (2000a) *The future of multi-ethnic Britain*, London: Runnymede Trust.

Parekh, B. (2000b) *Rethinking multiculturalism*, Cambridge, MA: Harvard University Press.

Pati, A. (2003) 'Passage from India', *The Guardian* (www.theguardian.com/society/2003/aug/27/primarycare.raceintheuk)

Pennie, P. and Best, F. (1990) *How the Black family is pathologised by the social services systems*, London: Association of Black Social Workers and Allied Professions.

Phillips, D. (2009) 'Parallel lives?', Paper presented to 'Rethinking Community Cohesion – Different Perspectives on Segregation and Community Relations' Conference, University of Birmingham, 14 October.

Platt, L. (2003) *Parallel lives?*, London: Child Poverty Action Group.

Rex, J. (1969) 'Race as a social category', *Journal of Biosocial Science*, Suppl 1, 145–52.

Rutter, J., Cooley, L., Jones, N. and Pillai, R. (2008) *Moving up together*, London: Institute for Public Policy Research.

Rutter, J., Cooley, L., Reynolds, S. and Sheldon, R. (2007) *From refugee to citizen: 'Standing on my own two feet'*, London: Refugee Support.

Sales, R. (2007) *Understanding immigration and refugee policy: Contradictions and continuities*, Bristol: Policy Press.

Sivanandan, A. (1982) *A different hunger: Writings on Black resistance*, London: Pluto Press.

Skellington, R. and Morris, P. (1996) 'Minority ethnic groups in the UK: A profile' in R. Skellington and P. Morris (eds) *'Race' in Britain today* (2nd edn), London: Sage/Open University, 64–73.

Solomos, J. (2003) *Race and racism in Britain* (3rd edn), Basingstoke: Palgrave Macmillan.

Southall Black Sisters (2008) 'Southall Black Sisters' Victory against Ealing Council – Judgement from Lord Justice Moses released'.

Tilki, M., Thompson, R., Robinson, L., Joss, B., Chan, E., Lewis, O. et al (2015) 'The BME third sector: Marginalised and exploited', *Voluntary Sector Review*, 6(1), 93–101.

Travis, A. (2010) 'Time for new approach to race relations, minister urges', *The Guardian*, 14 January (www.guardian.co.uk/world/2010/jan/14/john–denham–race–relations).

Troyna, B (1984) 'The "educational underachievement" of black pupils', *British Journal of Sociology of Education*, 5(2), 153-66.

Turner, A.W. (2008) *Crisis? What crisis? Britain in the 1970s*, London: Aurum Press.

Williams, F. (1996) '"Race", welfare and community care: A historical perspective', in W.I.U. Ahmad and K. Atkin (eds) *Race and community care*, Buckingham: Open University Press, 15-28.

Worley, C. (2005) '"It's not about race. It's about the community": New Labour and "community cohesion"', *Critical Social Policy*, 25(4), 483-96.

Yousaf, H. (2010) 'Threads of the Scottish tartan: The SNP's vision for race equality in Scotland', in J. McGrigor, R. Brown, H. Yousaf and J. Lamont (eds) *Achieving race equality in Scotland*, London: Runnymede Trust (www.runnymedetrust.org).

Part Two

'Race', ethnicity and welfare contexts

5

Poverty and income maintenance

Ian Law and Katy Wright

Overview

This chapter examines the relationship between poverty and ethnicity, assessing the impact of a range of policy interventions on Black and minority ethnic (BME) groups. This chapter:

- examines poverty and social exclusion among Gypsies/Travellers;
- looks at evidence on child and adult poverty within and across ethnic groups;
- evaluates explanations for ethnic differences in patterns of poverty;
- assesses the impact of welfare reforms and public spending cuts on BME;
- examines the links between immigration policy, social assistance and destitution;
- assesses the extent to which some minority ethnic groups are greater users of social assistance or certain other types of social security; and
- evaluates the impact of recent policy developments on minority ethnic groups.

Key concepts
benefits; income; poverty; wealth

Introduction

Complex factors have produced consistently higher poverty levels among Black and minority ethnic (BME) groups, while different patterns and levels exist across and within these groups. This chapter examines the relationship between poverty and ethnicity, and evaluates explanations for differing patterns of racial and ethnic outcomes. The chapter begins by looking specifically at poverty and social exclusion among Gypsies and Travellers, who historically have tended to be excluded from debates. Within this chapter, following common terminology, we refer to this 'group', which constitutes at least three distinct groupings, as Gypsy, Roma and Traveller (GRT). The chapter also considers the impact of austerity on different ethnic groups, before looking at the provision of social assistance and assessing the links with immigration policy and the ongoing creation of destitution among some groups of asylum-seekers. Subsequently, the pattern of take-up of state benefits by minority ethnic groups is examined and, finally, a selected set of policy interventions is evaluated, which shows a mixed picture of opportunities and challenges in this field. This chapter further develops the analysis of racism, ethnicity, migration and social security to be found in Law (2009).

Poverty

Low incomes and social exclusion (other forms of severe and chronic disadvantage) together constitute the notion of poverty used in this chapter (see The Poverty Site, 2010). Contemporary debates on poverty among minority ethnic groups in the UK tend to focus on groups where there is adequate empirical data from censuses and surveys, while groups that are not enumerated or that are 'hidden' within other categories are ignored in academic and policy debates. This chapter examines the latest evidence on ethnicity and poverty, beginning with an examination of poverty and marginalisation among GRT groups. In part because of the failure to enumerate GRT in UK censuses until 2011, their material conditions have frequently been ignored in accounts of ethnicity and poverty, and adequate focused research has been sadly lacking (Neale et al, 2008; NEP, 2010b). In the following section, child and adult poverty within and across ethnic groups is examined, together with other evidence on economic inequalities. The chapter demonstrates that racial and ethnic inequalities in patterns of poverty remain a constant and dynamic feature of British society.

Gypsies and Travellers

A focus on groups of colour in national policy development has created new forms of exclusion as the needs of other groups have been virtually ignored. The exclusion of GRT from censuses until 2011 contributed to the failure of progressive policy and practice interventions in ethnic relations to tackle the discrimination and inequalities they face. Furthermore, their historical omission from the concept of exclusion, from ethnic monitoring of public services and from policy debate and action has contributed to worsening outcomes in education and other key spheres of life (see also Chapters 6, 7, 8 and 11, this volume). However, the recent enumeration of this group has not led to improved outcomes due to a lack (or reversal) of policies aimed at tackling the needs of BME groups.

In the 2011 Census, 58,000 people identified themselves as Gypsy/Irish Traveller, representing 0.1% of the population of England and Wales (ONS, 2014). The origins and differentiation of groups within the overall GRT category are complex and include the formation of groups with both indigenous and non-UK roots. Migration to the UK, commencing in the 16th century (see Chapter 3, this volume), has been mainly driven by expulsion and repression in mainland Europe, together with the rejection of sedentary lifestyles and feudal bonds. Migrants have often been subject to oppressive vagrancy legislation, and a history of conflict between GRT and the state, particularly in relation to the enforcement of housing, urban planning and land control laws, has affected family travel and mobility (Morris and Clements, 1999). GRT populations fare badly in many dimensions of equality, including longevity, health, education, political participation, influence and voice, identity and legal security. Welfare outcomes are particularly poor (Cemlyn and Clark, 2005). For example, they have comparatively high levels of infant and maternal mortality, and lower life expectancy than any other group, partly as a result of difficulties accessing healthcare (European Commission, 2014; EHRC, 2016). Gypsies/Travellers have the lowest life expectancy of any ethnic group (Traveller Movement, 2015), 10 years lower than the national average for men and women, and GRT mothers are 20 times more likely to have experienced the death of a child (van Cleemput et al, 2004). Cemlyn and Clark confirm that many Gypsy and Traveller children are poor in multiple and different ways (Cemlyn and Clark, 2005). Many are financially poor, with multiple dimensions to the 'poverty' they face.

Census figures (ONS, 2014) show that Gypsies/Travellers are less likely than any other group to be economically active, with more than twice as many unemployed than among the overall population. This group is also more likely to be self-employed. Most are employed in elementary occupations, and GRT populations have the highest proportion of those with no qualifications. Their age profile tends to be younger, with over a third are aged under 20, compared to less than a quarter of England and Wales. Gypsy/Traveller culture has been identified as strongly family-orientated and child-centred, with family networks providing support in difficult times. GRT economies often involve family-based self-employed activities, which are flexible, adaptable and opportunistic in relation to gaps in mainstream economic markets. This includes traditional work like farming and scrapping, and newer activities such as market trading and construction. Previous economic outlets have declined, particularly in crowded urban environments (Power, 2004), while local authority restrictions on trading or operating businesses on official sites have undermined the Traveller economy (Ryder and Greenfields, 2015). Many find that simply being a Gypsy/Traveller and lacking basic literacy skills prevents them from accessing mainstream jobs or training. Consequently, access to social security benefits can be important, although research reveals significant discrimination and disadvantage in accessing the benefits system. Cemlyn and Clark (2005) found evidence that GRT groups were subject to surveillance on the assumption that they commit benefit fraud, with families denied benefits despite a lack of evidence of actual fraud. A lack of education, skills and qualifications among

GRT presents potential barriers to fulfilling the obligations of benefits claimants (Traveller Movement, 2013).

Conflicts have arisen around housing and caravan sites, media coverage and public hostility, with anti-Gypsy prejudice expressed more openly than against other groups. GRT populations have been criminalised for being homeless (those living on unauthorised encampments are very often legally homeless), and for pursuing nomadic ways of life. They have been collectively punished for the crimes of individuals, whereby whole settlements are evicted because of the behaviour of certain members (TLRP, 2007). Many families have been forced off land they own, and it is increasingly difficult to find stopping places. A lack of authorised sites has contributed to people establishing unauthorised sites, on which 16% of caravans are located (DCLG, 2016). However, the proportion of caravans on authorised sites has grown from 38% in 2007 to 54% in 2016, alongside a broader rise in the numbers of caravans (DCLG, 2016).

Despite conflict with residents and media hostility, in many areas efforts have been made to improve communication, social inclusion and provision of services to settled and non-settled GRT families. An evaluation of Scottish multi-agency partnership working concluded that many families had been helped to access the services they needed, many describing positive impacts on their health and well-being. The UK experience has provided examples of innovative practice across local authorities as new ways have been found to improve provision, although these developments have not benefited the GRT community as a whole (Macneil et al, 2005), and substantial inequalities remain. In many cases, progress has stalled or even reversed. After 2010, cuts to the Housing and Communities Agency (HCA) budget and changes to key planning policies directly affected traveller site provision. At the beginning of the 2010 coalition government, Matthew Brindley, spokesperson for the Irish Traveller Movement, stated:

> Over a decade's campaigning work has been destroyed overnight by this Coalition … if the communities don't have stable accommodation, that impacts on the health and education of our children, and the health and employment of our adults. Accommodation … is a catalyst to all the other severe problems faced by this incredibly vulnerable community. (cited in Law and Swann, 2016, p 40)

In particular, a lack of decent accommodation has severely negative health impacts, and poor conditions are common across both authorised and unauthorised sites (National Inclusion Health Board, 2016). Nevertheless, targets for Local Planning Authorities (LPAs) to make provision of land for Gypsy/Traveller sites were abolished under the Localism Act 2011, while Traveller Pitch Funding was withdrawn in 2015. The Government's *Planning policy for Traveller sites* (DCLG, 2012) devolved target-setting responsibility to local levels, while new definitions of Gypsies/Travellers in planning contexts exclude settled households, thereby reducing eligibility for planning permission (DCLG, 2015).

Comparing child and adult poverty

Minority ethnic groups constitute approximately 14% of the population (ONS, 2012), but a larger proportion of children, with over a quarter of state primary school pupils being from a minority ethnic background (DfE, 2011, p 2). Children from BME groups are over-represented among poor children; for example, 52% of Pakistani or Bangladeshi children and 45% of Black children are living in poverty, compared to 25% of White children (The Children's Society, 2013, p 4; Tinson et al, 2016, p 66). Between 2001 and 2007, racial and ethnic differentials decreased, and there was a decline in minority ethnic child poverty (but not among White British children), with Bangladeshi children experiencing the greatest fall in poverty rates. Overall, this data confirms, first, significant levels of diversity across ethnic groups; second, the persistence of greater poverty among BME groups; and, third, some impacts of poverty reduction measures on BME groups at greatest risk of poverty. Since 2010, overall poverty rates have stopped falling, and some are increasing again, as a result of cuts in benefits and public spending.

Platt's analysis showed that generally child poverty rates were higher than adult rates across all ethnic groups, with, for example, 54% of working-age Bangladeshi adults being in poverty (before housing costs, BHC) compared to 64% of Bangladeshi children, and 13% of White British working-age adults compared to 19% of children (Platt, 2009, pp 26-7). The general pattern of ethnic differentials in poverty rates was consistent among children, adults and all individuals (see Table 5.1).

Table 5.1: Children's poverty rates: rolling averages (BHC), Great Britain

	2001/02–2003/04 (%)	2002/03–2004/05 (%)	2003/04–2005/06 (%)	2004/05–2006/07 (%)
White British	20	20	19	20
Indian	28	28	30	27
Pakistani	59	56	53	53
Bangladeshi	72	66	65	58
Black Caribbean	31	27	30	26
Black African	38	38	37	35

Note: The poverty threshold is defined as 60% of median equivalent income before housing costs (BHC).

Bases: 2001/02-2003/04: 26,208; 2002/03-2003/04: 26,897; 2003/04-2005/06: 26,291; 2004/05-2006/07: 25,249, as presented in Platt (2009, p 25).

Source: HBAI weighted data 2001/02, 2002/03, 2003/04, 2004/05 and 2005/06, 2006/07

Explaining ethnic differences in poverty

How can we explain the differences in poverty rates across ethnic groups? It would be useful to start by examining the measurable factors that are linked to differences in poverty risks, such as employment status, migration history and family structure. Reasons for and timing of arrival have influenced employment, with earlier migrants concentrated in low-paid work (see Chapter 6, this volume) in manufacturing, which subsequently suffered from rapid de-industrialisation and restructuring. Later migrants were concentrated less in Northern industrial towns and more in the Midlands and London. Forced settlement in poorer areas (characteristic of more recent asylum-seeker dispersal) can limit educational opportunities, and restrict options for future generations. Multiple factors have contributed to high unemployment for minority groups, especially Caribbean, Pakistani and Bangladeshi groups, and higher rates of self-employment, particularly for Indian, Chinese and Pakistani groups. These include employment in vulnerable sectors, discrimination, concentration in poorer areas and, particularly for Pakistani, Bangladeshi and Black Caribbean groups, greater difficulty in obtaining high levels of qualifications (Simpson et al, 2006). The persistent role of ethnicity in differential labour market outcomes has been described as an 'ethnic penalty' (Heath and McMahon, 1997; Catney and Sabater, 2015).

BME women experience higher rates of poverty than White women, although a focus on household-level poverty has often obscured intra-household relations (Moosa and Woodroffe, 2009, p 43). Bangladeshi/Pakistani women have the highest rate of unemployment among women, and research (Heath and Cheung, 2006; Tyers et al, 2006; Berthoud and Blekesaune, 2007) confirms the persistence of this employment penalty over 30 years. Most Bangladeshi/Pakistani women are Muslims, suggesting religion may be more important than ethnicity in predicting employment penalties among women. Only people with disabilities are equally unlikely to move into employment as Muslim women. Intermittent absence from the labour market also impacts on male employment and therefore on incomes. Minority ethnic men are more likely to work part-time but again, this varies, with 35% of Bangladeshi men working part-time compared to 18% of Pakistani men, 10% of Caribbean men and 5% of White men (Khan, 2015, p 5). Overall, the ethnic employment gap is likely to remain significant for at least another century (Phillips, 2007). BME groups are disproportionately represented among the Department for Work and Pensions' (DWP) 'most disadvantaged customer group', facing complex barriers to work including employer attitudes, area-based factors, human capital and difficulties 'negotiating identities' between family life, religious and cultural values, and work (Hasluck and Green, 2007). When all measurable factors are taken into account, 'unexplained differences in poverty risk between otherwise similar families or children from different ethnic groups' (Platt, 2009, pp 57-8) may exist, demonstrating an 'ethnic poverty penalty'. This penalty invites further investigation, suggesting a need to target particular groups (for example, to increase pay or benefit take-up), and to monitor poverty across different ethnic groups to evaluate the effectiveness of mainstream measures.

Two studies examining stark ethnic differences in poverty rates and their causes concluded that they are determined by diverse factors including discrimination, patterns of educational qualification, labour market outcomes, housing locations, disability and ill health (Clark and Drinkwater, 2007; Palmer and Kenway, 2007). The National Equality Panel report (NEP, 2010a,b) confirmed 'deep-seated and systematic differences in economic outcomes' remained for different ethnic groups (NEP, 2010a, p 1). Median total household wealth, for example, varies considerably by ethnicity, from only £15,000 for Bangladeshi households to around £75,000 for Black Caribbean, £97,000 for Pakistani households and £200,000 or more for Indian and White British households. Bangladeshi/Pakistani households have a median equivalent net income of only £238 per week: the national median is £393 (NEP, 2010b, p 233).

In education, some BME groups improve their attainment from below the national average as they move through compulsory schooling, but, at 16, Pakistani, Black African and Black Caribbean boys' attainment in England remains well below the national average (see also Chapter 11, this volume). GRT children's attainment declines over the school years, with ethnic differentials steadily widening. This group, together with Black and Pakistani/Bangladeshi students, are less likely to go to prestigious universities or to get higher class degrees (NEP, 2010a, p 16). Despite Chinese, Indian and Black African populations having higher education qualifications than the White British population, most minority ethnic groups are less likely to be in paid employment than White British men and women. For some groups, differences in unemployment rates affect the 'second generation' as much as those born outside the UK. Pakistani/Bangladeshi Muslim men and Black African Christian men have an 'ethnic (or religious?) pay penalty', unexplained by factors such as age, occupation, family circumstances or qualifications, and earn 13%–21% less than White British Christian men (Longhi and Platt, 2008). Despite having some of the most successful educational outcomes, Chinese people faced an 'ethnic pay penalty' of 11% (NEP, 2010b, p 228). Levels of discrimination have been similar across all minority ethnic groups, affecting both men and women. The National Living Wage provides some protection against low wages, although minority ethnic group workers are more likely to be unaware of and not in receipt of the Living Wage (Low Pay Commission, 2007; Brynin and Longhi, 2015).

Welfare reforms and spending cuts

The spending cuts and welfare reforms rolled out since 2010 have disproportionately affected BME groups. The impacts of the cuts are complex, intersecting with the everyday experiences of marginalisation, poverty and discrimination already outlined (Sandhu et al, 2013). Austerity politics have included significant spending cuts to local authorities and government departments, welfare cuts and caps, the redrawing of welfare eligibility and an increased focus on benefits conditionality, sanctions and disallowances. As BME women tend to receive a higher proportion of their income from benefits and welfare, public sector cuts and reduced welfare spending have hit these groups particularly hard (Sandhu and Stephenson, 2015). Furthermore, Webster (2013) has suggested that there is evidence of differential treatment of White and BME groups in welfare sanctions. Between 2010 and 2015, around 631,000 public sector jobs were lost as a result of cuts, primarily in the North-East, the West Midlands and Yorkshire (SPERI, 2015, p 1). Traditionally, BME groups – particularly women – have been more likely to work in public sector roles, which have provided a 'springboard for ethnic minorities entering "middle class" jobs' (Catney and Sabater, 2015, p 67).

The Runnymede Trust has highlighted the increased threat of the financial exclusion of minority ethnic populations (Khan, 2008; Mawhinney, 2010). BME groups have lower levels of savings, lower take-up of insurance and poorer pensions (DWP, 2015). Furthermore, BME groups experience direct and indirect racial discrimination in accessing credit, while many are excluded from mainstream financial institutions and advice organisations. Research has also found that BME groups are often distrustful of mainstream financial institutions (Khan, 2010). Minority ethnic migrants do not necessarily understand welfare, benefits claims, tax or utilities systems, which leads to unpaid taxes, utilities arrears and failure to claim entitlements (Mawhinney, 2010, pp 5-6). In the five years to 2003/04, both in-work and out-of-work child poverty fell for the first time in 30 years (Macinnes et al, 2009, p 9), including a reduction in racial and ethnic inequalities. However, even before the economic crisis in 2008/09, child poverty was increasing. A national review of poverty and welfare following the 2010 General Election (Cabinet Office, 2010) confirmed that income inequality was at its highest level since 1961, with increases in severe poverty since 2004/05 and continuing ethnic differentials. While employment levels have increased, so has the number of working households in poverty. In-work poverty in 2014/15 was at a record high of 55% (Tinson et al, 2016, p 66). These broader rises in poverty help perpetuate the increased risk of financial exclusion among BME groups.

Welfare

Migration, welfare and destitution

British state policy towards migrants and minorities demonstrates a 'long pedigree of racism' (Craig, 2007). Regulation to exclude 'aliens', denizens (permanent settlers without British nationality) and particular racialised categories of British citizens from access to welfare benefits is evident in immigration legislation and wider social policy reforms from the Victorian period onwards. Poor Law rules, pension law, aliens' legislation and National Insurance criteria incorporated such practices (Williams, 1989). The British welfare state drew on eugenic notions of 'race' and nation to maintain imperialism, and to manage both the 'burden' of the Black, Asian, Irish and Jewish poor and the perceived threat of such groups to the jobs and wages of those in the 'new' mass traded unions. Post-Second World War welfare reforms and immigration legislation have continued racially exclusionary rules including residence tests, rules on 'recourse to public funds' and sponsorship conditions. New Labour amplified previous Conservative policy in relation to welfare, immigration and asylum (Morris, 2007; Somerville, 2007), reducing the entitlements of asylum-seekers, tightening requirements, availability tests, and migration controls, except for skilled migrants. The Immigration Act 1999 established the National Asylum Support Service (NASS) to arrange accommodation and provide vouchers at 70% of Income Support rates for adults (100% for child dependants). Following a campaign led by Bill Morris, then General Secretary of the Transport and General Workers' Union, cash replaced vouchers in 2002, but the provision of funds for basic support remains with NASS and distinct from social security, although tied into Income Support rates.

Measures reducing support for asylum-seekers have included withdrawing support from 'late' and unsuccessful applicants and some families. Increasing exclusion of this group from work and public services has led to widespread destitution (UK Parliamentary Joint Committee on Human Rights, 2007). A study by the Refugee Council focused on asylum-seekers in receipt of 'Section 4' support surveyed organisations across England and interviewed asylum-seekers, concluding that the use of vouchers was highly restrictive, 'causing unnecessary hardship and having a detrimental effect on many asylum-seekers' physical and mental well-being' (cited in NEP, 2010b, p 249). The Immigration Act 2016 introduced a number of new rules that affect BME groups and those seeking asylum. These include provision to ensure that 'all public sector workers in public-facing roles speak fluent English'; incentives for employing domestic workers in preference to skilled migrants; and the removal of support for failed asylum seekers. Since 2012, new rules mean that non-EEA (European Economic Area) nationals must meet a minimum income requirement of £18,600 to obtain a visa in order to join a spouse/partner in the UK, a move criticised for impacting on the right to family life, with even higher incomes required for bringing children.

Minority ethnic groups and benefits

Historically, all BME groups have shown greater use of means-tested benefits and lower use of non-income related benefits than the White population. The Runnymede Trust's analysis of the 2015 Budget (Khan, 2015) cited DWP evidence that tax credits provide 10% of Bangladeshi and 6% of Black household incomes, compared to 2% of White households. This greater dependence on means-tested benefits is due to numerous causes, including:

- *Greater poverty.* Platt (2007) has highlighted that over half of Pakistani, Bangladeshi and Black African children in Britain are growing up in poverty. Factors determining the stark ethnic differences in poverty rates include persistent discrimination, patterns of educational qualification, labour market outcomes, housing locations, disabilities and ill health (Clark and Drinkwater, 2007; Palmer and Kenway, 2007; Platt, 2009).
- *Excess unemployment.* This has led to higher claiming of Income Support and income-based Jobseeker's Allowance among all minority groups, but particularly Pakistani, Bangladeshi and Black Caribbean groups (ONS, 2000; DSS, 2001; NEP, 2010a, b). Unemployment rates are higher for all minority ethnic groups compared to the White population (EHRC, 2015, p 35), while youth unemployment among BME groups rose by 49% between 2010 and 2015 (Khan, 2015). Almost one-third (30%) of Bangladeshi/Pakistani young people aged 16-24 are unemployed compared to 11% of White and 19% of Black young people (Powell, 2018, p 2), with lower employment meaning more poverty (see also Chapter 6, this volume).
- *Different patterns of family structure.* For example, Bangladeshi groups have relatively large families, who are more likely to be in poverty and harder to support on the relatively low earnings they tend to receive (Berthoud, 2000; Bradshaw et al, 2006; Platt, 2007, 2009).
- *Long-term poverty among pensioners or the unemployed.* Some minority groups are less likely to have accrued assets and savings, are therefore more likely to need Income Support and support during periods of unemployment, as well as experiencing greater hardship in old age. Nearly 60% of Pakistani/Bangladeshi citizens had no savings compared to 28% of the population as a whole. Over 80% had savings below £1,500 (ONS, 2001).

Previous means-tested benefits including income-based Jobseeker's Allowance and Employment Support Allowance, Housing Benefit, Working Tax Credits and Child Tax Credits have been gradually replaced by Universal Credit since 2013. This single, means-tested payment is paid one month in arrears, directly into claimants' bank accounts. Welfare reforms have included caps on Housing Benefit, and on the number of bedrooms that can be funded. Such changes disproportionately affect BME households, which are more likely to be large, and to have fewer financial resources to fall back on and higher rates of poverty (Sandhu, 2016). The rolling back of state welfare provision has led to a rise in non-state forms of welfare such as food banks. A recent study of food banks in Bradford (Power et al, 2017) found that 'clients' are more likely to be White and Christian, which was linked to the fact that the majority of providers of emergency food are Christian, leading to the 'unintentional exclusion of ethnic and religious groups'.

Historically, welfare-to-work initiatives have had variable effectiveness for different ethnic groups. The New Deals were subject to ethnic monitoring of participation and outcomes, suggesting that different groups experienced different pathways (DfEE, 1999; DWP, 2002a; Hasluck and Green, 2007). For example, Indian groups tended to be over-represented in moves into employment, while Black African groups were more likely to take up further education and training. From 2011, existing welfare-to-work programmes, including the New Deal, were replaced with the Work Programme. Participation in the programme is mandatory, and failure to attend or to fulfil claimant obligations – accruing a certain number of job search hours, accepting places on particular schemes or attending interviews – results in the imposition of sanctions (highlighted in the Ken Loach's film, *I, Daniel Blake*). Sanctions involve benefits being stopped for four weeks for first offenders, or 13 weeks for those who have been sanctioned previously. As BME groups tend to claim for longer, the government suggested that the Work Programme, aimed at long-term claimants, would be particularly beneficial to them (DWP, 2011). However, research has suggested that the Work Programme is 'failing to meet the needs of minority ethnic people', with contractors spending less than half the intended amount on reaching these and other 'hard-to-reach' groups (Sandhu, 2016, p 5). As minority ethnic groups face multiple barriers to employment, it might be that the payment-by-results model used for the Work Programme provides a disincentive to work with them.

Impact of recent policy interventions

The Race Relations Amendment Act 2000 requires public authorities to produce 'race' equality strategies. The DWP's race equality document, *Equality, opportunity and independence for all* (2002b), assessed possible differential impacts of its services and policies, affirming a commitment to monitoring and evaluating the possible scale of the impact. It also committed the DWP to effective ethnic monitoring in all areas of delivery and among its employees, and to evaluations of future policy impact, on which it has failed to deliver. The Commission for Racial Equality's (CRE) final report in 2006 (before its amalgamation into the Equality and Human Rights Commission, EHRC) identified poor progress across all Whitehall departments in implementing 'race' equality strategies, although most of this work deals with employment rather than service delivery. Aspinall and Mitton (2007) confirmed the continuing failure to demonstrate compliance with 'race' equality requirements in the administration of benefits, particularly referring to local authority provision of housing and council tax benefits. However, simply reforming individual agencies' practice will not transform the delivery of social security to BME groups; rather, a process is needed that looks more fundamentally at the context of people's lives as, for example, the Social Exclusion Unit did (SEU, 2000), while also considering how policy regulations themselves are created and maintained.

Recent debate has highlighted the problem of hyper- or super-diversity, where professionals and managers face dilemmas in responding to the needs of culturally complex societies (Vertovec, 2006; Mir, 2007). The dangers of simplistic approaches to these questions are exemplified in discussion of 'ethnic managerialism' in the Benefits Agency (Law, 2016), where failure to identify needs leads to poor service, most recently in relation to BME women (Moosa and Woodroffe, 2009). The national evaluation of Sure Start, an initiative aimed at enhancing the life chances of young children living in disadvantaged neighbourhoods, identified a failure to address ethnicity (Craig et al, 2007). Outcomes for minority ethnic groups could not even be identified because of a failure to carry out appropriate ethnic monitoring – a notable failure of DWP activity for decades. Significant problems were again identified in a study of BME claimants of disability benefits (Jones and Tracy, 2010, pp 9-10), who reported lower levels of satisfaction with services, were less knowledgeable about benefits available to them and took longer to identify available help. Weaker knowledge and understanding of the benefits system had negative impacts on claimants' experiences, and many barriers to claiming remained in place.

Conclusion

In examining the relationship between poverty and ethnicity it is clear that significant diversity exists across ethnic groups, and that greater poverty persists among all BME groups. Poverty reduction measures have benefited those with highest risks of poverty, but indications suggest the worsening economic context and welfare cuts have had negative impacts. In the UK, there have been increases in severe poverty since 2004/05, with continuing differentials in terms of ethnicity. Gypsies/Travellers continue to be the worst affected, with high rates of mortality, suicide and substance abuse, worse health outcomes, declining educational outcomes, extremely low participation in secondary education, low employment rates and high poverty rates. The racialisation of migration and welfare has led to poor welfare outcomes for migrants and minorities. Past immigration policy has structured the settlement and opportunities of many minority groups and thus their relative dependence on social security. There are also explicit links between immigration rules and social security entitlements. Although there is significant diversity of circumstances and experiences among and within BME groups, there is a high risk of unemployment, poverty, reliance on means-tested benefits and under-claiming. Persistent disadvantage and complex barriers to work and benefits are experienced. The destitution created among some asylum-seekers, rising unemployment differentials and failure by the DWP to implement statutory 'race' equality strategies are further signs of poor future prospects.

Questions for discussion

- Why do Gypsies/Travellers tend to be ignored in debates over poverty and ethnicity?
- What is the likely impact of the economic recession on minority ethnic groups?
- What is the relationship between social security policy and immigration policy?
- How have 'welfare-to-work' policies and the introduction of the Minimum Wage impacted on minority ethnic groups?

Further reading

Craig, G. with Adamson, A., Ali, N., Ali, S., Atkins, L., Dadze-Arthur, A., Elliott, C., McNamee, S. and Murtuja, B. (2007) *Sure Start and Black and minority ethnic populations*, London: HMSO.

EHRC (Equality and Human Rights Commission) (2016) *England's most disadvantaged groups: Gypsies, Travellers and Roma* (www.equalityhumanrights.com/sites/default/files/is-england-fairer-2016-most-disadvantaged-groups-gypsies-travellers-roma.pdf).

Jones, M. and Tracy, I. (2010) *Ethnic minorities' experiences of claiming disability benefit*, Research Report No 609, London: DWP.

Khan, O. (2015) 'The 2015 Budget: Effects on black and minority ethnic people' (www.runnymedetrust.org/uploads/The%202015%20Budget%20Effect%20on%20BME%20RunnymedeTrust%2027thJuly2015.pdf).

National Inclusion Health Board (2016) *Impact of insecure accommodation and the living environment on Gypsies' and Travellers' health* (www.gov.uk/government/uploads/system/uploads/attachment_data/file/490846/NIHB_-_Gypsy_and_Traveller_health_accs.pdf).

Sandhu, K. (2016) *Universal Credit and impact on black and minority ethnic communities*, A Race Equality Foundation report (https://raceequalityfoundation.org.uk/community/universal-credit-and-impact-on-black-and-minority-ethnic-communities/).

References

Aspinall, P. and Mitton, L. (2007) 'Are English local authorities' practices on housing and council tax benefit administration meeting race equality requirements?', *Critical Social Policy*, 27, 381–414.

Berthoud, R. (2000) *Family formation in multi-cultural Britain: Three patterns of diversity*, Colchester: Institute for Social and Economic Research, University of Essex.

Berthoud, R. and Blekesaune, M. (2007) *Persistent employment disadvantage*, Research Report 416, London: DWP.

Bradshaw, J., Finch, N., Mayhew, E., Ritakallio, V.-M. and Skinner, C. (2006) *Child poverty in large families*, York: Joseph Rowntree Foundation.

Brynin, M. and Longhi, S. (2015) *The effect of occupation on poverty amongst ethnic minority groups*, York: Joseph Rowntree Foundation.

Cabinet Office (2010) *State of the Nation: Poverty, worklessness and welfare dependency in the UK*, London: Cabinet Office.

Catney, G. and Sabater, A. (2015) *Ethnic minority disadvantage in the labour market: Participation, skills and geographical inequalities*, York: Joseph Rowntree Foundation.

Cemlyn, S. and Clark, C. (2005) 'The social exclusion of Gypsy and Traveller children', in G. Preston (ed) *At greatest risk: The children most likely to be poor*, London: CPAG, 146-62.

Children's Society, The (2013) *A good childhood for everyone? Child poverty in the UK* (www.childrenssociety.org.uk/sites/default/files/tcs/2013_child_poverty_briefing_1.pdf).

Clark, K. and Drinkwater, S. (2007) *Ethnic minorities in the labour market: Dynamics and diversity*, York: Joseph Rowntree Foundation.

Craig, G. (2007) '"Cunning, unprincipled, loathsome": The racist tail wags the welfare dog', *Journal of Social Policy*, 36(4), 605-23.

Craig, G. with Adamson, A., Ali, N., Ali, S., Atkins, L., Dadze-Arthur, A., Elliott, C., McNamee, S. and Murtuja, B. (2007) *Sure Start and black and minority ethnic populations*, London: HMSO.

DCLG (Department for Communities and Local Government) (2012) *Planning policy for Traveller sites* (www.gov.uk/government/uploads/system/uploads/attachment_data/file/457420/Final_planning_and_travellers_policy.pdf).

DCLG (2015) *Planning policy for Traveller sites* (www.gov.uk/government/uploads/system/uploads/attachment_data/file/457420/Final_planning_and_travellers_policy.pdf).

DCLG (2016) 'Count of Traveller caravans July 2016: England' (www.gov.uk/government/uploads/system/uploads/attachment_data/file/569222/Statistical_Release_Traveller_Caravan_Count_July_2016.pdf).

DfE (Department for Education) (2011) 'Schools, pupils, and their characteristics' (www.gov.uk/government/uploads/system/uploads/attachment_data/file/219064/main_20text_20sfr122011.pdf).

DfEE (Department for Education and Employment) (1999) *Jobs for all*, London: DfEE.

DSS (Department of Social Security) (2001) *Family resources survey. Great Britain 1999-2000*, Leeds: Corporate Document Services.

DWP (Department for Work and Pensions) (2002a) 'New Deal for young people and long-term unemployed people aged 25+: Statistics to December 2001', Statistics First Release, February.

DWP (2002b) *Equality, opportunity and independence for all*, Race Equality Consultation Document, London: DWP.

DWP (2011) *Work Programme: Equality Impact Assessment* (www.gov.uk/government/uploads/system/uploads/attachment_data/file/220250/eia-work-programme.pdf).

DWP (2015) *Family resources survey: United Kingdom 2013/14* (www.gov.uk/government/uploads/system/uploads/attachment_data/file/437481/family-resources-survey-2013-14.pdf).

EHRC (Equality and Human Rights Commission) (2015) *Is Britain fairer? The state of equality and human rights 2015* (www.equalityhumanrights.com/sites/default/files/is-britain-fairer-2015.pdf).

EHRC (2016) 'England's most disadvantaged groups: Gypsies, Travellers and Roma' (www.equalityhumanrights.com/sites/default/files/is-england-fairer-2016-most-disadvantaged-groups-gypsies-travellers-roma.pdf).

European Commission (2014) *Roma health report: Health status of the Roma population. Data collection in the Member States of the European Union* (http://ec.europa.eu/health//sites/health/files/social_determinants/docs/2014_roma_health_report_en.pdf).

Hasluck, C. and Green, A.E. (2007) *What works for whom: A review of evidence and meta-analysis for the Department for Work and Pensions*, Research Report 407, London: Department for Work and Pensions.

Heath, A. and Cheung, S. (2006) *Ethnic penalties in the labour market: Employers and discrimination*, Research Summary 341, London: Department for Work and Pensions.

Heath, A. and McMahon, D. (1997) 'Education and occupational attainments: The impact of ethnic origins', in V. Karn (ed) *Ethnicity in the 1991 Census, Volume 4: Employment, education and housing among the ethnic minority populations of Britain*, London: The Stationery Office, 646–82.

Khan, O. (2008) *Financial inclusion and ethnicity*, London: Runnymede Trust.

Khan, O. (2010) *Saving beyond the High Street: A profile of saving patterns among Black and minority ethnic people* (www.runnymedetrust.org/uploads/publications/pdfs/SavingBeyondTheHighStreet-2010.pdf).

Khan, O. (2015) 'The 2015 Budget: Effects on Black and minority ethnic people' (www.runnymedetrust.org/uploads/The%202015%20Budget%20Effect%20on%20BME%20RunnymedeTrust%2027thJuly2015.pdf).

Jones, M. and Tracy, I. (2010) *Ethnic minorities' experiences of claiming disability benefit*, Research Report No 609, London: Department for Work and Pensions.

Law, I. (2009) 'Racism, ethnicity and migration', in J. Millar (ed) *Understanding social security*, Bristol: Policy Press, 75–92.

Law, I (2016) *Modernity, anti-racism and ethnic managerialism*, London: Springer.

Law, I. and Swann, S. (2016) *Ethnicity and education in England and Europe*, London: Routledge.

Longhi, S. and Platt, L. (2008) *Pay gaps across equalities areas*, London: Equality and Human Rights Commission.

Low Pay Commission (2007) *National Minimum Wage*, Low Pay Commission Report, Cm 7056, March, London: The Stationery Office.

Macinnes, T., Kenway, P. and Parekh, A. (2009) *Monitoring poverty and social exclusion*, York: Joseph Rowntree Foundation.

Macneil, M., Stradling, R. and Clark, A. (2005) *Promoting the health and wellbeing of Gypsy/Travellers in Highlands*, Inverness: Highlands Council.

Mawhinney, P. (2010) *Seeking sound advice, financial inclusion and ethnicity*, London: Runnymede Trust.

Mir, G. (2007) *Effective communication with service users*, London: Race Equality Foundation.

Modood, T., Berthoud, R., Lakey, J., Nazroo, J., Smith, P., Virdee, S. and Seishon, S. (eds) (1997) *Ethnic minorities in Britain: Diversity and disadvantage*, London: Policy Studies Institute.

Moosa, Z. and Woodroffe, J. (2009) *Poverty pathways: Ethnic minority women's livelihoods*, London: Fawcett.

Morris, L. (2007) 'New Labour's community of rights: Welfare, immigration and asylum', *Journal of Social Policy*, 36(1), 39-57.

Morris, R. and Clements, L. (eds.) (1999) *Gaining ground: Law reform for Gypsies and Travellers*, Hatfield: University of Hertfordshire Press.

National Inclusion Health Board (2016) *Impact of insecure accommodation and the living environment on Gypsies' and Travellers' health* (www.gov.uk/government/uploads/system/uploads/attachment_data/file/490846/NIHB_-_Gypsy_and_Traveller_health_accs.pdf).

Neale, M., Craig, G. and Wilkinson, M. (2008) *Marginalised and excluded*, York: York Travellers' Trust.

NEP (National Equality Panel) (2010a) *Summary: An anatomy of economic inequality in the UK*, London: Government Equalities Office/London School of Economics and Political Science.

NEP (2010b) *An anatomy of economic inequality in the UK*, London: Government Equalities Office/London School of Economics and Political Science.

ONS (Office for National Statistics) (2000) *Labour Market Trends*, London: The Stationery Office.

ONS (2001) *Social Trends 31*, London: The Stationery Office.

ONS (2012) 'Ethnicity in England and Wales: 2011' (www.ons.gov.uk/peoplepopulationandcommunity/culturalidentity/ethnicity/articles/ethnicityandnationalidentityinenglandandwales/2012-12-11#ethnicity-in-england-and-wales).

ONS (2014) '2011 Census analysis: What does the 2011 Census tell us about the characteristics of Gypsy or Irish travellers in England and Wales?' (www.ons. gov.uk/peoplepopulationandcommunity/culturalidentity/ethnicity/articles/ whatdoesthe2011censustellusaboutthecharacteristicsofgypsyoririshtravellers inenglandandwales/2014-01-21).

Palmer, G. and Kenway, P. (2007) *Poverty among ethnic groups: How and why does it differ?*, York: Joseph Rowntree Foundation.

Phillips, T. (2007) 'Equality and human rights: siblings or just rivals', *Benefits*, 15(2), 127-38.

Platt, L. (2007) *Poverty and ethnicity in the UK*, Bristol: Policy Press.

Platt, L. (2009) *Ethnicity and child poverty*, Research Report 576, London: Department for Work and Pensions.

Poverty Site, The (2010) *Relative poverty, absolute poverty and social exclusion*, York: Joseph Rowntree Foundation (www.poverty.org.uk/summary/social%20 exclusion.shtml).

Powell, A. (2018) *Unemployment by ethnic background*, House of Commons Briefing Paper 6385 (http://researchbriefings.files.parliament.uk/documents/SN06385/ SN06385.pdf).

Power, C. (2004) *Room to roam: England's Irish Travellers*, Action Group for Irish Youth/Community Fund.

Power, M., Doherty, B., Small, N., Teasdale, S. and Pickett, K. (2017) 'All in it together? Community food aid in a multi-ethnic context', *Journal of Social Policy* (http://eprints.whiterose.ac.uk/111978/7/div_class_title_all_in_it_together_ community_food_aid_in_a_multi_ethnic_context_div.pdf).

Ryder, A. and Greenfields, M. (2015) *Roads to success: Economic and social inclusion for Gypsies and Travellers*, An Irish Traveller Movement in Britain report (www.travellermovement.org.uk/wp-content/uploads/2015/09/Roads-to- Success-15-1.pdf).

Sandhu, K. (2016) *Universal Credit and impact on black and minority ethnic communities*, A Race Equality Foundation report (https://raceequalityfoundation.org.uk/ community/universal-credit-and-impact-on-black-and-minority-ethnic- communities/).

Sandhu, K. and Stephenson, M.A. (2015) 'Layers of inequality: A human rights and equality impact assessment of the public spending cuts on Black, Asian and minority ethnic women in Coventry', *Feminist Review*, 109(1), 169-79.

Sandhu, K., Stephenson, M.-A. and Harrison, J. (2013) *Layers of inequality: A human rights and equality impact assessment of the public spending cuts on Black Asian and minority ethnic women in Coventry*, A joint report of Coventry Women's Voices, Coventry Ethnic Minority Action Partnership, Foleshill (www. centreforwelfarereform.org/uploads/attachment/394/layers-of-inequality.pdf).

SEU (Social Exclusion Unit) (2000) *Minority ethnic issues in social exclusion and neighbourhood renewal*, London: Cabinet Office.

Simpson, L., Purdam, K., Tajar, A., Fieldhouse, E, Gavalas, V., Tranmer, M. Pritchard, J., and Dorling, D. (2006) *Ethnic minority populations and the labour market: an analysis of the 1991 and 2001 Census*, London: Department for Work and Pensions.

Somerville, W. (2007) *Immigration under New Labour*, Bristol: Policy Press.

SPERI (Sheffield Political Economy Research Institute) (2015) 'Public and private sector employment across the UK since the financial crisis', SPERI British Political Economy Brief No 10 (http://speri.dept.shef.ac.uk/wp-content/uploads/2015/02/Brief10-public-sector-employment-across-UK-since-financial-crisis.pdf).

Tinson, A., Ayrton, C., Barker, K., Barry Born, T., Aldridge, H. and Kenway, P. (2016) *Monitoring poverty and social exclusion*, York: Joseph Rowntree Foundation.

TLRP (Travellers Law Reform Project) (2007) *Response to discrimination law review: A framework for fairness: Proposals for a single Equality Bill for Great Britain – A consultation paper* (www.travellerslaw.org.uk/pdfs/single_equality_response.pdf).

Traveller Movement (2013) *Impact of universal credit and welfare reforms on the Gypsy and Traveller communities* (www.travellermovement.org.uk/wp-content/uploads/2014/01/Impact-of-universal-credit-and-welfare-reforms-on-the-Gypsy-and-Traveller-communities.pdf).

Traveller Movement (2015) 'Improving the health of Gypsies and Travellers' (www.travellermovement.org.uk/wp-content/uploads/2015/01/Gypsy-Traveller-Health-Briefing-2015.pdf).

Tyers, C., Hurstfield, J., Willison, R. and Page, R. (2006) *Barriers to employment for Pakistanis and Bangladeshis in Britain*, Research Summary 360, London: Department for Work and Pensions.

UK Parliamentary Joint Commission on Human Rights (2007) *The treatment of asylum seekers: Tenth report of Session 2006-07* (https://publications.parliament.uk/pa/jt200607/jtselect/jtrights/81/81ii.pdf).

van Cleemput, P., Parry, G., Peters, J., Moore, J., Walters, S., Thomas, K. and Cooper, C. (2004) *The health status of Gypsies and Travellers in England*, Sheffield: University of Sheffield.

Vertovec, S. (2006) *The emergence of super-diversity in Britain*, Centre for Migration, Policy and Society, Working Paper No 25, Oxford: University of Oxford.

Waite, L., Lewis, H., Hodkinson, S. and Dwyer, P. (2014) *Precarious lives*, Bristol: Policy Press.

Webster, D. (2013) JSA sanctions and disallowances, Report presented to the House of Commons Work and Pensions Committee (www.welfareconditionality.ac.uk/wp-content/uploads/2013/12/HofC-WPC-DW-CORR.-12-Sep-2013.pdf).

Williams, F. (1989) *Social policy: A critical introduction*, Cambridge: Polity Press.

6

Minority ethnic groups in the labour market

Baljinder Virk

Overview

This chapter examines the position of minority ethnic groups within the labour market. It presents:

- data on economic activity, employment and unemployment rates, types of employment, and earnings.
- explanations for the range of economic disadvantages experienced by these groups.

Key concepts
labour markets; economic activity; disadvantage; discrimination; (un)employment

Introduction

This chapter contextualises the position of minority ethnic groups in the labour market. It considers the four dimensions of labour market disadvantage suggested by Thurrow (1969): lower earnings; higher unemployment; reduced access to educational and training opportunities; and occupational crowding in less desirable jobs. It also considers other aspects of the labour market, including employment rates and industries of employment, which collectively portray the relative position of minority ethnic groups compared to the majority, White British population. Using largely census data, this chapter highlights the diversity between different groups. It then presents the literature on explanations for disadvantage. The evidence used in this chapter draws on historical references to provide a context with up-to-date evidence, where it is available, to see what improvements, if any, have been made since the first edition of this book was published. What is clear is that minority ethnic groups continue to experience disadvantage in a number of ways in the labour market (Catney and Sabater, 2015).

The growth of the minority ethnic population in Great Britain since the Second World War has been driven by three factors: immigration in response to a demand for labour; refugees seeking asylum; and natural rate of growth (see Chapter 3, this volume). The chapter in the first edition provides a short history of the major groups and dates of their immigration (see Virk, 2012, p 168). As Chapter 3 demonstrated, England and Wales has become more ethnically diverse, with the numbers and size of minority ethnic groups continuing to rise since 1991. Around one in five people (19.5% of the population overall) then identified with a minority ethnic group (ONS, 2014). Minority ethnic groups have a much younger age structure than the White population, and some minority groups contain more people per household than the average. Bangladeshi households are the largest, with a household average of 4.5, and Pakistanis are the second largest, with 4.1 (ONS, 2006). As a result, all other things being equal, minority ethnic groups will represent an expanding proportion of the labour market in the future (Owen et al, 2000).

As other chapters in this volume demonstrate, ethnic classification is far from straightforward. The broad ethnic groupings in national data categories mask significant diversity; for example, the 'White Other' census category contains those who might describe themselves primarily as Turkish, and within that group there are at least three distinct sub-groupings – mainland Turkish, Turkish Kurds and Cypriot Turks – who have very different labour market experiences and outcomes (Ennelli et al, 2005). Each Office for National Statistics (ONS) ethnic grouping includes people born in the specified region, and those born in Great Britain who are second or third generation. Those classified as being from a minority ethnic group, who have been born and educated in Great Britain, are likely to have a different experience of the labour market from recent migrants in the same ethnic classification. The 2011 Census was the first time that Gypsy or Irish Traveller and Arab were distinct categories. Ethnic groupings can also mask social class differences. Research on employment and the labour market is only slowly accommodating such differences, although it is rare for routinely collected data to reflect such subtleties and to allow a nuanced understanding of labour market experience.

Economic activity and employment rates

According to the 2011 Census, there were 36.3 million people aged 16-64 in England and Wales (ONS, 2014a). Of these, 7.5 million people (21%) identified with a group other than White British. (This section employs the full 18-category ethnic group classification used in the 2011 Census.)

There are marked variations in the economic activity and employment patterns of these different ethnic groups. (The economically active population includes people who are employed, self-employed, participating in government employment and training programmes, and doing unpaid family work and those who are unemployed according to the International Labour Organization's [ILO] definition.) Labour market participation varies considerably between the individual ethnic groups and within the broad ethnic group categories (see Table 6.1). In 2011 the highest employment rate of all the groups was for Other White – the second largest group, and includes numerous groups including Western European

Table 6.1: Economic activity of people aged 16-64, by ethnic group, England and Wales, 2011 Census

	In employment[a] (%)	Unemployed (%)	Inactive (%)	Total numbers (000s)
All	71	6	23	36,274
White	73	5	22	31,055
English/Welsh/Scottish/Northern Irish/British	73	5	22	28,732
Irish	73	5	22	338
Gypsy or Irish Traveller	40	10	50	36
Other White	77	5	19	1,949
Mixed/multiple ethnic group	60	11	30	638
White and Black Caribbean	56	14	30	225
White and Black African	59	11	29	81
White and Asian	62	8	31	171
Other Mixed	63	9	29	161
Asian/Asian British	60	7	33	2,937
Indian	70	6	24	1,026
Pakistani	49	9	42	705
Bangladeshi	48	10	41	275
Chinese	53	5	43	323
Other Asian	63	6	31	608
Black/African/Caribbean/Black British	61	13	26	1,241
African	59	13	28	667
Caribbean	67	12	22	408
Other Black	56	14	29	165
Other ethnic group	53	9	39	403
Arab	42	8	50	157
Any other ethnic group	59	9	32	246

Note: [a] Including self-employment.

Source: ONS (2014a)

and Polish groups. Of the non–White minority ethnic groups, the Indian group had the highest rate in employment (70%). In fact, the employment rates for the Asian/Asian British group has grown the most, from 53% (2001) to 62% (2014) (ONS, 2014a). The Indian group is followed by the Black Caribbean group (67%). The Gypsy or Irish Traveller and Arab groups had the lowest rates of employment. The groups experiencing the highest unemployment were Other Black and White and Black Caribbean (both 14%). Unemployment was also high for the African (13%) and Caribbean (12%) groups. The groups experiencing the lowest unemployment (5% per group) were the White British, Irish and Chinese. Gypsy or Irish Traveller and Arab groups were most likely to be economically inactive (both 50%). Pakistani and Bangladeshi groups were also most likely to be economically inactive (42% and 41% respectively).

Differences in labour market participation by gender

For some groups the patterns of labour market participation are similar for men and women. For example, the Other White group had the highest proportion of men (82%), and for women, but at a lower rate (72%). The rates were well above the average for the population (75% and 67% respectively). Gypsy and Irish Traveller men (49%) and women (31%) and Arab men (50%) and women (29%) had the lowest rates of all ethnic groups who were in employment. Bangladeshi and Pakistani women also had low rates of employment, but at much lower rates, around half of their male counterpart rates. Unemployment was highest among Other Black and White and Caribbean groups for both men and women (Other Black: men 17%; women 11%. White and Black Caribbean: men 16%; women 11%). The least likely group to be unemployed were both Chinese men and women (both 5% respectively). White British and White Irish women were also least likely to be unemployed (both 4%). Overall inactivity among women was 28%, 10 percentage points higher than for men (18%), and this was so across all ethnic groups. Figures 6.1 and 6.2 show the economic activity for men and women respectively.

For men, the highest rates of inactivity were for Chinese and Arab groups (both 40%), followed by Gypsy or Irish Traveller groups (39%); these were more than double the average rate (18%). For women, the highest rates of inactivity were for Arab (64%), Bangladeshi (61%), Pakistani (60%) or Gypsy or Irish Traveller (60%) groups. The reasons for economic inactivity vary between the groups and between gender and age. The main reason for male inactivity in the 2011 Census was being a student, being sick and having a disability, whereas the main reason for female inactivity was looking after the family and home.

Figure 6.1: Economic activity for men (aged 16-64) by ethnic group, England and Wales, 2011 Census

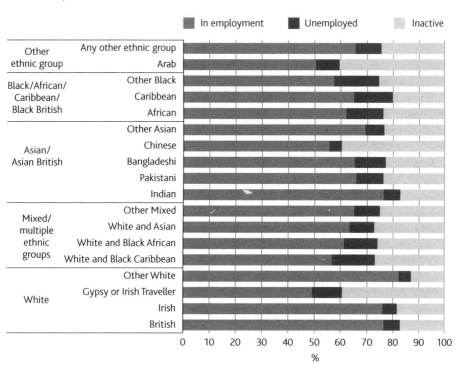

Source: ONS (2014a)

Types of employment

Industry

The representation of minority ethnic groups in industries and sectors is unevenly distributed. In comparison to White British employees, minority ethnic groups are under-represented in both the primary and secondary sectors, and over-represented in the tertiary or service sectors, where wages are generally lower and conditions generally less favourable. Certain minority ethnic groups are concentrated in particular industries (see Tables 6.2 and 6.3).

The 2011 Census shows that 37% of all men in employment worked in low-skilled occupations. However, over half of the men from Pakistani (57%), Black African (54%) and Bangladeshi (53%) backgrounds worked in low-skilled jobs. Chinese men were least likely to work in low-skilled occupations, followed by White Irish men. On the other hand, one-half of all women (59%) were more likely to work in low-skilled jobs. This was particularly more so for the Gypsy or Irish Traveller (71%), Bangladeshi (67%) and White and Black Caribbean (66%)

Figure 6.2: Economic activity for women (aged 16-64) by ethnic group, England and Wales, 2011 Census

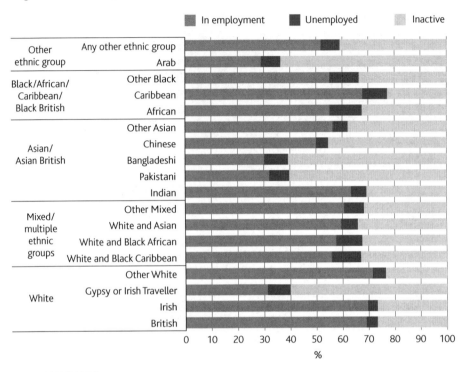

Source: ONS (2014a)

Table 6.2: The highest proportions of male employees from a specific minority ethnic group, 2011

Ethnicity	Industry	Proportion (%)
Bangladeshi	Accommodation and food service activities	36
Chinese	Accommodation and food service activities	31
Pakistani	Wholesale and retail trade; repair of motor vehicles and motor cycles	22
Indian	Wholesale and retail trade; repair of motor vehicles and motor cycles	21
Other Asian	Wholesale and retail trade; repair of motor vehicles and motor cycles	21

Source: ONS (2014a)

groups. Similar to the picture for men, the least likely to work in low-skilled jobs were Chinese (42%) and White Irish (45%) women.

Certain groups were concentrated in particular industries. Table 6.2 shows the industries with the highest proportion of men by group working in a particular

Table 6.3: The highest proportions of female employees from a specific minority ethnic group, 2011

Ethnicity	Industry	Proportion (%)
Black African	Human health and social work activities	39
Other Asian	Human health and social work activities	31
Black Caribbean	Human health and social work activities	29
Other Black	Human health and social work activities	27
White Irish	Human health and social work activities	25

Source: ONS (2014a)

industry. A high proportion of Bangladeshi and Chinese men (36% and 31%) were employed in accommodation and food service activities.

Overall, women are largely employed in human health and social work activities (see Table 6.3). Some minority ethnic groups are more concentrated in these sectors than White British women. For example 39% of Black African and 31% of Other Asian women are employed in this sector. Similarly 29% of Black Caribbean women were employed in this sector.

Occupation

The industrial distribution of employment powerfully influences the occupational distribution of work. Once again, there is a marked gender specialisation of work imposed on the contrasting specialisation in employment by ethnic group (Owen et al, 2000, p 78). The first edition of this chapter (see Virk, 2012) showed that one in five White British, Indian and Other Asian men were managers and senior officials in 2008. The groups least likely to be managers and senior officials are Other Black, White and Black African and Black African. While some Black African, Chinese, Indian and White and Asian men were even more likely than White British men to be employed in professional occupations, equally, other minority ethnic men were more likely to be employed in elementary occupations compared to White British men, suggesting a wide variation in experience within any particular ethnic grouping.

Chinese women were more likely to be employed as managers and senior officials and in professional occupations than White British women. This is also true for White and Asian women. However Indian women were less likely to be employed as managers and senior officials than White British women compared to men of their respective groups. Minority ethnic women were more likely than White British women to be employed in sales and customer service occupations. There is research showing Chinese and Indian groups, and especially girls, doing well at secondary school (see Shah, 2016).

Employment sector

In 2016, of the civil service employees who declared their ethnicity, 11.2% were from a minority ethnic group. While they are well represented in junior grades (12.8% of employees at executive officer and 11.7% at administrative responsibility level), they were not well represented at the more senior grades (7.0% at the senior civil service level) (ONS, 2016).

The Race Relations Amendment Act 2000 only applied to public or publicly funded bodies, and there is a consequent lack of data on minority ethnic groups employed in the private sector (Craig et al, 2010). Specific research on the number of minorities in professional and managerial positions in FTSE 100 companies found that only 40% of companies surveyed responded and, out of those, only 27 of the companies could provide a breakdown of the ethnicity of their employees. Of those that provided data, only 5.4% of their employees, 3.2% of junior and middle managers and only 1% of senior managers were from minority ethnic groups. Only three of 129 executive directors were from minority ethnic groups. Of the junior and middle managers, the Indian and Chinese groups were the only minority ethnic groups that were broadly in line with their representation in the wider employee population; among senior managers, the Indian group was the highest (Sanglin-Grant and Schneider 2000). Further, a recent report found that only 6% of top management roles are held by minority ethnic executives (Department for Business, Energy & Industrial Strategy, 2017; but note only one-half of the FTSE's 100 members had supplied meaningful information for the review, so the data are based on limited information).

Young people

There were over 6.6 million people aged 16-24 in England and Wales, and nearly one in four (23%) were from a minority ethnic group (2011 Census). As mentioned earlier, minority ethnic young people have a younger age profile, reflecting immigration and migration patterns. Around one-half of all young people were students (48%). The proportions varied across the different groups, with 87% of all young Chinese being students, and around three-quarters of Arab young people (76%). 'White Other' young people were the most likely to be in employment (43%). Gypsy or Irish Traveller groups had the highest proportion of young people who were unemployed (14%) – they also were most likely to be inactive and not a student (31%). White and Black Caribbean (13%) and Black Caribbean (12%) young people were most likely to be unemployed.

Earnings

There were wide variations in gross earnings from employment between the groups: among those working as employees, people in the Pakistani or Bangladeshi group received the lowest average hourly pay (£11.42 in the last three months of 2016), whereas Indian people received the highest (£4.39 per hour more) (Labour Force Survey, 2017). Legislation on the pay gap, the Ethnicity Pay Gap Bill, is to make provision for the publication of information related to the differences between ethnic groups. This will help with transparency to establish any pay differences.

Employment disadvantage experienced by minority ethnic groups

Based on the series of four Policy Studies Institute surveys and those of its predecessors, the position of minority ethnic groups in the labour market over time demonstrates the failure of policy from the 1960s to the1990s in addressing the labour market performance of minority ethnic groups. The first edition of this book presented the surveys and its key findings (see Virk, 2012).

Factors explaining labour market disadvantage among minority ethnic groups

Traditionally, two general explanations were put forward for the disadvantage experienced by minority ethnic groups in the labour market: migration and discrimination (see below). However, these factors cannot account for all the differences between the groups (Berthoud, 1999). Berthoud (2000) uses a six-factor framework to analyse the position of young Caribbean men in the labour market relative to other groups. This is used here to consider the labour market disadvantages experienced by other minority ethnic groups. The six factors are: migration; expectations and stereotypes; discrimination; family structures; alienation; and structure of the economy. It is important to remember that no single factor can explain minority ethnic disadvantage, that the interplay of factors is complex, and that many individuals experience multiple disadvantage. Some of the factors are more relevant than others when considering different groups, with some influencing labour market supply and others influencing labour market demand, an important consideration for potential policy solutions. The discussion below considers each factor in turn, drawing on available empirical evidence to explain its potential impact on employment.

Migration

Recent migrants may experience disadvantage in the labour market compared to longer-term residents. This can the result of a number of factors including lower or unrecognised educational qualifications; weaker social capital (network of contacts); and, by implication, fewer sources of reference in Britain to help them gain employment. Newer arrivals may also be unfamiliar with application procedures and interview techniques. Language skills are also an important factor, and poor language skills can reduce the range of job opportunities available. While most young minority ethnic people are fluent in English, language problems are prevalent for certain Asian groups in older age cohorts, most of whom are likely to have been born abroad (Modood et al, 1997). Over three-quarters of Bangladeshi women aged over 25 do not speak fluent English, and over 40% of Bangladeshi and Pakistani first-generation men are non-English-speaking, which impacts on their labour market engagement. For women this is used to explain their economic inactivity, whereas for men it explains high unemployment (Leslie and Lindley, 2001). Lack of English fluency has also been found to have a negative effect on earnings (Battu and Sloane, 2002; Dustmann and Fabbri, 2003). More recently Nandi and Fisher (2015) found a relationship between poor language skills and poverty. It would be expected that these issues would be less relevant the longer the individual has been in the host country, and so they tend to be eliminated for second and third generations (Hatton and Wheatley-Price, 1998). (Many migrant workers in Britain on a temporary basis also suffer significantly from poor English skills.) However, Heath et al (2000) found 'ethnic penalties' (that is, a pattern of discrimination related to factors such as pay, labour market status and so on as a result of identified ethnicity) to be of similar magnitude among both second and first generations.

Expectations and stereotypes

Expectations and stereotypes have been found to affect labour market success. Teachers' expectations are important and can impact on the academic success of pupils. In particular, Caribbean boys are expected, both by themselves and by their teachers, to under-achieve at school, which reduces their chance of success (Gillborn, 1990; Sewell, 1997; also see Chapter 11, this volume). This has a knock-on effect for those entering the labour market in terms of their prospects and the lower expectations of employers. In turn, this relative failure of young Caribbean men in the labour market may also contribute to lowering teachers' expectations in schools once again, resulting in a vicious circle. Stereotypes can also lead to a channelling of minority ethnic groups into specific occupations, for example, by those who help in making career choices (Cross et al, 1990). Expectations within minority ethnic households can also influence the supply of labour. For some women, employment choices have been found to be influenced by a number of factors, including cultural expectations, family and community pressures; this was found to be the case, for example, for Pakistani and Bangladeshi women in Oldham (Dale, 2008).

Discrimination

There are many sources of research suggesting the operation of discrimination in the UK labour market, including large-scale surveys, discrimination testing, investigations carried out by watchdogs and incidents that come to light at employment tribunals (see Virk, 2012, pp 180-3). It would not, however, be correct to say that the differences between minority ethnic employment and the general population are all due to discrimination. We need more research establishing when ethnicity makes a difference and when it does not.

Although statistical sources are useful, they are not sound proof that discrimination is the sole or major explanation for the disparities. Other such methods, relying on smaller sample sizes, have been used, such as discrimination testing. This method uses two or more testers, one belonging to the majority group and the other to minority groups. The testers are matched with the same credentials and apply for the same job. If, over a period of repeated testing, the majority group candidate is systematically selected over the minority ethnic candidate, this points to discrimination being in operation. An exercise of matched applications found net discrimination in favour of White names over minority ethnic applications to be 29% (DWP, 2009).

Discrimination testing focused on certain professions has also been undertaken. A study based on the medical profession found that NHS hospitals were twice as likely to select candidates with Anglo-Saxon names for interview over those with Asian names (Esmail and Everington, 1993); this is all the more remarkable given the very dependency of the NHS more generally on staff of minority ethnic backgrounds (see, for example, Rao, 2014). A similar study conducted in 1992 (Noon, 1993) examined evidence of racial discrimination among 100 of the UK's largest companies.

Experience of minority ethnic groups provides further corroboration of discrimination. The *Fourth national survey* reports (Modood et al, 1997) that 78% of economically active minority ethnic respondents thought that employers refused people jobs for racial or religious reasons. There was a slight difference in the opinions of the different ethnic groups, with the highest figure recorded among those of Caribbean origin, of which 95% believed that such discrimination existed. However, minority ethnic groups were more likely to believe that discrimination was widespread, with 18% believing that 'most' employers discriminate, compared to only 5% of White people. Evidence from minority ethnic groups themselves of discrimination may be criticised as subjective, although it has been found that minority ethnic groups under-estimated the discrimination to which they were exposed (Smith, 1977). Moreover, discrimination can be in the form of indirect discrimination (see Chapter 2, this volume), which may be harder to detect and prove. Recent research by the British Social Attitudes Survey found that as many as three out of every ten people were prepared to acknowledge explicitly that they were very or a little racially prejudiced (see www.natcen.ac.uk/blog/tag/racism).

The number of court cases due to discrimination may be an indicator of the extent of the problem (see Chapter 11, this volume). Race relations legislation has made racial discrimination illegal since 1965 (see Chapter 4); however, employment tribunals on the basis of racial discrimination made up only 1.5% of the total hearings of employment tribunals claims in 2009/10, with only 3% of claims being successful, and most being settled by means of conciliation, withdrawn or dismissed at the hearing (Ministry of Justice and Tribunals Service, 2010). That said, there is a year-on-year increase in employment tribunals based on discrimination on the grounds of religion or belief, although overall they are still tiny fractions of the total number of such cases and small in absolute terms; there were no claims in 2002/03, and 1,000 in 2009/10 (Ministry of Justice and Tribunals Service, 2010). Also 'hidden discrimination' (TUC, 2003) has now been identified and it is clear that institutional (indirect) racism in public services is prevalent in the UK (see Chapter 2, this volume). The imposition of significant charges to engage with employment tribunals may well have also discriminated against those in lower-paid jobs. (At the time of writing, the High Court has ruled these charges to be illegal and they are to be abolished.)

Family structures

Family structure impacts on some minority ethnic groups more forcefully than on others (Berthoud, 2000). In particular, over half (56%) of Black or Black British dependent children lived with a lone parent in 2009 compared to only almost one-quarter of White British children (23%) (ONS, 2010). Being brought up without a significant male role model may influence a young person's labour market engagement, for example, unemployment levels for single Black Caribbean men are twice as high as for those who are married or who live with a partner (Modood et al, 1997). In the case of Pakistani and Bangladeshi women, low activity levels are particularly characteristic of Asian Muslim women and are affected by the economic position of their husbands; the wives/partners of unemployed men have lower activity rates than the wives of men who have jobs (Modood et al, 1997).

Family structures may also be a factor for the high level of self-employment among certain minority ethnic groups (Basu, 1998), as the extended family may provide free labour or financial assistance. As mentioned earlier in this chapter, some minority ethnic groups have larger families than White British families, and childcare and family responsibilities, combined with disproportionately poor access to childcare, affect their supply of labour (Daycare Trust, 2000).

Alienation

Those who have experienced perceived, or real, exclusion from employment or other institutions, or have witnessed others in their community doing so, may develop a sense of alienation. Young Black Caribbean men may develop a sense of alienation as a consequence of their exclusion from employment (Wrench et al, 1997). Black Caribbean boys may develop a sense of resentment as a result of the stereotypes held about them by teachers, which is, in turn, perceived by the teachers as a potential threat, reinforcing the image (Gillborn, 1990; Sewell, 1997). As a result of being denied opportunities in the labour market, some may decide to adopt an alternative lifestyle. Many of these issues parallel the unemployment and disaffection among young White British men with poor academic achievements; class is obviously, then, a prominent factor. However, it is suggested that the disadvantages of young Black Caribbean men:

> may be seen as a general problem of exclusion and alienation during a period of widening economic inequality. On the other hand, important elements of the problems facing young Caribbean men are specifically racial and their response may also be based, in part, on a sense of ethnic identity and rejection. (Berthoud, 1999, p 4)

A study of young Bangladeshi men in inner-city London also found them to be alienated from the majority White British, as well as other minority ethnic, groups; this was so whether they were UK-born or Bangladeshi-born (Salway, 2008).

Structure of the economy

There is a lower demand for manual labour for those with limited qualifications and skills due to de-industrialisation and the shift from a manufacturing base since the main migrations of the 1950s-1970s occurred (DfEE, 2001). Further, minority ethnic groups tend to be highly concentrated in inner-city areas (Jones, 1993; Modood et al, 1997), where job opportunities are more restricted. That said, overall, minority ethnic groups are relatively less concentrated in declining industries than their White counterparts. However, some minority groups may be more affected than others: Indian men and women in particular are well-represented in manufacturing, which, as a sector, suffered a 31,000 loss in employment between 1995 and 2000 (Cabinet Office, 2000). Industry restructuring has also impacted on certain industries in particular geographical locations – for example, the decline of the textile industry has had a specific and negative effect on Pakistani and Bangladeshi groups in the North of England (Karn, 1997). Furthermore, there is also a spatial mismatch in that minority ethnic groups are not concentrated in areas where jobs are growing (Turok and Edge, 1999).

Minority ethnic groups tend to be affected by the business cycle more than their White counterparts (Jones, 1993; Lindley, 2005). This may be due to the occupations and industries in which they are employed being more sensitive to upturns and downturns in the economy. Berthoud's analysis of Labour Force Survey data (1999) found that unemployment among Black Caribbean and Black African groups was largely attributable to their sensitivity to variations in the economic environment. Recent research (Nandi and Fisher, 2015) found that most minority ethnic groups fared worse following the 2008 financial crisis and consequent recession.

Other factors affecting demand

It was shown earlier that employment rates for minority ethnic groups are lower than those of their White counterparts, reflecting, in part, the lack of labour market demand for them. This can be shaped by a number of factors. One of the dampeners of demand is the lack of companies providing employment opportunities in areas where minority ethnic groups live. Lower levels of business activity have been found in areas where such groups are concentrated, and the companies that do exist tend to be smaller than in White-dominant areas, which means reduced employment opportunities (Cabinet Office, 2000). In fact, the final report of the Cabinet Office study (2003) highlights geography as one of the key determinants of minority ethnic employment rates. Its analysis of Labour Force Survey data shows that minority ethnic employment rates are highest in Outer London and lowest in West Yorkshire and Greater Manchester. Geography has since shown disparities in the labour market outcomes in several studies (see, for example, Simpson et al, 2006; Lalani et al, 2014). Analysis of the 2011 Census shows that all minority ethnic groups in England are more likely to live in deprived neighbourhoods than White British groups (Jivraj and Khan, 2013). Finally, demand-side factors affecting minority ethnic groups include expectations and stereotypes of employers, discrimination, industrial restructuring (or de-industrialisation), geographical deprivation and poor levels of public infrastructure. All must be taken into account when trying to explain ethnic diversity within labour market participation. Local context, for example, might assume particular importance.

Other factors affecting supply

One explanation for minority ethnic labour market disadvantage focuses on human capital. This may be a particular factor for some groups; for example,

Black Caribbean and Pakistani/Bangladeshi students show the lowest levels of achievement at GCSE level. However, it cannot explain the disadvantage experienced by high-achieving groups, as GCSE attainment is highest among Indian and Chinese students, particularly girls, who outperform White British students (see Chapter 11, this volume).

Broadly speaking, one would assume that investment in education will lead to higher wages and better job prospects; however, over 30% of Indian, African Asian and Chinese groups exhibit levels of over-education for their jobs, compared to 20% of their White counterparts (Battu and Sloane, 2002). The same research found 36% of Bangladeshi workers to have fewer qualifications than were required for their job; in other words, they were under-educated. For the over-qualified, Berthoud (2000) found that the returns to education in terms of earnings were less for minority ethnic groups than they were for the White population; while a degree reaped an extra £80 per week for the White population, it only increased an Indian worker's weekly wage by £71 per week, the highest returns for a degree among all minority ethnic groups; the lowest returns for a degree were for the African group at a mere £27 per week, while Caribbean and Pakistani/ Bangladeshi graduates increased their earning power by £64 and £61 per week respectively. The most recent research in this area has found that, for any given level of qualification, White British men and women are more likely to be employed than minority ethnic groups (Machin et al, 2009).

Religion and culture have also been presented as significant supply factors (Weller et al, 2001; Ahmad et al, 2003; NEP, 2010). Lindley's (2002) analysis of the *Fourth national survey* found religion, as well as ethnicity, to be significant, that Hindu Indians appear to fare better in the labour market than Sikh Indians, and that, relative to other 'non-White religions', Muslims experience some unexplained employment 'penalty'. Hasmath (2012) defines a 'penalty' in that exclusionary discrimination is not the only potential explanation for ethnic penalties. Conditions such an individual's social network, a firm's working culture and a community's social trust are also a factor:

> The level of disadvantage is particularly acute for Muslim women. They are 71% more likely than white Christian women to be unemployed, even when they have the same educational level and language skills.... As well as suffering the disadvantages of Muslim men relating to employment opportunities, some women also face pressures from their communities around education and employment choices, and particular issues of discrimination within the workplace around dress. (House of Commons, 2016, p 6)

The explanation for this is likely to reflect a complex interplay between social-economic position and ethnic origin, some of which reflects local contexts, in addition to changing assumptions about how a person's ethnic origin assumes social meaning (see Chapter 2, this volume). We have seen growing evidence of how Islamophobia might impact on a person's labour market participation.

The review presented here is not exhaustive, and many other factors affect the supply of labour such as social class (Heath and McMahon, 1997) and housing tenure (see Chapter 7, this volume). Some barriers may not be exclusively related to ethnicity, but may be highly correlated with ethnicity, such as, for some groups (see Chapter 11), having a criminal record and ill health (see Chapter 12, this volume; see also Cabinet Office, 2000, for a more comprehensive literature review). In summary, however, the supply of minority ethnic groups in the labour market can be determined by factors including racial discrimination, human capital, religion and cultural factors, family structures, alienation, discouragement and social class among many others. Social mobility is now the dominant government discourse instead of group-based (whether based on ethnicity, gender or sexuality) disadvantage. It has become the priority for the government and figures in their diversity strategy. The issue of 'race' itself and racial discrimination has been substantially removed from policy discourse (Craig, 2013).

Conclusion

Despite minority ethnic groups having resided in large numbers in Britain for more than half a century and in many cases now having been British-born and educated, they still face disadvantage in the labour market. In general, minority ethnic groups are more likely to be unemployed and be in low-skill occupations and industries than the White British population. However, there is huge diversity among different minority ethnic groups, which is further complicated by gender and age. Differences within groups remain under-researched and need to be a greater feature of further work in this area; that said, there has been some work carried out in this area, including in relation to Gypsies and Irish Travellers.

Thurrow's (1969) dimensions of disadvantage are still prevalent in today's labour market. Although some minority ethnic groups have progressed, others suffer severe disadvantage. By all the indicators considered in this chapter, Pakistani and Bangladeshi groups fare worst, and this applies to both genders. Chinese and African Asian groups hold a position of broad parity with the White British population, whereas the Indian group who came directly from the subcontinent and the Black Caribbean group, who have been in Great Britain the longest, still experience some disadvantages. The evidence presented in this chapter also shows that Black Caribbean women fare much better than Black Caribbean men.

A number of factors have been put forward to explain some of these differences. These include migration, alienation, expectations and stereotyping, family structure, the structure of economy and discrimination, as well as other factors affecting the demand and supply of minority ethnic labour. There is also evidence that discrimination has most certainly gone beyond skin colour and is prevalent in terms of culture and religion. Additionally, there is evidence of hidden discrimination and institutional racism.

Although this chapter positions the groups in the labour market and provides some explanations, it does not look at the impact of policy measures on the groups. Despite various employment initiatives and legislation, significant disparities persist. Teasing out the complexity of this, while reflecting on the contested and changing definition of ethnicity, will be the challenge facing future research into this area. Differences within ethnic groupings are likely to be as important as difference between groupings.

Questions for discussion

- What strategies or policy measures could be introduced to eradicate difference, when accessing labour markets?
- To what extent do you think discrimination is a factor in the disadvantage minority ethnic groups face?
- To what extent do you think social class plays a role?

Online resources

www.ons.gov.uk/employmentandlabourmarket/peopleinwork/
employmentandemployeetypes/datasets/labourmarketstatusbyethnicgroupa09
  Up to date data can be retrieved from the quarterly Labour Force Survey.

www.ons.gov.uk/peoplepopulationandcommunity/culturalidentity/ethnicity/articles/eth
nicityandthelabourmarket2011censusenglandandwales/2014-11-13#characteristics-of-
ethnic-groups-in-employment
  Census analysis of labour market information by ethnicity.

www.equalityhumanrights.com/en/our-research/reading-lists
  Equality and Human Rights Commission: reading lists.

www.parliament.uk/womenandequalities
  Women and Equalities Committee: various reports.

www.ethnicity-facts-figures.service.gov.uk
  The government has launched a 'race' audit; this looks at the data on many areas of social policy, including labour market data.

References

Ahmad, F., Modood, T. and Lissenburgh, S. (2003) *South Asian women and employment in Britain: The interaction of gender and ethnicity*, London: Policy Studies Institute.

Basu, A. (1998) 'The role of institutional support in Asian entrepreneurial expansion in Britain', *Journal of Small Business and Enterprise Development*, 5(4), December, 317-26.

Battu, H. and Sloane, P.J. (2002) 'To what extent are ethnic minorities in Britain over-educated?', *International Journal of Manpower*, 23(3), 192-203.

Berthoud, R. (1999) *Young Caribbean men and the labour market: A comparison with other ethnic groups*, York: Joseph Rowntree Foundation.

Berthoud, R. (2000) 'Ethnic employment penalties in Britain', *Journal of Ethnic and Migration Studies*, 26(3), 389-416.

Cabinet Office (2000) *Ethnic minorities and the labour market: Interim analytical report*, London: Strategy Unit, Cabinet Office.

Cabinet Office (2003) *Ethnic minorities and the labour market*, Final report, London: Strategy Unit, Cabinet Office.

Catney, G. and Sabater, E. (2015) *Ethnic minority disadvantage in the labour market*, York: Joseph Rowntree Foundation.

Craig, G. (2013) 'The invisibilisation of "race" in public policy', *Critical Social Policy*, November, 712-20.

Craig, G., Adamson, S., Ali, N. and Demsash, F. (2010) *Mapping ethnic minorities in rapidly changing populations*, York: Joseph Rowntree Foundation.

Cross, M., Wrench, J. and Barnett, S. (1990) *Ethnic minorities and the careers service: An investigation into processes of assessment and placement*, Department of Employment, Research Paper No 73, London: HMSO.

Dale, A. (2008) *Pakistani and Bangladeshi women's labour market participation*, CCSR Working Paper 2008-02 (http://hummedia.manchester.ac.uk/institutes/cmist/archive-publications/working-papers/2008/2008-01-pakistani-and-bangladeshi-womens-labour-market-participation.pdf).

Daycare Trust (2000) *Investing in success*, London: Daycare Trust.

Department for Business, Energy & Industrial Strategy (2017) *Race in the workforce: The McGregor-Smith Review* (www.gov.uk/government/publications/race-in-the-workplace-the-mcgregor-smith-review).

DfEE (Department for Education and Employment) (2001) *Employer skills survey*, London: DfEE.

Dustmann, C. and Fabbri, F. (2003) 'Language proficiency and labour market performance of immigrants in the UK', *The Economic Journal*, 113(489), 695-717.

DWP (Department for Work and Pensions) (2009) *A test for racial discrimination in recruitment practices in British cities*, Research Report No 207, October.

Ennelli, P., Modood, T. and Bradley, H. (2005) *Young Turks and Kurds*, York: Joseph Rowntree Foundation.

Esmail, A. and Evertington, S. (1993) 'Racial discrimination against doctors from ethnic minorities', *British Medical Journal*, 306, March, 691–2.

Gillborn, D. (1990) *'Race', ethnicity and education*, London: Unwin Hyman.

Hatton, T.J. and Wheatley-Price, S. (1998) *Migration, migrants and policy in the UK*, London: Centre for Economic Policy Research.

Hasmath, R. (2012) *The ethnic penalty: Immigration, education and the labour market*, Aldershot: Ashgate.

Heath, A. and McMahon, D. (1997) 'Education and occupational attainments: The impact of ethnic origins', in V. Karn (ed) *Ethnicity in the 1991 Census, Volume 4: Employment, education and housing among ethnic minority populations in Britain*, London: Office for National Statistics, 91–113.

Heath, A., McMahon, D. and Roberts, J. (2000) "Ethnic differences in the labour market: A comparison of the samples of anonymised records and Labour Force Survey', *Journal of the Royal Statistical Society, Series A-Statistics in Society*, 163(3), 341–61.

House of Commons (2016) *Employment opportunities for Muslims*, HC 89, 11 August (https://publications.parliament.uk/pa/cm201617/cmselect/cmwomeq/89/8902.htm).

Jivraj, S. and Khan, O. (2013) *Ethnicity and deprivation in England: How likely are ethnic minorities to live in deprived neighbourhoods?*, York and Manchester: Joseph Rowntree Foundation and University of Manchester.

Jones, T. (1993) *Britain's ethnic minorities*, London: Policy Studies Institute.

Karn, V. (ed) (1997) *Ethnicity in the 1991 Census, Volume 4: Employment, education and housing among ethnic minority populations in Britain*, London: Office for National Statistics.

Lalani, M., Metcalf, H., Tufekci, L., Corley, A., Rolfe, H. and George, A. (2014) *How place influences employment outcomes for ethnic minorities*, York: Joseph Rowntree Foundation.

Leslie, D. and Lindley, J. (2001) 'The impact of language ability on employment and earnings of Britain's ethnic communities', *Economica*, 68(272), November, 587–606.

LFS (Labour Force Survey) (2017) Data downloaded from Nomis (www.nomisweb.co.uk/).

Lindley, J. (2002) 'Race or religion? The impact of religion on the employment and earnings of Britain's ethnic communities', *Journal of Ethnic and Migration Studies*, 28(3), July, 427–42.

Lindley, J. (2005) 'Explaining ethnic unemployment and activity rates: Evidence from the QLFS in the 1990s and 2000s', *Bulletin of Economic Research*, 57(2).

Machin, S., Murphy, R. and Soobedar, Z. (2009) *Differences in the labour market gains from higher education participation*, Report for NEP, London: London School of Economics and Political Science, CEP.

Ministry of Justice and Tribunals Service (2010) *Employment Tribunal and EAT Statistics 2009-2010 (GB)* (https://assets.publishing.service.gov.uk/government/uploads/system/uploads/attachment_data/file/218499/employment-trib-stats-april-march-2010-11.pdf).

Modood, T., Berthoud, R., Lakey, J., Nazroo, J., Smith, P., Virdee, S. and Beishon, S. (1997) *Ethnic minorities in Britain: Diversity and disadvantage*, London: Policy Studies Institute.

Nandi, A. and Fisher, P. (2015) *Poverty across ethnic groups through recession and austerity*, York: Joseph Rowntree Foundation.

NEP (National Employment Panel) (2010) *The structure of economic inequality in the UK*, London: National Equalities Office (www.equalities.gov.uk/pdf/NEP%20Report%20bookmarkedfinal.pdf).

Noon, M. (1993) 'Racial discrimination in speculative application: Evidence from the UK's top 100 firms', *Human Resource Management Journal*, 3(4), summer, 35-47.

ONS (Office for National Statistics) (2006) *Focus on ethnicity and religion* (https://webarchive.nationalarchives.gov.uk/20151014015843/http://www.ons.gov.uk/ons/rel/ethnicity/focus-on-ethnicity-and-religion/2006-edition/index.html).

ONS (2010) Social Trends 40: 2010 edition (https://webarchive.nationalarchives.gov.uk/20151014074142/http://www.ons.gov.uk/ons/rel/social-trends-rd/social-trends/social-trends-40/index.html).

ONS (2014a) 'Differences in labour market participation by gender', 2011 Census analysis: Ethnicity and labour market, England and Wales, 13 November (www.ons.gov.uk/peoplepopulationandcommunity/culturalidentity/ethnicity/articles/ethnicityandthelabourmarket2011censusenglandandwales/2014-11-13).

ONS (2014b) 'Characteristics of ethnic groups in employment', 2011 Census analysis: Ethnicity and labour market, England and Wales (www.ons.gov.uk/peoplepopulationandcommunity/culturalidentity/ethnicity/articles/ethnicityandthelabourmarket2011censusenglandandwales/2014-11-13#characteristics-of-ethnic-groups-in-employment).

ONS (2016) 'Civil Service statistics: 2016, Statistical bulletin' (www.ons.gov.uk/employmentandlabourmarket/peopleinwork/publicsectorpersonnel/bulletins/civilservicestatistics/2016).

Owen, D., Green, G., Pitcher, J. and Maguire, M. (2000) *Ethnic minority participation and achievements in education, training and the labour market*, Research Report No 225, October, London: Department for Education and Employment.

Rao, M. (2014) 'Inequality rife among black and minority ethnic staff in the NHS', *The Guardian*, 1 August (www.theguardian.com/healthcare-network/2014/aug/01/inequality-black-ethnic-minority-rife-nhs).

Salway, S. (2008) 'Labour market experiences of young UK Bangladeshi men: Identity, inclusion and exclusion in inner-city London', *Ethnic and Racial Studies*, 31(6), September, 1126-52.

Sanglin-Grant, S. and Schneider, R. (2000) *Moving on up? Racial equality and the Corporate agenda. A study of FTSE 100 companies*, A report for the Runnymede Trust, February, London: Runnymede Trust.

Sewell, T. (1997) *Black masculinities and schooling*, Stoke-on-Trent: Trentham Books.

Shah, S. (2016) 'Against the odds: Ethnic minority students are excelling at school', University of Leicester Press Office, 1 February (www2.le.ac.uk/offices/press/think-leicester/education/2016/against-the-odds-ethnic-minority-students-are-excelling-at-school).

Simpson, L., Purdam, K., Tajar, A., Fieldhouse, E., Gavalas, V., Tranmer, M., et al (2006) *Ethnic minority populations and the labour market: An analysis of the 1991 and 2001 Census*, London: The Stationery Office.

Smith, D.J. (1977) *Racial disadvantage in Britain: The PEP report*, Harmondsworth: Penguin.

Thurrow, L.C. (1969) *Poverty and discrimination*, Washington, DC: Brookings Institute.

TUC (Trades Union Congress) (2003) *Labour market programmes*, Briefing document.

Turok, I. and Edge, N. (1999) *The jobs gap in Britain's cities*, Bristol: Policy Press.

Virk, B. (2012) 'Minority ethnic groups in the labour market', in G. Craig, K. Atkin, S. Chattoo and R. Flynn (eds) *Understanding 'race' and ethnicity*, Bristol: Policy Press.

Weller, P., Feldman, A. and Purdam, K. (2001) *Religious discrimination in England and Wales*, Home Office Research Study 220, February, London: Home Office, Research, Development and Statistics Directorate.

Wrench, J., Hassan, E. and Owen, D. (1997) *Ambition and marginalisation: A qualitative study of under-achieving young men of Afro-Caribbean origin*, London: The Stationery Office.

7

Minority ethnic communities and housing

Gina Netto and Harris Beider

Overview

This chapter is concerned with Black and minority ethnic (BME) communities' experience of housing, specifically, their access to housing, housing circumstances and participation in housing markets. It:

- considers minority ethnic housing experiences within the context of immigration and settlement;
- introduces the concepts of direct and indirect racial discrimination;
- examines changes brought about by growing progress towards 'race' equality and increasing emphasis on community cohesion;
- pays particular attention to the role of the public sector, including Black-led housing associations and its recent decline, given its role in accommodating those on low incomes; and
- considers the implications of research for improving the position of BME communities in housing strategies, policy and delivery.

Key concepts
access; homelessness; housing association; participation; housing tenure

---

Introduction

Minority ethnic communities' experience within the housing system in the UK can be understood in the context of post-colonial immigration and settlement, growing progress towards 'race' equality and wider changes in providing housing for people on low incomes. More recently, it should also be viewed within the context of policy shifts, an increasingly hostile environment to migrants and the outcome of the referendum in the UK on European Union (EU) membership.

Drawing on research conducted in England and Scotland, this chapter begins by considering some of the key issues affecting minority ethnic groups' access to housing and their experiences within the housing system, including the sharp end of lack of access to housing, that is, homelessness and changes in housing tenure. It then considers minority ethnic participation within the system through the rise and decline of Black-led housing associations in England. Finally, the chapter concludes by considering some recent policy initiatives and their potential for overcoming some of the difficulties discussed.

In the UK, responsibility for housing resides within central government, with local authorities and voluntary sector agencies implementing centrally driven policies (Edgar, 2004), with some local variations. Social housing – which is subsidised by the state – is one of the main 'planks' of the housing safety net that provides a level of protection for poor and vulnerable UK nationals. Access to social housing – as in many other Western European countries – is conditional on citizenship status (Netto et al, 2015). Undocumented migrants or asylum-seekers are thus not eligible for social housing. Further, EU migrants have recently faced a tightening of eligibility criteria in order to reduce their access to social housing.

Compared to many other countries in Europe, the UK still has a relatively large social rented sector (Netto et al, 2015). However, the sector has shrunk considerably since the post-war period, and the housing market has changed from a predominantly rental one in the 1950s to one in which the majority of people live in their own homes. According to the English Housing Survey for 2012-13, the percentage of people in social housing has fallen from just under a third (31.4%) in 1980 to one in seven in 2000 (16.8%). As in many other Western European countries, the shortage of affordable housing for low-income groups has been a longstanding problem in the UK, and the phenomenon is currently viewed by some as constituting a 'housing crisis'. Despite this, equal access to the social rented sector is important for minority ethnic communities given the higher levels of poverty of certain ethnic groups (Platt, 2007; Netto et al, 2011) and their disproportionately high levels of representation in low-paid work (Low Pay Commission, 2013).

The decline in social housing has been attributed to a number of reasons, including lack of investment in local authority or council housing, the sale of council properties to tenants at discounted prices through the Right to Buy scheme and cuts in new house building (Phillips and Harrison, 2010). Other major changes in the housing environment since the 1950s are large-scale slum clearances, an increase in amenity levels and a decrease in overcrowding (Lakey, 1997). There have also been major shifts in the governance of housing through (often large-scale) transfers of stock from the local authority to housing associations. This has led commentators to argue that housing interventions since

1979 have taken place within an increasingly neoliberal environment (Phillips and Harrison, 2010). The continuing focus on home ownership in government policy in England (as opposed to increasing the supply of social housing) is likely to continue to reduce access to affordable housing and to reinforce these trends.

Edgar (2004) observes that housing policies for minority ethnic communities have tended mainly to concentrate on ensuring their access to the social rented sector, through providing good practice guidance and monitoring the policies and procedures of social landlords. A similar trend may be observed in a body of research that has documented disadvantage in the access and allocation of social housing and the need for greater awareness of the potential for institutional racism (Chahal, 2000; Netto et al, 2001, 2011; and see Box 7.1).

An understanding of direct and indirect racial discrimination as defined by the Race Relations Act 1976 is important for understanding changes in housing policy and practice, and its impacts on minority ethnic communities. It is also important to understand what is meant by 'institutional discrimination'.

Box 7.1: The Race Relations Act 1976 and racial discrimination

The Race Relations Act 1976 made it unlawful for local authorities to discriminate either directly or indirectly on racial grounds in the provision of goods, facilities and services.

Direct discrimination occurs when a person is treated less favourably on racial grounds than another person and may result in missed job opportunities or access to services, such as housing. In the housing field, the allocation policies of social housing organisations have been a major focus of attention as a means of addressing direct discrimination.

Indirect racial discrimination is defined as the imposition of conditions or requirements that, while not apparently discriminatory in themselves, have the effect of lowering the proportion of people from certain ethnic groups who are able to access services or qualify for jobs. Such discrimination may be reflected in the provision of housing that does not meet specific needs. An oft-cited example of such discrimination is the lack of availability of accommodation in the social rented sector that can accommodate large households. This is significant given the larger family sizes (and households) in certain communities.

Recognition of these forms of discrimination has now been extended in the Amendment to include 'institutional discrimination'. This is defined in the Macpherson Report (1999) as:

> The collective failure of an organisation to provide an appropriate and professional service to people because of their colour, culture and ethnic origin. It can be seen or detected in processes, attitudes and behaviour which amount to discrimination through unwitting prejudice, ignorance, thoughtlessness and racist stereotyping which disadvantages minority ethnic people. (Macpherson, 1999, 6.34)

The minority ethnic communities covered in this chapter are diverse, including long-established communities in the UK as well as recent arrivals. The latter include new economic migrants from EU Accession countries (A8 and A12), asylum-seekers and refugees. It is also worth acknowledging that significant differences exist in the housing needs, experiences and participation of minority ethnic communities, on the basis of class, age, gender, disability, religion, sexual orientation and generation.

Trends in minority ethnic settlement and patterns of disadvantage

As discussed in earlier chapters, migrants from South Asia and the West Indies mainly came from the late 1950s onwards to work in industries that faced difficulties in recruiting labour from the local population. These groups settled in different parts of the country, depending on employment opportunities. Phillips and Harrison (2010, p 223) note that in the earliest stages of post-war settlement, in the 1950s and 1960s, these migrants were forced by 'poverty, lack of knowledge of housing and blatant racist discrimination' into renting or buying poor-quality housing at the bottom end of the private market. The study notes that the development programmes in the early days of post-war slum clearance did not directly target the geographical areas in which black or Asian people were concentrated.

Many of the areas in which minority ethnic communities are concentrated are characterised by high unemployment, low pay and poor services and housing (Harrison with Davis, 2001; Edgar, 2004). As Simpson (2004) revealed, patterns of ethnic segregation or concentration are not in themselves problematic; they may provide valuable opportunities for mutual support within and across minority ethnic communities. It is potential restrictions in housing, environmental quality and job choice that are of concern (Harrison with Davies, 2001), or the coexistence of concentrations of minority ethnic households with the concentration of disadvantage (Lakey, 1997). Here, it is important to note the role of strategies adopted by individuals within these communities in contributing to changing spatial patterns. For instance, Simpson (2004) has argued that demographic evidence shows that Asian people are dispersing, supporting qualitative evidence of a desire to live in mixed neighbourhoods and gradual upward mobility (Phillips, 2002).

In the 1960s, direct and indirect racial discrimination continued to hinder access to good-quality housing and to influence patterns of settlement. Direct discrimination included allocation policies that disadvantaged individuals from certain ethnic groups by allowing them access to only poor-quality housing in the least desirable areas of the social rented sector. Other forms of direct discrimination could be seen in the racialised practices of estate agents who 'steered' individuals into certain areas (Phillips, 2002). Yet other forms of direct discrimination may be seen in the practices of building societies and banks that impose less favourable mortgage arrangements for minority ethnic communities than the majority population (Third et al, 1997). Indirect racial discrimination may be seen in the lack of larger-sized accommodation in the social rented sector, which disadvantages certain communities, where household sizes are typically larger than in the majority population, notably the Pakistani and Bangladeshi communities. Some housing authorities have introduced residence tests under powers in the Localism Act 2011 that disadvantage new arrivals, thus enabling another form of indirect discrimination.

One of the most important challenges to access for BME communities is the level of awareness within housing leaders. It could be argued that these issues of race and housing peaked with the publication of the Macpherson Report in 1999 and the final Housing Corporation BME Strategy. Since this point, the focus has shifted and reduced the salience of race and housing. Initially, New Labour's attention to social exclusion and poverty (SEU, 2000) demonstrated a move to tackle housing disadvantage. Phillips and Harrison (2010) note that, from 1997 onwards, New Labour's goal of tackling social exclusion included a well-defined geographical focus that was based on the premise that deprived neighbourhoods could be 'turned around' with wide-ranging government action addressing childcare, drugs, crime, unemployment and public health issues. The study observes that, in areas that were significantly occupied by minority ethnic populations, 'market renewal strategies' were explicitly linked to a community cohesion agenda that has been traced back to urban disturbances in several Northern English cities. These unrests gave rise to concerns that the largely Muslim Pakistani population living in these areas were living 'parallel lives' from the White population in the same area, and that there was a need to address ethnic segregation (Cantle, 2001). This framework, fixed on problematising 'race' issues and minority ethnic communities, blamed communities for patterns of residential segregation. Analysts have argued that the underlying factors that contributed to patterns of segregation were not acknowledged. For instance, structural constraints such as Islamophobia and the perception on the part of minority ethnic communities that racial harassment was more likely in certain geographical areas was not recognised (Phillips and Harrison, 2010; Netto and Abazie, 2012).

Analysis of statistical datasets has revealed many patterns of longstanding housing disadvantage, including that minority ethnic households were more likely to live in flats, maisonettes and bedsits and less likely to live in houses (Ratcliffe, 1997), and more likely to live in densely occupied housing and to lack exclusive use of the bath or WC (Owen, 1993). More recent research reveals that the disproportionate numbers of minority ethnic communities living in poor-quality and overcrowded housing have persisted (Phillips and Harrison, 2010; Netto et al, 2011). Research conducted by the think tank, the Human City Institute (Gulliver, 2016), confirms the persistent nature of BME disadvantage in housing. It should be noted that this is 30 years after the launch of the Black and Minority Ethnic Housing Strategy by the Housing Corporation in 1986. Key headline findings show the housing experiences for minority ethnic communities lag behind all other groups: they suffer from greater fuel poverty, overcrowding rates and are offered fewer opportunities to access social housing.

Trends in tenure patterns among minority ethnic households

As discussed earlier, one of the most important changes in the housing market in the UK is the shift towards owner-occupation. A comparison of statistical data between 1982 and 1994 in England found that rates of owner-occupation for all groups had increased, except for the Pakistani-origin population (Lakey, 1997). In an audit of Scotland-based research, Netto et al (2001) observed the identification of owner-occupation as the preferred option in a number of studies. However, the same studies have cautioned against a simplistic view of owner-occupation as a measure of upward mobility in the labour and housing markets, identifying 'reluctant' homeowners who had been forced to buy their homes due to fear or experience of racial harassment, lack of affordable, suitably sized accommodation for large households or a strong preference for a local area. Similarly, Harrison with Davis (2001) note that, although Indian and African Asian homeowners appear to have gained from investing in detached or semi-detached properties, 20% of Indian homeowners live in poor housing conditions, with many experiencing over-crowding (Phillip, 2006).

In terms of access to the social rented sector, Netto et al (2001) identified several areas of institutional discrimination against minority ethnic applicants in Scotland-based research, including allocation criteria such as waiting times and points for local connection to the area in which housing is sought, discretionary allocations procedures, as well as a failure to publicise vacancies. Encouragingly, more recent research conducted in England and Scotland indicated only a small amount of evidence that social housing providers may, unintentionally, discriminate against minority ethnic communities (Rutter and Latorre, 2009). It is likely that the Race

Relations Amendment Act 1976 and its Amendment (2000) increased awareness of the potential for discrimination through discretionary allocation processes and the need to counter this through ethnically monitoring and reviewing applicants and lets. More specifically, the Amendment placed a positive, enforceable duty on local authorities and registered social landlords to promote racial equality, and to produce and report on annual 'race' equality schemes. Although practice in this area is far from even, blatant discrimination appeared less likely to be evident.

The same study (Rutter and Latorre, 2009) also highlighted differential patterns of housing tenure between tenants born in the UK and those born overseas who had arrived in the UK in the last five years, with the latter being overwhelmingly housed in the private sector. This is consistent with a broader shift towards increased private renting. Contrary to much lurid press coverage of the issue, migrants to the UK in the last five years made up less than 2% of the total of those in social housing compared to the 90% of those who live in social housing who are UK-born. Of those who had migrated to the UK in the last five years, the majority were refugees who have been granted permission to remain in the UK. This highlights the need to counter common perceptions propagated by certain sections of the media that migrants displace UK-born citizens. Netto et al (2011) identify a number of approaches that can facilitate greater access to the social rented sector, including increasing the supply and appropriateness of housing, more effective communication between social housing providers and minority ethnic communities, and active engagement with voluntary organisations that work with these communities.

Phillips and Harrison's (2010) study reported that all the main minority ethnic groups were now well represented in the social rented sector. However, these gains in terms of equal access to housing appear to have been reversed by recent developments. Figures published by the Department for Communities and Local Government (DCLG, 2014) have revealed the proportion of new housing lets to minority ethnic communities has now declined. In that year, 16% of new social housing lets went to these communities compared to 17.3% in the previous year, despite an extra 17,763 lets. These figures represent a reversal of seven years of an increasing proportion of new lets going to minority ethnic households, taking the lettings to these communities to a similar level to that of 2010/11. New powers given by councils to change allocations policies and encouragement by the government to introduce local connection requirements may help to explain these changes. It is also likely that equal access to housing may be threatened by the recent introduction of 'right to rent' rules that prevent housing associations and private rented sector landlords from renting to people who do not have 'leave to remain' in the UK (Home Office, 2016). These rules may make landlords reluctant to rent to other migrants and encourage discriminatory behaviour. In the next section, we consider the sharp end of lack of access to accommodation, that is, homelessness.

Homelessness and extreme housing exclusion in minority ethnic communities

Research carried out by Gulliver (2016) has revealed that homelessness has risen rapidly for BME communities and sharpened in 'Austerity Britain'. As the report states:

> Homelessness has grown proportionately more for BME groups over the last two decades from 17 to 37 per cent of the total. (Gulliver, 2016, p 3)

However, despite the high profile that has been accorded to homelessness on the policy agenda, until relatively recently little attention has been paid to revealing the nature and extent of homelessness in minority ethnic communities (Harrison with Phillips, 2003). Netto's Scotland-based study (2006) identifies four main factors as contributing to homelessness in minority ethnic communities. These include changes in household formation as a result of having to leave the home of a relative or friend due to over-crowding, relationship breakdown, marital difficulties, intergenerational conflict and domestic abuse; financial difficulties due to low income, unemployment and lack of access to affordable housing; constrained housing options and loss of independent tenancies; and policies and legislation relating to the position of asylum-seekers and refugees and minority ethnic women escaping domestic violence. Consistent with other research (Gervais and Rehman, 2005), Netto et al (2006) found that, in contrast to homelessness in the majority population, problems associated with substance abuse were not a major contributory factor to homelessness in these communities, and that repeat homelessness was rare. However, hidden homelessness on an appreciable scale, as indicated by the overrepresentation of these communities in overcrowded and poor-quality housing, is evident (Netto et al, 2006). Worryingly, access to homelessness services by minority ethnic communities – including the finding and providing of accommodation services, advice giving on welfare benefits and facilitating access to employment – is typically problematic. Netto and Gavrielides (2010) have argued the case for closer cooperation between mainstream and minority ethnic agencies in addressing the barriers to accessing these services. Areas identified for closer partnership working include increasing awareness of homelessness services in these communities, widening access to early intervention, maintaining ongoing support to vulnerable individuals and informing policy development.

In addition, Netto et al (2015) have drawn attention to the situation of people facing extreme housing exclusion, that is, 'rooflessness', severe overcrowding or residing in very poor or insecure housing conditions, and who do not have access to state support. A key route into these circumstances includes a lack of eligibility for benefits or social housing for various categories of migrants who are not entitled to support from the state, including undocumented and economic migrants and asylum-seekers. Undocumented migrants, that is, migrants without any legal permission to be in the country of residence, from both EU and non-EU countries, have no recourse to public funds. Economic migrants from the EU are not entitled to access public funds or social housing in the first three months of their stay in Britain. Afterwards their entitlements depend on their situation (and may be none or very limited), but in general these have been eroded by recent legislative changes. Asylum-seekers who are fleeing war or political conflict in their countries of origin have no right to work and, in the process of claiming asylum in the UK, have limited support and are vulnerable to destitution. Refused asylum-seekers are especially vulnerable since they generally have no recourse to public funds; only under stringent conditions can they apply for very limited state support (Netto, 2017). However, their pressing housing needs remain and require responses.

In the next section we review the role of minority ethnic participation within the social housing sector in England. Specifically, we scrutinise the impact and outcomes of the Black and minority ethnic housing policies implemented by the Housing Corporation from 1986 to 2003. Of course, this is now over 10 years ago and seems historic. The Housing Corporation was replaced by the Homes and Communities Agency, and there was no separate new Black and minority ethnic housing policy after 2003. We suggest that there has been a substantial decline in the significance of issues related to minority ethnic communities.

We argue that, while the Housing Corporation's Policy was an innovative programme, its impact has been mixed, with few demonstrable outcomes. Instead, there has been a decline in the significance of issues related to minority ethnic communities in housing generally, and the role of Black and minority led-housing associations specifically. A number of reasons are put forward including changing macro policy priorities, organisational performance and regulatory focus. This suggests a need for organisations to reconfigure to meet new policy challenges.

A new discourse on 'race' and housing in the social rented sector

In 1986, 10 years after the Race Relations Act 1976, and five years after serious urban riots (see Benyon and Solomos, 1987), the Housing Corporation launched a Black and minority ethnic housing policy designed to 'encourage, run and create separate black run organisations as a channel for providing rented housing' (Harrison, 1995, p 88). The language was stark and contrasts with the current policy approach to equalities in its radicalism. The 1986 BME Housing Policy was about capacity building Black leadership and providing alternative sources of housing for minority communities. Implicit in this was the recognition that the so-called mainstream (or White-led) housing associations had not addressed the issue of race equality. The outcomes were dramatic. Direct and targeted investment by the Housing Corporation resulted in the registration of 44 BME housing associations. This was important for two reasons. Symbolically, these community-based organisations were given an opportunity to address housing and related disadvantage in minority communities. This was achieved by building new social housing and levering investment into neighbourhoods, which led to renewal. Practically, BME housing organisations created employment and management openings for minority activists as either employees or committee members.

A second five-year plan – *An independent future* – started in 1992 (Housing Corporation, 1992) and concentrated on making BME housing associations financially viable. One of the consequences of the Housing Act 1988 was enabling housing associations to get investment from the private sector to build and manage housing. This was problematic for BME housing associations. Since they were new organisations, they did not have sufficient time to accumulate the level of reserves needed to subsidise rents (Royce, 1996). Asset value, management capacity and governance were the key indicators taken into account by financiers. BME housing associations were viewed as high risk.

The final Housing Corporation policy – *An enabling framework* – from 1998 to 2003 was shaped by the desire to meet the need of minority consumers, irrespective of whether they were tenants of a BME housing association. To this end the focus was on meeting the needs of minority tenants of all housing associations:

> towards ensuring that the expectations of black and minority ethnic communities are achieved, whether through the provision of adequate social housing by the full-range of landlords (only some of which will be black-led) or through enabling members of the community to effectively participate in the delivery of services, through equality in the workplace, in management and in board membership. (Whitehead et al, 1998, p 5)

Improving governance and business performance rather than either consolidation or empowerment were the key watchwords from 1998.

It could be argued that the three policies show a declining significance of race/ethnicity as a result of three main factors. First, BME associations were small organisations and vulnerable to changes in policy and economic climate. The perception of high rents ensured the Housing Corporation regulatory spotlight was firmly placed on this sub-sector (Whitehead et al, 1998). Second, development costs became complex and expensive, requiring investment in human capital, partnership agreements and legal scrutiny. Third, equality legislation, combined with inspection by the Housing Corporation (latterly the Homes and

Communities Agency) and the Audit Commission, led to improved performance on these issues by the social housing sector as a whole. A debate developed on the added value given by BME housing associations (CIH, 2004). The wider challenges of race, communities and residence continue to be discussed by policy and academic communities (see Beider, 2009).

Declining interest in race and housing: the problem with regulation and representation

There are a number of problems with housing regulation and 'race' that follow from the policy discussion above. First, regulators have moved to accommodate 'race' within the much wider prism of equality and/or diversity. This parallels the direction from race relations to community cohesion and the Race Relations Act 1976 to the Equality Act 2010 respectively. It could be argued that the movement towards accommodating 'race' within the much wider lens of equalities was a signal that addressing racism is no longer important as a policy priority. Indeed, this has driven the complaints by many Black organisations against the all-embracing Equality and Human Rights Commission (EHRC), which replaced the Commission for Racial Equality in 2007. We are seeing a similar trend in the housing sector, with more resources and priority being afforded to non-race-equality areas by both the Housing Corporation and Audit Commission. For example, the Housing Corporation published a new Good Practice Note 8 on Equalities and Diversity that stressed the importance of housing associations dealing with wider issues other than 'race', such as disability and sexuality (Housing Corporation, 2004b). This followed an internal publication that significantly embraced the wider equality agenda in which 'race' is not mentioned specifically but seen within the context of other levels of disadvantage. A decade after the Macpherson Report (1999), it could be argued that the policy and regulatory regimes are challenging housing organisations less on 'race' equality and more on community cohesion (Home Office, 2001).

The inference is that 'race' equality should not be seen as an end itself, but merely as part of the wider landscape that helps to address the problems identified by the community cohesion report (Home Office, 2001). Macpherson called for institutional racism to be addressed and 'race' equality to be promoted while common norms and shared spaces were discussed as community cohesion (see Beider, 2012). Housing regulation has become all-embracing and less nuanced at a time when society in the UK is becoming more diverse and fragmented. The need is for specific regulatory interventions on minority housing issues, and yet relatively little has been said about the needs and aspirations of new migrants, who arguably have the greatest housing needs. Recent migration from Eastern Europe, Africa and the Middle East has changed the landscape for housing, 'race' and representation policy in England. Many 'new' BME communities have very little in common with 'old' BME communities from the Caribbean, India and Pakistan (Beider and Goodson, 2005).

There are a number of problems that need to be considered in adapting the framework for race and representation to respond to these societal changes. First, representation should take account of new barriers to involvement including language, expectations and awareness of institutions among newcomer communities. New groups may be excluded from being represented within housing institutions because of basic language barriers.

Second, the impact of change on 'old minorities' in the jostling for power and general community politics needs to be explicitly acknowledged. The perception that hard-won influence and resources will be diverted to 'new minorities' requires a careful response. Research has shown that some old communities (that is, established minority groups) are resistant to new communities (that is, refugees and asylum-seekers) accessing political networks and representation on local area-based committees (Beider, 2005). In some instances this could be viewed as 'recycled racism'. Old minorities are blaming new minorities for neighbourhood decline, and for placing pressures on public resources, for example, by requiring larger family housing. This was very much the way that racism manifested itself against migrants from the Caribbean and Indian subcontinent during the 1950s and 1960s. It could be argued that the new groups are perceived as the 'undeserving' poor. Housing regulation and policy discussion is reluctant to acknowledge and indeed understand these complex power-related conflicts. The focus on representation at one end and on building cohesive communities at the other misses important drivers for community change.

Third, the expectations placed on 'BME delegates' in representative models of involvement require reassessment. A singular representative cannot represent fragmented and complex communities from minority groups. Yet there is an implicit assumption within the housing regulatory literature that housing organisations should have a representative management committee and senior staff (Housing Corporation, 2002, 2004a). This could lead to tokenism of the worst type, where housing associations simply use their networks to identify an appropriate person from a minority group so as to tick the box marked 'diverse representation'. Moreover, empowering individuals rather than addressing racism and social justice leads to debates peppered with the terms of 'leaders' and 'community leaders' to refer to people who have typically been identified and selected by institutions to speak on behalf of communities. This is problematic as a means of fully engaging with communities. It is doubtful whether 'leaders' really represent the diverse groups that compose any community of interest (Mullins et al, 2004) since they may be out of touch with young people or women but are requested/put under pressure to speak on their behalf. More fundamentally, the discussion about community leaders is racialised, since there is seldom any discussion about 'community leaders' applying to discussion in White communities.

At the same time as these changes are taking place in policy and society, the social housing sector has also been changed by a process of rationalisation, merger and restructuring. There is a strong trend towards streamlining, reducing the size and number of committees and limiting formal local accountability arrangements. It is widely recognised that traditional forms of representation and governance are no longer fit for purpose (Future Shape of the Sector Commission, 2006). The move towards rationalisation has meant that many smaller associations are joining larger groups. This is especially evident within the specialist BME housing association sector, with very few continuing to exist as independent organisations. Instead, they are becoming part of larger housing associations, which results in concerns about the representation and engagement of minority groups; formal independence has been traded for the promise of wider influence, but the impact on accountability to minority communities is unresolved. The largest BME housing association collapsed because of governance and financial problems that shook the confidence in this sub-sector. The demise of the voice of BME housing, the Federation of Black Housing Organisations (FBHO) in 2008, deepened the sense of gloom (albeit a new representative body, BME National, replaced it in 2009).

Rationalisation may mark the end of the BME housing sector but the decline has been in place for a considerable period. Despite concerns about the performance of some Black-led housing associations, there is clear evidence that specialist support led to the emergence of new and important organisations that met the needs of BME communities and helped the social housing sector as a whole to improve performance (CIH, 2004). Moreover, the knowledge and professional skills provided by BME housing professionals permeated the wider housing sector, leading to greater racial and cultural awareness and opportunities for leadership of mainstream housing associations. This level of support will not be afforded to new groups, where there is evidence to suggest that housing needs are not being met by housing associations. Problems in awareness, understanding and engagement of new communities may not be easily resolved by housing associations (Markkanen, 2009). The concluding section of this chapter now considers policy initiatives and developments that offer some potential for improving the housing circumstances of minority ethnic communities.

Implications for housing strategies, policy and service delivery

Effective responses to minority ethnic communities need to be embedded within an overall policy context that eliminates unlawful discrimination and promotes racial equality and good race relations. *The code of practice for rented housing* produced by the Commission for Racial Equality (CRE, 1991) remains a useful source of reference. In England, Harrison with Phillips (2003) noted many signs of progress in measures taken to improve the housing circumstances of minority ethnic communities. These include an explicit commitment to racial equality by the UK government; guidance on the development of local authority strategies through consultation with minority ethnic organisations; more encouragement to take tougher action against racial harassment; and the role of the National Housing Inspection system in monitoring performance and change. More generally, there is a need for regulatory bodies to consider how the regulatory framework can be used to ensure compliance with the Equality and Human Rights Act 2010. The Act has provided further opportunities to increase understanding of equality law by bringing together different forms of anti-discriminatory legislation and making it easier to understand. However, commentators have argued that the commitment to tackling 'race' equality in housing, as in other areas, has been diluted within a broader equality context and, as other chapters note, the issue of 'race' has generally been downgraded.

Fair and transparent allocation of housing and the need for ongoing support

Fair and transparent allocation policies obviously continue to play an important role in ensuring equal access to housing for all sections of the population. Netto (2006) calls for allocation policies to give more weight to hidden homelessness in minority ethnic communities and to recognise fear of racial harassment as a major deterrent to living in certain areas, thus narrowing housing options. In a study on refugee pathways to housing, settlement and support in Glasgow, Netto and Abazie (2012) acknowledge the challenges faced by housing providers in allocating housing to refugees in perceived safe areas given the limited stock available in the city, but argue that more can be done to reduce the gap between policies and procedures for tackling racial harassment, and the experience of refugees living in these areas. In order to ensure that minority ethnic communities are not intentionally or inadvertently discriminated against, Blackaby and Chahal (2000, p 90) suggest that a number of areas in the allocations process should be ethnically monitored, including the proportions of ethnic groups that are offered and let dwellings; comparisons of waiting time between different groups; and whether there are differences between ethnic groups in terms of why offers are refused, including refusals on the grounds of fear of racial harassment.

Choice-based lettings (CBL) approaches in which social landlords advertise homes for let and applicants take the initiative in bidding for vacancies offer greater transparency than discretionary procedures. Such approaches have the potential for individuals from minority ethnic communities to achieve better outcomes than traditional allocation policies since they place house-seekers rather than housing officers in the driving seat, reducing the possibility that an applicant may be made an 'inappropriate offer' (for example, in an area that may be perceived to be unsafe for individuals from minority ethnic communities). The results of evaluative studies of CBL systems have been encouraging in terms of increased interest from minority ethnic communities (Pawson et al, 2006). However, such schemes are not likely to be equally accessible to all sections of the population, and may hinder the ability of those who lack access to computing facilities, have literacy issues or are not fluent enough in English to make bids within the time frame allowed. The effectiveness of such schemes in ensuring more equitable outcomes for minority ethnic communities (as well as other vulnerable groups) is therefore reliant on the incorporation of specific support services that will ensure accessibility for all minority ethnic communities.

Monitoring of homelessness services

There is a clear need for regulatory bodies such as the Homelessness Directorate to set well-defined expectations of the monitoring of service provision. With particular reference to ensuring that an equitable service is provided to homeless applicants from minority ethnic communities, Blackaby and Chahal (2000, p 69) suggest monitoring aspects of service provision by undertaking:

- a breakdown of the ethnic origins of people seeking advice and information, compared to a breakdown of the ethnic origin of households in the local area;
- a comparison of the ethnic origins of people applying as homeless, accepted as homeless and accommodated in various types of housing – hostels, bed and breakfast and permanent accommodation; and
- a comparison between the various ethnic groups of the length of time homeless people spend in temporary accommodation.

In addition, given the radical cutting back of the welfare net, increased pressure on homelessness services in the UK and extreme housing exclusion, Netto et al (2015) argue that further consideration needs to be given to learning from international contexts. In a study involving country-based experts in 11 developed and developing countries, a number of innovative lessons are identified for increasing housing supply, including better use of empty properties; new forms of housing design for high-quality, more affordable, permanent and temporary housing; and encouraging the development of community-based communal housing solutions and community self-build. The study also considers what would have to change in the UK in order for these approaches to be implemented.

Future of Black-led housing organisations

In the last section we reviewed the rise and decline of the Black-led housing sector in parallel to macro-policy intervention. The role of the Housing Corporation's BME housing policies from 1986 to 2003, the publication and positive impact of the Macpherson Report in 1999 and finally, the emergence of community cohesion following the riots in 2001 have informed this debate. As discussed, the emphasis on community cohesion has contributed to a period of stagnation and decline for the Black-led housing sector. A rigid determination to focus on similarities between communities and an emphasis on common norms and shared public spaces inevitably raised concerns about the value of housing associations that not only described themselves as 'Black', but were rooted in the anti-racist struggles of the past. At a stroke, Black-led housing organisations became out of step with mainstream policy and began to look dated. Macro policy has played an important role in the development and decline of the Black-led housing sector. However, it has also been argued that the decline of the Black-led housing sector cannot be simply blamed on the problematic nature of community cohesion policy. Recent flaws in governance have been documented by research and in the housing media. A successful future for Black-led housing associations could lie in returning to their origin and rise, that is, as community-based organisations that advocated for greater investment in a range of public service areas. In this way Black-led housing associations could use their considerable experience of organisational change, accessing private finance and leadership skills to influence public policy change. Given the shift in the direction of policy and politics signalled by the previous coalition and the current Conservative governments, emphasising localism, entrepreneurism and working on housing, as well as other policy domains, may lead to the emergence of a new type of Black-led housing association, but this time without any clear level of political or financial support from government.

Moving ahead, those organisations committed to addressing the issues of equity in housing need to focus on meeting the needs of established and emerging minority communities, the latter even more so given the scale of the 'crisis' of migrants coming to Europe since 2015. Moreover, the hostile political atmosphere surrounding the issues of immigration leading up to the 2016 EU referendum demonstrates that the issues of race and difference are highly combustible. Brexit means that BME housing associations – rooted in awareness of diverse communities and neighbourhoods and a tradition of campaigning for 'race' equality – should be well positioned to capitalise on meeting new housing needs, considering alternative responses and raising the profile of 'race' equality in housing in partnership with other housing organisations.

Conclusion

Although some progress has been made in tackling the housing disadvantage experienced by minority ethnic communities in the UK, it is clear that serious challenges remain. The political environment has deteriorated since the first BME strategy was launched in 1986 and the publication of the Macpherson Report into the murder of Stephen Lawrence in 1999. 'Race' has been weakened as a public policy priority with the rise of community cohesion and integration by successive governments. Positive interventions on meeting the needs of minority communities has also been severely curtailed by an increasingly toxic debate on migration, which reached its nadir with the vote to leave the EU in 2016. The Grenfell fire in 2017 shows that minority and poor communities continue to be located in very poor housing nearly 20 years after the Macpherson Report addressed the problem of institutional racism. Addressing housing inequalities – including the disproportionate numbers of minority ethnic groups who experience homelessness – involves a sound understanding of the broader social inequalities that they face, and appreciation of the diversity within these communities at the local level. Evidence-based policy-making and the political will to tackle racial inequalities and discrimination in housing is urgently needed.

Questions for discussion

- What are the main patterns of housing disadvantage experienced by minority ethnic communities?
- What are the main causes of homelessness in minority ethnic communities? How can homelessness in these communities be reduced or prevented?
- What are the factors that have contributed to the rise and fall of black-led housing associations?

Further reading

Cabinet Office (2017) 'Race Disparity Audit' (www.gov.uk/government/publications/race-disparity-audit). This briefing of a wide-ranging audit reveals how people from different ethnic backgrounds are treated in key policy areas, including housing.

EHRC (Equality and Human Rights Commission) (2017) *Following Grenfell: The human rights and equality dimension* (https://equalityhumanrights.com/sites/default/files/following-grenfell-the-human-rights-and-equality-dimension.pdf). This reports on what the EHRC is doing following the fire at Grenfell Tower, which led to the deaths of 70 people, including many people from minority ethnic groups. It highlights the importance of access to safe, adequate and affordable housing for all vulnerable groups.

Finney, N. and Harris, B. (2013) 'Understanding ethnic inequalities in housing: Analysis of the 2011 Census', *Health & Place*, 46, 82-90 (https://www.sciencedirect.com/science/article/pii/S135382921630226X). This paper analyses key ethnic inequalities in housing, including recent trends relating to tenure and ethnicity, based on census data.

GLA (Greater London Authority) (2013) *Trends in housing tenure* (https://files.datapress.com/london/dataset/2011-census-housing/2015-11-03T11:21:36/CIS2013-06%20Trends%20in%20Housing%20Tenure.pdf). This briefing tracks tenure changes in London's housing stock, including a focus on ethnicity, based on three sets of census data.

Markannen, S. and Harrison, M. (2012) '"Race", deprivation and the research agenda: Revisiting housing, ethnicity and neighbourhoods', *Housing Studies*, 28(3), 409-28. This article explores the connections between UK ethnic relations and housing neighbourhoods.

Netto, G., Fitzpatrick, S., Sosenko, F. and Smith, H. (2015) *International lessons on tackling extreme housing exclusion* (www.jrf.org.uk/report/international-lessons-tackling-extreme-housing-exclusion). This report brings together lessons from a study of 11 countries to reveal innovative approaches to tackling the housing exclusion of vulnerable groups.

References

Beider, H. (2005) 'Housing, social capital and integration', Paper presented to ENHR Conference, Reykjavik, 29 June–3 July.

Beider, H. (2009) 'Guest Introduction: Rethinking race and housing', *Housing Studies*, 24(4), 405–15.

Beider, H. (2012) *Housing, race and community cohesion*, Oxford: Wiley–Blackwell.

Beider, H. and Goodson, L. (2005) *Black and minority ethnic communities in the Eastern Corridor: Aspirations, neighbourhood 'choice' and tenure*, Birmingham: Birmingham City Council.

Benyon, J. and Solomos, J. (eds) (1987) *The roots of urban unrest*, Oxford: Pergamon Press.

Blackaby, B. and Chahal, K. (2000) *Black and minority ethnic housing strategies: A good practice guide*, London: Chartered Institute of Housing, Federation of Black Housing Organisations and the Housing Corporation.

Cantle, T. (2001) *Community cohesion: A report of the Independent Review Team*, London: Home Office.

Chahal, K. (2000) *Ethnic diversity, neighbourhoods and housing*, York: Joseph Rowntree Foundation.

CIH (Chartered Institute of Housing) (2004) *The future of BME housing associations*, Coventry: CIH.

CRE (Commission for Racial Equality) (1991) *The code of practice for rented housing*, London: CRE.

DCLG (Department for Communities and Local Government) (2014) *Annual report and accounts 2014-15* (www.gov.uk/government/publications/dclg-annual-report-and-accounts-2014-to-2015).

Edgar, B. (2004) *Policy measures to ensure access to decent housing for migrants and ethnic minorities*, University of Dundee and University of St Andrews, Joint Centre for Scottish Research Universities of Dundee and St Andrews.

Future Shape of the Sector Commission (2006) *Working brief*, London: London and Quadrant Group.

Gervais, M. and Rehman, H. (2005) *Causes of homelessness amongst ethnic minority populations*, London: Department for Communities and Local Government.

Gulliver, K. (2016) *Forty years of struggle: A window on race and housing, disadvantage and exclusion*, Birmingham: Human City Institute.

Harrison, M. (1995) *Housing, 'race', social policy and empowerment*, Aldershot: Avebury.

Harrison, M. with Davis, C. (2001) *Housing, social policy and difference: Disability, gender, ethnicity and housing*, Bristol: Policy Press.

Harrison, M. with Phillips, D. (2003) *Housing and black and minority ethnic communities: Review of the evidence base*, London: Office of the Deputy Prime Minister.

Home Office (2001) *Community cohesion: A report of the independent reviewing team*, London: HMSO.

Home Office (2016) *Code of practice on illegal immigrants and private rented housing* (www.gov.uk/government/publications/right-to-rent-landlords-code-of-practice/code-of-practice-on-illegal-immigrants-and-private-rented-accommodation-for-tenancies-starting-on-or-after-1-february-2016).

Housing Corporation (1992) *An independent future: Black and minority ethnic housing association strategy 1992-1996*, London: Housing Corporation.

Housing Corporation (2002) *Regulatory code, Good practice note*, London: Housing Corporation.

Housing Corporation (2004a) *BME association rent restructuring grant announced*, London: The Housing Corporation.

Housing Corporation (2004b) *Regulatory code, Good practice note*, London: Housing Corporation.

Lakey, J. (1997) 'Neighbourhoods and housing', in T. Modood and R. Berthoud with J. Lakey, J. Nazroo, P. Smith, S. Virdee and S. Beishon, *Ethnic minorities in Britain: Diversity and disadvantage*, London: Policy Studies Institute, 184-223.

Low Pay Commission (2013) *National Minimum Wage*, Low Pay Commission Report, Cm 8565, London: The Stationery Office (www.gov.uk/government/publications/national-minimum-wage-low-pay-commission-report-2013).

Macpherson, Sir W. (1999) *The Stephen Lawrence inquiry*, London: HMSO.

Markkanen, S. (2009) *Looking to the future: Changing black and minority ethnic housing needs and aspirations*, London: Race Equality Foundation.

Mullins, D., Beider, H. and Rowlands, R. (2004) *Empowering communities, improving housing: Involving black and minority ethnic tenants and communities*, London: Office of the Deputy Prime Minister.

Netto, G. (2006) 'Vulnerability to homelessness: Use of services and homelessness prevention in Black and minority ethnic communities', *Housing Studies*, 21(4), 581-603.

Netto, G. (2017) Written submission, Equality and Human Rights Committee, Scottish Parliament Inquiry into Destitution, Asylum and Insecure Immigration Status in Scotland (www.parliament.scot/parliamentarybusiness/Current Committees/103215.aspx).

Netto, G. and Abazie, H. (2012) 'Racial harassment in the social rented sector: The case for a community development approach', *Urban Studies*, 50(4), 674-90.

Netto, G. and Gavrielides, T. (2010) *Linking black and minority ethnic organisations with mainstream homeless service providers*, Better Housing Briefing 15, London: Race Equality Foundation.

Netto, G., Sosenko, F. and Bramley, G. (2011) *A review of poverty and ethnicity in Scotland*, York: Joseph Rowntree Foundation (www.jrf.org.uk/publications/review-poverty-and-ethnicity-scotland).

Netto, G., Fitzpatrick, S., Sosenko, F. and Smith, H. (2015) *International lessons on tackling extreme housing exclusion*, York: Joseph Rowntree Foundation (www.jrf.org.uk/report/international-lessons-tackling-extreme-housing-exclusion).

Netto, G., Arshad, R., deLima, P., Almeida Diniz, F., MacEwen, M., Patel, V. and Syed, R. (2001) *Audit of research on minority ethnic issues in Scotland from a 'race' perspective*, Edinburgh: Scottish Executive.

Owen, D. (1993) *Ethnic minorities in Great Britain: Housing and family characteristics*, 1991 Census, Statistical Paper 4, National Ethnic Minority Data Archive, Centre for Research in Ethnic Relations, Warwick: University of Warwick.

Pawson, H., Donohoe, A., Jones, C., Watkins, D., Fancy, C., Netto, G., et al (2006) *Monitoring the longer-term impact of choice-based lettings*, London: Department for Communities and Local Government (https://researchportal.hw.ac.uk/en/publications/monitoring-the-longer-term-impact-of-choice-based-lettings).

Phillips, D. (2002) *Movement to opportunity? South Asian relocation in Northern cities*, End of Award Report, Economic Social and Research Council R000238038, Leeds: School of Geography, University of Leeds.

Phillips, D. and Harrison, M. (2010) 'Constructing an integrated society: Historical lessons for tackling black and minority ethnic housing segregation in Britain', *Housing Studies*, 25(2), 221-37.

Platt, L. (2007) *Poverty and ethnicity in the UK*, Bristol: Policy Press.

Ratcliffe, P. (1997) '"Race," ethnicity and housing differentials in Britain', in V. Karn (ed) *Ethnicity in the 1991 Census, Volume 4: Employment, education and housing among the ethnic minority populations of Britain*, London: The Stationery Office.

Royce, C. (1996) *Financing Black and minority ethnic housing associations*, York: Joseph Rowntree Foundation.

Rutter, J. and Latorre, M. (2009) *Social housing allocation and immigrant communities*, Manchester: Equality and Human Rights Commission.

SEU (Social Exclusion Unit) (2000) *Minority ethnic issues in social exclusion and neighbourhood renewal*, London: Cabinet Office.

Simpson, L. (2004) 'Statistics of racial segregation: Measures, evidence and policy', *Urban Studies*, 41(3), 661–81.

Third, H., Wainwright, S. and Pawson, H. (1997) *Constraint and choice for minority ethnic home owners in Scotland*, Edinburgh: Scottish Homes.

Whitehead, C., Marshall, D., Royce, C., Saw, P. and Woodrow, J. (1998) *A level playing field? Rents, viability and value in BME housing associations*, York: Joseph Rowntree Foundation.

8

Understanding the influence of ethnicity on health

Saffron Karlsen, Marilyn Roth and Laia Bécares

Overview

There is substantial evidence identifying marked ethnic inequalities across different measures of health and mortality. By highlighting examples of ethnic inequalities in health and explaining the drivers of these inequities, this chapter provides an understanding of the inter-relationships between minority ethnic status and structural factors, thereby emphasising the value of an intersectional approach. This chapter:

- presents evidence on the patterning of health across different ethnic groups;
- outlines different approaches to analysing the relationships between ethnicity and health;
- establishes how different analytical approaches shape our understanding of ethnic inequalities; and
- explains how social structures influence health experience.

Key concepts
ethnic density; social exclusion; racist victimisation; social identification

Introduction

There is compelling evidence regarding the health disadvantage experienced by many, although not all, people from minority ethnic groups living in the UK (see Nazroo, 2001; Sproston and Mindell, 2006; Bécares, 2015), Europe and elsewhere, including the USA (Williams, 2001), Latin America (Pan American Health Organization, 2001), South Africa (Sidiropoulos et al, 1997), Australia (McLennan and Madden, 1999) and New Zealand (Harris et al, 2006). This disadvantage persists for adults and children (Panico and Kelly, 2007), and across many indicators of morbidity and mortality (Salway et al, 2010).

Table 8.1 presents ethnic inequalities in a range of health indicators using data from the Health Survey for England (HSE) 2004 (Sproston and Mindell, 2006). Despite being over a decade old – and with no comparable data collected since – HSE 2004 remains the most comprehensive source with which to examine the health of different ethnic populations in England. For example, the 'Ethnicity Facts and Figures' website (www.ethnicity-facts-figures.service.gov.uk) presents the latest government data available with which to examine these issues, but no information on ethnic variations in physical health. Table 8.1 compares the likelihood of people with different ethnicities experiencing different forms of poor health, with the relative likelihood, or risk, of experiencing poor health among the wider (or general) population. The risk of the general population is set at 1 to make it easier to establish the differences between the groups. Those groups that have a risk greater than 1 have a risk of poor health greater than that of the general population, while those with risks below 1 have a risk of poor health lower than that of the general population.

The figure in brackets shown for each minority ethnic category is the standard error. This is used to establish whether any difference between this group and the general population is large enough to be statistically significant (and not simply driven by sampling issues affecting the findings).

There are some similarities in the likelihood of experiencing certain health outcomes between different minority ethnic groups. For example, Indian, Pakistani and Bangladeshi men and women and Black Caribbean women have between two-and-a-half and five-and-a-half times the risk of diabetes when compared to their counterparts in the general population. By contrast, men in several minority ethnic groups (Indian, Pakistani, Bangladeshi and Chinese) have a significantly lower risk of obesity than men in the general population. Certain ethnic groups appear to be at greater risk than the general population on a number of health indicators. Pakistani and Bangladeshi people have greater risk of poor health than the general population on almost all of the measures examined, although the size of risk (and the extent to which this difference is statistically significant) varies by health outcome.

While the differences in the health experiences of people with different ethnicities are well established, evidence gaps remain. Population projections (which use existing data to estimate the nature of future populations) suggest that Bangladeshi and Pakistani men and women have lower expected life expectancies at birth and greater risk of persistent disability compared with other ethnic groups (Wohland et al, 2015). However, we have little actual data on ethnic differences in mortality rates to see if these projections are correct (Salway et al, 2010a). There are also groups under-represented in statistics, including new migrant groups, such as White minorities, Gypsies and Travellers, and asylum-seekers

Table 8.1: Age-standardised[a] risk ratios for specific health outcomes, by minority ethnic group and gender

	Bad/very bad self-reported health	Limiting longstanding illness	GHQ12 score 4 or more	Any CVD	Diabetes	BMI over 30 (obese)	Raised waist:hip ratio	Hypertension
				Relative risks (standard errors)[b]				
Men								
General population[c]	1.00 (6%)	1.00 (23%)	1.00 (11%)	1.00 (14%)	1.00 (4%)	1.00 (23%)	1.00 (33%)	1.00 (32%)
Black Caribbean	1.37 (0.37)	1.00 (0.14)	1.21 (0.22)	0.73 (0.17)	2.05 (0.54)	1.03 (0.15)	**0.73 (0.13)**	1.37 (0.19)
Black African	0.81 (0.25)	**0.63 (0.12)**	0.88 (0.17)	**0.25 (0.10)**	1.98 (0.60)	0.79 (0.14)	0.77 (0.18)	1.21 (0.22)
Indian	1.45 (0.27)	1.12 (0.12)	**1.32 (0.19)**	0.91 (0.15)	**2.86 (0.43)**	**0.60 (0.08)**	1.15 (0.11)	1.15 (0.13)
Pakistani	**2.33 (0.42)**	1.17 (0.14)	**1.56 (0.28)**	1.28 (0.24)	**2.72 (0.54)**	**0.76 (0.12)**	**1.46 (0.13)**	0.98 (0.19)
Bangladeshi	**3.77 (0.55)**	**1.52 (0.15)**	**1.83 (0.35)**	0.16 (0.69)	**3.87 (0.78)**	**0.22 (0.05)**	**1.34 (0.16)**	**0.63 (0.14)**
Chinese	0.75 (0.20)	**0.57 (0.10)**	0.76 (0.15)	**0.58 (0.14)**	1.29 (0.36)	**0.26 (0.06)**	**0.66 (0.13)**	0.78 (0.13)
Irish	1.41 (0.33)	1.11 (0.13)	1.08 (0.21)	1.16 (0.22)	0.67 (0.22)	1.07 (0.15)	0.98 (0.12)	1.13 (0.18)
Women								
General population[c]	1.00 (7%)	1.00 (27%)	1.00 (15%)	1.00 (13%)	1.00 (3%)	1.00 (23%)	1.00 (30%)	1.00 (29%)
Black Caribbean	**1.90 (0.31)**	1.20 (0.11)	1.27 (0.17)	0.89 (0.13)	**3.03 (0.49)**	**1.43 (0.13)**	**1.42 (0.14)**	**1.58 (0.19)**
Black African	1.68 (0.36)	0.83 (0.11)	1.19 (0.19)	0.83 (0.24)	1.80 (0.61)	**2.00 (0.17)**	**1.64 (0.23)**	1.71 (0.37)
Indian	1.39 (0.24)	0.86 (0.09)	0.99 (0.13)	**0.72 (0.12)**	**2.46 (0.46)**	0.89 (0.08)	1.15 (0.11)	0.91 (0.12)
Pakistani	**3.54 (0.49)**	**1.60 (0.14)**	**1.73 (0.24)**	0.93 (0.16)	**5.32 (0.87)**	**1.48 (0.14)**	**1.77 (0.16)**	1.01 (0.18)
Bangladeshi	**4.02 (0.57)**	**1.22 (0.11)**	1.37 (0.23)	0.83 (0.18)	**3.20 (0.77)**	0.89 (0.12)	**2.29 (0.17)**	1.43 (0.22)
Chinese	**0.55 (0.20)**	**0.46 (0.08)**	0.83 (0.15)	**0.56 (0.15)**	1.72 (0.48)	**0.32 (0.07)**	1.00 (0.16)	1.12 (0.20)
Irish	0.74 (0.19)	**0.80 (0.09)**	0.95 (0.13)	0.83 (0.14)	0.84 (0.24)	0.88 (0.10)	**1.27 (0.13)**	0.95 (0.14)

Notes:

[a] Age standardisation was conducted separately for men and women: expressing male data to the overall male population and female data to the overall female population. No age standardisation has been introduced to remove the effects of the different age distributions of men and women. This should be borne in mind when comparing data for men and women.

[b] The figures in bold show differences that are statistically significant.

[c] Standardised risk ratio and observed prevalence are displayed for the general population.

Source: HSE 2004; general population figures from HSE 2003

and refugees. Evidence collected during the 2011 England and Wales Census suggests that White Gypsy and Irish Traveller groups experience considerable health disadvantages, even when compared with Bangladeshi and Pakistani people (Bécares, 2015). More detailed work is needed to explain why these occur (see also Chapter 5, this volume).

We now present an overview of evidence regarding the different explanations of these ethnic health inequalities. Assumptions about the nature of ethnic inequalities affect the ways in which research is conducted. This informs our understanding of how and why these patterns emerge, and the policies developed to address them (see Chapter 2, this volume).

Understanding the drivers of ethnic inequalities in health and disease

It is important to consider the centrality of racism to any attempt to explain ethnic inequalities in health. Not only are personal experiences of racism and harassment likely to influence health, but racism as a social force will also play a central role in structuring the social and economic disadvantage faced by minority ethnic groups: 'a racism that has its roots in colonial history' (Nazroo, 2003, p 282).

Theoretical explanations justifying particular approaches to the investigation of ethnic health inequalities have tended to focus either on genetic/biological or cultural/behavioural differences between groups, or on the social processes that produce and perpetuate the social disadvantage experienced disproportionately by people with minority ethnic backgrounds and the consequences these have for their health (see Chapter 10, this volume). Ethnic groups are social constructs that vary across time and place and are generally poor proxies for genetic markers (Mukherjee, 2016). There is great variation in the extent to which certain genetic traits are concentrated among particular ethnic groups, and in how these might impact on their health experience. Despite this, research investigating ethnic health inequalities has often emphasised genetic/biological explanations over those that describe more structural influences (Graves and Rose, 2006; see also Chapter 7, this volume). Indeed, approaches used to classify individuals into ethnic categories often rely on genetic markers (such as skin colour) or ancestral location (whose environmental factors also affect genes), encouraging recourse to 'genetic' explanations with little theoretical reflection on the limitations of this 'evidence' (Morning, 2014).

We consider racism as having a central role in the development of ethnic inequalities in health, which influences health directly and encourages the perpetuation of social disadvantage (which subsequently affects health). We also argue, however, that while approaches exploring genetic/biological, cultural/ behavioural and social/structural factors have traditionally been considered unrelated and even competing, there are ways in which they reflect similar structural processes of social exclusion and mistreatment, which affect both the circumstances of people's lives and approaches to health research and policy development. This highlights the value of adopting more intersectional approaches, which explore the potential interrelationships between different dimensions of discrimination and disadvantage.

We begin by examining the evidence exploring the health implications of socioeconomic disadvantage and victimisation, which is experienced disproportionately by people with minority ethnic backgrounds in the UK and elsewhere. We then discuss how examining other influences on ethnic health inequalities can improve our understanding of the impact of structural disadvantage on the lives of people with minority ethnic backgrounds. Finally, we explore the additional insights offered by more creative theoretical approaches to the investigation of the relationships between ethnicity and health.

Structural components of ethnic differences in health: socioeconomic disadvantage

There is a large body of research exposing the health consequences of poor socioeconomic status (Marmot Review, 2010). Given the concentration of many people with minority ethnicities in socioeconomic disadvantage (Karlsen and Pantazis, 2017; see also Chapters 5, 9 and 10, this volume), it is not surprising that this has been found to be an important driver of ethnic health inequalities among both adults (Nazroo, 2003) and children (Kelly et al, 2008). Yet, analytical approaches often treat these structural forces as issues that *disguise* the explanations of these inequalities rather than as explanations in their own right. This is done implicitly, when statistical models exploring the relationship between ethnicity and health are 'adjusted' to remove the effects of socioeconomic status, in the expectation that this will uncover this important 'ethnic' effect. Unfortunately, such approaches rarely demonstrate either theoretically or empirically what the remaining 'ethnic' effect in a model might be (Nazroo, 1998). As a consequence, ethnicity is treated as an essentialised 'risk' factor with innate characteristics that inevitably produce poor health and higher mortality, without reflection on the processes producing these effects and the broader contextual factors that influence them.

Such models also assume that inclusion in a particular socioeconomic category has similar implications for people regardless of ethnicity. However, empirical evidence suggests that this is often not the case, with people with minority ethnicities more disadvantaged than White people, even within the same socioeconomic bands (Karlsen and Pantazis, 2017). For example, within each occupational band, people from minority ethnic groups are often on less prestigious occupational grades with lower incomes, poorer job security, less social working hours and more stressful working conditions, all of which have been shown to independently affect health (see Marmot Review, 2010). There is evidence that unemployed people in minority ethnic groups have on average been unemployed for longer than their White counterparts, and a higher proportion of Pakistani and Bangladeshi households are lacking one or more basic household amenities compared with those in other ethnic groups, regardless of their housing tenure. Strikingly, Pakistani and Bangladeshi people in the highest occupational category have been found to have average weekly incomes similar to that of White people in the lowest occupational category (Nazroo, 2001).

The use of such measures, therefore, cannot completely remove the socioeconomic differences between these different ethnic groups. These approaches simply encourage researchers to *think* that they have done so and that any ethnic difference remaining is due to 'something else', which is usually assumed to be something related to cultural, behavioural or biological factors innate to particular minority ethnic populations. The use of more sensitive measures of social position suggest a much greater role for socioeconomic status in generating ethnic inequalities in health than has previously been acknowledged (Karlsen et al, 2012).

The socioeconomic disadvantage experienced by people with minority ethnicities has a significant impact on their health. This disadvantage reflects particular histories of migration, an associated lack of social and cultural capital to seek jobs in the labour market (see Chapters 2 and 3, this volume) and experiences of exclusion, victimisation and racialisation. The residential concentration of people from minority ethnic groups in neighbourhoods with greater socioeconomic disadvantage (Jivraj and Khan, 2015) has also been described as one of the mechanisms by which racism operates to restrict their lives, as a social manifestation of both individual prejudices and institutional discrimination (Acevedo, 2000). While the particular manifestation of the processes changes over time (and is experienced in different ways for different groups), the effects of earlier, negative experiences tend to persist. These issues therefore remain pertinent for both more recent and older migrants. More recently, empirical evidence has examined more directly other ways in which racism can influence the health experiences of people from different ethnic backgrounds.

Structural components of ethnic differences in health: racist victimisation

Evidence from the UK, USA and elsewhere indicates that racism is experienced in a number of ways and has a significant impact on adults' and children's mental and physical health (Harris et al, 2006; Mohseni and Lindström, 2008; Priest et al, 2013; Paradies et al, 2015). Racism has been found to affect health directly, through the negative physical and psychological consequences of interpersonal racist, verbal or physical violence (Karlsen and Nazroo, 2002a), or through living in fear of such incidents (Karlsen and Nazroo, 2004). Prejudice, via institutional racism, also justifies the social and economic disadvantage in which minority ethnic people are concentrated, which subsequently impacts on health (see Chapter 3, this volume). These various manifestations of racist harassment and discrimination have been shown to have separate effects on health (Karlsen and Nazroo, 2002a; see also Chapter 10, this volume).

Long-term exposure to racism and a devalued status has been found to damage self-esteem, invalidate self-worth and block aspirations (Krieger, 2000). It may shape the content and frequency of stressful life events and may limit the range of feasible responses to them, in addition to the social support available. Associations have been reported between experiences of interpersonal racism and health behaviours such as smoking, problematic alcohol use and being overweight (Shariff-Marco et al, 2010). Racism in healthcare and other statutory services is associated with delayed screening for prostate cancer (Shariff-Marco et al, 2010); poor self-rated health, physical functioning, mental health; and smoking and symptoms of cardiovascular disease (Harris et al, 2006). Racism experienced in child or young adulthood is associated with higher rates of cigarette smoking, alcohol use and illicit drug use, and lower healthcare utilisation and greater dissatisfaction with any healthcare received (Priest et al, 2013). Growing up in a racist environment – where children's neighbours and family members frequently report experiences of racism – is also detrimental to children's socioemotional and cognitive development (Kelly et al, 2013; Bécares et al, 2015).

An individual's responses to their experiences of victimisation and social exclusion directly influences their health. Positive, action-orientated responses – where people challenge or report their experiences – are less damaging than more negative and emotion-focused forms of coping such as ignoring the problem or taking psychoactive substances (Noh and Kaspar, 2003). Such responses are clearly related to people's opportunities do so.

Establishing the role of racism in shaping ethnic inequalities in health is hindered by problems of measurement (Karlsen and Nazroo, 2017). Recognition of reportable incidents of racism is not straightforward. Moreover, some coping mechanisms might actually discourage acknowledgement of these experiences (Ruggiero and Taylor, 1995). Racism can also be subtle, making it less easy to identify. While racism is considered to generate and perpetuate the socioeconomic disadvantage experienced disproportionately by many people with minority ethnicities, direct evidence of such victimisation is difficult to establish. These issues have obvious implications for the collection of empirical evidence.

Moreover, the relationships between such structural inequality and health are not straightforward. The role of 'ethnic density' in explaining health outcomes demonstrates this. The poverty associated with many localities with increased levels of minority ethnic concentration has a negative impact on health. Yet areas with higher concentrations of minority ethnic residents, or particular ethnic density, have also been shown to have protective effects on their residents' physical and mental health (Das-Munshi et al, 2010; Bécares et al, 2012, 2014; Bécares, 2014). The 'ethnic density effect' suggests that the enhanced mutual social support and stronger sense of community and belongingness offered by living in close proximity to others with the same ethnic background as oneself can limit, or protect against, the direct and indirect health consequences of racism (Bécares et al, 2009) and the stigma associated with lower socioeconomic status (Pickett and Wilkinson, 2008).

Figure 8.1 shows the likelihood of reporting poor health for minority ethnic people who report interpersonal racism relative to those who live in areas with similar levels of ethnic density but did not report such experiences. Experiences of racism had the highest health effect in areas with the highest levels of ethnic density for Caribbean people (shown by the gradual increase in the black line). However, a (non-significant) protective effect of ethnic density can be observed for Bangladeshi, Indian and Pakistani people, for whom the detrimental association between experienced discrimination and poor health is smaller at higher levels of ethnic density, shown by the gradual downward slope of the other lines in the figure (Bécares et al, 2009).

Strong empirical evidence supports the critical role of structural and social factors in the development of ethnic health inequalities, despite the limitations inherent in the methodological approaches often used to investigate them. We now describe how recognition of the behavioural influences on ethnic health inequalities – evidence that has traditionally been considered to disprove the significance of social/structural factors – is affected by the methods adopted to investigate them, which may mask the structural factors that influence them.

Cultural components of ethnic inequalities in health and disease

Research and policy initiatives frequently draw attention to the health implications of people's 'traditional' lifestyles. Such lifestyles may protect health, through the opportunities for improved access to social support, socio-communal engagement or access to economic and other resources offered by close religious or other cultural networks (Roth and Kobayashi, 2008; Salway et al, 2010a). However, historically research approaches have largely focused on 'traditional' cultures as the *cause* of poor health outcomes (as discussed in Chapter 2, this volume).

Empirical evidence suggests that there is great variation in the extent to which individuals adopt particular health-related behaviours (such as smoking), *within* as well as *between* ethnic groups. Table 8.2 presents ethnic inequalities in a range of health-related behaviours, using the same method as Table 8.1. These figures show how understandings of the health consequences of minority ethnic cultures or lifestyles varies dramatically according to the indicator used, including for

Figure 8.1: Association between racism and poor self-rated health at varying levels of own-ethnic density among people who have experienced racism, relative to those who have not

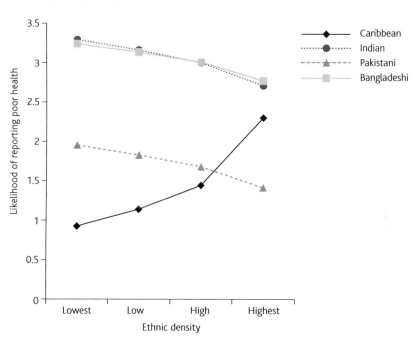

Note: Analyses adjusted to take account of the effects of differences in age, sex, individual socioeconomic status and area deprivation in the sample.

Source: Adapted from Bécares et al (2009)

those groups typically considered to have poorer health (such as Bangladeshi and Pakistani people). For example, ethnic variations in levels of alcohol, fruit and vegetable consumption and mean fat intake suggest that the health of those with (non–White) minority ethnicities should – other things being equal – be better than that of other groups. However, ethnic variations in the use of cooking salt, cigarette smoking and physical activity suggest minority ethnic 'lifestyles' (for some, but not all) that may impact negatively on health. Some health behaviours (such as tobacco chewing) are underestimated among some groups (Roth et al, 2009). But despite this, the health implications of these lifestyles are neither sufficiently consistent – nor poor enough – to imply the almost ubiquitous minority ethnic health disadvantage outlined above.

We would argue that the relationships between ethnicity and health-related behaviours need to be understood in light of the evidence exposing the impact of socioeconomic disadvantage and racism on health and health-risk taking. Research combining data from HSE 2006, 2007 and 2008 shows that the significantly higher rate of smoking among Bangladeshi, compared with White British, men

Table 8.2: Age-standardised risk ratios[a] for health behaviours, by minority ethnic group and gender

	Current cigarette smoker	Drank alcohol three or more days a week in the past year	Did at least 30 minutes of moderate physical activity on at least five days a week	Ate at least five portions of fruit and vegetables a day[b]	Mean fat intake score	Added salt during cooking
			Relative risks (standard errors)			
Men						
General population[c]	1.00 (24%)	1.00 (41%)	1.00 (37%)	1.00 (23%)	1.00 (24.3)	1.00 (56%)
Black Caribbean	1.02 (0.12)	0.75 (0.08)	1.03 (0.09)	1.40 (0.16)	0.85 (0.04)	1.38 (0.07)
Black African	0.80 (0.11)	0.47 (0.08)	0.84 (0.09)	1.40 (0.16)	0.82 (0.03)	1.38 (0.08)
Indian	**0.78 (0.09)**	0.44 (0.05)	0.75 (0.06)	1.64 (0.15)	0.76 (0.02)	1.69 (0.04)
Pakistani	1.08 (0.11)	0.05 (0.02)	0.64 (0.07)	1.47 (0.14)	0.84 (0.04)	1.69 (0.04)
Bangladeshi	**1.43 (0.11)**	0.01 (0.01)	0.58 (0.07)	1.48 (0.20)	0.89 (0.04)	1.73 (0.04)
Chinese	0.81 (0.13)	0.49 (0.07)	0.74 (0.07)	1.66 (0.16)	0.80 (0.03)	1.42 (0.07)
Irish	**1.30 (0.13)**	1.23 (0.10)	1.05 (0.08)	1.14 (0.13)	0.98 (0.04)	0.83 (0.07)
Women						
General population[c]	1.00 (23%)	1.00 (26%)	1.00 (25%)	1.00 (27%)	1.00 (21.2)	1.00 (53%)
Black Caribbean	1.08 (0.11)	0.42 (0.06)	1.17 (0.10)	1.16 (0.09)	0.84 (0.04)	1.33 (0.07)
Black African	0.34 (0.07)	0.28 (0.08)	1.03 (0.10)	1.23 (0.11)	0.92 (0.04)	1.60 (0.08)
Indian	0.23 (0.04)	0.21 (0.04)	0.81 (0.07)	1.37 (0.11)	0.81 (0.02)	1.78 (0.05)
Pakistani	0.19 (0.04)	0.01 (0.01)	0.46 (0.06)	1.19 (0.11)	0.91 (0.04)	1.70 (0.06)
Bangladeshi	0.11 (0.04)	0.00 (0.00)	0.32 (0.06)	1.00 (0.13)	0.84 (0.04)	1.79 (0.05)
Chinese	0.32 (0.07)	0.37 (0.08)	0.59 (0.07)	1.65 (0.13)	0.90 (0.06)	1.49 (0.08)
Irish	1.11 (0.11)	1.06 (0.11)	1.08 (0.11)	1.24 (0.12)	1.00 (0.02)	0.87 (0.08)

Notes:

[a] See Table 8.1 for an explanation on how age standardisation was carried out in HSE 2004.

[b] The figures in bold show differences that are statistically significant.

[c] Standardised risk ratio and observed prevalence displayed for the general population.

Source: HSE 2004; general population figures from HSE 2003

is explained by socioeconomic differences between them (Karlsen et al, 2012). Moreover, the smoking rate of Pakistani men is significantly *lower* than that of White British men after adjusting for socioeconomic differences between the groups. Attributing such variations in smoking rates to cultural, rather than socioeconomic, factors therefore seems short-sighted.

'Cultural factors' also affect people's interactions with health and other statutory services: in terms of both how people from minority ethnic groups engage with services and how services respond to their needs. Establishing whether ethnic variations in the uptake of statutory services exist is problematic. This is partly caused by problems establishing the ethnicity of people using health and other services. There are also issues relating to the need to establish whether any ethnic (or other) difference in service use is associated with a need that is not being met, or simply differences in the prevalence of particular symptoms or conditions. Despite these problems, research identifies important ethnic differences in health service use. Nazroo et al (2009) found that people from some minority ethnic groups were more likely than White majority groups to have visited their GP in the last two weeks. However, people in all minority ethnic groups, including Irish and Chinese people, were less likely to visit a dentist for check-ups and Indian, Pakistani, Bangladeshi and Chinese people had significantly lower levels of hospital utilisation. Gypsies and Travellers, and asylum-seekers and refugees, have also been found to have poor access to GPs and other primary and secondary care services (Aspinall and Watters, 2010).

Ethnic differences have been found in access to secondary services, particularly for cardiovascular disease (Sekhri et al, 2008) and maternity care, which partly explains the stark ethnic differences in maternal mortality (Lewis, 2007). There are particular concerns relating to the experiences of people from different Black groups, as well as Gypsies and Travellers and asylum-seekers and refugees, engaging with mental health services. Men with African and Caribbean backgrounds are up to 6.6 times more likely to be admitted as inpatients or detained under the Mental Health Act, are twice as likely to be detained in secure services, and stay for twice as long in those services compared with others (Mental Health Taskforce, 2016; see also Chapter 10, this volume). There are, therefore, ethnic differences in the medical treatment received, even for those with similar symptoms/diagnoses. African-Caribbean people have been shown to be more likely to receive medication as the primary source of treatment for mental health problems, and are less likely to receive psychotherapy, or talking therapies, than those in other ethnic groups (McKenzie et al, 2001). Perhaps even more striking is community-based evidence that does not identify symptomatic differences, which would justify these ethnic variations in inpatient stays (Nazroo and King, 2002). Racism within mental health services continues to be a problem (CQC, 2015).

While cultural factors, such as variations in symptom presentation, may contribute to ethnic differences in service use, the doctor–patient dynamic may also be affected by negative stereotypes and racist behaviour (see Chapter 2, this volume). For example, migrants in Sweden described a need to become acclimatised to the Swedish health system, to identify the particular expectations of Swedish health providers, which were argued to vary from those of providers in pre-migration locations (Akhavan and Karlsen, 2013). These cultural disconnects constitute a mismatch between majority institutional cultures and minority ones, and are not the result of the problematic behaviours of individuals. However, care providers interviewed in this study did not recognise this learning process, instead resorting to negative stereotypes to justify variations in behaviour. Other studies have found evidence of providers' negative stereotypes and preconceptions about the characteristics and preferences of particular ethnic groups, which in some cases have affected treatment recommendations (Chowbey et al, 2008; Mir and Sheikh, 2010). Such negative outcomes are not always intentional. Physicians' implicit, or unconscious, stereotyping has been found to directly affect the diagnosis and treatment of African American patients as well as a wide range of indicators of poor visit communication, including clinician verbal dominance, lower patient positive affect, less patient-centredness and poorer ratings of care, particularly (but not only) for Black patients (van Ryn et al, 2006).

A recurring theme in research studies describes the sense among minority ethnic service users of being unwelcome and isolated, and of providers being dismissive and disrespectful (Bharaj and Salway, 2008; Worth et al, 2009). Figures produced by the Care Quality Commission (CQC) in 2008/09 suggest that people of Asian/Asian British ethnicity are 50% and Chinese people 70% less likely than White British people to report that they were always treated with dignity and respect by their GP. Service engagement is directly affected by prior experiences with those services. People who have been treated poorly during interactions with health and other services, or who know people who have been treated in this way, will be discouraged from further engagement with those services, and, where they do occur, these interactions will induce additional stress. As a consequence, opportunities to access the health benefits associated with screening or timely engagement with services following the onset of symptoms may be lost, with implications for health and life. Salway et al (2010a) outline three interrelated ways in which the delivery of health services can undermine the health and healthcare experiences of people with minority ethnic backgrounds:

* failure to understand and accommodate specific cultural preferences;
* failure to establish effective communication; and
* discriminatory attitudes and behaviours that directly compromise care and cause significant distress among patients and their family carers.

Effective communication is clearly problematic for those with limited proficiency in English. It is also hampered by factors related to the ways in which services are provided. Traditional understandings of health and illness, which may not correlate with biomedical ideas, do affect how some people choose to manage and treat their health problems, including engagement with health services, which they perceive as less accommodating of their perspectives (Mackenzie et al, 2003). There is evidence, for example, that people from some minority ethnic groups, such as Chinese people, are more likely to self-medicate and use complementary and alternative medicine (CAM) than White British people. However, there is also evidence of a direct association between CAM use by Black Americans and experience of racism, both generally and in interactions with healthcare services. It is therefore important to recognise that such 'cultural' differences in health–related behaviour may be driven by experiences of unfair treatment and the limitations this places on treatment choice. This trend must be considered in the context of the healthcare system and the degree to which cultural preferences are understood, respected and accommodated (Fink, 2002). Lack of access to information and a lack of familiarity with health systems can affect people's ability to engage with and to exercise choice with regards to their healthcare, particularly (but not only) new migrants and those with poor English-language skills. The available evidence speaks of the ways in which the *institutional cultures* of statutory services can perpetuate existing structural disadvantages, limiting people's access to resources that may otherwise improve their health.

Creative approaches to the study of ethnic inequalities in health

We have described several broad approaches relating to structural/social and cultural/behavioural influences on ethnic health inequalities. We have explained how each can inform our understanding of inequalities and how the approaches used to investigate them affect our perception of their nature. We end with a discussion of developments in the investigation of ethnic health inequalities, which can offer additional insight into the drivers of inequalities and opportunities for fruitful future research. These explore the role of religion, migration and social identification. Each adopts a more creative approach towards the investigation of which aspects of 'ethnicity' might be important for health, which can enable us to identify more clearly the drivers of these inequalities and to put in place effective policy to address them.

Like ethnicity, religion is an important source of personal identity, group cohesion and social and political mobilisation for 'majority' and 'minority' people. Religion has the potential to provide health benefits (Kinnvall, 2002), to operate as a focus for victimisation and discrimination (Karlsen and Nazroo, 2014) and as a resource against social and economic exclusion (Maselko et al, 2011). Consequently, investigation of religious or ethnic/religious inequalities may offer valuable opportunities to develop a better appreciation of the drivers of ethnic inequalities in health.

Karlsen and Nazroo (2010) used combined data from HSE 1999 and 2004 to show that people in the predominantly Indian Sikh and Hindu groups and Indian, Pakistani and Bangladeshi Muslims have a significantly increased risk of reporting their health to be fair or poor compared with White British people. Hindus have a 59%, Sikhs a 217%, Indian Muslims a 268%, Pakistani Muslims a 226% and Bangladeshi Muslims a 294% (almost three times) increased risk of fair or poor health compared with White British people (Karlsen and Nazroo, 2010). Importantly, this approach shows the stark differences in the health experience of the different Indian (Hindu, Sikh and Muslim) groups, which is lost in approaches that use a single combined 'Indian' category.

There is compelling evidence regarding the significant socioeconomic disadvantage experienced by Muslims (with a range of ethnicities) and Sikhs, and the implications these have for their health experience (Karlsen and Nazroo, 2010). Evidence regarding the shifting focus of racism onto Muslims (Karlsen and Nazroo, 2014), and the ways in which NHS services struggle to deliver religiously sensitive care and ensure their (particularly Muslim) clients are treated with respect (Salway et al, 2010b), speak again to the social/structural rather than biological/behavioural explanations for these patterns. This remains an under-exploited but potentially fruitful avenue for further exploration.

Nazroo et al (2007) examined more specifically the impact of sociopolitical context in their investigation of the apparent health advantages of Caribbean American people relative to Caribbean people living in the UK (and African American people). They concluded that the health differences were explained by migration from the Caribbean to the USA taking place later than that to the UK, into a different 'race' relations context, at a time when, perhaps, migrants were able to take advantage of the civil rights movement in a way that the pre-existing Black population (and the population in the UK) was not (Nazroo et al, 2007, p 825).

Understanding the characteristics of migration – and the implications these have for racism and socioeconomic disadvantage – is important. Social forces define who migrates, where they migrate to and their migrant experience, including:

- social and economic forces that drive migration;
- selection of the population into migrant and non-migrant groups;
- social and economic and political contexts into which migrants arrive; and
- how these contexts develop over time and across generations.

Such research can also begin to account for the super-diversity (Vertovec, 2007; see also Chapter 3, this volume) that is now considered to characterise migration to the UK and elsewhere, which has been produced by significant changes in the reasons for and the origins of people's migration and their experiences before, during and after their move. Again, evidence exploring this remains lacking.

This chapter has drawn attention to the methodological limitations of existing research, and the opportunities to address these. Studies are beginning to respond to some of these opportunities to recognise more fully the impact of racism on the lives of minority ethnic people, and how the effects of racism accumulate throughout the life course and across generations, to reproduce and perpetuate ethnic health inequalities. These studies can identify the health impact of cumulative exposure to racism, which show incremental negative long-term effects on the mental health of minority ethnic people (Wallace et al, 2016).

Finally, comprehensive understanding of the interrelationships between aspects of minority ethnic status, structural factors and health can only be achieved by allowing for the dynamic and multidimensional nature of ethnicity and the different ways that ethnicity forms part of people's lives. Racially motivated social exclusion has been found to be strongly associated with the ways people think about, and define, themselves, and the social groups of which they feel able to consider themselves part (Karlsen, 2006; Karlsen and Nazroo, 2015). Such *racialisation* – the way that racist victimisation and exclusion affects our self-perception – along with socioeconomic exclusion, has been found to play an important role in explaining ethnic inequalities in health (Karlsen and Nazroo, 2002b). Again, this work remains limited.

Conclusion

Developing a better understanding of the relationships between ethnicity and health is an important focus for ethnically diverse countries like the UK. This chapter described how ethnic inequalities in health persist across a broad range of health outcomes, and the different ways in which ethnic inequalities in health are explained. It highlighted several ways in which the approach used to *investigate* ethnic health inequalities influences how these inequalities are *understood,* which, in turn affects what strategies and policies are used to address them. Ethnic health inequalities need to be considered as structural, associated with factors such as socioeconomic disadvantage and social exclusion, rather than as generated by biological or cultural differences between groups. We also need to consider how these influences interact to shape the health (and other related) experiences in the daily lives of people with different ethnicities. Without an appropriate understanding of the drivers of ethnic health inequalities, we cannot hope to develop effective policies to address them.

Questions for discussion

- What are the main drivers of ethnic health inequalities?
- In what ways can 'culture' be considered to influence them?

- Why have structural/social explanations traditionally been given less research attention?
- How are more creative approaches to the study of ethnic health inequalities able to offer additional insight into the association between ethnicity and health?

Online resources

www.ethnicity-facts-figures.service.gov.uk

The latest government evidence examining ethnic inequalities, including those relating to health, is available on their 'Ethnicity Facts and Figures' website.

www.equalityhumanrights.com/en/race-report-healing-divided-britain

Empirical evidence on the persistence of ethnic inequalities on a range of indicators including levels of race hate crime is available via the Equality and Human Rights Commission (EHRC).

www.ethnicity.ac.uk

Detailed evidence regarding a range of ethnic inequalities, including health, based on analyses of the 2011 England and Wales Census and other sources, is provided by the Centre on Dynamics of Ethnicity at the University of Manchester.

Further reading

Bécares, L. (2015) 'Which ethnic groups have the poorest health?', in A. Jivraj and L. Simpson (eds) *Ethnic identity and inequality in Britain: The dynamics of diversity*, Bristol: Policy Press, 123-39.

Karlsen, S. (2007) 'Ethnic inequalities in health: The impact of racism', Better Health Briefing 3, London: Race Equality Foundation (https://raceequalityfoundation.org.uk/wp-content/uploads/2018/03/health-brief3.pdf).

Nazroo, J.Y. and Williams, D.R. (2006) 'The social determinants of ethnic/racial inequalities in health', in M. Marmot and R.G. Wilkinson, *Social determinants of health* (2nd edn), Oxford: Oxford University Press, 238-66 (https://scholar.harvard.edu/davidrwilliams/dwilliam/publications/social-determination-ethnicracial-inequalities-health).

References

Acevedo, G.D. (2000) 'Residential segregation and the epidemiology of infectious diseases', *Social Science & Medicine*, 51, 1143-61.

Akhavan, S. and Karlsen, S. (2013) 'Practitioner and client explanations for ethnic disparities in Swedish health care use – A qualitative study', *Journal of Immigrant and Minority Health*, 15(1), 188-97.

Aspinall, P.J. and Watters, C. (2010) *Refugees and asylum seekers: A review from an equality and human rights perspective*, Equality and Human Rights Commission, Research Report 52.

Bécares, L. (2014) 'Ethnic density effects on psychotic symptomatology among Latino ethnic groups: An examination of hypothesized pathways', *Health & Place*, 30, 177-86.

Bécares, L. (2015) 'Which ethnic groups have the poorest health?', in A. Jivraj and L. Simpson (eds) *Ethnic identity and inequality in Britain. The dynamics of diversity*, Bristol: Policy Press, 123-39.

Bécares, L., Nazroo, J. and Jackson, J. (2014) 'Ethnic density and depressive symptoms among African Americans: Threshold and differential effects across social and demographic subgroups', *American Journal of Public Health*, 104(12), 2334-41.

Bécares, L., Nazroo, J. and Kelly, Y. (2015) 'A longitudinal examination of maternal, family, and area-level experiences of racism on children's socioemotional development: Patterns and possible explanations', *Social Science & Medicine*, 142, 128-35.

Bécares, L., Nazroo, J. and Stafford, M. (2009) 'The buffering effects of ethnic density on experienced racism and health', *Health & Place*, 15, 670-8.

Bécares, L., Shaw, R., Nazroo, J., Stafford, M., Atkin, K., Albor, C., et al (2012) 'Ethnic density effects on physical morbidity, mortality and health behaviors: A systematic review of the literature', *American Journal of Public Health*, 102(12), e33-e66.

Bharj, K. and Salway, S. (2008) *Addressing ethnic inequalities in maternity service experiences and outcomes: Responding to women's needs and preferences*, London: Race Equality Foundation, Better Health Briefing, no 11.

Chowbey, P., Salway, S., Gerrish, K., Ismail, M. and Moullin, M. (2008) *Responding to diverse needs: Eating disorders in 'BME communities' in Sheffield*, Sheffield: South Yorkshire Eating Disorders Association.

CQC (Care Quality Commission) (2015) *Right here, right now: People's experiences of help, care and support during a mental health crisis* (www.cqc.org.uk/content/right-here-right-now-mental-health-crisis-care-review).

Das-Munshi, J., Bécares, L., Dewey, M., Stansfeld, S. and Prince, M. (2010) 'Understanding the effect of ethnic density on mental health: Multi-level investigation on survey data from England', *British Medical Journal*, 341, c5367.

Fink, S. (2002) 'International efforts spotlight traditional, complementary, and alternative medicine', *American Journal of Public Health*, 92(10), 1734-9.

Graves, J.L. and Rose, M.R. (2006) 'Against racial medicine', *Patterns of Prejudice*, 40(4-5), 481-93.

Harris, R., Tobias, M., Jeffreys, M., Waldegrave, K., Karlsen, S. and Nazroo, J. (2006) 'Racism and health: The relationship between experience of racial discrimination and health in New Zealand', *Social Science & Medicine*, 63, 1428-41.

Jivraj, S. and Khan, O. (2015) 'How likely are people from minority ethnic groups to live in deprived neighbourhoods?', in A. Jivraj and L. Simpson (eds) *Ethnic identity and inequality in Britain: The dynamics of diversity*, Bristol: Policy Press, 199-213.

Karlsen, S. (2006) 'A quantitative and qualitative exploration of the processes associated with ethnic identification', PhD Sociology, Department of Epidemiology and Public Health, UCL.

Karlsen, S. and Nazroo, J.Y. (2002a) 'The relationship between racial discrimination, social class and health among minority ethnic groups', *American Journal of Public Health*, 92(4), 624-31.

Karlsen, S. and Nazroo, J.Y. (2002b) 'Agency and structure: The impact of ethnic identity and racism on the health of minority ethnic people', *Sociology of Health and Illness*, 24(1), 1-20.

Karlsen, S. and Nazroo, J.Y. (2004) 'Fear of racism and health', *Journal of Epidemiology and Community Health*, 58(12), 1017-18.

Karlsen, S. and Nazroo, J.Y. (2010) 'Religious and ethnic differences in health: Evidence from the Health Surveys for England 1999 and 2004', *Ethnicity & Health*, 15(6), 549-68.

Karlsen, S. and Nazroo, J.Y. (2014) 'Ethnic and religious variations in the reporting of racist victimization in Britain: 2000 and 2008/2009', *Patterns of Prejudice*, 48(4), 370-97.

Karlsen, S. and Nazroo, J.Y. (2015) 'Ethnic and religious differences in the attitudes of people towards being "British"', *The Sociological Review*, 63(4), 759-81.

Karlsen, S. and Nazroo, J.Y. (2017) 'Measuring and analysing "race", racism and racial discrimination', in J.M. Oakes and J.S. Kaufman (eds) *Methods in social epidemiology*, San Francisco, CA: Jossey-Bass, 43-68.

Karlsen, S. and Pantazis, C. (2017) 'Ethnicity, poverty and social exclusion: Towards a better understanding of ethnic variations in socioeconomic position', in E. Dermott and G. Main (eds) *Poverty and social exclusion, Volume 1: The nature and extent of the problem*, Bristol: Policy Press, 115-34.

Karlsen, S., Millward, D. and Sandford, A. (2012) 'Investigating ethnic differences in current cigarette smoking over time using the Health Surveys for England', *European Journal of Public Health*, 22(2), 254-6.

Kelly, Y., Bécares, L. and Nazroo, J. (2013) 'Associations between maternal experiences of racism and early child health and development: Findings from the UK Millennium Cohort Study', *Journal of Epidemiology and Community Health*, 67, 35-41.

Kelly, Y., Panico, L., Bartley, M. and Marmot, M. (2008) 'Why does birthweight vary among ethnic groups in the UK? Findings from the Millennium Cohort Study', *Journal of Public Health*, 31, 131-7.

Kinnvall, C. (2002) 'Nationalism, religion and the search for chosen traumas: Comparing Sikh and Hindu identity constructions', *Ethnicities*, 2(1), 79-106.

Krieger, N. (2000) 'Discrimination and health', in L. Berkman and I. Kawachi (eds) *Social epidemiology*, Oxford: Oxford University Press.

Lewis, G. (2007) *The Confidential Enquiry into Maternal and Child Health (CEMACH). Saving mothers' lives: Reviewing maternal deaths to make motherhood safer – 2003-2005*, London: CEMACH.

Mackenzie, E., Taylor, L., Bloom, B., Hufford, D. and Johnson, J. (2003) 'Minority ethnic use of complementary and alternative medicine (CAM): A national probability survey of CAM utilizers', *Alternative Therapies in Health and Medicine*, 9(4), 50-6.

Marmot Review (2010) *'Fair society, healthy lives': Strategic review of health inequalities in England post 2010* (www.instituteofhealthequity.org/resources-reports/fair-society-healthy-lives-the-marmot-review/fair-society-healthy-lives-full-report-pdf.pdf).

Maselko, J., Hughes, C. and Cheney, R. (2011) 'Religious social capital: Its measurement and utility in the study of the social determinants of health', *Social Science & Medicine*, 73, 759-967.

McKenzie, K., Samele, C., van Horn, E., Tattan, T., van Os, J. and Murray, R. (2001) 'Comparison of the outcome and treatment of psychosis in people of Caribbean origin living in the UK and British Whites: Report from the UK700 trial', *The British Journal of Psychiatry*, 178, 160-5.

McLennan, W. and Madden, R. (1999) *The health and welfare of Australia's Aboriginal and Torres Strait Islander peoples*, Commonwealth of Australia: Australian Bureau of Statistics.

Mental Health Taskforce (2016) *The five year forward view for mental health* (www.england.nhs.uk/mental-health/taskforce).

Mir, G. and Sheikh, A. (2010) '"Fasting and prayer don't concern the doctors ... they don't even know what it is": Communication, decision-making and perceived social relations of Pakistani Muslim patients with long-term illnesses', *Ethnicity & Health* (www.tandfonline.com/doi/full/10.1080/13557851003624273).

Mohseni, M. and Lindström, M. (2008) 'Ethnic differences in anticipated discrimination, generalised trust in other people and self-rated health: A population-based study in Sweden', *Ethnicity & Health*, 13(5), 417-34.

Morning, A. (2014) 'And you thought we had moved beyond all that: Biological race returns to the social sciences', *Ethnic and Racial Studies*, 37(10), 1676-85.

Mukherjee, S (2016) *The gene: An intimate history*, New York: Vintage.

Nazroo, J.Y. (1998) 'Genetic, cultural or socio-economic vulnerability? Explaining ethnic inequalities in health', *Sociology of Health and Illness*, 20(5), 710-30.

Nazroo, J.Y. (2001) *Ethnicity, class and health*, London: Policy Studies Institute.

Nazroo, J.Y. (2003) 'The structuring of ethnic inequalities in health: Economic position, racial discrimination and racism', *American Journal of Public Health*, 93(2), 277-84.

Nazroo, J. and King, M. (2002) 'Psychosis – Symptoms and estimated rates', in K. Sproston and J. Nazroo (eds) *Minority Ethnic Psychiatric Illness Rates in the Community (EMPIRIC)*, London: The Stationery Office.

Nazroo, J.Y., Falaschetti, E., Pierce, M. and Primatesta, P. (2009) 'Ethnic inequalities in access to and outcomes of healthcare: Analysis of the health survey for England', *Journal of Epidemiology and Community Health*, 63(12), 1022-7.

Nazroo, J.Y., Jackson, J., Karlsen, S. and Torres, M. (2007) 'The black diaspora and health inequalities in the US and England: Does where you go and how you get there make a difference?', *Sociology of Health and Illness*, 29(6), 811–30.

Noh, S. and Kaspar, V. (2003) 'Perceived discrimination and depression: Moderating effects of coping, acculturation and ethnic support', *American Journal of Public Health*, 93(2), 232-8.

Pan American Health Organization (2001) *Equity in health: From an ethnic perspective*, Washington, DC: Pan American Health Organization.

Panico, L. and Kelly, Y. (2007) 'Ethnic differences in childhood cognitive development: Findings from the Millennium Cohort Study', *Journal of Epidemiology and Community Health*, 61(Suppl 1), A36.

Paradies, Y., Ben, J., Denson, N., Elias, A., Priest, N., Pieterse, A., et al (2015) 'Racism as a determinant of health: A systematic review and meta-analysis', *PLoS One*, 10(9), e0138511.

Pickett, K.E. and Wilkinson, R. (2008) 'People like us: Ethnic group density effects on health', *Ethnicity & Health*, 13, 321-34.

Priest, N., Paradies, Y., Trenerry, B., Truong, M., Karlsen, S. and Kelly, Y. (2013) 'A systematic review of studies examining the relationship between reported racism and health and wellbeing for children and young people', *Social Science & Medicine*, 95, 115-27.

Roth, M.A. and Kobayashi, K.M. (2008) 'The use of complementary and alternative medicine among Chinese Canadians: Results from a national survey', *Journal of Immigrant and Minority Health*, 10(6), 517-28.

Roth, M.A., Aitsi-Selmi, A., Wardle, H. and Mindell, J. (2009) 'Under-reporting of tobacco use among Bangladeshi women in England', *Journal of Public Health*, 31(3), 326.

Ruggiero, K.M. and Taylor, D.M. (1995) 'Coping with discrimination: How disadvantaged group members perceive the discrimination that confronts them', *Journal of Personality and Social Psychology*, 68(5), 826-38.

Salway, S., Hyde, M. and Karlsen, S. (2010a) 'Race and ethnicity', in P. Allmark, S. Salway and H. Piercy (eds) *Life & Health: An evidence review and synthesis for the Equality and Human Rights Commission's Triennial Review 2010*, Sheffield: Centre for Health and Social Research, Sheffield Hallam University, 371-503.

Salway, S., Hyde, M. and Karlsen, S. (2010b) 'Religion and belief', in P. Allmark, S. Salway and H. Piercy (eds) *Life & Health: An evidence review and synthesis for the Equality and Human Rights Commission's Triennial Review 2010*, Sheffield: Centre for Health and Social Research, Sheffield Hallam University, 620-92.

Sekhri, N., Timmis, A., Chen, R., Junghans, C., Walsh, N., Zaman, J., et al (2008) 'Inequity of access to investigation and effect on clinical outcomes: Prognostic study of coronary angiography for suspected stable angina pectoris', *British Medical Journal* (www.bmj.com/content/bmj/336/7652/1058.full.pdf).

Shariff-Marco, S., Klassen, A.C. and Bowie, J.V. (2010) 'Racial/ethnic differences in self-reported racism and its association with cancer-related health behaviours', *American Journal of Public Health*, 100(2), 364-74.

Sidiropoulos, E., Jeffery, A., Mackay, S., Forgey, H., Chipps, C. and Corrigan, T. (1997) *South Africa Survey 1996/97*, Johannesburg: South African Institute of Race Relations.

Sproston, K. and Mindell, J. (eds) (2006) *Health Survey for England 2004: The health of minority ethnic groups*, London: The Information Centre.

van Ryn, M., Burgess, D., Malat, J. and Griffin, J. (2006) 'Physicians' perceptions of patients' social and behavioral characteristics and race disparities in treatment recommendations for men with coronary artery disease', *American Journal of Public Health*, 96(2), 351-7.

Vertovec, S. (2007) 'Super-diversity and its implications', *Ethnic and Racial Studies*, 30(6), 1024-54.

Wallace, S., Nazroo, J. and Bécares, L. (2016) 'Cumulative exposure to racial discrimination across time and domains: Exploring racism's long term impact on the mental health of ethnic minority people in the UK', *American Journal of Public Health*, 106(7), 1294-300.

Williams, D.R. (2001) 'Racial variations in adult health status: Patterns, paradoxes and prospects', in N. Smelser, W.J. Wilson and F. Mitchell (eds) *America becoming: Racial trends and their consequences, National Research Council Commission on Behavioral and Social Sciences and Education*, Washington, DC: National Academy of Sciences Press, 371-410.

Wohland, P., Rees, P., Nazroo, J. and Jagger, C. (2015) 'Inequalities in healthy life expectancy between ethnic groups in England and Wales in 2001', *Ethnicity & Health*, 20(4), 341-53.

Worth, A., Irshad, T., Bhopal, R., Brown, D., Lawton, J., Grant, E., et al (2009) 'Vulnerability and access to care for south Asian Sikh and Muslim patients with life limiting illness in Scotland: Prospective longitudinal qualitative study', *British Medical Journal*, 338, b183.

9

Ethnicity, disability and chronic illness

Simon Dyson and Maria Berghs

Overview

This chapter will help readers to understand how patterns of disablement and chronic illness may partly derive from levels of material deprivation. It also:

- illustrates the value of looking at the interactions not only between ethnicity and disablement, but also between other factors such as age, gender and socioeconomic status; and
- shows why it is important to interpret official figures on disability and ethnicity with care, and how cultural explanations from a policy perspective might worsen inequalities.

It will help readers to understand the changing policy contexts associated with increased racism and disability discrimination.

Key concepts
care; disability; embodiment; impairment

Introduction

This chapter examines the situation of people from minority ethnic groups who have a disability or are living with a chronic illness. First, we discuss the complex relationship between the (general) overrepresentation of minority ethnic groups living in material deprivation (see Chapter 8, this volume) and the significance of this for the prevalence of impairments. Second, we consider the implications of a social model of disability for minority groups, arguing that ethnicity and disablement need to be theorised within a framework of intersectionality, as explained earlier, in Chapter 2. Gender, life course and socioeconomic position – and, in addition, societal norms and values related to impairment and disability – are central to this analysis. This is why we specifically and critically examine the position of minority ethnic groups in official statistics on disablement. Third, we consider how a service provider's assumptions might lead to impoverished service quality. Finally, we look at the changing policy context for disablement and ethnicity, and how neoliberal policy questions the entitlements of people with disabilities and of minority groups, and in particular their rights to 'deserving' citizenship.

Ethnicity, disability and health

Having reminded ourselves in Chapter 2 that there are divisions within minority ethnic communities, in terms of country of birth, migration status, gender, sexuality, religion, language, age, socioeconomic status, and residential location, we next need to consider that there may be patterns of association between ethnic minority groups, disablement and levels of chronic illness. There are two ways of thinking of this relationship: structural or identity-sensitive, although these are not mutually exclusive (see Chapter 2). Structural refers primarily to levels of material deprivation, lower social standing and lack of control over work processes. Identity refers to cultural or identity-sensitive processes. Figure 9.1 illustrates the cyclical relationship between historical-material structural processes and how they become linked to inequalities. Cultural values and beliefs can

Figure 9.1: Structural inequalities and identity-sensitive discrimination matrix

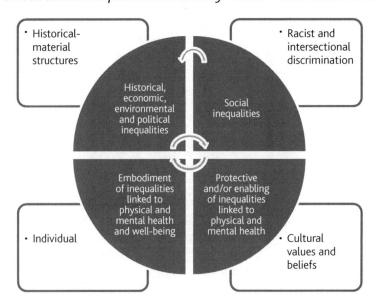

become protective or enabling of health inequalities and affect whether or not they become individually embodied.

While there is systematic evidence of racism leading to physical and mental ill health (see also Chapter 8), more meta-analysis is needed about variations of exposure to – and the long-term effects of – racism (Paradies et al, 2015; Wallace et al, 2016; see also Chapter 8). For instance, exposure to racist violence or racist micro-aggressions can lead to high blood pressure (Krieger et al, 2008) and increased risk of diabetes, and to heart disease prompted by repeated health-damaging flight-or-fight hormones (Wilkinson, 2002). The effects of racism on health are now also becoming linked to understanding the social determinants of chronic illness (Cockerham et al, 2017). Similarly, while micro-aggressions were initially defined in the 1970s in terms of the adverse effects of indirect racism, they are now said to comprise:

> The brief and commonplace daily verbal behavioural and environmental indignities, whether intentional or unintentional that communicate hostile, derogatory or negative racial, gender, sexual-orientation and religious slights and insults to the target person or group. (Sue, 2010, p 5)

Despite this, overt disability discrimination or experiences of (dis)ableism have not been conceptualised fully. These can, likewise, have a negative effect on health. Such processes have been theorised as 'psycho-emotional disablism' (Reeve, 2002) or 'internalised ableism' (Campbell, 2008), but we know very little about how those processes link to differing forms of racism and health. While disability or racist hate crimes are clearly identity-sensitive mechanisms, other processes such as cultural meanings and framings of chronic illnesses such as mental illness (Dein et al, 2008; see also Chapter 10, this volume), diabetes (Keval, 2015), or heart disease (Kaiser et al, 2015) are not generally linked to inequalities in health status, which are almost all explained by material-structural factors (Pickett and Wilkinson, 2015). In popular debates on how health, ethnicity, disease and chronic illness become correlated, ethnicity as 'genetic' or culture as 'risky' are typically viewed as causes of health inequalities. Analyses of agency and structure are ignored (Keval, 2015).

Although the cultural and individual experiences of disablement are important, consideration should be given to the influence of material-structural factors in the very genesis of impairment and chronic illness (see Chapter 8). There are strong correlations between childhood disability and socioeconomic deprivation (Berghs et al, 2016), and particularly so among children with disabilities from Black and minority ethnic (BME) or lone parents or parents with a disability (Blackburn et al, 2010). Structural factors and greater socioeconomic deprivation are linked to higher rates of impairments: material deprivation and poor diet (spina bifida) and lack of access to the best health services (birth trauma and cerebral palsy). Impairment, therefore, is linked with social stratification. The frequency of 'birth defects' is associated with levels of material deprivation, and, since different ethnic communities live with disproportionate levels of relative poverty, their rates of impairment will vary correspondingly (Knowles et al, 2017). Social deprivation, lack of education and ethnicity are, for example, linked together in understanding why and how long mothers took the folate supplements that are necessary to prevent spina bifida (Brough et al, 2009). There is also a knock-on effect of impairment and future ill health for children growing up in deprivation (Wilkinson, 2002; Pickett and Wilkinson, 2015).

Of course, the putative relationship of *material deprivation, belonging to a minority ethnic group* and *prevalence of impairments* represents a vast over-simplification, as the following, examining the relationship between socioeconomic position, ethnicity and intellectual disabilities, indicates (see Box 9.1). The relationship varies according to moderate or severe impairment, type of intellectual disability and which particular minority ethnic groups are being considered.

Box 9.1: Deprivation, ethnicity and intellectual disability

Emerson (2012) examined links between social deprivation, ethnicity and intellectual and developmental disability. Material and environmental factors are important, but so are social factors. Infant health and identification of disability depends on consistent access to and trust in service provision. Despite structural and social explanations, it is not yet clear why certain disabilities are identified in particular ethnic groups:

> Lower household socio-economic position was associated with increased rates of identification of intellectual and developmental disabilities especially less severe forms of intellectual disability. Higher area deprivation was independently associated with increased rates of identification of less severe forms of intellectual disability but decreased rates of identification of profound multiple intellectual disability and autism spectrum disorder. Minority ethnic status was, in general, associated with lower rates of identification of intellectual and developmental disabilities. Exceptions to this general pattern included higher rates of identification of less severe forms of intellectual disability among Gypsy/Romany and Traveller children of Irish heritage, and higher rates of identification of more severe forms of intellectual disability among children of Pakistani and Bangladeshi heritage. (Emerson, 2012, p 218)

Having looked at the way in which chronic illness and impairments are related to wider socioeconomic inequalities in society, the next section examines the conceptualisation of ethnicity in disability studies.

Disentangling ethnicity, disability and chronic illness

There is no consensus on what constitutes 'disability'; the purpose of bureaucratic labels used to define and measure disability; and the self-identification of people who might be considered or consider themselves disabled. What counts as impairment is also fiercely contested, and this adds further layers of complexity to debates about disability. Impairment may be congenital; acquired through birth trauma, illness or accident; or experienced at various points across the life course. In the UK, organisations for people with disabilities advocate a social model of disability as a way of understanding disability. The social model developed as a critique of a 'medical model', which views impairment as located in an individual needing rehabilitation, medicine and/or cure. By contrast, the social model of disability makes a distinction between impairment (as biological, sensory, cognitive and so on) and 'disability' that is the outcome of societal oppression (Oliver and Barnes, 2012). The social model focuses on enabling society to ensure greater inclusion of people with disabilities. To distance itself from 'dis–abling' attitudes (for instance, that a person with a disability represents a tragic, passive victim, to be pitied or conceived as not 'normal'), the social model actively separates itself from disease models. Despite significant political changes in ensuring societal inclusion, the social model has itself come under criticism as being theoretically 'outdated' (Shakespeare and Watson, 2001) and ignoring diversity (Ottosdottir and Evans, 2016), especially in accounting for ethnicity.

Feminist disability scholars have highlighted how the social model, by focusing on structure, has neglected understandings of impairment as personal, located in a body and linked to chronic illness (Thomas, 2007). It has, for example, downplayed the extent to which we both *are* a body and *have* a body (Hughes, 2009), and therefore the importance of embodiment. Embodiment means that people do not just have a body; they experience the world through their bodies and this experience is linked to a gendered, cultural and material context; social identity; and disability discrimination and racism (Campbell, 2008; Erevelles, 2014). This critical disability stance argues that, rather than giving just a materialist explanation of impairment and disability, both impairment and disability are socially and culturally constructed (Goodley, 2016; Meekosha and Shuttleworth, 2016). Here, intersectionality and the impact of class, gender, sexuality and ethnicity become important to understand the embodied experiences of impairment and disability.

There is also a struggle within the social model about whether to classify chronic illnesses as disability. Some people with a chronic illness, genetic disorder or disease may not view themselves as 'disabled' but identify more with a biomedical diagnosis of impairment and the possibility of a future cure (Hughes, 2009; Ottosdottir and Evans, 2016). Hence, there has been a stand-off between disability theorists who have tended to regard some clinicians and medical sociologists as essentialising 'disability', that is, treating it as an internal attribute of a person rather than as an oppressive social relationship (Thomas, 2007). There are also some conditions where the relationship between disease, chronic illness and disability seems to be constantly evolving and intertwined. Further, structural inequalities, deprivation and discrimination affect the way in which certain conditions are viewed as public health priorities, and thus develop across the life course (see also Chapter 8, this volume). Box 9.2 focuses on newborn screening for sickle cell disease (SCD) to illustrate this point.

Box 9.2: Sickle cell disease

All infants in England are screened at birth for SCD, irrespective of ethnicity (Dyson, 2005). This is part of the routine newborn screening (the 'heel prick test') aimed at early diagnosis and as part of prevention. Hence, if detected at birth, SCD morbidity and mortality can be reduced by the administration of daily penicillin, vaccinations and health education for parents on signs and symptoms that constitute a medical emergency, for example, how to avert or deal with a 'painful crisis', a characteristic and difficult feature of SCD caused by the sickle shape of the abnormal blood cells and the occlusion of blood supply to particular organs/muscles. At an early diagnostic stage, SCD is framed neither as a chronic illness, nor as disablement, but as a life-threatening genetic disease or disorder to which preventive public health measures can be applied. However, as children age with SCD, parents are given complicated messages about the management of SCD. Some of this advice is again of a preventive and supportive nature (staying hydrated and warm to avoid acute painful episodes), but equally some is about how SCD, in common with other chronic illnesses, can be 'managed' at the individual level. This is despite the fact that there is more than one illness or process of disablement occurring together with SCD. These processes may arise from an effect of the disease itself, ageing, poor environment and/or the stressors of inequality (Pickett and Wilkinson, 2015) and/or the experience of racism (Krieger et al, 2008), but they can also be exacerbated by the lack of access to specialised care and medicine.

Box 9.2 also reminds us how the social model of disability does not necessarily help us with respect to understanding the body in pain. Achieving progressive changes to the social environment does not alter the experience of pain for conditions where the 'biological predominates' (Scambler and Newton, 2010), such as in SCD, which is characterised by 'painful crises' (Wailoo, 2017a, b). This means that, no matter how much the social model emphasises that people are 'disabled' by society and that this is different from the physical aspects of impairment, some types of medical conditions continue to exert their 'effects', such as pain, despite attempts to construct enabling environments (Thomas, 2012). A deeper understanding of how the physical or mental condition is linked to chronicity and impairment has been a weakness of theoretical models trying to explain disability. In particular, the social model – and disability studies in general – struggles with theorising how pain can become racialised or linked to other forms of discrimination based on sexuality and gender, as well as on the wider intersections of inequality (Campbell, 2008; Annamma et al, 2013; Erevelles, 2014; Wohland et al, 2015). For instance, the association of drug addiction with younger people of black and African Caribbean background, from poorer socioeconomic backgrounds in the USA (and the UK), led to the withholding of effective pain medication during the 1990s. Black sickle cell patients were often treated as potential drug addicts, while their experience of pain (a characteristic feature of their chronic condition) was contested (Wailoo, 2017a, b).

Finally, the social model has also tended to emphasise independence from professional control and 'independent living' through welfare provision, such as personal budgets and direct payments (Thomas, 2007; Oliver and Barnes, 2012). Feminist writers have been critical of this stance. They note that we are embedded in relationships of caring and interdependence across the life course (Erevelles, 2014), and how the intersectionality of caring relationships are unequal for women and minority ethnic groups (Nishida, 2017). Critical disability studies has argued for the importance of differing experiences, values and needs among people with disabilities as a way of comprehending what care or lack of care entails for impairment and disability (Erevelles, 2014). With respect to minority ethnic populations, services can essentialise relationships of dependence in emphasising 'caring' as part of a community identity and intergenerational responsibilities of family.

In response to such criticisms, Thomas (2012) has argued that the social model is really a social–relational model and that 'a sociology of disability' needs to be developed. She argues that this would be akin to equality and diversity studies, and would examine, 'engagements with gender, "race", sexuality, age and social class' (Thomas, 2012, p 209). Other strands of disability studies, for instance, critical disability studies, argue for processes for the decolonisation of Western-based definitions of 'disability' (Grech and Soldatic, 2016). This would mean reconceptualising what terms such as 'impairment', 'disability' and 'chronic illness' mean for different ethnic groups. It remains to be seen how successful such efforts will be, and if other models of understanding disability – such as a human rights approach – may have more salience in the future (Berghs et al, 2016). In the next section, we illustrate how ethnicity remains the lens through which relationships between culture and care are understood by services, even as they try to develop cultural competence, in which practitioners are encouraged to ensure their assumptions about different cultural practices and values do not become the basis of inequalities (Atkin et al, 2014).

Chronic illness, disability and ethnicity

Ethnicity has been challenged as the dominant framework for analysing the health and social care relationships of minority ethnic groups. Care has been seen as an emergent component of life histories and family relationships, and cannot be prejudged by locating the people concerned within a particular ethnic or religious grouping (Chattoo and Ahmad, 2008). Further, people with disabilities have other identities (that is, age, ethnicity, sexuality, gender, religion) that may be more salient to them. Young people with disabilities of South Asian descent, for example, negotiate their lives in multifaceted ways. They may draw contingently on different aspects of both Western and British Pakistani Muslim culture (Hussain et al, 2002), as well as on discourses that emphasise solidarity with disability or those that emphasise difference (Islam, 2008).

In response to a changing society in the UK, health and social care have slowly begun to develop culturally competent care, but still struggle to accommodate the complexity of intersectionality. The following examples (see Box 9.3) illustrate the importance of revealing the relationships between ethnicity, disability and age.

Box 9.3: Ethnicity, disability and age: differences in understanding social networks and personalised care

Dementia as part of the process of ageing is an issue that affects all ethnic groups. A particular concern in the provision of services is how to interpret personalised care in a culturally competent manner for BME communities. Personalised care places an emphasis on ensuring an individual is in control of their care, but the following examples illustrate why personalised care may also mean understanding the social and cultural needs and values linked to identity. While it is important to understand cultural values, a sole focus on ethnicity over other aspects of a person's identity may lead to group essentialism, leading to a lack of understanding of a person's needs and inadequate service provision.

Regan (2016) notes that, while Asian people with dementia are under-represented in services, vascular dementia is more common in the BME population in the UK. This is due to cardiovascular and other risk factors linked to health inequalities. Young onset dementia is also more prevalent in the BME population. She gives an in-depth case study of Mr Q, a Muslim Pakistani man experiencing early onset dementia in his fifties. Mr Q has a cardiovascular condition and a history of mental health issues. He is widowed and unable to access any family, community or religious support. He is 'desperate' to access not only culturally competent dementia care, but also health and social care services that acknowledge the correlation between his age, health and mental health needs.

When we consider good practices in health and social care, we often neglect culturally competent care for older LGBT people. Westwood et al (2015) give an example of an older gay African Caribbean man experiencing the first signs of dementia. They argue that his identity may be constructed by service providers in terms of his gender, ethnicity and impairment, while his need for services that focus on social inclusion and embeddedness in the gay community is neglected.

Service provision equally struggles with how to implement culturally competent care alongside understanding the nuances within disability. Service provision and the d/Deaf community fail to address the exclusion of minorities. Evidence suggests that services also struggle with identifying and accommodating new ethnic populations, such as people from Eastern Europe and Roma children (Cline and Mahon, 2010; Swanwick et al, 2016).

As indicated in Box 9.3, understanding complexity in relation to offering health and social care across the life course will become increasingly important as the UK population ages. Access to palliative and social care has tended to be poorly developed for those from minority ethnic communities (Culley and Dyson, 2009). The proportion of people with disabilities in the UK population is expected to increase, and public health services will have to ensure that they prepare for a diverse ageing population with disability and complex health needs. Ten million people in England, for example, experience significant difficulty with day-to-day activities linked to long-term conditions, and this population includes those with lifelong and later-life conditions. As ageing is associated with functional decline, nearly half of those living with impairments are aged 60 or over (see Berghs et al, 2016). As we have argued, structural factors and greater socioeconomic deprivation, affecting minority ethnic populations in particular, have an impact on the prevalence of impairment and future disability.

Moreover, people with disabilities live with other physical conditions, such as coronary heart disease, diabetes and respiratory conditions, alongside mental health problems. There are marked social gradients in disability across the life course, with evidence of enduring effects associated with deprivation in childhood (see below). In addition, and at each stage of the life course, people with disabilities are disproportionately exposed to the social factors that contribute to health inequalities, including proximal risk factors such as smoking, obesity and lack of physical activity, alongside the broader determinants associated with educational and employment opportunities, poverty and poor housing, and inequitable access to services (Berghs et al, 2016). These environmental disadvantages are, in turn, disabling and create further barriers to social inclusion. In the next section, we examine the relationship between disability and ethnicity, specifically how official statistics reflect the connection between the two, and the implications of this for policy.

Ethnicity and disability in official statistics and statutory services

We have seen how ethnic inequalities in health status cannot simply be explained by inequalities in the level of material deprivation facing different communities (see Chapter 8, this volume). This alerts us to the fact that, in examining patterns of disablement, *ethnicity does not constitute an explanation in its own right*. With this in mind – and with all the caveats about understating variation in terms of gender, age, level of material deprivation, religion, language and so on – we can take a look at Table 9.1 below. This represents a great improvement on early Office of Population Censuses and Surveys (OPCS) disability surveys, criticised by Oliver (1992), who challenged the main question posed by these surveys in terms of what was wrong with the person with a disability rather than what was wrong with society. Table 9.1 takes into account the findings of the *Review of Equality Data* (ONS, 2007) and the need to ensure measurement of the disablement process, but also to gather statistical data through the International Classification of Functioning, Disability and Health (ICF).

In Table 9.1, an adult is deemed to have a 'participation restriction' if they experience at least one barrier to participation in at least one of the following life areas: education and training; employment; economic life and living standards; transport; leisure, social and cultural activities; social contact; accessibility of

Table 9.1: Mean count of participation restriction by ethnic group and impairment status, 2009–11, adults aged 16 and over

Ethnic group	Mean count of adults without impairment	Mean count of adults with impairment	Mean count for all adults	Sample size (=100%)
White	1.9	2.9	2.2	33,010
Mixed	2.5	3.0	2.6	250
(British) Asian	2.2	3.1	2.4	1,640
(British) Black	2.7	3.4	2.8	650
Chinese/Other	2.3	3.3	2.5	550
Total	2.0	3.0	2.3	36,090

Source: Adapted from ODI (2011, p 41, Table 3.6)

housing; or accessibility outside the home. Furthermore, perhaps cognisant of Oliver's (1992) criticism (above), this survey extends the notion of barriers to include discrimination; the attitudes of other people; inaccessible buildings, public transport and information; limited income; not having anyone to meet or speak to; as well as lack of support, equipment and adjustments.

Bearing in mind the very broad categories constructed for comparison (both adults with impairment and ethnic groups), we can delineate some general patterns. First, a comparison of adults without impairment across ethnic groups suggests that there are reasons other than ethnicity associated with restrictions on participation in society. In all cases *reported* restrictions are higher in minority ethnic groups compared to White groups. However, there are good reasons for supposing that this table underestimates the degree of disadvantage. Mixing White people of good and poor health statuses means that the differences in reported restrictions in adults without impairments are likely to give a false impression of the real degree of differences, say, between White English and BME groups.

This brings us to the issue of statutory support for people with chronic ill health or with a disability from minority ethnic groups. If services are statistically established in the first instance with provision for White groups in mind, then minority ethnic people with a disability may be expected to fit in with existing provision (Ahmad and Bradby, 2008; Raghavan et al, 2013). The outlook of service providers could make this worse if they believe that minority ethnic people with a disability should 'know where to find us' (Temple et al, 2008) or are 'coping' (Raghavan et al, 2013). Furthermore, disadvantage (for instance, in terms of material deprivation, housing or transport) has tended to be associated with poorer service delivery, along with lowered expectations, complicated bureaucratisation and a lack of understanding of services by the disadvantaged clients (Raghavan et al, 2013). A lack of translated materials (or audio interpretations of materials if people do not read the script of the language they speak) may also result in low awareness and reduced take-up of services (Raghavan et al, 2013). While some specialised services have become more culturally competent, especially for second- and third-generation service users (Malik et al, 2017), cuts affecting services to people with disabilities and strained services, especially for asylum-seekers with a disability, are now the norm (Yeo, 2017). Ottosdottir and Evans (2016) argue that limited research on the needs of refugees and asylum-seekers also affects the development of those services. Further, Phillimore and Bradby (2016) warn that the lack of evidence about newer minority ethnic groups and their health needs will affect future service provision.

A limited service response is one where a specialist worker for minority ethnic issues is appointed, with all cases of minority ethnic people with disabilities then offloaded onto that key worker or specialist, leaving them over-burdened and reducing quality of service as a consequence (Raghavan et al, 2013). More culturally competent services may develop from strong leadership enacting anti-racist policies and enabling policies for people with disabilities, encouraging White staff to develop their skills by working across differences without being judged, being proactive in reaching out to the communities themselves to understand their needs, and recruiting a workforce that reflects the diversity of the communities served (Phillimore and Bradby, 2016). The changing policy context makes this challenging.

Changing policy contexts

The Chronically Sick and Disabled Persons Act 1970 was institutionally able to link chronic illness and disablement, not only because it predated the social model of disability, but also because an ethos of responding to want and need prevailed. The subsequent historical transition from liberal to neoliberal social policy has seen such policies ruthlessly applied to people with disabilities. The embodied effects of neoliberal policies also become racialised in explaining how disability and chronic illness intersect with ethnicity. It has also led to the questioning of the right to health of minorities as well as the criminalisation of established minority groups through racist policing of low-income communities, increased 'stop and searches', and higher levels of imprisonment (Bowling and Phillips, 2007), with health and mental health effects on those people and communities. The popular press often conflates the adverse circumstances of poor 'illegal migrants' with criminality through legal discourses on incarceration, often of migrants who have committed no crime (Bosworth, 2014; Yeo, 2017).

The prevailing attitude of service providers has been to develop mainstream services and then expect BME groups to fit in with existing provision, rather than to generate culturally inclusive services that are consonant with present and future needs (Phillimore and Bradby, 2016). In periods of severe economic retrenchment and the imposition of austerity measures, as is currently being experienced by the poor in the UK, the case for proper attention to the rights of minority ethnic people with disabilities and migrants is lost because it is constructed as outside the realms of 'citizenship' (Ottosdottir and Evans, 2016). In such instances, cuts to White-orientated services would need to be even greater if one were to establish services, for example, for the numbers of medical consultants per sickle cell patient, on an equitable basis (Dyson and Atkin, 2013).

In the early 2000s, people with disabilities from BME communities had little influence in shaping new guidelines on the provision of social care that emphasised personal independence and user-led organisations (Stuart, 2006; Wright, 2016). The value of 'independence' (as in personal independence payments) is Eurocentric, and to this we should add that, historically, organisations for people with disabilities have failed to include minority ethnic people with disabilities, such that government reliance on user-led organisations effectively institutionalises the exclusion of people with disabilities from minority ethnic groups (Stuart, 2012).

Wealth can not only create stronger charities in an area of social care, but also, through the funding of policy organisations and think tanks, help shape the wider policy agenda in regressive ways. Slater (2014) calls this *agnotology*, or the social construction of ignorance, in which messages about the 'deserving' and 'undeserving' person with chronic ill health or a disability are promulgated to the extent that a particular political viewpoint receives extensive airing and reinforcement in the media. For example, if someone with chronic ill health or a disability fails to find work, this can be represented as an individual failure of effort or character (Wright 2016), rather than, say, being attributed to structural barriers to employment. Such notions then become accepted as 'common-sense' wisdom. Further, people living with cystic fibrosis and SCD equally deserve appropriate support. However, in 2016 the Cystic Fibrosis Trust, serving 10,500 people living with cystic fibrosis, had an income of over £12 million (equivalent to £1,142 per person affected) compared to the Sickle Cell Society, serving 15,000-20,000 people, had an income of £0.3 million (or £20 per person affected). When the state shifts its responsibilities to the voluntary sector, this effectively institutionalises inequalities in provision between different groups, as charities raising money from communities overrepresented in terms of material deprivation will not generate the same resources in the first instance.

Likewise, Stewart (2016) documents how government policy-makers, working with US insurance companies as advisers, have implemented the (massively flawed) assessment of people with disabilities for welfare payments by actively undermining the very notion of social security. The very renaming of social security as 'welfare' reflects a policy move whereby suspicion is cast on 'entitlement' to Employment and Support Allowance (ESA) for disability, chronic illness and ill health. Within policy discourses, an unemployed person with a disability is viewed as an 'active welfare subject' and is morally responsible for not being employed (Wright, 2016). This has been powerfully illustrated in the film *I, Daniel Blake* by director Ken Loach. In this, policy-makers have been aided by controversial models such as the biopsychosocial model, heavily criticised by disability theorists for its conceptual inadequacy and 'victim-blaming' of people with disabilities (Shakespeare et al, 2017). The public climate also led to hate crimes against people with disabilities becoming a legal issue, but there are no data on the links between disability and racism, higher incidences of detention under the Mental Health Act and the incarceration of people with mental health issues (EHRC, 2017).

Reducing public support and imposing austerity measures entails the possibility that the state's failure in health and social care provision will open the door for neoliberal services based on US corporate insurance schemes, delimiting social security policies in the future. Such moves towards stigmatising minority ethnic and disabled populations through 'blame' mean that acceptance of diversity or even super-diversity (Phillimore and Bradby, 2016), and the creation of 'cultures of equivalence', no longer function at a public, policy or service level (Clair et al,

2016). Despite legal protections, the Equality and Human Rights Commission (EHRC, 2017) found that inequalities for people with disabilities had increased, especially for those with mental health issues or learning disabilities. Social security reforms have also had a negative impact, with more people with disabilities living in poverty, experiencing more material deprivation and being food-poor (EHRC, 2017).

Conclusion

This chapter has examined how the concepts of ethnicity, disablement and chronic illness may be related. We have explored the limitations of the social model of disability, how ethnicity and disablement need to be looked at together and a more nuanced approach to the intersectionality of age, gender and socioeconomic status is required. Hence, interpreting official statistics on the patterns of ethnicity and disability, based on particular definitions and understandings of both ethnicity and disability, we need to use both as markers that help direct us in our search to identify the key pathways to inequalities rather than as explanatory variables *per se*. We further noted that inequalities in the extent and mode of delivery of services may contribute to the exclusion of minority ethnic people with a disability. Finally, we considered the changing neoliberal policy context, and how more recent forms of social security provision, and the abdication of responsibility from the state to the charity and private sectors, have reinforced the exclusion of people with disabilities from minority ethnic communities, and have worsened levels of inequality.

Questions for discussion

- What might be some of the reasons for the marginalisation of minority ethnic groups within the disabled people's movement, and vice versa?
- To what extent does the life course impact on the experience of chronic illness and disability?
- What policy initiatives might address the historical legacy of different economic resources within non-governmental and third sector organisations?

Online resources

www.raceequalityfoundation.org.uk
  Research on disability, discrimination and disadvantage can be found on the Race Equality Foundation website.

www.equalityhumanrights.com/sites/default/files/being-disabled-in-britain.pdf
  The Equality and Human Rights Commission's report, *Being disabled in Britain: A journey less equal.*

www.who.int/disabilities/world_report/2011/en/
  Disability as an international issue is conceptualised in the *World report on disability* (World Health Organization, 2011).

Further reading

Dyson, S.M. and Atkin, K. (eds) (2014) *Genetics and global public health: Sickle cell and thalassaemia,* London: Routledge.
Pryma, J. (2017) '"Even my sister says I'm acting like a crazy to get a check": Race, gender, and moral boundary-work in women's claims of disabling chronic pain', *Social Science & Medicine,* 181, 66-73.
Shakespeare, T. (2013) *Disability rights and wrongs revisited,* London: Routledge.

References

Ahmad, W. and Bradby, H. (2008) 'Ethnicity and health: Key themes in a developing field', *Current Sociology,* 56(1), 47-56.
Annamma, S.A., Connor, D. and Ferri, B. (2013) 'Dis/ability critical race studies (DisCrit): Theorizing at the intersections of race and dis/ability', *Race Ethnicity and Education,* 16(1), 1-31.
Atkin, K., Chattoo, S. and Crawshaw, M. (2014) 'Clinical encounters and culturally competent practice: the challenges of providing cancer and infertility care', *Policy & Politics,* 42(4), 581-96.
Berghs, M., Atkin, K., Graham, H., Hatton, C. and Thomas, C. (2016) 'Implications for public health research of models and theories of disability: A scoping study and evidence synthesis', *Public Health Research,* 4(8).
Blackburn, C.M., Spencer, N.J. and Read, J.M. (2010) 'Prevalence of childhood disability and the characteristics and circumstances of disabled children in the UK: Secondary analysis of the Family Resources Survey', *BMC Pediatrics,* 10(1), 21.
Bosworth, M. (2014) *Inside immigration detention,* Maidenhead: Open University Press.
Bowling, B. and Phillips, C. (2007) 'Disproportionate and discriminatory: Reviewing the evidence on police stop and search', *The Modern Law Review,* 70(6), 936-61.

Brough, L., Rees, G.A., Crawford, M.A. and Dorman, E.K. (2009) 'Social and ethnic differences in folic acid use preconception and during early pregnancy in the UK: Effect on maternal folate status', *Journal of Human Nutrition and Dietetics*, 22(2), 100-7.

Campbell, F.A.K. (2008) 'Exploring internalized ableism using critical race theory', *Disability & Society*, 23, 151-62.

Chattoo, S. and Ahmad, W.I.U. (2008) 'The moral economy of selfhood and caring: Negotiating boundaries of personal care as embodied moral practice', *Sociology of Health and Illness*, 30(4), 550-64.

Clair, M., Daniel, C. and Lamont, M. (2016) 'Destigmatization and health: Cultural constructions and the long-term reduction of stigma', *Social Science & Medicine*, 165, 223-32.

Cline, T. and Mahon, M. (2010) 'Deafness in a multilingual society: A review of research for practice', *Educational and Child Psychology*, 47(2), 41-9.

Cockerham, W.C., Hamby, B.W. and Oates, G.R. (2017) 'The social determinants of chronic disease', *Social Science & Medicine*, 52(1), S5-S12.

Culley, L.A. and Dyson, S.M. (2009) *Ethnicity and healthcare practice: A guide for the primary care team*, London: Quay Books.

Dein, S., Alexander, M. and Napier, A.D. (2008) 'Jinn, psychiatry and contested notions of misfortune among east London Bangladeshis', *Transcultural Psychiatry*, 45(1), 31-55.

Dyson, S.M. (2005) *Ethnicity and screening for sickle cell/thalassaemia*, Oxford: Elsevier Churchill Livingstone.

Dyson, S.M. and Atkin, K. (2013) 'Achieve equity in access to sickle cell services', *Health Services Journal*, 26 November.

EHRC (Equality and Human Rights Commission) (2017) *Being disabled in Britain: A journey less equal*, London: EHRC.

Emerson, E. (2012) 'Deprivation, ethnicity and the prevalence of intellectual and developmental disabilities', *Journal of Epidemiology and Community Health*, 66(3), 218-24.

Erevelles, N. (2014) 'Thinking with disability studies', *Disability Studies Quarterly*, 34(2), 1-16.

Goodley, D. (2016) *Disability studies: An interdisciplinary introduction*, London: Sage.

Grech, S. and Soldatic, K. (eds) (2016) *Disability in the global South: The critical handbook*, New York: Springer.

Hughes, B. (2009) 'Disability activisms: Social model stalwarts and biological citizens', *Disability & Society*, 24(6), 677-88.

Hussain, Y., Atkin, K. and Ahmad, W.I.U. (2002) *South Asian disabled young people and their families*, Bristol/York: Policy Press/Joseph Rowntree Foundation.

Islam, Z. (2008) 'Negotiating identities: The lives of Pakistani and Bangladeshi young disabled people', *Disability & Society*, 23(1), 41-52.

Kaiser, B.N., Haroz, E.E., Kohrt, B.A., Bolton, P.A., Bass, J.K. and Hinton, D.E. (2015) '"Thinking too much": A systematic review of a common idiom of distress', *Social Science & Medicine*, 147, 170-83.

Keval, H. (2015) 'Risky cultures to risky genes: The racialised discursive construction of South Asian genetic diabetes risk', *New Genetics and Society*, 34(3), 274-93.

Knowles, R.L., Ridout, D., Crowe, S., Bull, C., Wray, J., Tregay, J., et al (2017) 'Ethnic and socioeconomic variation in incidence of congenital heart defects', *Archives of Disease in Childhood*, 102, 496-502.

Krieger, N., Chen, J.T., Waterman, P.D. Hartman, C., Stoddard, A.M., Quinn, M.M., et al (2008) 'The inverse hazard law: blood pressure, sexual harassment, racial discrimination, workplace abuse and occupational exposures in US low-income black, white and Latino workers', *Social Science & Medicine*, 67(12), 1970-81.

Malik, K.J., Unwin, G., Larkin, M., Kroese, B.S. and Rose, J. (2017) 'The complex role of social care services in supporting the development of sustainable identities: Insights from the experiences of British South Asian women with intellectual disabilities', *Research in Developmental Disabilities*, 63, 74-84.

Meekosha, H. and Shuttleworth, R. (2016) 'What's so "critical" about critical disability studies?', in L. Davis (ed) *The disability studies reader*, New York and London: Routledge, 175-94.

Nishida, A. (2017) 'Relating through differences: disability, affective relationality, and the US public healthcare assemblage', *Subjectivity*, 10(1), 89-103.

ODI (Office for Disability Issues) (2011) *ODI Life Opportunities Survey: Wave 1 results* (www.gov.uk/government/statistics/life-opportunities-survey-wave-one-results-2009-to-2011).

Oliver, M. (1992) 'Changing the social relations of research production?', *Disability, Handicap & Society*, 7(2), 101-14.

Oliver, M. and Barnes, C. (2012) *The new politics of disablement*, Basingstoke: Palgrave Macmillan.

ONS (Office for National Statistics) (2007) *Report from the Review of Equality Data*, London: ONS.

Ottosdottir, G. and Evans, R. (2016) 'Disability and chronic illness', in F. Thomas (ed) *Handbook of migration and health*, Cheltenham and Northampton, MA: Edward Elgar Publishing.

Paradies, Y., Ben, J., Denson, N., Elias, A., Priest, N., Pieterse, A., et al (2015) 'Racism as a determinant of health: A systematic review and meta-analysis', *PLOS One*, 10(9), e0138511.

Pickett, K.E. and Wilkinson, R.G. (2015) 'Income inequality and health: A causal review', *Social Science & Medicine*, 128, 316-26.

Phillimore, J. and Bradby, H. (2016) 'Public policy, immigrant experiences, and health outcomes in the United Kingdom', in D. Raphael (ed) *Immigration, public policy, and health: Newcomer experiences in developed nations*, Toronto: Canadian Scholars Press, 133–56.

Raghavan, R., Pawson, N. and Small, N. (2013) 'Family carers' perspectives on post-school transition of young people with intellectual disabilities with special reference to ethnicity', *Journal of Intellectual Disability Research*, 57(10), 936–46.

Reeve, D. (2002) 'Negotiating psycho-emotional dimensions of disability and their influence on identity constructions', *Disability & Society*, 17(5), 493–508.

Regan, J.L. (2016) 'Ethnic minority, young onset, rare dementia type, depression: A case study of a Muslim male accessing UK dementia health and social care services', *Dementia*, 15(4), 702–20.

Scambler, S. and Newton, P. (2010) '"Where the biological predominates": Habitus, reflexivity and capital accrual within the field of Batten disease', in G. Scambler and S. Scambler (eds) *New directions in the sociology of chronic illness and disabling conditions*, Basingstoke: Palgrave Macmillan, 77–105.

Shakespeare, T. and Watson, N. (2001) 'The social model of disability: An outdated ideology?', in S.N. Barnartt and B.M. Altman (eds) *Research in Social Science and Disability, Volume 2: Exploring theories and expanding methodologies: Where we are and where we need to go*, Bingley: Emerald Group Publishing Limited, 9–28.

Shakespeare, T., Watson, N. and Alghaib, O.A. (2017) 'Blaming the victim, all over again: Waddell and Aylward's biopsychosocial (BPS) model of disability', *Critical Social Policy*, 37(1), 22–41.

Slater, T. (2014) 'The myth of "Broken Britain": Welfare reform and the production of ignorance', *Antipode*, 46(4), 948–69.

Stewart, M. (2016) *Cash not care: The planned demolition of the UK welfare state*, London: New Generation Publishing.

Stuart, O. (2006) *Will community-based support services make direct payments a viable option for Black and minority ethnic service users and carers?*, London: Social Care Institute for Excellence.

Stuart, O. (2012) 'Not invited to the party? BME adults and the personalisation of social care', in G. Craig, K. Atkin, S. Chattoo and R. Flynn (eds) *Understanding 'race' and ethnicity*, Bristol: Policy Press, 133–50.

Sue, D.W. (2010) *Microaggressions in everyday life: Race, gender and sexual orientation*, Hobokon, NJ: John Wiley & Sons.

Swanwick, R., Wright, S. and Salter, J. (2016) 'Investigating deaf children's plural and diverse use of sign and spoken languages in a super diverse context', *Applied Linguistics Review*, 7(2), 117–47.

Temple, B., Young, A. and Bolton, J. (2008) '"They know where to find us …" Service providers' views on Early Support and minority ethnic communities', *Disability & Society*, 23(3), 223–34.

Thomas, C. (2007) *Sociologies of disability and illness: Contested ideas in disability studies and medical sociology*, Basingstoke: Palgrave Macmillan.

Thomas, C. (2012) 'Theorising disability and chronic illness: Where next for perspectives in medical sociology?', *Social Theory and Health*, 10(3), 209-28.

Wailoo, K. (2017a) 'Sickle cell disease – A history of progress and peril', *The New England Journal of Medicine*, 376, 805-7.

Wailoo, K. (2017b) 'Thinking through the pain', *Perspectives in Biology and Medicine*, 59(2), 253-62.

Wallace, S., Nazroo, J. and Bécares, L. (2016) 'Cumulative effect of racial discrimination on the mental health of ethnic minorities in the United Kingdom', *American Journal of Public Health*, 106(7), 1294-300.

Westwood, S., King, A., Almack, K., Suen, Y.T. and Bailey, L. (2015) 'Good practice in health and social care provision for LGBT older people in the UK', in J. Fish and K. Karban (eds) *Lesbian, gay, bisexual and trans health inequalities: International perspectives in social work*, Bristol: Policy Press, 145-58.

WHO (World Health Organization) (2011) *World report on disability*, Geneva: WHO.

Wilkinson, R.G. (2002) *Unhealthy societies: The afflictions of inequality*, London: Routledge.

Wright, S. (2016) 'Conceptualising the active welfare subject: Welfare reform in discourse, policy and lived experience', *Policy & Politics*, 44(2), 235-52.

Wohland, P., Rees, P., Nazroo, J. and Jagger, C. (2015) 'Inequalities in healthy life expectancy between ethnic groups in England and Wales in 2001', *Ethnicity & Health*, 20(4), 341-53.

Yeo, R. (2017) 'The deprivation experienced by disabled asylum seekers in the United Kingdom: symptoms, causes, and possible solutions', *Disability & Society*, 32(5), 1-2.

10

Understanding 'race', ethnicity and mental health

Frank Keating

Overview

The disparities in mental health and mental health service provision for Black and minority ethnic (BME) communities in the UK are well documented, but have not been adequately understood or theorised. This chapter:

- reviews how ethnicity and mental (ill) health have been theorised;
- examines policy and practice responses in the UK, including ethnic-specific service provision in mainstream services;
- explores the advantages and disadvantages of current provision; and
- pays specific attention to diversity within and across groups, particularly women, refugees and asylum-seekers and Gypsies and Travellers.

Key concepts
culture; gender; mental health; service delivery

Introduction

Meeting the mental health needs of people from Black and minority ethnic (BME) communities is an area for public concern. A substantial body of research shows that these groups are disproportionately represented in mental health statistics (Bhui and O'Hara, 2014). On the one hand, there is evidence of overrepresentation in relation to diagnoses such as schizophrenia, while on the other, there is under-representation in relation to diagnoses such as affective disorder. Moreover, these groups receive the services they do not want and not those that they need. The Care Quality Commission (CQC), the health watchdog in England, annually monitors the use of the Mental Health Act 2007, which provides the legal framework to detain people who are deemed mentally ill for compulsory treatment. The 2015/16 report found that there is inequality in the use of the Act between different populations. It reported, for example, that Black men were more likely to be compulsorily detained in hospital compared to White men (CQC, 2016). This disturbing situation persists despite the fact that needs, issues and concerns for BME people with mental health problems have been pushed to the fore of the policy agenda (DH, 2014).

Achieving good mental healthcare for individuals from these communities is one of the biggest challenges for mental health services in England and Wales (DH, 2014; Mental Health Providers Forum and Race Equality Foundation, 2015), because disparities in rates of mental illness, treatment, care and outcomes remain. Explanations for this seemingly intractable situation are varied. It is anticipated that the impact of current austerity measures will exacerbate this situation.

The following sections provide an overview of the policy context in the UK, explore how mental illness is theorised in the context of 'race' and ethnicity, discuss the implications for certain minority groups and offer suggestions for good practice. This chapter predominantly draws on research and practice evidence with African and Caribbean men in England. It acknowledges diversity in mental health services, but notes the limited research with wider groups, and in other UK countries. Generalisations are therefore limited, although experiences of racism and discrimination are common and well documented in other chapters of this book.

Policy context in the UK

There has been a significant lack of policy response to reducing the racial disparities in mental health, at both national and local levels. A tragic, but significant, marker for BME communities was the death of David (Rocky) Bennett in 1998 while being restrained by nursing staff on a medium-secure ward. After a long struggle by his family to achieve justice, an inquiry concluded that mental health services were institutionally racist (Blofeld, 2003). The government subsequently published an action plan for *Delivering race equality* (DRE) in England and Wales (DH, 2005), the first national plan to address inequalities in mental health for BME groups. This plan had three building blocks: the development of more and appropriate and responsive services; better quality information; and increased community engagement.

Laudable as these intentions were, they contained weaknesses. DRE focused on organisational change, but failed to appreciate the heterogeneity in communities and the complex identities and practices they contained. It also failed to appreciate that the inequalities in mental health for Black people that exist cannot be separated from the general inequalities that these communities experience in society. Moreover, the problem seems to have been framed in the context of culture; therefore the focus was on developing a culturally competent workforce. In the final report and recommendations for future action it was noted that participants rated their experience of 'race' equality and cultural capability training positively, but at three-month follow-up these gains were lost (Wilson, 2010). Fernando (2006) argues that a focus on culture can in itself be racist and has to be examined in this context. Cultural competence has arguably led to a narrow focus on aspects such as dietary requirements, religious and spiritual practices, and appropriate environments. These factors are important, but often mean that more serious issues of institutional processes and practices that discriminate against BME communities are overlooked and left intact (see Gunaratnam, 2008).

The DRE programme did offer opportunities to redress the situation through its programme of community engagement, whereby it funded 80 community projects to assess the needs of BME communities and established community development worker (CDW) posts in mental health trusts (DH, 2009). These projects seemed to have a narrow focus on needs assessment despite the needs of these communities already being documented in research; what was required instead were strategies for meeting these needs. Walker and Craig (2009) evaluated the role of DRE mental health CDWs, and found that they were mainly involved in community engagement, scoping and mapping activities and mental health awareness; very few had direct involvement in service delivery or development. They concluded that CDWs are in a position to facilitate engagement with BME communities, but must be located in strategic partnership structures to support 'race' equality. In reality, most were in marginal positions, remote from policy-making centres, poorly paid and supported, with limited budgetary scope, and unable to make effective use of their findings. Fountain and Hicks (2010), in their evaluation of the community engagement dimension of DRE, found that some of the benefits identified were greater awareness of community needs, better access to services and improved links between communities, providers and commissioners. The final reports of the DRE programme acknowledge that the roots of the inequalities for BME communities lie in social, not biological, factors, so 'the responsibility for remedial action extends to all the agencies that influence public mental health and well-being' (NMHDU, 2010, p 2; see also Wilson, 2010). There have been more recent policy developments that will be reviewed here.

First is the strategy for mental health in England (DH, 2011), which makes explicit reference to the need for reducing inequalities in mental health. This policy directive informed other initiatives such as the *Closing the gap* report (DH, 2014), which listed 25 priorities for healthcare, among which two specifically focused on BME communities. These relate to increasing access to mental health services and identifying the mental health needs of offenders sooner. This is pertinent given the broader crisis in accessing mental health services for BME communities (Jeraj et al, 2015). There are glimmers of hope. For example, there is now a commissioning guide on mental health services for BME communities with recommendations to include a patient and carer standard for 'race' equality (Joint Commissioning Panel for Mental Health, 2014). The review of acute psychiatric care (Crisp et al, 2015) recommended that there should be strategies to reduce the overuse of the Mental Health Act for BME communities, and that this should be closely monitored. It also recommended that procurement of services from black voluntary services (BVS) organisations should be prioritised.

Second, the personalisation agenda is enshrined in the Care Act 2014 (HM Government, 2014). This is a model of care that enables a person to choose their care provider and decide how resources will be spent to meet their needs. This offers opportunities for more tailor-made care, and, in the case of BME people, more culturally relevant care (Moriarty, 2014). It is interesting to note that Webber et al (2014) found that the uptake for personal budgets for people with mental health problems is much lower than for other service user groups regardless of ethnicity. Moriarty (2014) posits that the evidence on the experience of BME communities of personal budgets is limited, and it is therefore difficult to arrive at definitive conclusions on its effectiveness for these communities. Moreover, Joannou et al (2011) suggest that this model is not unproblematic in relation to BME communities. Specifically in mental health, the principles enshrined in this model of care seem to go against the fundamental issues that underpin how BME communities experience mental healthcare within the context of relations of power, coercion and control, as explained later. If this agenda is going to yield positive outcomes for BME communities, the coercive nature of their experiences of mental healthcare requires drastic attention.

Third, the Immigration Act 2016 (HM Government, 2016) aims to reduce illegal immigration by making it difficult for migrants to work in the UK and restricting support for those whose claims to asylum have been rejected. It seems that the discourse of refugees and asylum-seekers has shifted from one that aims to respond to human need to one that focuses on economic need, which means that mental health needs will still go unmet, and may even be exacerbated by these policy and legislative developments. Despite these developments, there are still concerns that addressing racial inequalities in mental health do not seem central to current policy initiatives. In fact, Nazroo (2015, p 1066) argues that 'questions of racial inequality have disappeared from the policy agenda' because of a purported belief that Britain is now a post-racial society.

Theorising mental illness

The mental health arena transcends disciplinary boundaries, including psychiatry, nursing, psychology and social work. This offers significant challenges in defining what mental illness means. I have argued that the discourse on mental illness is fraught with tensions and contradictions (Keating, 2016). Definitions of mental (ill) health are influenced by cultural, social and political forces. Unfortunately, biomedical explanations, deriving from psychiatry, have dominated the discourse, and the search for more social and sociological explanations has been hampered. The underlying assumption of the more medically orientated approach is that psychiatric symptoms are universal and uniformly manifested.

There are competing perspectives on what constitutes mental illness (Rogers and Pilgrim, 2014). Bracken and Thomas (2005) argue that our knowledge of mental illness and distress is incomplete, and that new ways of thinking about them are continually emerging. Coppock and Hopton (2000) suggest that there is ample evidence to show that mental illness is not merely a biological issue, but is also affected by social and political circumstances. Moreover, subjective perceptions, cultural frameworks and the invisibility of mental illness make it less tractable than physical illness. Users of mental health services have also challenged how mental health is construed, and proposed that social models of mental health are more helpful (Beresford et al, 2010). Regardless of the perspective or approach to understanding mental illness, it is clear that when a person is assigned a label of mental illness, they take on an identity that is stigmatised and negatively valued (Fernando, 2006; Glasgow Anti-Stigma Partnership, 2007). Mental illness can be deeply dehumanising and alienating. It is generally regarded with anxiety and fear, which leads to rejection and exclusion. People with mental health problems continue to be among the most disadvantaged and socially excluded groups in society (SEU, 2004).

The World Health Organization (WHO) views mental health as:

> a state of well-being in which the individual realises his or her own abilities, can cope with the normal stresses of life, can work productively and fruitfully, and is able to make a contribution to his or her community. (2010, revised 2014)

This definition assumes that there is a universal dimension to an understanding of mental health, ignoring that these understandings are relative and contextual (Fernando, 2014). Fernando (2014) also argues that in global contexts it is unhelpful to apply definitions universally. Moreover, little is known about whether BME communities share or subscribe to this understanding of mental health. Defining mental illness is ultimately a political, social and cultural issue, and more work is needed to explore the views and perspectives of BME communities on mental (ill) health and how this may affect their willingness to seek help when needed.

Ethnicity and mental health

One enters a contested area of knowledge when concepts such as 'race', ethnicity and mental illness are linked. Most authors propose that a key to understanding issues of 'race', culture and ethnicity is to be clear about how these are defined. I would argue differently. Following the lead of Cooper et al (2005; see also Chapter 2, this volume), 'race' and 'ethnicity' should be viewed as social constructions, with different individual and societal meanings depending on the context in which they are applied. Important to consider are the meanings attached to 'race' and its sub-components of 'ethnicity', culture and racism. These concepts carry what Knowles (1999, p 125) terms 'the edifice of negative social meanings'. One cannot, therefore, assume that all people from BME groups will assign similar meaning and value to being cast in the role of the 'other' and, by implication, in an inferior position. They may not therefore identify themselves as part of an institutionally racist situation. Ethnicity also constitutes only one dimension, albeit an important one, of the identities of BME people, but it intersects with other social divisions such as age, ability, class, gender and sexuality.

Dressler (1993) argues that epidemiology has failed to formulate useful theories of ethnicity that can be employed to evaluate ethnic group differences in mental health. He offers a review of traditional models, and suggests one that usefully explains the disparities in mental health for minority groups (see Box 10.1). He posits that an understanding of the inequalities and disparities in health (and, I would assert, mental health too) can provide insights into the social processes that underpin these inequalities (see also Chapter 8, this volume). More importantly, such an understanding can form a useful basis for strategies to address or even overcome inequalities in mental health.

Box 10.1 Explanations for health inequalities

Dressler (1993), writing about health inequalities in the USA, reviewed three models that have been used to explain ethnic differences in health, and offers a fourth that can be utilised to achieve a fuller understanding. These models are relevant to a UK context as they reflect how inequalities in mental health have been theorised in the UK.

Racial-genetic model
This model is premised on the hypothesis that phenotypic and genetic features, such as skin colour, predispose certain groups (that is, minorities) to ill health. Despite the fact that such views have been refuted, there is a body of research that still attempts to use ethnicity as a signifier for mental illness (Singh, 2005).

Health-behaviour lifestyle model
A basic premise of this model is that differences between ethnic groups are a function of unhealthy behaviours such as smoking, alcohol and drug misuse. In the UK, this hypothesis has been used to link schizophrenia with the excessive use of cannabis. Thus

the term 'cannabis psychosis' has been introduced and offered as an explanation for the elevated rates of schizophrenia for certain groups such as African Caribbean people. However, there is inconclusive evidence of the association between excessive use of cannabis and psychosis. Hence this model does not provide adequate explanations for inequalities in mental health.

A socioeconomic model

This model posits that the differences in mental health between certain groups can be ascribed to factors such as poverty, education, employment and so on. Such an explanation may be of partial use, especially given that BME groups in the UK fare worse across all social indicators such as education, employment, housing and so on. Cooper et al (2008) have shown that socioeconomic status alone does not account for these differences. Further, this model does not take into account factors such as differential access to these resources, and therefore cannot fully explain the inequalities that these groups experience in mental health.

A social-structural model

Building on the socioeconomic model, this hypothesis states that the structural position of BME groups in society and the continued discrimination against them in a racialised society contributes significantly to the inequalities in mental health. In the UK this has been explored and confirmed by several authors, for example, Karlsen and Nazroo (2002), McKenzie et al (2008) and Sharpley et al (2001). More specifically, Cooper et al (2008) found that perceived disadvantage mediated the relationship between ethnicity and psychosis.

Source: Adapted from Dressler (1993)

Hence, key thinkers in this area have sought biological explanations for disparities in diagnosis of mental (ill) health, while others have looked for more social explanations (Morgan et al, 2004; McKenzie, 2006), and still others offer racism as a causal factor (Fernando, 2014; McKenzie, 2006; Nazroo, 2015). Blofeld's (2003) inquiry into the death of Rocky Bennett (referred to earlier) cogently illustrated how racism was at play in his mental healthcare.

However, none of these hypotheses fully explain why the mental health situation for Black people has persisted over the last 30 years. For example, the hypothesis that racism based on skin colour is a causal factor does not explain the mental health disparities for Irish communities in England (Rogers and Pilgrim, 2014). Life stressors have also been suggested as a causal factor, but Gilvarry et al (1999) found no differences in life stressors between White and Black ethnic groups, but did find that Black people will attribute adverse life events to racism. Karlsen

(2007; see also Wallace et al, 2016) also illustrated how adverse life events can have a damaging effect on the mental health of Black people. The implications of this are that people from minority groups may therefore be disinclined to use services that they perceive to be prejudiced against them.

There are more recent theoretical developments to explain the intersections between ethnicity and mental health. For example, critical race theory offers a framework for analysing the endemic nature of racism and the devastating impact on the lived experiences of BME communities (Delgado and Stefancic, 2017). Critical race theory was developed to challenge liberal views of structural inequality that positioned 'race' as analogous to class-based discrimination (Rollock and Gillborn, 2011). It offers a radical framework to enable a critical examination of 'race', racism and the intersections of power and law (Rollock and Gillborn, 2011). Another example is intersectionalities, a theory that examines and explains how different social divisions interconnect and intertwine to inform identity (Crenshaw, 1991; see also Chapter 2, this volume). I have reviewed these developments elsewhere (Keating, 2015, 2016).

Discrimination, disadvantage and mental health

Karlsen (2007) demonstrated the connections between racial discrimination and poor health, concluding that people from BME groups experience poorer health as a result of negative attitudes towards them (see Chapter 8, this volume). They also often find themselves in situations considered as reinforcing risk factors for mental illness. These include exclusion from school (84% of children excluded from schools are boys from Caribbean backgrounds); social deprivation as a result of unemployment; the prevalence of crime and drug cultures; and overrepresentation in prison populations (White, 2006). The evidence also shows that the current economic crisis and austerity measures affect BME communities disproportionately (EHRC, 2016). Khan (2015) reviewed the impact of budget cuts in the UK on BME communities, and predicted that they are likely to be adversely impacted in the areas of part-time employment, child poverty, benefits caps and so on. For BME groups these experiences are all underpinned or informed by their experiences of racism, which may influence their help-seeking behaviour. The reason for not seeking help may be fear of the possible consequences such as loss of status, control, independence and autonomy (White, 2006). The problems are compounded for minority groups because of their perceptions of mental health services and a belief that these services will discriminate against them (Keating and Robertson, 2004). More importantly, there exists a real and potent fear that engagement with mental health services will lead to their death (Keating and Robertson, 2004). Fountain and Hicks (2010) found that fear of engagement was also related to the social repercussions that may arise as a result of accessing mental health services. I therefore argue that, before we can improve aspects of mental health service delivery, such as access to care, appropriate treatment and so on, we need a critical understanding of the connections between culture, ethnicity, 'race', racism and mental illness.

Another issue to consider is the impact of racial disadvantage and discrimination on individuals, their families and communities. Patel and Fatimilehin (1999) suggest that the impact of racism is psychological, social and material. The effects of these are likely to be detrimental to mental health; for some they will be minimal, but for others the effects will be of great significance to their emotional well-being (Karlsen, 2007). Hence, the cumulative effects of racial discrimination have been established. In a recent analysis of the Longitudinal Household Survey in the UK, Wallace et al (2016) found that exposure to racial discrimination over a period of time has incremental negative effects on the mental health and well-being of BME groups. The impact of racism has to be analysed in the context of histories of migration, alienation, subordination and the way in which these groups have been and continue to be stigmatised in society.

'Blackness' and 'madness': the negative spiral

Keating et al (2002) have demonstrated that stereotypical views of Black people, racism, cultural ignorance, stigma and the anxiety associated with mental illness often combine to undermine the way in which mental health services assess and respond to the needs of BME communities. Other authors have directed attention to the disproportionate rate of hospital admissions, adverse pathways to care, such as the involvement of the police, and overuse of the Mental Health Act for some groups (Morgan et al, 2004; Moffat et al, 2006). So, for African and Caribbean men, being seen as 'big, Black, bad, dangerous and mad' can lead to conceptions that they are less deserving of treatment that would lead them to pathways of recovery (Keating, 2016). Meerai et al (2016) offer a useful critique of the associations with the label 'mad' and the dominant stereotypes of Black male identities and the resultant treatment they receive in mental health services.

Minority ethnic groups with mental health problems face at least four negative forces that underpin their experiences:

- how BME people are treated in society;
- how people with mental health problems are perceived in society;
- the power of institutions to control and coerce people with mental health problems; and
- the perceptions of BME people that mental health services are discriminatory and dangerous.

These experiences in society have an impact on their mental and emotional well-being. These experiences, in turn, influence how they experience and perceive mental health services. Their (historical and contemporary) marginal position in society affects how they are treated in mental health services – and these various experiences interact to produce what Trivedi (2002) terms 'a spiral of oppression'. Black people do not trust mental health services and those who work in mental health services fear them, which means that there is lack of engagement on both sides. The spiral is presented in Figure 10.1, and the challenge for mental health professionals is therefore to break this spiral.

Figure 10.1: The spiral of oppression

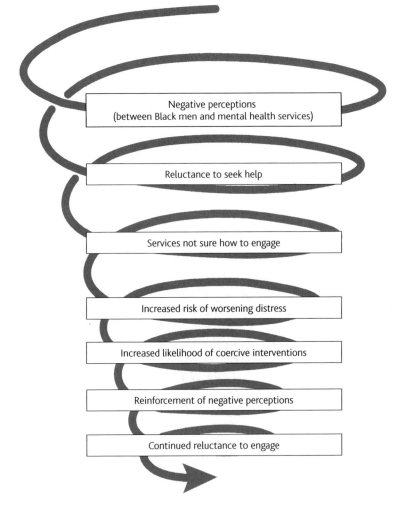

Negative perceptions
(between Black men and mental health services)

Reluctance to seek help

Services not sure how to engage

Increased risk of worsening distress

Increased likelihood of coercive interventions

Reinforcement of negative perceptions

Continued reluctance to engage

Source: Keating (2007)

Establishing mental health status in minority ethnic groups

Assessing or finding out the true extent of mental illness in BME communities is difficult and complex. There is conflicting and contradictory evidence on who is affected by mental illness in these communities. The first systematic attempt at gathering information on the mental health status of BME groups in hospital settings in England and Wales was derived from the 'Count Me In' census in 2006 (Healthcare Commission, 2007). This was later extended to include community mental health settings.

The rates that have been presented show significant differences for certain minority groups. Differences between groups are to be expected, but when these differences are due to social factors and the allocation of or access to resources, they should be construed as disparities or inequalities (Schwartz and Meyer, 2010). There are commonalities across groups, but there is also diversity within and across groups. A common finding is that the risk of psychosis is elevated in nearly all BME groups compared with the White British group (Bhui and O'Hara, 2014).

In addition, the following common experiences across BME groups have been documented in relation to disparities in mental health diagnosis, access to services and outcomes. These groups commonly experience:

- stigma, stereotypical views, racism and negative social repercussions, which ultimately lead to these groups being reluctant to seek help;
- cultural barriers, including language, particularly for some Black African people and older generations of South Asian and Chinese people;
- culturally inappropriate or insensitive services;
- services that are unable to engage with contextual factors; and
- social risk factors such as unemployment, poverty and educational attainment (Bhui et al, 2003; DH, 2007; Fountain and Hicks, 2010).

Experiences that are particular to certain minority ethnic groups are summarised as follows.

South Asian sub-groups commonly experience:

- loneliness and isolation, particularly Bangladeshi groups;
- higher rates of alcohol misuse for men, particularly Pakistani and Muslim men who drink;
- difficulties in access to healthcare such as primary care services (Nazroo et al, 2009);
- higher rates of suicide and self-harm for women; and
- lack of knowledge about services, particularly among older people (DH, 2007; McKenzie et al, 2008; Hurcombe et al, 2010).

African and Caribbean groups commonly experience:

- elevated rates of schizophrenia;
- aversive pathways to care;
- greater involvement of the police in admission to mental healthcare;
- controlling and harsher treatments;
- high rates of suicide for young men with a diagnosis of schizophrenia; and
- low access to psychological support (DH, 2007; Bhui et al, 2003; Fountain and Hicks, 2010; Sharpley et al, 2001; Bhui and O'Hara, 2014).

There are other ethnic groups about whose mental health little is known. For example, the mental health needs of the Chinese community are underresearched, with difficulties with language and socioeconomic status defined as significant risk factors for mental (ill) health (Au and Tang, 2009). A mixed-methods study exploring the mental health needs of the Chinese community in Birmingham (Huang and Spurgeon, 2006) found a high level of psychiatric morbidity compared to the general population. Particularly affected were older people, students and migrant workers. The evidence shows that Chinese people in the UK continue to use traditional medicines for mental health problems, and it is important for mainstream services to find ways of working that can incorporate and accommodate such practices into providing appropriate mental healthcare for these communities (Tighe and Tran, 2010). However, a scoping exercise in Scotland focusing on perceptions of mental well-being in Chinese and Pakistani communities drew 52% of its English-written literature from China (Newbigging et al, 2008). Researchers may thus need to look outside Europe more often for their sources.

Issues for particular groups

Women

Significant levels of need have been identified for BME women, yet there are low levels of service use. Figures suggest that more women than men will experience some form of mental health problem (Bird, 1999; Wilson, 2001; McManus et al, 2009). The National Psychiatric Morbidity Survey (McManus et al, 2009), for example, reported that the rates for common mental disorder among women were higher for Asian women. Black British women are four times more likely to be detained under the Mental Health Act 1983 compared to White British women (Crisp et al, 2015). Edge (2010) also points out that there is evidence that women from BME groups, in particular, African Caribbean groups, are at increased risk of mental health problems in the perinatal period. However, Kotecha (2009, p 71) argues that 'a potent mix of gender blindness and negative views of minority cultures further contributes to BME women's mental health needs being neglected across the spectrum of research, policy development, service provision and practice'. For example, a policy document relating to women's mental health (DH, 2002) paid scant attention to the issues for women from BME groups. A review of this policy in 2010 (NMHDU, 2010) reports that there are still significant gaps in personalised services for women from these groups. It found that a number of community engagement projects have been developed through the DRE programme (DH, 2005), but these are largely in the voluntary sector, and there is still a need to ensure equal access to mental healthcare for the diverse needs of women (Fountain and Hicks, 2010; NMHDU, 2010).

McKenzie et al (2008) found that the rates of suicide for older Asian women was double that of the general population. Earlier evidence showed a higher rate for young Asian women (Raleigh, 1996), but McKenzie et al (2008) found that the rate for younger Asian women was only marginally raised. They conclude that there are a number of factors that may explain the fall in rates for younger Asian women, such as demographic change and how stress is managed in these communities, but this needs further research attention. They recommend further research to explain the increased rates for older Asian women, and that this group be a target for a prevention strategy. Refugee and asylum-seeker women require specific attention. Gill and Banga (2009) suggest that these women are less likely to access services because of their lack of awareness of the options available. Domestic violence and abuse have also been identified as significant risk factors for mental distress due to barriers to reporting abuse and a desire to protect 'family honour'. Consequently, it has been suggested that a range of accessible services are needed to support women, specifically those with children, women at risk of suicide, and refugees and asylum-seekers (Wilson, 2001; Gill and Banga, 2009; Kotecha, 2009; Edge, 2010). Services should respond to a diverse range of needs, and gender and ethnicity should be key variables in measuring service access and outcomes for BME women.

Refugees and asylum-seekers

Millions of people have been uprooted and displaced after the Second World War and as a result, the Geneva Convention (UNHCR, 2010) was drafted to provide protection for people who felt that they did not have protection in their own countries. During the 1990s new internal conflicts arose in various parts of the world that sparked a rapid increase in the numbers of people fleeing war and persecution. The UK has been receiving refugees and asylum-seekers alongside other European nations, although it should be noted that it takes in fewer refugees and asylum-seekers than other countries in Europe. There are various debates on the presence of refugees and asylum-seekers in the UK, underpinned by myths and stereotypes that often result in discrimination and exclusion (Allsop et al,

2014). The current situation for refugees and asylum-seekers is made worse by austerity measures such as changes in entitlements to benefits and cuts to social benefits, which means that poverty is central to their lived experience (Allsop et al, 2014).

Refugees and asylum-seekers are among the most vulnerable and isolated groups in the UK (Patel, 2009; Sen, 2016). Refugees experience stress, acculturation difficulties, losses and life events that are mediators for mental disorder. However, the refugee experience is not a natural dimension of the human experience, and should therefore not be automatically associated with mental ill health. These experiences can lead to higher levels of distress, depression and anxiety (Vostanis, 2014; Sen, 2016). As for other migrant groups and more settled communities, there are problems with access to mental health services for refugees and asylum-seekers. This is often compounded by their eligibility and lack of entitlement to services, or the fact that their distress resulting from traumatic experiences is pathologised by mental health professionals. Identifying mental illness within refugee groups is problematic because of difficulties in communication, in cultural explanatory models for mental illness and in their economic and political contexts and public perceptions of their status (Watters and Ingleby, 2004; Patel, 2009). Professionals need to be aware of the health and social care needs of refugees and asylum-seekers, but also alert to the risk of suicide (Bhui et al, 2006). Gaining access to sustainable housing (Jones and Mullins, 2009) and sustainable employment are key factors that can have a positive impact on the emotional well-being of refugees and asylum-seekers. Mental health promotion strategies should aim to reduce isolation, and promote opportunities for employment and education, underpinned by a partnership approach to overcome the discrimination and isolation of these communities (Burnett and Peel, 2001; Burnett, 2009).

Gypsies and Travellers

Gypsies and Travellers have a longstanding presence in the UK, yet they continue to be treated with hostility and misunderstanding (Cemlyn, 2008). As discussed in Chapter 8, they experience significant levels of disadvantage, reflected in their lower access to health generally and to mental health services in particular. Current austerity measures referred to earlier are likely to increase the levels of disadvantage experienced by these groups (Lau and Ridge, 2011). Matthews (2008) found scant reference to the health needs of these groups in the policy arena. Gypsies and Travellers experience significant health inequalities. For example, they are more likely to have a long-term health condition and to experience higher rates of depression and anxiety (Lane et al, 2014). Cultural beliefs associated with mental health also affect their willingness to seek help for mental health problems. This is often compounded by a lack of sensitivity and understanding on the part of health professionals (Parry et al, 2007). It has been suggested that a piecemeal approach to service provision for Gypsies and Travellers contributes to the high levels of social exclusion they experience in health and social care services (Cemlyn, 2008). Improving the cultural competence of professionals and outreach services and partnership working with Gypsies and Travellers can go some way to combat the discrimination and exclusion they face (Parry et al, 2007; Cemlyn, 2008).

Experiencing mental health services

Psychiatry is the only branch of medicine that legitimately allows healthcare professionals to forcibly treat, restrain and control individuals with mental health problems. These functions of providing care, control and accommodation are delivered through a network of mental health services such as community mental health teams and early interventions teams (Rogers and Pilgrim, 2014). Mental health professionals have the power to name and rename emotional distress. Rogers and Pilgrim (2014) argue that racial biases mean that these groups are disproportionately dealt with by specialist mental health services, and as these services are characterised by coercive practices, this constitutes structural disadvantage. Contributing to the disadvantages that BME groups experience in mental health services is the 'risk agenda' dominating mental health policy over the recent past.

Minority groups' experiences of mental health services are characterised by access to services they do not want and the lack of receipt of services they need (Keating et al, 2002). There is evidence of complex pathways into mental healthcare often involving the police and the criminal justice system (Moffat et al, 2006). The England and Wales 'Count Me In' census of 2009 demonstrated that referral rates from general practitioners and community mental health teams were lower than average for some minority ethnic groups. Overall, admission rates were higher for minority ethnic groups, at 23% of the total inpatient population, although they only constitute 8% of the general population. Rates of detention under the Mental Health Act 1983 were between 19% and 38% higher than average. These rates were particularly elevated for Black groups (especially men) and higher than average for Pakistani groups. Higher rates of control and restraint applied mainly to Black groups, but also to White Irish and White Other groups. Certain groups – in particular Indian, Bangladeshi, Black Caribbean and Other Black groups – were more likely to be subject to Community Treatment Orders (CQC, 2011, 2016).

It is clear that individuals from these minority groups do not receive equal care. This situation seems unchanging, as illustrated by a study exploring the views and experiences of mental health service users of African and Caribbean communities in Birmingham (Rabiee and Smith, 2007). This found that service users have negative perceptions of mainstream mental health services. The service user survey as part of the BME 'Count Me In' census of 2005 in England and Wales reported that Black service users were most disadvantaged in inpatient services, reported higher levels of dissatisfaction with their care, and were more likely to experience harsher treatments such as control and restraint (Mental Health Act Commission, 2006).

Experience in the Black-led voluntary sector

There is evidence that the BVS sector offers appropriate and relevant support to minority groups (Keating et al, 2002; Fountain and Hicks, 2010; Knifton et al, 2010). They work from conceptual frameworks of mental distress that embrace the whole person instead of narrowly defined categories of mental illness (Saheliya et al, 2008; Fernando and Keating, 2009; Mohammed, 2010). Services in this sector are valued because they make critical observations about psychiatry and its limitations, but they also include an understanding of the political reality of the experiences of minority ethnic groups (Moffat et al, 2006; Mohammed, 2010). However, these services face problems of short–term contracts, inadequate funding and limited opportunities for developing robust infrastructures (Mental Health Providers Forum and Race Equality Foundation, 2015). It has been predicted that the austerity measures referred to above are also more likely to affect BVS organisations. The intelligence (knowledge and skills) potentially gleaned from services in this sector has not been incorporated into mainstream service delivery, nor has there been an extensive evaluation of their contribution to reducing inequality.

Responding positively

This section provides some pointers to ways in which the disparities in mental health for BME groups can be addressed.

Suggestion 1: Talking 'race', talking mental illness

Practitioners need to make connections between a person's lived experience, their behaviour and their distress. In research on *Breaking the circles of fear*, Keating et al (2002) found that mental health professionals were fearful of talking about issues of 'race' and culture, fearing being cast as racist or 'getting it wrong'. Inevitably, by *not* talking about these issues, they get it wrong. An important starting point is to engage in a dialogue about 'race' and mental illness. Engaging with and reflecting on the inequality, discrimination and oppression that arise from social divisions in society is deeply challenging. It is an invitation to examine who we are: our experiences of advantages and disadvantage, power and powerlessness, inclusion and exclusion (Williams and Keating, 2005).

Suggestion 2: Creating safe spaces of entry

The pathways into services for some BME groups have been described as problematic (Keating et al, 2002; CQC, 2011; Bhui and O'Hara, 2014). BME people are more likely to come into contact with services via the police or criminal justice system or at the instigation of family members. Given the fraught nature of the relationships between BME communities, the police and other institutions of social control, and the deep mistrust they have of them, it is important to find alternative ways of engaging these groups with mental health services, but more so, to help them deal with the stresses of racism and everyday life more effectively. BME groups need safe points of 'entry' into talking about their emotional distress. Individuals from minority ethnic groups need to be encouraged to talk about their concerns, in non-stigmatising and safe environments. Safe spaces can only be created when mental health services change their negative perceptions of these communities, work to establish positive relationships with them and offer services addressing their lived experiences. They need to work to establish positive relationships with these communities by building and sustaining effective partnerships with BME service user groups and survivor-led service organisations (Kalathil, 2013).

Suggestion 3: People need care that helps them to find their way back to a meaningful existence, meaningful relationships, meaningful connections and a restored identity

When BME people come into contact with mental health services they are offered standard medicalised responses to their situation and needs (Fountain and Hicks, 2010). Service users report that mental health workers view them only in terms of their diagnosis and tend to deal with their illness in isolation from other aspects of their lives (Keating et al, 2002). This narrow focus on biological factors means that other contributing factors to their distress or impacting on their treatment often go undetected, untreated and unresolved. This leads service users to conclude that the services are 'inhumane' (Kalathil, 2013) and treat them without respect and dignity. We need social care and welfare services to provide responses that speak to people's life circumstances, including their lived experience of racism, inequality and discrimination. This means incorporating their experience and viewpoints into an assessment of their situation, making sense of their everyday activities of life. Practitioners are required to document the concrete details of people's lives. A significant aspect of understanding lived experience is to identify sources of oppression and tease out the overlaps and intersections between 'race', ethnicity, culture, age, class, gender, religion, disability and sexuality. Partnerships between BME survivor-led and BVS organisations should be developed. Examples are work in Scotland that has involved partnerships with BME voluntary organisations and engaging BME service users in definitions of mental well-being (Newbigging et al, 2008; Saheliya et al, 2008; Knifton et al, 2010).

Conclusion

Eradicating disparities in mental health treatment and outcomes for BME people requires changes in how these communities are viewed. Making services more humane at the interpersonal level is deeply important. Everyone values positive relationships: they are key to good emotional and social functioning. People who have been excluded and marginalised and who have suffered emotional distress are in greater need of positive relationships. Mental health services should build positive working relationships with BME individuals, and engage with the ideals they have of themselves. The overrepresentation and negative experiences of Black men in mental health services call for a multidisciplinary and multi-agency approach involving service providers such as the criminal justice system, the educational system and others outside the field of mental health.

There should be a greater focus on prevention and early intervention, and an active programme of mental health promotion aimed at minority groups. There is a small, but growing, Black service user movement, and their efforts should be supported. Improving mental and emotional well-being for BME communities should be anchored in history, broader societal conditions and their lived experiences, including experiences of racism, but also how they have survived in the face of adversity. We need services that address cultural diversity and challenge inequality, and professional cultures that enable practitioners to reflect on these issues in the quest to promote and provide mental health services that are just, fair and equal.

In exploring the relationship between mental (ill) health, ethnicity and racism, it is clear that we encounter complex issues affecting access to mental healthcare and the appropriateness of services to BME communities. There have been measures at national and local levels to address the disparities that BME groups face. Progress in engaging communities has been limited (Fountain and Hicks, 2010). Addressing racism and racial inequalities in mental health seems to be the most effective route to improving the mental health and well-being of these communities.

Questions for discussion

- Why do BME communities experience difficulties in accessing appropriate mental healthcare?
- Explore ways in which mental healthcare for BME groups can be improved.

- A number of theoretical positions and examples of how they play out in practice are mentioned. Discuss the pros and cons of each, and note the evidence used to support your discussion.

Online resources

www.blackmentalhealth.org.uk
   Black Mental Health UK is a community-based, Black-led human rights campaigning group to address inequalities in mental health for African and Caribbean communities.

www.raceequalityfoundation.org.uk
   The Race Equality Foundation seeks to use evidence about discrimination and disadvantage to promote race equality in health, housing and social care.

www.rota.org.uk
   Race on the Agenda is a social policy think tank focusing exclusively on issues that affect BME communities.

Further reading

Bhugra, D., Craig, T. and Bhui, K. (2010) *Mental health of refugees and asylum seekers*, Oxford: Oxford University Press.
Fernando, S. (2010) *Mental health, race and culture* (3rd edn), Basingstoke: Palgrave Macmillan.
Sewell, H. (2008) *Working with ethnicity, race and culture in mental health: A handbook for practitioners*, London: Jessica Kingsley Publishers.

References

Allsop, J., Nando, S. and Phillimore, J. (2014) *Poverty among refugees and asylum seekers in the UK*, Birmingham: Institute for Research into Superdiversity.
Au, S. and Tang, R. (2009) 'Mental health services for Chinese people', in S. Fernando and F. Keating (eds) *Mental health in a multi-ethnic society: A multidisciplinary handbook*, London: Routledge, 235-58.
Beresford, P., Nettle, M. and Perring, R. (2010) *Towards a social model of madness or distress? Exploring what services users say*, York: Joseph Rowntree Foundation.
Bhui, K. and O'Hara, J. (2014) 'Ethnic inequalities, complexity and social exclusion', in S. Davies (ed) *Annual report of the Chief Medical Officer 2013*, London: Department of Health, 275-84.

Bhui, K., Stansfeld, S., Hull, S., Priebe, S., Mole, F. and Feder, G. (2003) 'Ethnic variations in pathways to and use of specialist mental health services in the UK: Systematic review', *The British Journal of Psychiatry*, 182, 105-16.

Bhui, K., Craig, T., Mohamud, S., Warfa, N., Stansfeld, S.A., Thornicroft, G., et al (2006) 'Mental disorders among Somali refugees: Developing culturally appropriate measures and assessing socio-cultural risk factors', *Social Psychiatry and Epidemiology*, 41, 400-8.

Bird, L. (1999) *The fundamental facts*, London: Mental Health Foundation.

Blofeld, J. (2003) *Independent Inquiry into the Death of David Bennett*, London: Department of Health.

Bracken, P. and Thomas P. (2005) *Postpsychiatry: Mental health in a postmodern world*, Oxford: Oxford University Press.

Burnett, A. (2009) 'The Sanctuary Practice in Hackney', in S. Fernando and F. Keating (eds) *Mental health in a multi-ethnic society: A multidisciplinary handbook*, London: Routledge, 217-25.

Burnett, A. and Peel, M. (2001) 'Health needs of asylum seekers and refugees', *British Medical Journal*, 322, 544-7.

Cemlyn, S. (2008) 'Human rights and Gypsies and Travellers: An exploration of the application of a human rights perspective to social work with minority communities', *British Journal of Social Work*, 38, 153-73.

Cooper, C., Morgan, C., Byrne, M., Dazzan, P., Morgan, G., Hutchinson, G., et al (2008) 'Perceptions of disadvantage, ethnicity and psychosis', *The British Journal of Psychiatry*, 192, 185-90.

Cooper, L., Beach, M.C., Johnson, R.L. and Inui, T.S. (2005) 'Delving below the surface: Understanding how race and ethnicity influence relationships in health care', *Journal of General Internal Medicine*, 21, S21-S27.

Coppock, V. and Hopton, J. (2000) *Critical perspectives on mental health*, London: Routledge.

Crenshaw, K. (1991) 'Mapping the margins: Intersectionality, identity politics, and violence against women of color', *Stanford Law Review*, 43(6), 1241-99.

Crisp, N., Smith, G. and Nicholson, K. (eds) (2015) *Old problems, new solutions – Improving acute psychiatric care for adults in England*, London: Commission on Acute Adult Psychiatric Care.

CQC (Care Quality Commission) (2011) *Count Me In 2010: Results of the 2010 National Census of inpatients and patients on supervised community treatment in mental health and learning disability services in England and Wales*, London: CQC.

CQC (2016) *Monitoring the Mental Health Act in 2015/16*, London: CQC.

Delgado, R. and Stefancic, J. (2017) *Critical race theory: An introduction*, New York: New York University Press.

DH (Department of Health) (2002) *Women's mental health: Into the mainstream*, London: DH.

DH (2005) *Delivering race equality in mental health care: An action plan for reform inside and outside services and the government's response to the Independent Inquiry into the Death of David Bennett*, London: DH.

DH (2007) *Positive steps: Supporting race equality in mental healthcare*, London: DH.

DH (2009) *Delivering race equality in mental health care: A review*, London: DH.

DH (2011) *No health without mental health: Mental health strategy for England*, London: DH.

DH (2014) *Closing the gap: Priorities for essential change in mental health*, London: DH.

Dressler, W.D. (1993) 'Health in the African American community: Accounting for health inequalities', *Medical Anthropology Quarterly*, 7(4), 325-45.

Edge, D. (2010) 'Perinatal mental health care for black and minority ethnic (BME) women: A scoping review of provision in England', *Ethnicity and Inequalities in Health and Social Care*, 3(3), 24-32.

EHRC (Equality and Human Rights Commission) (2016) *Healing a divided Britain: The need for a comprehensive race equality strategy*, London: EHRC.

Fernando, S. (2006) 'Stigma, racism and power', *Ethnic Network Journal*, 1(1), 24-8.

Fernando, S. (2014) *Mental health worldwide: Culture, globalisation and development*, Basingstoke: Palgrave Macmillan.

Fernando, S. and Keating, F. (2009) 'The way ahead', in S. Fernando and F. Keating, *Mental health in a multi-ethnic society: A multidisciplinary handbook*, London: Routledge, 235-58.

Fountain, J. and Hicks, J. (2010) *Delivering race equality in mental health care: Report on the findings and outcomes of the community engagement programme 2005-2008*, Preston: University of Central Lancashire.

Gill, A. and Banga, B (2009) *Black, minority ethnic and refugee women, domestic violence and access to housing*, London: Race Equality Foundation.

Gilvarry, C.M., Walsh, E., Samele, C., Hutchinson, G., Mallet, R., Rabe-Hesket, S., et al (1999) 'Life events, ethnicity and perceptions of discrimination in patients with severe mental illness', *Social Psychiatry and Psychiatric Epidemiology*, 34(11), 600-8.

Glasgow Anti-Stigma Partnership (2007) *Mosaics of meaning full report. Exploring stigma and discrimination towards mental health problems with black and minority ethnic communities in Glasgow* (www.seemescotland.org).

Gunaratnam, Y. (2008) 'Care, artistry and what might be', *Ethnicity and Inequalities in Health and Social Care*, 1(1), 9-17.

Healthcare Commission (2007) *Count Me In: Results of the 2006 national census of inpatients in mental health hospitals and facilities in England and Wales*, London: Healthcare Commission.

HM Government (2014) *The Care Act 2014*, London: The Stationery Office.

HM Government (2016) *The Immigration Act 2016*, London: The Stationery Office.

Huang, S. and Spurgeon, A. (2006) 'The mental health of Chinese immigrants in Birmingham, UK', *Ethnicity & Health*, 11(14), 365-87.

Hurcombe, R., Bayley, R. and Goodman, A. (2010) *Ethnicity and alcohol: A review of the UK literature*, York: Joseph Rowntree Foundation.

Jeraj, S., Shoham, T. and Islam-Barrett, F. (2015) *Mental health crisis review: Experiences of black and minority ethnic communities*, London: Race Equality Foundation.

Joannou, D., Fernando, M., Harrison-Read, C. and Wickramasinghe, N. (2011) 'Impacting on diversity practice in an outer London Borough', *Ethnicity and Inequalities in Health and Social Care*, 2, 71-81.

Joint Commissioning Panel for Mental Health (2014) *Guidance for commissioners of mental health services for people from black and minority ethnic communities*, London: Royal College of Psychiatrists.

Jones, P.A. and Mullins, D. (2009) *Refugee community organisations: Working in partnership to improve access to housing services*, London: Race Equality Foundation.

Kalathil, J. (2013) *Dancing to our own tunes: Reassessing black and minority ethnic mental health service user movement*, London: NSUN in partnership with Catch-a-Fyia.

Karlsen, S. (2007) *Ethnic inequalities in health: The impact of racism*, Better Health Briefing Paper 3, London: Race Equality Foundation.

Karlsen, S. and Nazroo, J.Y. (2002) 'The relationship between racial discrimination, social class and health among ethnic minority groups', *American Journal of Public Health*, 92, 624-31.

Keating, F. (2007) *A Race Equality Briefing: African and Caribbean men and mental health*, London: Race Equality Foundation.

Keating, F. (2015) 'Linking "race", mental health and a social model of disability', in H.S. Spandler, J. Anderson and B. Sapey (eds) *Madness, distress and the politics of disablement*, Bristol: Policy Press, 127-38.

Keating, F. (2016) 'Racialised communities, producing madness and dangerousness', *Intersectionalities: A Global Journal of Social Work Analysis, Research, Policy and Practice*, 5(3), 173-85.

Keating, F. and Robertson, D. (2004) 'Fear, black people and mental illness: A vicious circle?', *Health and Social Care in the Community*, 12(5), 439-47.

Keating, F., Robertson, D., Francis, F. and McCulloch, A. (2002) *Breaking the circles of fear. A review of the relationship between mental health services and African and Caribbean communities*, London: Sainsbury Centre for Mental Health.

Khan, O. (2015) *The 2015 Budget: Effects on Black and minority ethnic people*, London: Runnymede Trust.

Knifton, L., Gervais, M., Newbigging, K., Mirza, N., Quinn, N., Wilson, N. and Hunkins-Hutchinson, E. (2010) 'Community conversation: Addressing mental health stigma with ethnic minority communities', *Social Psychiatry and Psychiatric Epidemiology*, 45(4), 497-504.

Knowles, C. (1999) 'Race, identities and lives', *The Sociological Review*, 47(1), 110–35.

Kotecha, N. (2009) 'Black and minority ethnic women', in S. Fernando and F. Keating (eds) *Mental health in a multi-ethnic society: A multidisciplinary handbook*, London: Routledge, 58–71.

Lane, P., Spencer, S. and Jones, A. (2014) *Gypsy, Traveller and Roma: Experts by experience*, Cambridge: Anglia Ruskin University.

Lau, A. and Ridge, M. (2011) 'Addressing the impact of social exclusion on mental health in Gypsy, Roma and Traveller communities', *Mental Health and Social Inclusion*, 15(3), 129–37.

Matthews, Z. (2008) *The health of Gypsies and Travellers in the UK*, Better Health Briefing 12, London: Race Equality Foundation.

McKenzie, K. (2006) 'Racial discrimination and mental health', *Psychiatry*, 5(11), 383–7.

McKenzie, K., Bhui, K., Nanchahal, K. and Blizard, B. (2008) 'Suicide rates in people of South Asian origin in England and Wales: 1993-2003', *The British Journal of Psychiatry*, 193, 406–9.

McManus, S., Meltzer, H., Brugha, T., Bebbington, P. and Jenkins, R. (2009) *Adult psychiatric morbidity in England: Results of a household survey 2007*, Leeds: NHS Information Centre for Health and Social Care.

Meerai, S., Abdillahi, I. and Poole, J. (2016) 'An introduction to anti-Black sanism', *Intersectionalities: A Global Journal of Social Work Analysis, Research, Polity and Practice*, 5(3), 18–35.

Mental Health Act Commission (2006) *Count Me In: The National Mental Health and Ethnicity Census 2005 service user survey*, Nottingham: Mental Health Act Commission.

Mental Health Providers Forum and Race Equality Foundation (2015) *Better practice in mental health for Black and ethnic minority communities*, London: Race Equality Foundation.

Moffat, J., Sass, B., McKenzie, K. and Bhui. K. (2006) *Improving pathways into mental health care for Black and ethnic minority groups: A systematic review of the grey literature*, London: Queen Mary School of Medicine and Dentistry.

Mohammed, R. (2010) 'From the editor', *Agenda*, 34, 5–6.

Morgan, C., Mallett, R., Hutchinson, G. and Leff, J. (2004) 'Negative pathways to psychiatric care and ethnicity: The bridge between social science and psychiatry', *Social Science & Medicine*, 58, 739–52.

Moriarty, J. (2014) *Personalisation for people from Black and minority ethnic groups*, London: Race Equality Foundation.

Nazroo, J. (2015) 'Ethnic inequalities in severe mental disorders: Where is the harm?', *Social Psychiatry Psychiatric Epidemiology*, 50, 1065–7.

Nazroo, J.E., Falaschetti, E., Pierce, M. and Primatesta, P. (2009) 'Ethnic inequalities in access to and outcomes of healthcare: Analysis of the Health Survey for England', *Journal of Epidemiology and Community Health*, 63(12), 1022-7.

Newbigging, K., Bola, M. and Shah, A. (2008) *Scoping exercise with Black and minority ethnic groups on perceptions of mental wellbeing in Scotland*, NHS Health Scotland/University of Central Lancashire.

NMHDU (National Mental Health Development Unit) (2010) *Working towards women's well-being: Unfinished business*, London: NMHDU.

Parry, G., van Cleemput, P., Peters, J., Walters, S., Thomas, K. and Cooper, C. (2007) 'Health status of Gypsies and Travellers in England', *Journal of Epidemiology and Community Health*, 61, 98-204.

Patel, N. (2009) 'Developing psychological services for refugee survivors of torture', in S. Fernando and F. Keating (eds) *Mental health in a multi-ethnic society: A multidisciplinary handbook*, London: Routledge, 122-35.

Patel, N. and Fatimilehin, I. (1999) 'Racism and mental health', in C. Newness, G. Holmes and C. Dunn (eds) *This is madness: A critical look at psychiatry and the future of mental health services*, Ross-on-Wye: PCC Books.

Rabiee, F. and Smith, P. (2007) *Being understood, being respected: An evaluation of the statutory and voluntary mental health service provision for members of African and African Caribbean communities in Birmingham*, Birmingham: University of Central England and ACAR.

Raleigh, V.S. (1996) 'Suicide patterns and trends in people of Indian subcontinent and Caribbean origin in England and Wales', *Ethnicity & Health*, 1, 55-63.

Rogers, A. and Pilgrim, D. (2014) *A sociology of mental health and illness*, London: McGraw-Hill Education.

Rollock, N. and Gillborn, D. (2011) 'Critical Race Theory (CRT)', British Educational Research Association (www.bera.ac.uk/researchers-resources/publications/critical-race-theory-crt).

Saheliya, Outside the Box, Health in Mind, Scottish Recovery Network, NHS Lothian and NHS Health Scotland (2008) *Finding strength from within: Report on three local projects looking at mental health and recovery with people from some of the Black and minority ethnic communities in Edinburgh*.

Schwartz, S. and Meyer I.H. (2010) 'Mental health disparities research: The impact of within and between groups analysis on tests of social stress hypotheses', *Social Science & Medicine*, 70(8), 1-17.

Sen, P. (2016) 'The mental health needs of asylum seekers and refugees: Challenges and solutions', *BJPsych International*, 13(12), 30-2.

SEU (Social Exclusion Unit) (2004) *Mental health and social exclusion*, London: Office of the Deputy Prime Minister.

Sharpley, M., Hutchinson, G., Murray, R.M. and McKenzie, K. (2001) 'Understanding the excess of psychosis among the African Caribbean population in England: Review of current hypotheses', *The British Journal of Psychiatry*, 178(Supplement 40), s60–s68.

Singh, P. (2005) *No home, no job: Moving on from transitional spaces*, London: Off the Streets and into Work.

Tighe, M. and Tran, C.T.L. (2010) 'Improving access to traditional Chinese medicine: Lessons in pluralism from a UK Chinese national healthy living centre', *Ethnicity and Inequalities in Health and Social Care*, 3(3), 38–43.

Trivedi, P. (2002) 'Racism, social exclusion and mental health: A Black service user's perspective', in K. Bhui (ed) *Racism and mental health: Prejudice and suffering*, London: Jessica Kingsley Publishers, 71–82.

UNHCR (2010) *Convention and Protocol relating to the Status of Refugees*, Geneva: UNHCR.

Vostanis, P. (2014) 'Meeting the mental health needs of refugees and asylum seekers', *The British Journal of Psychiatry*, 204, 176–7.

Walker, R. and Craig, G. (2009) *Community development workers for Black and minority ethnic mental health: Embedding sustainable change*, London: National Mental Health Development Unit.

Wallace, S., Nazroo, J. and Becares, L. (2016) 'Cumulative effect of racial discrimination on the mental health of ethnic minorities in the United Kingdom', *American Journal of Public Health*, 106(7), 1294–3000.

Watters, C. and Ingleby, D. (2004) 'Locations of care: Meeting the mental health and social care needs of refugees in Europe', *International Journal of Law and Psychiatry*, 27, 549–70.

Webber, M., Treacy, S., Carr, S., Clark, M. and Parker, G. (2014) 'The effectiveness of personal budgets for people with mental health problems: A systematic review', *Journal of Mental Health*, 23(3), 146–55.

White, A. (2006) 'Men and mental well-being – Encouraging gender sensitivity', *The Mental Health Review*, 11(4), 3–6.

WHO (World Health Organization) (2014) *Mental health: A state of well-being* (www.who.int/features/factfiles/mental_health/en/).

Williams, J. and Keating, F. (2005) 'Social inequalities and mental health', in A. Bell and P. Lindley (eds) *Beyond the water towers: The unfinished revolution in mental health services 1985-2005*, London: Sainsbury Centre for Mental Health.

Wilson, M. (2001) 'Black women and mental health: Working towards inclusive services', *Feminist Review*, 68, 24–51.

Wilson, M. (2010) *Delivering Race Equality Action Plan: A five year review*, London: National Mental Health Development Unit.

11

UK education policy and 'race'

Uvanney Maylor

Overview

Utilising critical race theory, this chapter questions notions of 'race' equality and explores the role of 'race' in student in/exclusion and the disparity in educational outcomes between students of different ethnic backgrounds and genders. It also analyses recent government policy interventions in addressing educational inequalities, and the continuing persistence of racism in student experiences in the UK. The chapter focuses on:

- the absence of 'race' and racism in government education policy and its impact on the attainment and experiences of students of compulsory school age from Black Asian, Minority, Ethnic (BAME), Gypsy, Roma and Traveller communities;
- the increasing Islamophobia in schools, which has been influenced by the government's Prevent strategy and emphasis on British values; and
- exemplars of BAME students challenging contentions of low achievement and 'Islamic terrorism'.

Key concepts
British values; critical race theory; educational attainment; Islamophobia; equality

Introduction

This chapter is concerned with the significance of 'race' in UK education policy particularly since 2012, and the impact it has had on students' educational experiences and attainment. However, at the outset it is important to state that, while student attainment at age 16 in England, Scotland and Wales is referenced in this chapter, much of the content focuses on 'race' in English education policy. This is because Scotland, Northern Ireland and Wales have devolved political and administrative powers from the government of Westminster (England), and hence are responsible for shaping and delivering their own education systems (DfE,

2016a; Scottish Government, 2016; Welsh Government, 2016). Notwithstanding its devolved powers, Northern Irish educational policy is omitted as its educational provision is divided by religion, with Protestant and Catholic students largely attending separate schools. In contrast to the rest of the UK, Northern Ireland does not measure school performance data by ethnicity owing to schools being predominantly White and the fact that religious affiliation is synonymous with ethnicity (Doherty and Poole, 2002). The sectarian nature of educational provision in Northern Ireland, combined with the omission of ethnicity as a unit of analysis, makes comparative analysis of student attainment across UK countries difficult.

There are two other key reasons for the greater focus on England. First, of the constituent countries, England has the most ethnically diverse school population, with 31% of students from Black, Asian, Minority, Ethnic (BAME) backgrounds attending primary schools, and 28% in secondary schools (DfE, 2017b). In Welsh schools BAME students account for 9% of students (Lewis and Starkey, 2014), although the actual numbers are quite small (Welsh Government, 2017). In Scotland, while BAME students account for 7% of students, the White minority ethnic student population is 1.5 times greater than that of the BAME student population (Scottish Government, 2016). Second, although there is an established history of ethnically diverse educational provision, since 2012 there has been a return to assimilationist/integrationist ideals in English education (first evident in the 1960s) in the guise of 'British values' (DfE, 2014). The central focus of this chapter is 'race' in educational policy and it takes as its starting point that 'race' is a social construct. Next, it is important to briefly outline the theoretical framework underpinning the discussion (see also Chapter 2, this volume).

Theoretical framing

As the central focus of this chapter is 'race' in educational policy, assuming that 'race' is a social construct, it is important to outline the theoretical framework underpinning the discussion (see also Chapter 2, this volume). The theoretical framework applied here is critical race theory (CRT), which developed from legal studies in the USA. CRT has five main tenets, the first and perhaps most important being that racism is endemic and permanent in US society (Ledesma and Calderon, 2015). Despite different histories and ethnic compositions, the US experience is applicable to examining 'race' and racism within education policy in the UK (Gillborn, 2008). Through concepts of 'White supremacy' and 'Whiteness as property', CRT critiques dominant White ideologies/privileges as 'a system of opportunities and benefits conferred upon (White) people simply because they are White' (Solórzano and Yosso, 2002). Another CRT tenet, 'interest convergence', contends that progression is often experienced by 'people of Colour' when their interests converge with those of White people. CRT gives credence to knowledge and counter-stories by people of Colour and their intersectional experiences (for example, where class intersects with gender and 'race') as they are useful in challenging White majority perspectives (Crenshaw, 1991). As CRT critiques liberal ideologies of meritocracy and notions of colour-blindness, it is useful in examining educational experiences and ideological policy discourses.

CRT advocates developing new racialised educational insights and securing educational change through interrogating and challenging educational inequalities, and critiquing policy discourse and enactment. Fundamental to a CRT approach in this chapter is a better understanding of what is currently happening in schools and higher education classrooms in terms of racial/cultural sensitivity in teaching, and learning to facilitate equitable student experiences/outcomes for majority and minority ethnic groups. Equitable outcomes are underscored by the notion of equal opportunity, which is:

> associated with the idea that students of Colour should have access to the same opportunities that is curriculum, instruction, funding [and] facilities as White students. This emphasis on sameness is important because it helped boost the arguments for equal treatment. (Ladson-Billings and Gillborn, 2004, pp 59-60)

Further, it is assumed that without equal treatment and equal opportunities there cannot be equitable outcomes. English government perspectives on the role of 'race' in facilitating equitable outcomes for all students are explored next.

Race equality: in/exclusion of 'race'

At the time of writing in early 2018, the Department for Education (DfE) website lists 24 key education policies that help us examine the place of 'race' in English education policy (see www.gov.uk/government/organisations/department-for-education). The areas covered indicate that the DfE is concerned not just with school types, funding, leadership, student participation and the curriculum, but also with the structural factors that may affect student experience such as poverty, poor health and disability. Surprisingly, despite England's ethnic diversity (ONS, 2012), what appears to be missing is specific reference to 'race' as a key variable affecting student participation, experience and outcomes. For any mention of 'race' or issues to do with 'race'/ethnicity one has to go to the equality link, which covers broader equality, diversity and inclusion issues. This link relates to equal opportunities in employment working patterns, recruitment and retention, learning and development (that is, education and training), equality and diversity actions – focusing especially on gender and caste discrimination.

Why is there a policy vacuum on 'race' within education when 'race' is a protected characteristic within the Equality Act 2010? Arguably, 'equality' has become a euphemism for 'race'. Prompted by the Equality and Human Rights

Commission's (EHRC) (2016) findings of racial inequalities in education, employment and health in England, Scotland and Wales, Prime Minister May launched a public audit to 'reveal racial disparities and help end the burning injustices many people experience across Britain' (May, 2016; Ross, 2016). When launching the review, the Prime Minister did not specify the 'burning injustices' that affect people's educational experiences. However, she drew attention to Black Caribbean children being '3 times more likely to be permanently excluded from school than (their) peers', and 'White working-class boys being less likely than any other group to go to university' (May, 2016). The disproportionate exclusion of Black children in comparison to students from other ethnic groups is not, however, a new phenomenon (Gillborn, 2006). Such an emphasis ignores the persistently low attainment of Black Caribbean boys (DfE, 2017b) and the absence of measures to address this.

The Prime Minister's comments epitomise CRT contentions of White supremacy, which is illustrated by the government's need to prioritise the poor educational outcomes of the majority community over that of minority groups. Hence the Prime Minister found it necessary, while highlighting Black school exclusion, to draw attention away from the severity of Black Caribbean children's experience of exclusion and raise concerns about the attainment of White working-class boys. It was noticeable that the Prime Minister emphasised White boys' class and gender to the exclusion of their 'race'/ethnicity (that is, British), whereas ethnicity was foregrounded when referring to Black Caribbean school exclusion. Such identification serves to normalise/pathologise (Phoenix et al, 2002) Black school exclusions as individual, behavioural issues inherent in the community. The negative positioning of Black vis-à-vis White students is further exemplified by the following comment by Prime Minister Theresa May:

> If you're Black, you're treated more harshly by the criminal justice system than if you're white. If you're a White, working-class boy, you're less likely than anybody else to go to university. (May, 2016)

May's observation above echoed the former Prime Minister David Cameron's comment that '1 in 10 of the poorest White boys go into higher education', in contrast to young Black men, who were 'more likely to be in a prison cell than studying at a top university' (quoted in Ross, 2016). At the time, Cameron questioned the cause of the 'overrepresentation of Black people in the criminal justice system'. He asked if the cause was related to 'class divisions or a lack of equal opportunity ... or is it something worse – something more ingrained, institutional and insidious?' However, he stopped short of saying that it was institutional, and instead blamed 'social inequality', 'poor parenting' and young people lacking 'access to vital, life enriching experiences, mentors and support networks'. Neither prime minister drew attention to the educational inequalities or racism experienced by Black students. Identifying Black boys as potential criminals also suggests that any concerns about their educational performance and future outcomes are misplaced. However, MP David Lammy's 2017 recommendations concerning the review commissioned by the Prime Minister are a stark reminder of the level of discrimination BAME people experience in the criminal justice system and education.

Racism has been defined as 'a system of domination and oppression with a historical basis that divides and organises society in ways that structurally disadvantage certain minority groups on the basis of their ascribed ethnicity or race' (Ashe and Nazroo, 2016, p 9). As explained above, the sub-subsuming of 'race' within the Equality Act 2010 can lead to 'race'-informed educational inequality being hidden and somewhat overridden by other inequalities such as class and gender (as in the case of White working-class boys). This begs the question: how does a focus on equality help to remove the racial disparities (alluded to by the Prime Minister) in student outcomes? Moreover, there is no specific reference to racial inequality in the government's five-year strategic education plan (2015-20), which is underpinned by broader notions of equality and social justice (DfE, 2016b) and is to be achieved 'by ensuring that irrespective of location, prior attainment or economic or social background, children and young people have access to high-quality provision' (DfE, 2016b, p 8). From a CRT perspective, what is missing from the government's desire to deliver educational social justice is an understanding that social justice does not just happen through providing access, but requires learning opportunities and resources to be equitable so that all students can fully participate in them (Hayes and Juarez, 2012). Also essential is an understanding of how social inequalities are produced and the role that schools (underpinned by educational policy) play in reproducing and legitimating racial inequality. That is how policy discourse and enactment can simultaneously exclude the very students it would seek to include. This is exemplified in the later discussion on academy schools.

Despite the strategic plan referring to students' social background, no consideration is given to student ethnicity. Instead, a commitment to high expectations for all students led the government emphatically to declare that it was 'unapologetically ambitious for every child and young person', and '[wanting to] ensure there are no forgotten groups' (DfE, 2016b, p 11). While the strategic plan does not refer to specific ethnic groups, given the continued under-attainment and exclusion of Black and Gypsy/Roma and Traveller students (DfE, 2017b), these students would appear to be two groups that the government has forgotten in their educational provision. Moreover, it is concerning that, given that the EHRC (2016, p 7) called for the structural problems contributing to the 'continuing disadvantage experienced in some White communities' to be comprehensively addressed, the government interpreted this as meaning White British and not also including Gypsy/Roma and Traveller students. Perhaps this is because Gypsy/

Roma and Traveller attainment is attributed to culturally informed prolonged absences from school at various stages of their education (DCLG, 2012).

Another key priority in the strategic plan is for schools to develop students so they can have 'fulfilling careers' and 'make a positive contribution to British society' (DfE, 2016b, p 35). However, this is less likely to happen without a focus on 'race'/ethnicity and the implementation of an education system tailored to students' individual needs. This is something the Welsh Assembly has sought to do through implementation of a minority ethnic achievement grant designed to support the attainment of minority ethnic students (Lewis and Starkey, 2014), a grant that was, incidentally, previously discontinued in English schools by the British government.

School attainment

Key Stage 4 (KS4) attainment is reviewed here since it is a key government indicator of student success at age 16 and the potential to progress to advanced-level study or training culminating in employment or progression to higher education. When considering student ethnicity attainment data, it is worth noting that a review of qualifications in England and Wales in 2011 led to KS4 attainment measure changes in both countries between 2013 and 2017. For example, in England up to 2015-16, the KS4 attainment measure was 5+ A*-C GCSEs (General Certificate in Secondary Education) including English and mathematics. In 2016 two new KS4 performance measures were implemented, 'attainment 8' (measures average achievement in up to eight subjects including English, mathematics and three subjects that count in the English Baccalaureate, encompassing English, mathematics, science, a language, and history or geography) and 'progress 8' (captures the progress made on average from the end of primary to the end of secondary school) (DfE, 2017b, p 3). Importantly, attainment 8 and progress 8 measures are now compared with student characteristics, namely, gender, special educational needs (SEN), disadvantage (includes students adopted from care, those who are looked after and those eligible for free school meals, FSM), ethnicity and having English as an additional language (EAL), which is compared with having English as a first language (DfE, 2017b).

There are differences in the reporting of outcomes according to ethnicity. For example, in Scotland, Chinese attainment is reported alongside Asian students under the category 'Asian Chinese', whereas in England and Wales the category only consists of Chinese students. In Scotland, the attainment of African, African Other, Caribbean and Black students is reported together as African/Black/Caribbean. In England, since 2016, the term 'major grouping variable' has been used to note the broad ethnic categories of White, Asian, Mixed, Chinese, Black and Any Other ethnic group, but the 'minor grouping variable' is used when referring to within-group attainment such as Black Caribbean within Black and

Bangladeshi within Asian (DfE, 2017b). An overview of KS4 student attainment in England, Scotland and Wales is provided below. Notably, changes in performance measures, the way ethnicity data is reported and a different examination system in Scotland make KS4 attainment comparisons difficult.

Wales

Welsh government (2017) data concerning students achieving the equivalent of 5 GCSEs grade A★-C at KS4, Level 2 for the years 2014–16, reveals that Chinese students (96%) were the highest achievers, followed by Indian (94%), Bangladeshi (92%), Mixed White and Asian (90%) and Mixed White and African (89%) students. The attainment of Black African students was similar to that of White British students, at 85%. No results were recorded for Traveller students. This may be due to the size of this group (38 students). Gypsy/Gypsy Roma students had the lowest attainment (54%), although their actual numbers (78) are quite small. There is a 22% gap between the attainment of Gypsy/Gypsy Roma students and the next lowest attainers, those with Any Other White background (76%), and a 24% gap with Black Caribbean students (who have low numbers, 50) (at 78%).

When the lower attainment, particularly of Black Caribbean and Gypsy/ Gypsy Roma students, is mapped onto the Level 2 inclusive threshold, including a grade A★-C in English or Welsh as a first language and mathematics, both groups grossly under-achieve compared to students from other ethnic groups. The attainment of these student groups reflects their attainment in 2013–15 where they were less likely than White students to achieve five GCSEs (Welsh Government, 2016). Arguably continuing low attainment reflects student ability; however, it is noticeable that, except for Chinese students (whose cohort size is small), all other ethnic groups under-performed at this level. This leads one to question the purpose of the examination changes introduced in 2013–14 and whose attainment they were designed to enhance?

Scotland

Reviews of Scottish attainment data revealed that between 2012 and 2016, Asian Chinese students were the highest attainers, followed by Asian Indian students (CES, 2016). The next highest were Asian Pakistani students, whose attainment was equal to that of students with mixed ethnicities. In 2013/14 and 2014/15, Asian Chinese students had the highest level of achievement at Level 5 (indicator for further education), 97% and 95% respectively.

In 2013/14 and 2014/15, 91% and 88% respectively, Asian Chinese students achieved one or more Scottish qualifications at Level 6 (indicator for higher education). While data for 2014/15 showed a decrease in attainment for Asian Chinese students, their attainment was in excess of other students including students identifying as Asian Other (78%) with Level 6 qualifications; 2014/15 appeared to be a problem year as, in 2015/16, Asian Chinese attainment at Level 5 was 96% and at Level 6 it had also improved to 92%. Children, Education and Skills (CES) data (2016) also revealed that between 2010 and 2016, of all ethnic groups, Asian Chinese school leavers had the highest proportion in positive follow-up destinations (for example, higher education).

In 2014/15, at Level 5, African/Black/Caribbean students (94%) fared better than White Scottish students (85%). In 2014/15 a similar pattern was evident for African/Caribbean/Black students (75%), who performed better than White Scottish students (60%) at Level 6. Moreover, in 2015/16, African/Caribbean/Black (57%) students were also more likely to be found studying in higher education than White Scottish (36%) students, which demonstrates their commitment to increased knowledge. Even though the percentage of African/Caribbean/Black students studying in higher education was slightly lower than that of Asian Indian (59%) students, it was comparable with Asian Pakistani and Asian Other students, at 56% (CES, 2016). Although the qualifications studied for by students in Scotland, Wales and England are different, it is noticeable that, when compared with their counterparts in England and Wales, African/Caribbean/Black students in Scotland perform much better while also outperforming White Scottish students.

England

A five-year review of educational attainment in England, Wales and Scotland by the EHRC (2016) found that in England Chinese and Indian students (particularly girls) were the highest achievers of 5A*-C GCSEs including English and mathematics, with Bangladeshi students consistently achieving above the national average. Such attainment contrasted with that of Pakistani, Mixed White/Black Caribbean, Other White, Other Black and Black Caribbean students whose performance was constantly below the national average, whereas Gypsy/Roma (14%) and Traveller (18%) students (albeit with smaller numbers in school) performed the lowest. When GCSE attainment data is compared by ethnicity, gender and socioeconomic status in England, White boys eligible for free school meals had the lowest educational attainment in 2013. The scale of deterioration in White male achievement was evident in 2015, when only 24% of White boys eligible for FSM achieved five A*-C GCSEs. This represented a 33% gap for White boys eligible for FSM compared with the national attainment average of 57%. The next lowest achievers were Black Caribbean boys eligible for FSM (32%), which represented a 25% difference vis-à-vis the national average.

Government reporting of assessment performance data in England changed in 2016, and this change included the DfE reporting of student attainment according to 'major' ethnic categories, namely, Chinese, Asian, White and Black

(DfE, 2017b). Such categorisation revealed little change in student attainment according to ethnicity. Asian and Chinese students attained above the national average at A★-C in English and mathematics, and in achievement of the English Baccalaureate (EBacc). The attainment of mixed ethnic students was above the national average for EBacc entry and achievement, but below the national average for A★-C in English and mathematics, while White and Black students attained below the national average for A★-C in English and mathematics, and EBacc achievement (DfE, 2017b).

As well as 'major ethnic' categories, the reporting of FSM student attainment is done according to 'selected minor ethnic' groupings. The differentiation between 'major' and 'minor' ethnic groups suggests that the government is interested in conveying a more nuanced understanding of attainment across all ethnic groups. However, the omission of some groups within the 'minor' category contradicts that assumption. It is not clear why only the attainment of 'selected minor' ethnic groups are reported. Moreover, what informs the 'selection' of such groups? If 'minor' refers to student population size in English schools, one would expect the ethnic groups with small student numbers such as Black (5.2%), Chinese (0.4%), Mixed (4.3%) and Any Other ethnic group (1.5%) to be included within the 'minor' category (DfE, 2017b). What accounts for Chinese students being included as both a 'major' and a 'minor' group? Moreover, it is unclear why the attainment of all the constituent parts of the Asian (9.6%) category is broken down within 'minor' to reflect gendered FSM attainment by Bangladeshi, Indian and Pakistani students, but not all of the Black category (only Black Caribbean is reported), or any of the Mixed category when the broader categories are broken down.

It is equally mystifying why White British students as a major ethnic group are discussed within the 'minor' category with regard to the impact of FSM entitlement on White British attainment. This could be because the attainment of White British students sits well below the national average (DfE, 2017b), yet the attainment of Gypsy/Roma and Traveller students who are a 'minor' ethnic group in terms of population size, and with previously reported extremely low attainment (EHRC, 2016), is not reported, maintaining the continued policy invisibilisation of this politically unpopular group. It is further concerning that the attainment of Black African students eligible for FSMs was not reported within the 'minor' grouping when, as evidenced by the EHRC (2016), the attainment of Black African students, despite being above the national average in 2012/13, had fallen below the national average by 2015. This would suggest any increases or falls experienced by this group need monitoring and explicit reporting. Both the inclusion and the omission of particular ethnic groups in the reporting of student attainment raises questions about the government's stated commitment to fostering educational social justice for its lower-achieving students.

The importance of understanding the attainment of all students by ethnicity is evidenced by the government's assessment of 'minor' ethnic groups by gender and

FSM entitlement that reveals the extent to which differential attainment exists within and across ethnic groups. Across all ethnic groups girls outperform their male counterparts (DfE, 2017b). However, White British (39%), Black Caribbean (44%) and Pakistani (46%) girls perform below the national average (49%), like their male counterparts (White British boys, 33%; Black Caribbean boys, 36%; Pakistani boys, 42%). Without this disaggregation, it would not be evident that, despite the high performance of Asian students as a group, Indian boys with FSM entitlement (46.5%) perform worse than Bangladeshi boys (48%), and that both perform below the national average, which contrasts with their female counterparts, whose attainment is above average, at 51% and 52% respectively. There is also an interesting attainment gap of 6% between high-achieving Chinese students, with Chinese boys eligible for FSMs attaining 56% and Chinese FSM girls 62%. FSM attainment exemplified above illustrates the ways in which gender, class and 'race' are intertwined in student outcomes (Strand, 2014a, b).

Discussion of Key Stage 4 data

Notably, regardless of how KS4 performance is measured in England, Scotland and Wales, Chinese and Indian students are consistently the highest achievers across the board. In England and Wales attainment gaps persist between White and Gypsy Roma/Travellers and Black Caribbean students, whose attainment remains below the national average (DfE, 2017b; Welsh Government, 2017). This notwithstanding, in both Scotland and England, Black students fare much better than their White Scottish and White British counterparts (CES, 2016; DfE, 2017b).

Clearly, educational performance is nuanced by 'race'; however, the government's doggedly colour-blind approach to education means that they have sought to explain differential attainment through students' socioeconomic background, gender and whether they have SEN (DfE, 2017b). Such an approach also ignores research that demonstrates that educational outcomes are racialised. For example, Indian and Chinese high attainment has been attributed to having a strong motivation to achieve and supportive families for whom the pursuit of educational capital is considered essential for upward social mobility (Francis et al, 2008; Basit, 2013). This contrasts with the (wrongly) assumed lack of value placed on education by and lower parental involvement of Black parents, often used to explain the lower attainment of Black students (Maylor, 2014).

If, as the government contends, poverty is a key factor in the lower attainment of students from lower socioeconomic backgrounds (DfE, 2016a), one would expect all FSM students to have similar outcomes. As shown above, however, there is a huge differential between majority and minority ethnic FSM students with the highest and lowest attainment in England. In relation to the low attainment of Black students, contentions about the influence of poverty on their attainment are called into question because, even where Black (African and Caribbean) students have middle-class backgrounds, they still under-achieve (Rollock et al, 2015). Thus, class does not appear to impact outcomes for Black children positively. Moreover, teachers' lower expectations of Black children – informed by notions of White supremacy (Gillborn, 2013; Ladesma and Calderon, 2015) – only serve to perpetuate the attainment disadvantage Black students experience. Institutional racism, namely, 'discrimination through unwitting prejudice, ignorance, thoughtlessness and racist stereotyping' (Macpherson, 1999, p 28) negates high aspirations and the ability to achieve highly, particularly among Black, Gypsy/ Roma and Traveller students (Mirza, 2006; Rhamie, 2007; Levinson, 2015). Embedding 'race' in education policy is imperative if the government's stated commitment to educational social justice is to be experienced as more than rhetoric, and the aspirations and achievements of Black males at an individual level (reflected in Box 11.1 below) are to be understood and to become commonplace.

Box 11.1: Black men attending elite universities

Black African and Caribbean males are under-represented at elite universities (Boliver, 2016; HEFCE, 2017). This is also reflective of the very low state school intakes at universities such as Cambridge, Oxford and Durham. However, as illustrated by research (Dumangane, 2016), Black men are increasingly challenging deficit school/societal positioning of Black boys/men through studying at prestigious universities (see also Watkiss, 2017).

In concluding this section, it is important to also consider the absence of 'race' in government discourse about academy school provision. Academies account for two-thirds of secondary and one-fifth of primary schools in England, with a third of BAME students attending sponsored academies (DfE, 2016a). Yet academy attainment data are not disaggregated by ethnicity (DfE, 2017a). Without such an analysis it is difficult to discern the social justice impact of academy outcomes for all students, which is essential given that much research (Hutchings et al, 2015; Worth, 2016) contends that attainment in some academies may be detrimental to students from disadvantaged backgrounds, which includes BAME students.

Promoting British values, preventing terrorism and valuing diversity

So far it has been argued that British educational policy follows a colour-blind approach to racial and ethnic disadvantage in relation to gender and socioeconomic position. This section explores how a White supremacist belief and fears of a threat to Whiteness under the pretext of British values reinforces rather than challenges such an approach (discussed under 'securitisation' in Chapter 2, this volume).

While an embedding of 'race' remains absent from English educational policy, perhaps the most glaring example of the existence of racism and an implicit focus on 'race' in English education policy is the wide-ranging government policy emphasis on British values and the Prevent strategy, introduced in 2011 and revised in 2015 under the Counter-Terrorism and Security Act 2015 by the then coalition government. Prevent aims to 'prevent people from being drawn into terrorism' (HMI, 2015, p 2, para 5). The strategy makes clear that the government considers the greatest terrorism threat to come from Islamist terrorist organisations and extremist ideology. The latter is defined as: 'vocal or active opposition to fundamental British values, including democracy, the rule of law, individual liberty and mutual respect and tolerance of different faiths and beliefs' (HMI, 2015, p 2, para 5). British values are considered essential to citizens 'building a common home together' (Cameron, quoted in Dearden, 2015). The idea of building a 'common home' relates to British society recognising a common British identity, despite having different ethnicities, cultures, faiths/ beliefs and languages.

One might question what the Prevent strategy and British values have to do with English education policy? The emphasis on British values does not feature explicitly in current Conservative education policy, but it underpins expectations of teaching and learning, as teachers are required to emphasise and not undermine fundamental British values in their teaching (DfE, 2014; Starkey, 2018). Ostensibly, promoting British values in teaching is considered essential to building a harmonious multi-ethnic society. However, the government would seem to be mostly concerned about societal cohesion being undermined by people with a Muslim heritage. Muslims have been (and continue to be) labelled as terrorists because of ongoing bombings in England, continental Europe and the USA (discussed in Maylor, 2016). The emphasis on the promotion of British values in schools has led to a rise in Islamophobia, which is a form of cultural racism (Ashe and Nazroo, 2016) and one that has not been systematically evidenced against other religions in British schools. (This does not discount outbursts of anti-Semitic behaviour, but these have rarely been evidenced in schools and are not, as is the anti-Muslim rhetoric, reflected systematically in policy.)

Opportunities were sought to identify Muslim transgressors/non-conformists of British values, as exemplified during 2014-15, when between 21 and 25 schools (with a predominance of Muslim- but notably Pakistani-heritage children) in Birmingham, England were accused of attempting to undermine British values through appointing Muslim school governors. These schools were separately investigated by Birmingham City Council and the DfE, an investigation that infamously became known as the 'Trojan horse affair' because it was initially instigated by an anonymous letter to Birmingham City Council. The DfE investigation can be considered a formal response to the perceived 'ideological challenge of terrorism' (HMI, 2015, p 2) posed by these schools, as the investigation was led by a former head of counter-terrorism. Theresa May (then Home Secretary) accused the then Education Secretary (Michael Gove) of not sufficiently addressing an 'Islamist plot to take over Birmingham schools' (BBC News, 2014a), and charged Ofsted (Office for Standards in Education) with identifying schools at risk of radicalisation and rooting out 'Islamic terrorism' (HMI, 2015, p 2). 'Terrorist' schools found guilty by Ofsted of attempting to 'impose and promote a narrow faith-based ideology in secular schools' (Sir Michael Wilshaw, cited in BBC News, 2014b) were publicly humiliated, were placed in special measures and had their funding withdrawn and governor changes imposed.

These actions of the DfE and the government could be interpreted as religious discrimination, as, when no evidence of an Islamist plot was found, they failed to publicly acknowledge their mistake over schools accused of terrorism, which Ofsted had declared to have good governance and to provide an 'outstanding'/'good' education (BBC News, 2014a). Moreover, it is not clear what led to a school rated as 'outstanding' in 2012 to be put into 'special measures' following an Ofsted re-inspection in 2014. It is possible to surmise that the government were not concerned about Muslim student performance *per se* in Birmingham, as notably Pakistani and Bangladeshi children have a higher GCSE attainment than White British children (DfE, 2017b). Analysis of student performance in faith schools has also shown that Muslim faith schools (albeit there are only eight in England) are high-performing schools with an average attainment at age 16 of 59% compared with the average of 51% achieved by mainstream secular schools (DfE, 2017b). Box 11.2 challenges stereotyped notions of Muslims as terrorists, and illustrates not only the capacity of Muslim students to achieve, but also to be positive role models for all.

An outcome of the 'Trojan horse' investigation has been increased surveillance of school governance, ethos and curriculum content since September 2015. There has also been greater government emphasis on schools 'building resistance' against (perceived) threats of Islamic terrorism through the promotion and teaching of British values (DfE, 2014; BBC News, 2015). However, it is noticeable that the government's position on British values is inconsistent when it comes to predominantly White schools. This was exemplified by a nursery school in Lincolnshire, England, which in 2016 was downgraded from 'outstanding' to 'good' following an Ofsted inspection that observed that the school's teaching did not reflect an understanding of Britain as an ethnically diverse society (Mail Online, 2016). While this was just one school, in contrast to the Birmingham schools, there was no DfE investigation (or indeed one conducted in front of the media) into what is being taught in this nursery (and other predominantly White schools) about Britain's ethnic/cultural diversity. Moreover, despite school and parental accusations of the Ofsted report being racist, no questions were raised by the government about school governance or students experiencing a curriculum that did not reflect the multi-ethnic composition of the wider society. This response diverges from the position adopted by the New Labour government which, while committed to British values and equally fearful of Islamic terrorism – following a review of diversity in the school curriculum – stipulated that all state schools needed to have a common understanding of how Britain became a multi-ethnic society (Ajegbo et al, 2007).

The vehement parental reaction to the downgraded Ofsted inspection report is also reflected in the increasing numbers of primary school children being excluded for espousing racist views (Perraudin, 2016). Sadly, however, White racism has been exacerbated by the UK referendum decision (Brexit) in June 2016 to leave the European Union (EU), and is likely to worsen as the break-up with Europe is finalised within an atmosphere charged with enhanced expressions of English nationalism and xenophobia (Lesińska, 2014).

Box 11.2: Role modelling and achievement

The Windsor Fellowship supports BAME young people to achieve and to become role models through its mentoring and development programmes targeting secondary-aged and undergraduate students. Below, two graduates explain the benefits derived from the Windsor Fellowship's undergraduate programme, which 'combines residential training seminars, a paid work placement with a sponsoring organisation and volunteering [during] the second year of a three-year undergraduate degree or in the third year of a four-year undergraduate degree'.

> 'After completing my undergraduate studies, I immediately started work as a Research Assistant at a charity called ENGAGE, whose objectives include increasing political and media awareness among British Muslims as well as challenging Islamophobia.... I benefited greatly from my two years on the LPU [leadership programme for undergraduates]; as well as meeting some brilliant people, having a safe environment to develop professional skills and learn about the world of work was invaluable. I entered post-graduate employment with self-confidence and a desire to continue to learn and

develop.' (Nadiya Takolia, University of Warwick, Politics and International Studies, Home Office Fellow)

'I am Director for Sales for Europe, Middle East and Africa for an American software company specialising in Enterprise Social Media Management called Shoutlet ... the success I have had in this role, is directly related to the journey through the Windsor Fellowship since I was 14 with the most recent programme being the LPU [which] gave me the confidence to engage and build relationships with people at all levels of a business.... Being a Fellow has had a significant impact in my day to day career and it is a big part of who I am. The LPU has taught me to embrace and learn from failures and balance my emotions in celebrating my successes ... the LPU is geared not just to showcase yourself as an academic with a 2:1 but as a human being with a lot to offer geared with the mindset to achieve despite any challenges that come in your way.' (Nikhilkumar Adhia, London School of Economics and Political Science, House of Commons Fellow)

Source: www.windsor-fellowship.org/testimonials

Conclusion

The United Nation's (UN) Committee on the Elimination of Racial Discrimination (2016) recommended that the UK educate teachers to promote respect for diversity and to challenge racial inequality and racism, but three difficulties undermine this requirement:

- the prevalence of a predominantly White teacher and leadership workforce who do not have an understanding of student diversity (NASUWT, 2017), and the ways in which stereotyped perceptions about particular ethnic groups can negatively impact on student outcomes;
- the lack of understanding of the power of majority Whiteness (Gillborn, 2013) and its ability to 'individualise a problem' (for example, low student ability or a lack of belief in British values), which is fundamentally 'structural and systemic in nature' (Ashe and Nazroo, 2016, p 38);
- the government's persistent colour-blind educational policy to maintain the status quo has led to a failure to challenge institutional racism.

This means that ensuring social justice and equitable outcomes for students from different ethnic/racial backgrounds is an unlikely outcome. As Britain is a multi-ethnic society, it remains unacceptable in 2018 that educational policy continues to ignore an essential identity category ('race'). This serves to underscore inequitable educational experiences and outcomes encountered by BAME students.

Questions for discussion

- In what ways does ignoring 'race' underscore inequitable educational outcomes for White and BAME students?
- Can you think of any challenges that the young men (see Box 11.1) might have faced in getting to the University of Cambridge and being a minority there?
- How far do you think the Windsor Fellowship (see Box 11.2) or similar schemes can prepare students to promote British values/community cohesion, resist Islamophobia and become role models?

Online resources

www.windsor-fellowship.org/programmes
For Windsor Fellowships in conjunction with STEM (science, technology engineering and mathematics), the Bank of England, the National Audit Office, the Welsh government and the USA.

Further reading

Clycq, N., Nouwen, M. and Vandenbroucke, A. (2014) 'Meritocracy, deficit thinking and the invisibility of the system: Discourses on educational success and failure', *British Educational Research Journal*, 40(5), 796-819.

Osler, A. (2016) *Human rights and schooling: An ethical framework for teaching for social justice*, New York: Teachers College Press.

Wright, C., Maylor, U. and Becker, S. (2016) 'Young black males: Resilience and the use of capital to transform school "failure"', *Critical Studies in Education*, Special Issue: Exclusion, alternative programmes, schools and social justice, 57(1), 21-34.

References

Ajegbo, K., Kiwan, D. and Sharma, S. (2007) *Curriculum review: Diversity and citizenship*, London: Department for Education and Skills.

Ashe, S.D. and Nazroo, J. (2016) *Equality, diversity and racism in the workplace: A qualitative analysis of the 2015 Race at Work Survey*, Manchester: ESRC Centre on Dynamics of Ethnicity, University of Manchester.

Basit, T. (2013) 'Educational capital as a catalyst for upward social mobility amongst British Asians: A three-generational analysis', *British Educational Research Journal*, 39(4), 714-32.

BBC News (2014a) 'May and Gove in row over extremism in schools', 14 June (www.bbc.co.uk/news/education-27691901).

BBC News (2014b) 'Trojan Horse report finds "aggressive Islamist ethos" in schools', 18 July (www.bbc.co.uk/news/uk-england-birmingham-28349706).

BBC News (2015) 'Overlapping "Trojan Horse" inquiries criticised by MPs', 17 March (www.bbc.co.uk/news/education-31905704).

Boliver, V. (2016) 'Exploring ethnic inequalities in admission to Russell Group universities', *Sociology*, 50(2), 247-66.

CES (Children, Education and Skills) (2016) *Summary statistics for schools in Scotland*, No 7, 13 December.

Crenshaw, K. (1991) 'Mapping the margins: Intersectionality, identity politics, and violence against women of color', *Stanford Law Review*, 43(6), 1241-99.

DCLG (Department for Communities and Local Government) (2012) *Progress report by the ministerial working group on tackling inequalities experienced by Gypsies and Travellers*, London: DCLG.

Dearden, L. (2015) 'David Cameron extremism speech', *The Independent*, 20 July (www.independent.co.uk/news/uk/politics/david-cameron-extremism-speech-read-the-transcript-in-full-10401948.html).

DfE (Department for Education) (2014) *Guidance on promoting British values in schools*, London: DfE.

DfE (2015) 'Permanent and fixed period exclusions in England: 2013 to 2014', Statistical first release (www.gov.uk/government/uploads/system/uploads/attachment_data/file/449433/SFR27_2015_Text.pdf).

DfE (2016a) 'Revised GCSE and equivalent results in England: 2014 to 2015. Main text', Statistical first release 01/2016 (www.gov.uk/government/statistics/revised-gcse-and-equivalent-results-in-england-2014-to-2015).

DfE (2016b) 'DfE strategy 2015-2020: World-class education and care', DFE-00087-2016, London: DfE (www.gov.uk/government/uploads/system/uploads/attachment_data/file/508421/DfE-strategy-narrative.pdf).

DfE (2017a) *Experimental statistics: Multi-academy trust performance measures: England, 2015 to 2016*, Statistical first release 02/2017, 19 January.

DfE (2017b) *Revised GCSE and equivalent results in England*, Statistical first release, 03-2017, London: DfE.

Doherty, P. and Poole, M. (2002) 'Religion as an indicator of ethnicity in Northern Ireland an alternative perspective', *Irish Geography*, 35(2), 75-89.

Dumangane, C. (2016) 'Exploring the narratives of the few: British African Caribbean male graduates of elite universities in England and Wales', Unpublished PhD thesis, School of Social Science, Cardiff University.

EHRC (Equality and Human Rights Commission) (2016) *Healing a divided Britain: The need for a comprehensive race equality strategy report*, London: EHRC.

Francis, B., Archer, L. and Mau, A. (2008) *British-Chinese pupils' identities, achievement and complementary schooling: Full research report ESRC end of award report*, RES-000-23-1513, Swindon: Economic and Social Research Council.

Gillborn, D. (2006) 'Citizenship education as placebo: "Standards", institutional racism and education policy', *Education, Citizenship and Social Justice*, 1(1), 83–104.

Gillborn, D. (2008) *Racism and education: Coincidence or conspiracy?*, London: Routledge.

Gillborn, D. (2013) 'The policy of inequity: Using CRT to unmask White supremacy in education policy', in M. Lynn and A. Dixson (eds) *Handbook of critical race theory in education*, London: Routledge, 129–39.

Hayes, C. and Juárez, B. (2012) 'There is no culturally responsive teaching spoken here: A critical race perspective', *Democracy and Education*, 20(1), 1–14.

HEFCE (Higher Education Funding Council for England) (2017) *Student characteristics: Ethnicity* (www.hefce.ac.uk/analysis/HEinEngland/students/).

HMI (Her Majesty's Inspectorate) (2015) *Revised Prevent Duty Guidance for England and Wales: Guidance for specified authorities in England and Wales on the duty in the Counter-Terrorism and Security Act 2015 to have due regard to the need to prevent people from being drawn into terrorism*, London: HMI.

Hutchings, M., Francis, B. and Kirby, P. (2015) *Chain effects: The impact of academy chains on low-income students*, London: The Sutton Trust.

Ladson-Billings, G. and Gillborn, D. (2004) *The Routledge/Falmer reader in multicultural education*, London: RoutledgeFalmer.

Ledesma, M. and Calderon, D. (2015) 'Critical theory in education: A review of past literature and a look to the future', *Qualitative Inquiry*, 21(3), 206–22.

Lesińska, M. (2014) 'The European backlash against immigration and multiculturalism', *Journal of Sociology*, 50(1), 37–50.

Levinson, M. (2015) '"What's the plan?" "What plan?" Changing aspirations among Gypsy youngsters, and implications for future cultural identities and group membership', *British Journal of Sociology of Education*, 36(8), 1149–69.

Lewis, S. and Starkey, J. (2014) *Welsh Government social research*, No 59/2014.

Macpherson, W. (1999) *The Stephen Lawrence inquiry*, CM 4262-1, London: The Stationery Office.

Mail Online (2016) '"Outstanding" rural nursery is downgraded by Ofsted for not teaching toddlers about ethnic diversity and not having enough pictures of Black and Asian people on walls', 27 April (www.dailymail.co.uk/news/article-3561380/Nursery-downgraded-Ofsted-failing-teach-ethnic-diversity.html).

May, T. (2016) Statement from the new Prime Minister Theresa May, 13 July (www.gov.uk/government/speeches/statement-from-the-new-prime-minister-theresa-may).

Maylor, U. (2014) *Teacher training and the education of Black children: Bringing color into difference*, New York and London: Routledge.

Maylor, U. (2016) '"I'd worry about how to teach it": British values in English classrooms', Special Issue: Fundamental British Values, *Journal of Education for Teaching: International Research and Pedagogy*, 42(3), 314–28.

Mirza, H.S. (2006) '"Race", gender and educational desire', *Race Ethnicity and Education*, 9(2), 137–58.

NASUWT (National Association of Schoolteachers Union of Women Teachers) (2017) *Visible minorities, invisible teachers: BME teachers in the education system in England*, London: NASUWT.

ONS (Office for National Statistics) (2012) *Ethnicity and national identity in England and Wales 2011*, London: ONS.

Perraudin, F. (2016) 'Rise in primary school pupils suspended for racist abuse', *The Guardian*, 29 December (www.theguardian.com/education/2016/dec/26/rise-in-primary-school-pupils-suspended-for-racist-abuse).

Phoenix, A., Frosh, S. and Pattmann, R. (2002) *Young masculinities: Understanding boys in contemporary society*, Basingstoke: Palgrave Macmillan.

Rhamie, J. (2007) *Eagles who soar: How Black learners find the path to success*, Stoke-on-Trent: Trentham Books.

Rollock, N., Gillborn, D., Vincent, C. and Ball, S. (2015) *The colour of class: The educational strategies of the Black middle classes*, London and New York: Routledge.

Ross, T. (2016) 'David Cameron: "Black people more likely to be in prison than at a top university"', *The Telegraph*, 31 January (www.telegraph.co.uk/news/politics/david-cameron/12131928/Labours-David-Lammy-to-lead-government-race-review.html).

Scottish Government (2016) *Delivering excellence and equity in Scottish education: A delivery plan for Scotland*, 28 June (www.gov.scot/Publications/2016/06/3853).

Solórzano, D.G. and Yosso, T.J. (2002) 'A critical race counterstory of race, racism, and affirmative action', *Equity and Excellence in Education*, 35(2), 155–68.

Starkey, H. (2018) 'Fundamental British values and citizenship education: Tensions between national and global perspectives', *Geografiska Annaler: Series B, Human Geography*, doi:10.1080/04353684.2018.1434420.

Strand, S. (2014a) 'Ethnicity, gender, social class and achievement gaps at age 16: Intersectionality and "getting it" for the White working class', *Research Papers in Education*, 29(2), 131–72.

Strand, S. (2014b) 'School effects and ethnic, gender and socio-economic gaps in educational achievement at age 11', *Oxford Review of Education*, 40(2), 223–45.

UN (United Nations) Committee on the Elimination of Racial Discrimination (2016) *Concluding observations on the twenty-first to twenty-third periodic reports of United Kingdom of Great Britain and Northern Ireland* (http://tbinternet.ohchr.org/Treaties/CERD/Shared%20Documents/GBR/CERD_C_GBR_CO_21-23_24985_E.pdf).

Watkiss, J. (2017) 'Just 15 black male students began their studies at Cambridge University in a single year', Cambridgeshire Live, 3 May (www.cambridge-news.co.uk/news/just-15-black-male-students-12979189).

Welsh Government (2016) *KS4 performance measures in Wales: Changes and comparability*, Cardiff: Welsh Government.

Welsh Government (2017) *Academic achievement by pupil characteristics, 2016,* Statistical first release, Cardiff: Welsh Government.

Worth, J. (2016) *Analysis of academy school performance in 2015*, Slough: NFER.

12

Young people, 'race' and criminal justice

Bankole Cole

Overview

This chapter:

- appraises the political response to youth offending and welfare in Britain over the past 30 years;
- examines whether adequate provision is made for young offenders of different ethnicities and gender;
- reviews the extent to which ethnicity should be a key factor in the provision of welfare for youths involved in the criminal justice system; and
- examines the UK experience, wherever possible, in context of Europe.

Key concepts
crime; criminal justice; offending; policing

Introduction

In most societies, young people are often portrayed as 'the future generation'. Behind this image is the notion that the state and society ought to care for its young people, providing what it believes is required for them to grow into useful adults. The age groups constituting 'youth' vary between different countries. In Europe, 'youths' consist of children aged 0-14 and young people aged 15-29. Figures for 2014 suggest that, of the 507 million inhabitants in the 28 countries of the European Union (EU-28), 79 million (16%) were children aged 0-14 and 90 million (18%) were young people aged 15-29. In total, almost 170 million EU inhabitants (33.3%) were under the age of 30 in 2014 (EU, 2015a). During 2014, children accounted for 18% and young people 20% of the UK population (total: 37%), the third highest figure in the EU–28 (EU, 2015a, p 23). Two urban conurbations in the UK – Inner London (43.4%) and the West Midlands (41.8%) – were among the top five areas in Europe with the highest shares of youths (0–29 years) in the total population in 2014 (EU, 2015a, p 24). This chapter aims to discuss the extent to which 'ethnicity' is significant in the provision of state support to youths who have broken the law or are at risk of offending, including those at risk of being victims of crime. The focus of the chapter is on young people below 18 years of age (often referred to as 'juveniles') as the youth justice system in most countries deals with this group of 'youths'. Offenders aged between 18 and 20 are often referred to as young adults and those over 21 as adults. Both of these groups are often processed through the adult criminal justice system.

Ethnicities, youth and crime

The numbers of young people involved in the criminal justice system appear to have been decreasing worldwide. In 2010, youths made up an average of 9.3% of the total numbers of convicted criminal offenders per 100,000 of the population among the surveyed 28 EU countries (European Institute for Crime Prevention and Control, 2014). In England and Wales, 27,900 young people were sentenced in the year ending March 2016. This represents a fall of 10% compared with the previous year, and of 71% since the year ending March 2006 (YJB/MoJ, 2017).

However, according to Section 95 statistics on 'race' and the UK criminal justice system (published since 1992, following the Criminal Justice Act 1991), Black, Asian, Minority, Ethnic (BAME) young people are disproportionately represented in the total number of youths caught up within the youth justice system, from 'stop and search' through to sentencing. For example, in the year ending March 2016, BAME young people accounted for 21,900 (25%) of arrests of young people, with 10,800 (12%) being from a Black ethnic group. In the same year, BAME young people accounted for 41% of the under-18 custodial population, with Black youths alone accounting for 21% of young people in custody (YJB/MoJ, 2017).

BAME youths are also overrepresented as victims of crimes compared with their White counterparts (MoJ, 2015; Uhrig, 2016). Available crime data in England and Wales shows that BAME youths are disproportionately represented among those experiencing racially motivated antisocial behaviour and crimes, while the perpetrators of these offences are disproportionately White youths (Scottish Executive, 2005; Jansson, 2006; Craig et al, 2009; Times Online, 2009). Of particular concern is the number of BAME youths becoming increasingly involved in weapons-related crimes, both as offenders and as victims. In the year ending March 2015, the percentage of BAME young people convicted of or cautioned for possession of a knife or other offensive weapons was 39% compared with 16% for adults (YJB/MoJ, 2016, p 78). Reports have also indicated that BAME youths are disproportionately represented in youth criminal gang membership and activities (HM Government, 2007; Scottish Government Social Research, 2010a, b). The fact that criminal justice statistics in the USA and most EU countries have also shown significant BAME youth overrepresentation as offenders and victims of crimes (see Kalunta-Crumpton, 2010) raises important questions as to whether addressing youth offending requires different explanations and solutions according to 'race'.

The context

Since the end of the Second World War, Europe has been witnessing a significant rise in its BAME populations, both Whites and non-Whites. The majority of the immigrants that settled in Britain, especially immediately after the war, were from Britain's former colonies (see Bowling and Phillips, 2002; see also Chapter 2, this volume). The majority of these post-war immigrants settled in the poorest and most deprived neighbourhoods of big cities, effectively ghettoised as a result of prejudice and discrimination from their hosts, and also because these offered the cheapest housing. As most of the immigrants were also employed in the lowest-paid jobs, social mobility was limited and access to support services poor. The result was that many remained permanently living in these areas, more so as White neighbours moved out into more affluent areas (see also Chapter 7, this volume). Thus, the descendants of these immigrants, now British citizens, have grown up in some of Britain's most deprived inner-city areas.

Although the factors that trigger youth offending are many, the key factors such as association with criminal adults and peers, drug misuse, poverty and unemployment are often associated with living in deprived neighbourhoods (see Bradshaw et al, 2004; Government Office for London, 2007). The EU reported that, in 2013, the proportion of children in the EU-28 experiencing severe material deprivation was 1.4 percentage points higher than the corresponding ratio for the whole population, and stood at 11% (EU, 2015a, p 184). This report noted that 'the gap was largest in the United Kingdom, Romania and Hungary' (EU, 2015a, p 184). In the same year, 13% of people aged 15-24 and 30% of people aged 25-29 in the EU were not in employment, education or training (NEET) (EU, 2015a, p 42). In the UK, figures for October to December 2016 showed that 12% of all people aged 16-24 (about 862,000 young people) were NEET. In terms of ethnicity, the figures released for April-June 2016 showed that BAME youths aged 16-24 were disproportionally represented among the youths in the NEET category, accounting for 11% of the total (126,000 youths). Office for National Statistics (ONS) figures also showed that the unemployment rate for Black men aged 16-24 in London in September 2016 was 29% compared with 15% of Whites of the same age group (ONS, 2017).

Research evidence has also shown that BAME youths encounter significant racial discrimination in employment, education and housing, resulting in their being even more socially excluded than their White counterparts. Their experiences in the UK during the 1950s/1960s, of social rejection, stigma and prejudice are well documented. Black youth subcultures and music were stereotyped as inspiring violence, and Black youths generally were associated with low-level criminality such as illegal drug use and alleged trafficking (mainly in cannabis) and prostitution (pimping) (Bowling and Phillips, 2002). These stereotypes of Black youths were supported and orchestrated by selective and predominantly negative media reporting on black youths and their communities, which led to an increase in police presence in inner-city areas, where the majority of young Black people lived (Solomos, 1988; Cole, 2010). By the 1970s, concerns were already growing in Black inner-city communities of being over-policed and under-protected by police forces that were allegedly indiscriminately targeting Black youths for 'stop and searches', using excessive force during arrests and generally harassing their communities (Bowling and Phillips, 2002).

In 1975, the London Metropolitan Police (Met) produced the first ethnically coded statistics for street robbery in the capital. In spite of the fact that these figures were based on inadequate racial classifications (see Fitzgerald and Sibbitt, 1997), the Met announced that young Black youths in London were disproportionally involved in street robbery (mugging), the victims of which were mainly Whites. On the basis of these data, the Met and other police forces in Britain began a campaign of surveillance and quasi-militaristic policing of Britain's inner cities in the quest to clamp down on 'muggers' (see Hall et al, 1978). Police tactics included increased use of legal provisions in the Vagrancy Act 1824 to stop, question and search people on the streets. It was alleged that the majority of people stopped and searched were Black youths, who were repeatedly searched in ways that were considered indiscriminate and possibly racist (see Chapter 2, this volume). This police action exacerbated the already strained relationship between the police and inner-city Black youths (Gaskell and Smith, 1985; Gaskell, 1986; Solomos, 1988), and it was one of the key factors that led to the inner-city disorders (riots) of the 1980s, in which Black youths were heavily involved (Keith, 1993). According to Lea and Young (1993), these 'riots' were a definitive reaction to the political and economic marginalisation of Black youths and the characterisation of their lifestyles and communities as criminal; they were also directed at the police's heavy-handedness and racist policing of their communities apparently with the support of a possibly racist and uncaring government (Gilroy, 1982).

The legacy of Lord Scarman

In April 1981, Lord Scarman was appointed to inquire into the reasons behind the disorders in Brixton, London. What was remarkable about the Scarman Report (1981) was its attempt to find an explanation for the disturbances beyond the violence on the streets that incorporated aspects of social policy and welfare that were at the root of the problem. The report provided an analysis of the social and economic conditions in Brixton on the eve of the disturbances, comparing them with those in other inner-city areas where similar disturbances had occurred. Scarman concluded that, while differences undoubtedly existed between these areas, the similarities were even more striking. He described these similarities as: 'A high ethnic minority population, high unemployment, a declining economic base, a decaying physical environment, bad housing, lack of amenities, social problems including family breakdown, a high rate of crime and heavy policing' (Scarman, 1981, p 12).

Scarman explained how the disproportionate experience of deprivation and poverty of BAME, mainly Black Caribbean, (Black) youths, in the affected inner cities, and their clashes with the police, are inextricably linked: first, in terms of how, by living much of their lives on the streets, Black youths are more likely than other youths to come into contact with the police, especially as they are more likely to be involved in street crimes (Scarman, 1981, p 11); and, second, how 'unimaginative and inflexible policing can make the tensions which deprivation engenders greatly worse' (Scarman, 1981, p 100). Accordingly, Scarman highlighted the importance of considering the welfare problems that Black inner-city youths are faced with when policy decisions are being made about why they disproportionately offend (Scarman, 1981, pp 4–16). Scarman stressed the point that White youths also suffer from deprivations, but that Black youths do so to a much greater degree. More importantly, Scarman emphasised the part that racial discrimination had played in limiting access to employment and state welfare for Black youths. In addition, he argued that racial discrimination was also intrinsic in the actions of the police that had led to the disturbances. However, he dismissed the view that British police officers were generally racist. Instead, he argued that the racism that existed within some of Britain's police forces was caused by a handful of 'rotten apples' among the police officers (Scarman, 1981, pp 64–74). This position was later dismissed by the Macpherson Report (1999) in which the British police were described as being 'institutionally racist' (see Chapter 2, this volume).

Finally, Scarman talked about conflicting policies between local and central governments being 'a source of confusion and reduced drive' (Scarman, 1981, p 101). Whereas there was evidence that some efforts were being made to address racial disadvantage, Scarman maintained that there wasn't a sufficiently well-coordinated programme for combating the problem. He was also dismayed that the private sector was not fully involved in the process. As he put it, 'the private sector is not an alternative to adequate public sector involvement: both are needed' (Scarman, 1981, p 102). Scarman insisted that, unless a clear lead was given by government in this area, 'there can be no hope of an effective response' (Scarman, 1981, p 108). However, he expressed concern that 'a policy of direct coordinated attack on racial disadvantage inevitably means that the ethnic minorities will enjoy for a time a positive discrimination in their favour' (Scarman, 1981, p 135). He feared that this could provide a legitimate and understandable backlash from the majority British White population. Accordingly, he concluded that 'special programmes for ethnic minority groups should only be instituted where the need for them is clearly made out' (Scarman, 1981, p 109).

South Asian youths

A crucial deficiency in the Scarman report was the over-emphasis that was placed on youths of African Caribbean origin, in spite of the fact that British South Asian youths, who are mainly of Indian, Pakistani and Bangladeshi origins, also took part in the inner-city riots, for example, in Birmingham. British South Asian youth were initially perceived as generally 'law-abiding' – a view that is believed to emanate from their adherence to strong religious moral ethics and cultures (see Wardak, 2000); recent UK crime statistics have, however, been showing a steady increase in their involvement in crimes, with disproportionate numbers being imprisoned for serious crimes (Uhrig, 2016; YJB/MoJ, 2016). Like their Black counterparts, Asian youths in Europe are generally socially excluded and are known to experience racial discrimination disproportionately, for example, in employment and education (see EU, 2015b). Asian residents have also been known to be disproportionately victimised by racist far-right groups who challenge their European citizenship status and disrespect their cultures and religions. In the UK, frequent taunting of Asian youths and their families by far-right groups led to the first violent street clash between National Front/British National Party (BNP) supporters and Asian youths in Dewsbury, West Yorkshire, in 1989. This prompted media stories of emerging Asian youth gangs that might be fighting against years of racist victimisation but also had criminal intentions (Webster, 1997). Racist taunting of Asian youths and their communities continued in the UK, and was one of the main causes of violent clashes between South Asian youths and BNP supporters in what became known as the 'Northern cities riots', which took place in 2001 in Oldham, Burnley, Bradford and Leeds.

The Cantle Report into the causes of the 2001 riots, like the Scarman Report, acknowledged deprivation and youth disillusionment as significant causes, but blamed the riots on deep-rooted segregation, whereby people of different ethnicities in some parts of Britain had not 'mixed' but lived 'parallel' and polarised lives (Cantle, 2001). The counter-argument that the segregation was not voluntary but forced by deep-rooted racism and the alienation of Asian youths and their communities was underplayed in the reports on these riots. Allegations of discriminatory policing were also ignored (Kundnani, 2001). Instead, the ruling (Labour) government's response to these riots was to call for public debates on citizenship and to encourage local authorities to work 'harder' on promoting 'community cohesion' (Home Office, 2001).

In recent years, South Asian youths of Islamic faith have also been at the centre of serious crime debates in Europe, following the waves of terrorist attacks in the continent, especially since the 9/11 terrorist attacks. It is generally believed that the threat of terrorism in Europe is posed much more by 'home-grown' radicalised Muslim youths who are European citizens than by radicalised Muslims from abroad. This appears to be proven by the fact that the terrorist attacks in 2016/17 in France, Belgium, Germany and the UK were carried out mainly by Muslim youths who had legal residence status or were citizens of these countries. Concerns about European Muslim youths travelling to fight in Muslim countries of the Middle East against Western troops have existed since the 1980s, but it was the rise of organised global Islamic terrorist groups like Al Qaeda and the Islamic State, and their systematic grooming ('radicalisation') and mobilisation of Muslim youths in Europe to fight in troubled Islamic countries like Syria, Afghanistan and Iraq, and the call for them to perform *jihad* in their own countries, that has placed Muslim youths and their communities at the centre of counter-terrorism policies in many European countries.

Although the majority of Muslim youths who are known to have been 'radicalised' came from deprived communities and to have experienced racial discrimination and exclusion that might have provoked their hatred for the society in which they live and resulted in support for a violent Islamic ideology and *jihad*, radicalisation is a complex transformative learning process that is brought about by a variety of factors (Bouhana and Wikstrom, 2011; Wilner and Dubouloz, 2011; Lynch, 2013). The result has been counter-productive, as measures to prevent radicalisation and counter-terrorism in Europe became focused on Muslim youths and communities (DCLG, 2007; Kundnani, 2012; and see Chapter 2, this volume).

The Prevent strategy in the UK and Europe includes a variety of measures aimed at preventing people from being drawn into or adopting violent extremist ideologies. These measures are to be rooted in 'communities at risk', and include community engagement approaches aimed at mobilising relevant groups and institutions at the local level, to challenge violent extremist ideologies among 'suspect' groups and to promote support for 'mainstream voices'; disrupt those who promote violent extremism and their institutions; support vulnerable individuals, for example, by giving them appropriate advice and education about the dangers of being 'radicalised'; and increase the capacity (resilience) of communities to resist violent extremism and to address the grievances that extremist 'ideologues' are exploiting (HM Government, 2011). However, experiences of discrimination or exclusion, unemployment and housing problems or being victimised are not regarded as grievances for the purpose of Prevent, as they could apply to any form of social discontent and violence (see HM Government, 2008b). In contrast, Prevent allows links to be made between criminality and radicalisation, and therefore encourages those concerned with youth offending to identify youths with whom they are working who may become interested in violent extremism, and to consider measures that could be incorporated into their intervention in order to rehabilitate such offenders and to divert them away from being 'radicalised'.

There is a strong focus in Prevent on enabling communities to easily identify individuals who are vulnerable to radicalisation and, where a 'vulnerable person' is identified, to create points of referral for them to access interventions to address the root causes of their radicalisation. Some of the interventions that have been suggested for those who are vulnerable to radicalisation include:

- referral to youth mentoring projects;
- engagement with positive role models;
- providing positive alternative activities such as volunteering; and
- projects aimed at developing a stronger faith understanding.

Most significant are the powers that have been given to schools in the UK to identify children prone to being drawn into terrorism/violent extremism and to refer them to the government early intervention programme called 'Channel' (HM Government, 2010, 2012a, b, 2015). The success of these programmes, if any, is yet to be researched fully. Instead, it has been alleged that counter-terrorist measures in Europe have led to an increase in Islamophobia, social divisions and racial hatred – factors that are likely to further aid the processes of radicalisation (Spalek and Lambert, 2008; Kundnani, 2012).

Refugee and asylum-seeking young people

The numbers of children and young people fleeing from persecution and extreme poverty in countries experiencing political conflicts, and seeking asylum in European countries, have been increasing in recent years. Of significant concern has been the increasing numbers of these youths who have travelled to Europe unaccompanied. In 2016, over 90% of the 7,567 children who crossed the Mediterranean into Europe were unaccompanied (UNHCR, 2016). Unaccompanied and asylum-seeking children (UASC) are becoming an increasingly significant part of the refugee and asylum-seeker youth populations in Europe. Refugee and asylum-seeking youths depend on state authorities in the countries of their arrival to safeguard their welfare and uphold their rights. Unfortunately, however, many European countries are experiencing difficulties coping with the unprecedented refugee numbers, and this has led to poor reception conditions, as well as major gaps in the provision of appropriate welfare arrangements, due to inadequate funding, leading to the services provided being usually sub-standard. In the UK, refugee and asylum-seeking youths and their families are generally housed in poor inner-city areas, with limited or no support networks, education and employment opportunities. Delays in the processing of applications for support, the insecurity of residence and restrictions to benefits and work have driven many of these asylum-seeking youths and their parents into poverty (Cooper, 2009). Like the resident British minority youths, they have also experienced racial prejudice and victimisation (Hemmerman et al, 2007).

Whereas there are no reliable official statistics on the offending rates of asylum-seeker or refugee youths, the association of these groups with crime has been the subject of much media and public attention in the UK since early 2000 (Malloch and Stanley, 2005; Cooper, 2009). One 2007 report maintained that there has been an increase in the numbers of young asylum-seekers and refugees with significant post-traumatic stress conditions increasingly becoming engaged in gang activities in London. Concern was expressed that these foreign youths were having a disproportionately negative impact on their UK peer groups (MPS, 2007). David Green, Director of the CIVITAS think tank, asserted:

> We are importing 15, 16, 17 and 18-year-olds brought up in countries with an anarchistic warlord culture, in which carrying knives and guns is routine. That is no exaggeration. We are asking for trouble if we do not confront this issue. (quoted in Mail Online, 2007)

The fact that some of the youths who took part in the 2016/17 terrorist attacks in Europe are believed to have entered Europe as asylum-seekers has raised doubts about the genuineness of asylum-seeking youths from Islamic countries, and this has damaged the degree of public sympathy for these young people. Consequently, the crime problems in which minority ethnic youths are, statistically, disproportionally involved now range widely in the UK and Europe from street crimes and weapons-related offences to terrorism.

Welfare vs criminal justice

In Britain, criminal justice responses to youth offending have varied slightly depending on the government in power. These variations are between what is commonly referred to as the 'welfare' and 'justice' approaches to youth justice. Although the differences between both have been contested, 'welfare' is largely associated with a rehabilitative approach, while 'justice' describes a youth justice system that is focused on punishment or retribution (Muncie, 2009). This section provides a review of UK youth justice policies under various governments since 1979.

Conservative governments (1979-97)

The Conservative governments of the 1980s/1990s did not act on Scarman's preference for a 'race'-related welfare approach to youth offending. Instead, the policing recommendations in the report were given priority, with new laws passed in 1984 and 1986, giving the police more powers in criminal investigations and in policing public disorder, respectively.

The UK Conservative Party's approach to youth justice is rooted in the neo-conservative theory of crime, and generally embraces the 'justice' model of youth justice (Muncie, 2009; see also Chapter 11, this volume). The Conservatives see crime as 'a matter of choice and a course of action freely chosen by pathological individuals with no self-control who [threaten] the very moral fabric of society' (Muncie, 2009, p 140). The causes of youth offending are believed to include indiscipline; weakened social bonds; lack of secure family upbringing or parental irresponsibility; family breakdown (absent fathers); underachievement in school mainly as a result of truanting, idleness or being work-shy; and moral decline, epitomised, for example, by the misuse of drugs. Thus, youth crime is placed within the larger context of societal decline – the result of the 'ill-effects of modernisation and affluence, which have led to the erosion of traditional values based around morality and duty to the family and wider community' (Gunter, 2010, p x). Accordingly, young offenders were to be treated as candidates for 'correction', not 'welfare'.

The moral panic in the 1980s/1990s that youth offending was fast rising provided the governing Conservative Party with justification for adopting a punitive stance on youths breaking the law. A new Criminal Justice Act, passed in 1991, was based on the principle of 'just deserts', with a strong focus on individual and parental responsibility. The law introduced a variety of sanctions that could be used for children and young people who commit crimes, as well as for their parents. This punitive stand on youth offending was matched, however, by the Conservative government's poor record on youth welfare. For example, youths not in full-time education were, in 1991, denied social security benefits. In addition, the reduction in the amount of affordable accommodation, the result of market-driven government housing policies, led to increased youth homelessness (see Hutson and Liddiard, 1994). Furthermore, Conservative youth employment and training initiatives to 'help' youths gain employment left many young people in precarious situations of economic uncertainty and disaffection, including high unemployment, with minority ethnic minority youths generally, and girls in particular, most affected (Griffin, 1985; Cockburn, 1987).

Offending was not perceived in terms of 'race' or racial differences in youth experiences. Young people who committed crimes were seen as having similar characteristics in terms of life experiences and exposure to criminogenic factors. As a result, a 'one-hat-fits-all' approach was adopted in youth justice during the 1980s and early 1990s, in spite of research evidence that continued to show BAME youths' disproportionate exposure to these criminogenic factors.

New Labour (1997-2010)

The 'New Labour' government that came to power in the UK in 1997 was greatly influenced by the left realist criminological theory of crime (Matthews and Young, 1992; Young, 1997). This view believes that, whereas the root causes of crime lie in 'relative' deprivation and social exclusion, the explanation for social action should be the same, and people should be seen as being responsible for their actions. A left realist approach to youth crime, therefore, would tackle youth social and economic exclusion head-on, but at the same time, mete out appropriate punishments to those breaking the law. This position was captured in the New Labour slogan of 'Tough on crime, tough on the causes of crime' (Home Office, 1997a, b, c). But, according to Young (2002), New Labour, in fact, adopted a 'weak' definition of exclusion, viewing it as a self-imposed condition by a lazy and idle underclass – a view it shared with previous Conservative governments.

Muncie (2009) argued that the New Labour era was a culmination of different youth justice discourses ranging from the liberal justice position of viewing youths as rational actors to neoliberal and neo-conservative positions of seeing youths as irresponsible, dangerous and immoral. These views have produced youth policies ranging from measures to clamp down on youth anti-social behaviour right through to more legal provisions to ensure that youths, on the one hand, face up to their offending behaviour while parents, on the other, take responsibility for their child's criminal or deviant behaviour. Muncie concluded that, under New Labour, 'there appears an almost universal political consensus that the root cause of youth crime lies in a breakdown of morality associated with dysfunctional families and a feckless underclass' (2009, p 146). As a result, laws were enacted that placed youth offending on a par with that of adults, in terms of their subjection to the criminal law and the criminal justice system (Cavadino and Dignan, 2007). For example, the Crime and Disorder Act 1998 abolished the old legal tradition of *doli incapax* (someone who cannot be legally held responsible for their actions) for 10- to 13-year-olds and introduced, instead, a range of 'early intervention' child orders for children under the age of 10, 'to catch them before they start'. New Labour scaled up the managerialisation process started by the Conservatives. The 1998 Act created the Youth Justice Board for England and Wales, a new executive, non-departmental public body (NDPB) responsible for the supervision, monitoring and assessment of all aspects of the youth justice system. Multi-agency Youth Offending Teams (YOTs) were created, to manage the local delivery of youth justice services. Most importantly, the focus of New Labour's youth justice programme was allegedly 'prevention'. On this platform initiatives were encouraged that combined the efforts of public, private, voluntary and faith groups (the third sector) and communities to address and prevent the causes of youth crime (Home Office, 2009; Neuberger, 2009).

Unlike its Conservative predecessors, Labour appeared to want to tackle 'race' issues in youth justice. In 2006, the House of Commons Home Affairs Committee (HAC) inquired into the persistent problem of the over-representation of Black youths in the criminal justice system. In May 2007, the Committee published its report, with 67 main recommendations (House of Commons HAC, 2007). In many ways, this report is a replay of the Scarman Report published 25 years earlier. Like Scarman, the Committee identified the causes of Black youths offending as emanating mainly from their disproportionate subjection to social exclusion; educational under-achievement compounded by high levels of school exclusion; high unemployment rate; a lack of positive role models for young Black people (especially boys) as a result of the predominance of single-parent families (absent fathers) within Black communities; mental health problems; homelessness; misuse of drugs; living in unsafe and criminal communities; and the negative effect of popular music and culture on Black youths (House of Commons HAC, 2007). The Committee was particularly concerned about the disproportionate involvement of Black youths in criminal youth affiliations ('gangs'), especially that both male and female youths were joining gangs as a 'protective measure' against victimisation by gang members (House of Commons HAC, 2007, pp 1-4; Home Office, 2002). Finally, like Scarman, the HAC report maintained that, whereas racial discrimination within the criminal justice system might be a contributory factor, it was so 'only in some instances' (House of Commons HAC, 2007, p 45).

The Committee has been criticised for focusing mainly on Black youths and ignoring youths of other ethnicities (Bowling and Phillips, 2006). However, in response to the Committee report (HM Government, 2007, 2008a, 2009), the Labour government made efforts to show that, unless otherwise specified, the majority of ongoing initiatives were meant for youths of all ethnicities. The common denominator, it was claimed, was youths living in 'challenging' or deprived environments who are offending or at risk of offending. (See Box 12.1 for a list of initiatives linked to youth offending supported under New Labour.)

Box 12.1: Youth crime prevention initiatives under New Labour

Family and personal support
- Initiatives to ensure that parenting support services are accessible, appropriate and relevant to BAME families' needs.
- Ensuring that available drug treatment facilities for youths are accessible to and are meeting the needs of youths of all ethnicities.
- Engaging youths at risk of offending in positive activities that would involve them in expressing their creativity positively in music, creative arts and other cultural activities and sports, to empower young people and raise their self-esteem,

confidence and aspirations, hence endowing them with the skills and knowledge that are required to join the workforce and ultimately diverting them away from offending.

- Supporting youths who are victims of crime, to make sure that they do not turn to crime in response to being a victim.
- Helping young offenders leaving custody reintegrate into the labour market and get accommodation on release.

School and education

- Expansion of schools and community mentoring schemes to include mentoring by peers and ex-offenders for young adults in prisons.
- Increased efforts to reduce the school exclusion rate of Black youths.
- Ensuring that all schools fully meet their responsibilities under the Race Relations (Amendment) Act 2000 to eliminate unlawful discrimination and promote equality of opportunity among, and good relations between, persons of all ethnic groups.
- Ensuring that proper educational provision is made for young people excluded from school.
- Ensuring that the school curricula are relevant to the needs of Black youths as well as empowering them.
- Making schools safer by expanding the Safer Schools partnerships scheme and increasing after-school police patrols in known high-crime areas.

Community

- Increasing awareness of, and access to, safe spaces in areas of high deprivation, in which young people can meet informally and gain access to information about organised (positive) activities, help and advice.
- Tackling gang membership more seriously by setting up more youth gang exit programmes, paying more attention to the provision of 'safe houses', providing mentoring and positive activities in the communities for youths caught up in youth affiliations but not yet involved in crime, arresting gang members, and providing more support at schools to help youths say 'no' to gang membership.
- Tackling gun and knife crimes by giving continuing financial support to existing national initiatives such as the Tackling Gangs Action Programme (TGAP) and Tackling Knives Action Programme (TKAP), and encouraging the development of similar initiatives elsewhere.
- Using the media to raise awareness among youths about the dangers of becoming involved in violent crimes.
- Ensuring that support provided by the YOTs meet the needs of young Black people.
- Tailoring support and services that youths receive within the criminal justice system to individual needs, not age, and ensuring continuity of support when an offender moves from the youth justice system into an adult one.

> • Improving the youths' trust and confidence in the use of police 'stop and search' powers, and encouraging youths from minority ethnic backgrounds to choose the police as a future career option.
> • Engaging with young people, for example, through local youth forums set up by the police and local Crime and Disorder Reduction Partnerships (CDRPs) in which young people can meet to talk about their concerns.
>
> For full details, see HM Government (2007, 2008a, 2009).

Particular emphasis was put on working with faith groups in order to reach out to youths in communities perceived to be 'hard to reach' (Cabinet Office, 2006, 2007; MoJ, 2008; MoJ and NOMS, 2008). Faith groups, especially Muslim ones, were used to raise awareness of government youth initiatives, thereby increasing programme and project take-up rates in these communities. Faith groups were also involved in the setting up of gang exit and safe haven programmes to support youths wanting to leave gangs and those avoiding victimisation or pressure to join gangs (NOMS/YJB, 2007; DCLG, 2008).

On first reading, the above list of initiatives appears to have a strong 'welfare' edge to it. A closer look reveals that the welfare issues that are mostly connected with BAME youth offending – unemployment, homelessness and experiences of racial discrimination and exclusion – are not stressed in any of them. More important is the lack of provision for monitoring and accountability. There were many projects established, but no overall coordination provided, and many were not properly evaluated.

Conservative-Liberal Democrats coalition government (2010-15)

The coalition government that came to power in 2010 inherited a decreasing population in youth offending. In contrast, however, was an ever-increasing reoffending rate, with over 60% of young people leaving custody reoffending within a year (Gove, 2015; YJB/MoJ, 2015c). A House of Commons Justice Committee report on youth justice appeared to put the blame of youth offending on the shoulders of 'other agencies', arguing:

> There is a limit to what criminal justice agencies can achieve in preventing offending: young people in the criminal justice system are disproportionately likely to have high levels of welfare need and other agencies have often failed to offer them support at an early stage. (House of Commons Justice Committee, 2013, p 3)

The government supported the Committee's view on the critical importance of effective early intervention and the crucial role that various agencies could play in preventing youth offending, but in its response to the Committee report, it singled out lack of education as a criminogenic factor that required significant attention (MoJ, 2013). Thus, in a consultation Green Paper published in 2013 entitled *Transforming youth custody: Putting education at the heart of detention*, the coalition government proposed to establish a network of secure colleges across England and Wales to replace existing youth custodial provisions. In addition, the number of contracted education hours in Young Offender Institutions was to be doubled (MoJ, 2014).

Conservative government (2015-)

The succeeding 2015 Conservative government, in its party manifesto, *Strong leadership, a clear economic plan, a brighter more secure future*, made no explicit references to youth offending or youth justice, suggesting that there was to be no fundamental break with policies of the previous coalition administration. Accordingly, the policy to place education at the centre of youth justice was adopted. However, shortly after taking up office, amidst criticisms of secure colleges becoming modern–day borstals and the immense costs that the construction of the colleges would incur, the Conservative government took a dramatic U-turn not to proceed with the secure colleges project. Instead, in September 2015, Charles Taylor was asked to lead a departmental review of the youth justice system for the Ministry of Justice. His interim findings supported the government's view that the youth justice system would be more effective and better able to rehabilitate young people if education was at its heart. However, in place of the secure colleges, Taylor recommended the introduction of secure schools delivering core subjects such as English and mathematics, as well as a range of work training, and the setting up of apprenticeship schemes with employers post-sentence to ensure that young ex-offenders are earning or learning on release. The secure schools would be:

> Smaller custodial establishments of up to 60-70 places ... located in the regions that they serve. They should be set up within schools legislation, commissioned in England in a similar way to alternative provision free schools, and governed and inspected as schools. Rather than seeking to import education into youth prisons, schools must be created for detained children which bring together other essential services, and in which are then overlaid the necessary security arrangements. (Taylor, 2016, p 40)

It is alarming to note that 'race' continued to slip into the oblivion as an explanation for youth offending, as the factor that makes it obvious – racism –

continues to be unacknowledged. Meanwhile, the Youth Justice Board (YJB) has been busy researching how best to address reoffending (YJB, 2014, 2015a). This has resulted in the publication of a reoffending toolkit that is designed to provide better understanding and analysis of the characteristics of the reoffending cohort, and help YOTs develop strategies to prevent further reoffending. The reoffending toolkit includes a disproportionality toolkit that allows YOTs to gain a broader understanding of when, where, how and why ethnicity-based disproportionality arises in their local youth justice system (YJB, 2015a, p 10). However, the disproportionality tool only enables a YOT to see 'at a glance' whether there is any over-representation of any particular ethnic groups in their local youth justice system. The YJB is yet to provide a tool that will enable YOTs to provide a deeper analysis or explanation of any disproportionality by ethnicity and how it might be addressed (YJB, 2015b, pp 9-10). The favoured approach is to continue to address common risk and needs factors based on the Ministry of Justice's definition of what works in managing children and young people who offend (MoJ, 2016b).

Gender, youth and justice

Studies conducted on gender and the criminal justice system have shown that the reasons why young women enter the criminal justice system are slightly different from those of young men (Smith and McAra, 2004; Gelsthorpe, 2006; Gelsthorpe and Sharpe, 2006). Like ethnicity, gender is yet to be fully understood in the delivery of youth services to young girls, especially those from minority ethnic backgrounds who are also disproportionately represented in the criminal justice system. The youth justice system appears to treat young women of all ethnicities in a similar way (YJB, 2009). It is often assumed that the risk factors for young women's offending are the same as those for boys, namely, peer pressure, failure in education, family issues and drug/alcohol misuse.

Although arguments in favour of 'gender-responsive strategies' and initiatives for women are developing (Shaw and Hannah-Moffat, 2000, 2004; Hedderman, 2004), the bulk of the arguments that have been put forward so far have been for adult women. Research has shown that young women (girls) in the youth justice system do not respond in the same way to treatment as their male counterparts (YJB, 2009). This area needs further research. With regard to ethnicity, there is as yet no concrete evidence on whether the offending behaviour of young women of different ethnicities differs; after all, it was only in 2010 that the first partially detailed set of racially coded statistics on UK women was published (MoJ, 2010). At least, however, this process has started.

Conclusion

It is doubtful whether governments can accommodate the criminal justice and related welfare needs of youths of all ethnicities. Dell and Boe (2000) have argued that to prioritise 'race' or ethnicity in addressing offending behaviour would be to assume that offending behaviour arises more from racial experience than from shared common life histories. According to them:

> Individuals differ due to their racialized experiences but they also resemble one another due to common life experiences. The overall implication is that caution must be exercised in focussing … exclusively on race. The lack of attention to similarity across racial categories may result in overlooking or minimizing elements of individual shared life histories that may contribute to understanding and identifying criminogenic factors (risk and needs). (Dell and Boe, 2000, p iv)

The need to prioritise 'shared experiences' over 'race' is promoted by those claiming that the 'race' or ethnicity dimension is over-played, and that in today's multicultural, modern Britain, for example, we should 'celebrate' shared experiences rather than emphasise difference (Mirza, 2010). Cole (2008), however, argues that racialised experiences should not be undermined. Scarman has shown that disadvantage in education, housing and employment, which minority ethnic youths disproportionally suffer, is a key factor in understanding their over-involvement in crime. There is no clear evidence that this situation has changed significantly today. Research in England and Wales shows that the most frequent form of explanation offered to account for offending by Black and Asian offenders is racism in society generally, and within the criminal justice system specifically (Denney, 1992; Calverley et al, 2004; Cole and Wardak, 2006). Cole (2008) argues that the risk of reoffending is high where offenders are confronted by racism after completing a sentence, which means that a significant factor in their offending remains ever-present. 'Celebrating' difference is not divisive. In fact, it is a fundamental requirement of true democracy. However, it is not expected that there will be any significant change in the approach to 'race' under UK Prime Minister Theresa May's government, as youths, not to mention BAME and foreign youths, do not appear as a priority in any of the policy issues that have been advanced as important to her government. In summary:

• British and European crime and criminal justice system statistics reveal that there are differences in youth offending and victimisation by ethnicity.
• The Scarman Report into the 1980s riots set a precedent by alerting governments to the importance of prioritising welfare over criminal justice

(policing) as the way of addressing the offending behaviour of BAME youths who predominantly live in Britain's most deprived inner cities.

- Subsequent political responses to youth offending and welfare appear to have ignored 'ethnic' differences and focused on tackling known criminogenic needs, irrespective of ethnicity – a cautionary move, perhaps, acknowledging the warnings given by Scarman of a possible 'backlash' if policies were instituted that directly favoured Blacks for reasons that are considered unfair by the general (White) population.
- New Labour, through its vigorous pursuance of multi-agency partnerships in youth crime prevention initiatives, appears to have acknowledged Scarman's recommendation regarding the involvement of all sectors in youth justice. The reality, however, is that government control of the process continued at a distance through monopoly of youth justice policies and funding.
- The current move to give education a priority in the youth justice system is welcomed, but has yet to be tested.
- Low priority continues to be given to female youths.
- The youth justice and welfare systems have yet to provide adequately for youths of all ethnicities, but the question remains as to whether ethnicity or 'shared experiences' should be the guiding principle.

Questions for discussion

- What are the causes of the disproportionate representation of BAME youths in the criminal justice system? How can these be addressed through a reform of the state welfare system?
- What should be the priority in welfare provisions for youths who are at risk of offending and those who offend: ethnicity or 'shared experiences'?
- How should gender be approached within welfare provision for youths of all ethnicities involved in the criminal justice system?

Further reading

Bhui, S. (ed) (2009) *Race and criminal justice*, London: Sage.

MoJ (Ministry of Justice) (2016) *Statistics on women and the criminal justice system 2015 – A Ministry of Justice Publication under Section 95 of the Criminal Justice Act 1991*, London: The Stationery Office.

References

Bouhana, N. and Wikstrom, P.O.H. (2011) *Al Qaida influenced radicalization: A rapid evidence assessment guided by situational action theory*, London: Home Office, Office for Security and Counter Terrorism.

Bowling, B. and Phillips, C. (2002) *Racism, crime and justice*, London: Longman.

Bowling, B. and Phillips, C. (2006) *Young Black people and the criminal justice system*, Submission to the House of Commons Home Affairs Committee Inquiry, October, London: King's College.

Bradshaw, J., Kemp, P., Baldwin, S. and Rowe, A. (2004) *The drivers of social exclusion: A review of the literature for the Social Exclusion Unit in the Breaking of Cycle series*, London: Office of the Deputy Prime Minister.

Cabinet Office (2006) *Partnership in public services: An action plan for third sector involvement*, London: HM Treasury/Cabinet Office.

Cabinet Office (2007) *The future role of the third sector in social and economic regeneration: Final report*, London: HM Treasury/Cabinet Office.

Calverley, A., Cole, B., Kaur, G., Lewis, S., Raynor, P., Sadeghi, S., et al (2004) *Black and Asian offenders on probation*, Home Office Research Study 277, London: Home Office.

Cantle, T. (2001) *Report of the Community Cohesion Review Team* (Cantle Report), London: HMSO.

Cavadino, M. and Dignan, J. (2007) *The penal system: An introduction* (3rd edn), London: Sage.

Cockburn, C. (1987) *Two-track training: Sex inequalities and the YTS*, London: Macmillan.

Cole, B. (2008) 'Working with ethnic diversity', in S. Green, E. Lancaster and S. Feasey (eds) *Addressing offending behaviour*, Cullompton: Willan, 402-25.

Cole, B. (2010) 'Race, crime and criminal justice in Britain', in A. Kalunta-Crumpton (ed) *Race, crime and criminal justice: International perspectives*, Basingstoke: Palgrave Macmillan, 25-50.

Cole, B. and Wardak, A. (2006) 'Black and Asian men on probation: Social exclusion, discrimination and experience of criminal justice', in S. Lewis, P. Raynor, D. Smith and A. Wardak (eds) *Race and probation*, Cullompton: Willan, Chapter 5.

Cooper, C. (2009) 'Refugees, asylum seekers and criminal justice', in S. Bhui (ed) *Race and criminal justice*, London: Sage, 137-53.

Craig, G., Adamson, S. Cole, B., Law, I. and Chan, C.K. (2009) *Hidden from public view? Racism against the UK's Chinese population*, London: Department for Communities and Local Government.

DCLG (Department for Communities and Local Government) (2007) *The role of Muslim identity politics in radicalization*, London: DCLG.

DCLG (2008) *Face to face and side by side: A framework for partnership in our multi-faith society*, London: CLG Publications.

Dell, C.A. and Boe, R. (2000) *An examination of Aboriginal and Caucasian women offender risk and needs factors*, Ottawa: Research Branch, Correctional Services of Canada.

Denney, D. (1992) *Racism and anti-racism in probation*, London: Routledge.

EU (European Union) (2015a) *Being young in Europe today*, Eurostat Statistical Books, Luxembourg: Publications Office of the European Union.

EU (2015b) *Overview of youth discrimination in the European Union Report 2015*, Luxembourg: Publications Office of the European Union.

European Institute for Crime Prevention and Control (2014) *European sourcebook of crime and criminal justice statistics* (5th edn), Helsinki: HEUNI.

Fitzgerald, M. and Sibbitt, R. (1997) *Ethnic monitoring in police forces: A beginning*, London: Home Office.

Gaskell, G. (1986) 'Black youth and the police', *Policing*, 2(1), 26–34.

Gaskell, G. and Smith, P. (1985) 'Young Blacks' hostility to the police: An investigation into its causes', *New Community*, 12(1), 66–74.

Gelsthorpe, L. (2006) 'The experiences of female minority ethnic offenders: The other "other"', in S. Lewis, P. Raynor, D. Smith and A. Wardak (eds) *Race and probation*, Cullompton: Willan, Chapter 6.

Gelsthorpe, L. and Sharpe, G. (2006) 'Gender, youth and justice', in B. Goldson and J. Muncie (eds) *Youth crime and justice*, London: Sage, 47–61.

Gilroy, P. (1982) 'The myth of Black criminality', *The Socialist Register*, 47–56.

Gove, M., MP (2015) Written statement to Parliament: 'Youth justice', 11 September (www.gov.uk/government/speeches/youth–justice).

Government Office for London (2007) *Indices of Deprivation*, Corporate Information and Analysis Team, London: Government Office for London.

Griffin, C. (1985) *Typically girls?*, London: Routledge.

Gunter, A. (2010) *Growing up bad? Black youth, 'road' culture and badness in an East London neighbourhood*, London: The Tufnell Press.

Hall, S., Critcher, C., Jefferson, T., Clarke, J. and Roberts, B. (1978) *Policing the crisis: Mugging, the state and law and order*, London: Macmillan.

Hedderman C. (2004) 'The "criminogenic" needs of women offenders', in G. McIvor (ed) *Women who offend*, London: Jessica Kingsley Publishers, Chapter 11.

Hemmerman, L., Law, I., Simms, J. and Sirriyeh, A. (2007) *Situating racist hostility and understanding the impact of racist victimisation in Leeds*, Leeds: Centre for Ethnicity and Racism Studies.

HM Government (2007) *The government's response to the House of Commons Home Affairs Select Committee Report: Young Black people and the criminal justice system*, London: The Stationery Office.

HM Government (2008a) *Home Affairs Select Committee Inquiry: Young Black people and the criminal justice system. First annual report*, December, London: The Stationery Office.

HM Government (2008b) *The Prevent strategy: A guide for local partners in England*, London: HM Government.

HM Government (2009) *Home Affairs Select Committee Inquiry: Young Black people and the criminal justice system. Second annual report*, December, London: The Stationery Office

HM Government (2010) *Channel: Supporting individuals vulnerable to recruitment by violent extremists*, London: HM Government.

HM Government (2011) *Prevent strategy*, London: HM Government.

HM Government (2012a) *Channel: Protecting vulnerable people from being drawn into terrorism*, London: HM Government.

HM Government (2012b) *Channel: Vulnerability assessment framework*, London: HM Government.

HM Government (2015) *Counter-Terrorism and Security Act, 2015*, London: HM Government.

Home Office (1997a) *No more excuses – A new approach to tackling youth crime in England and Wales*, London: HMSO.

Home Office (1997b) *Preventing children offending: A consultative document*, London: HMSO.

Home Office (1997c) *Tackling youth crime*, London: HMSO.

Home Office (2001) *Building cohesive communities: A Report of the Ministerial Group on Public Order and Community Cohesion*, London: HMSO.

Home Office (2002) *Shootings, gangs and violent incidents in Manchester*, Crime Reduction Research Series Paper 13, London: HMSO.

Home Office (2009) *Engaging communities in criminal justice*, London: HMSO.

House of Commons HAC (Home Affairs Committee) (2007) *Young Black people and the criminal justice system. Second report of Session 2006-07*, Vol 1, London: HMSO.

House of Commons Justice Committee (2013) *Youth justice, Seventh report of Session 2012–13*, Vols 1/2, London: The Stationery Office.

Hutson, S. and Liddiard, M. (1994) *Youth homelessness: The construction of a social issue*, London: Macmillan.

Jansson, K. (2006) *Black and minority ethnic groups' experiences and perceptions of crime, racially motivated crime and the police: Findings from the 2004/05 British Crime Survey*, London: Home Office.

Kalunta-Crumpton, A. (ed) (2010) *Race, crime and criminal justice: International perspectives*, Basingstoke: Palgrave Macmillan.

Keith, M. (1993) *Race, riots and policing: Lore and disorder in a multi-racist society*, London: UCL.

Kundnani, A. (2001) 'From Oldham to Bradford: The violence of the violated', in Institute of Race Relations (eds) *The three faces of British racism*, London: Institute of Race Relations.

Kundnani, A. (2012) 'Radicalisation: The journey of a concept', *Race & Class*, 54(2), 3–25.

Lea, J. and Young, J. (1993) *What is to be done about law and order?* (revised edn), London: Pluto Press.

Lynch, O. (2013) 'British Muslim youth: Radicalisation, terrorism and the construction of the "other"', *Critical Studies on Terrorism*, 6(2), 241–61.

Macpherson, W. (1999) *The Stephen Lawrence inquiry: Report of an inquiry by Sir William Macpherson*, London: HMSO.

Mail Online (2007) 'Immigrants from war-torn countries fuelling gang crime' (www.dailymail.co.uk/news/article-451995/Immigrants-war-torn-countries-fuelling-gang-crime.html).

Malloch, M.S. and Stanley, E. (2005) 'The detention of asylum seekers in the UK: Representing risk, managing the dangerous', *Punishment & Society*, 7(1), 53–71.

Matthews, R. and Young, J. (eds) (1992) *Issues in realist criminology*, London: Sage.

Mirza, M. (2010) 'Rethinking race', *Prospect*, October, 31–2.

MoJ (Ministry of Justice) (2008) *Third sector strategy: Improving policies and securing better public services through effective partnerships' (2008-2011)*, London: MoJ.

MoJ (2010) *Statistics on women and the criminal justice system – A Ministry of Justice publication under Section 95 of the Criminal Justice Act 1991*, London: HMSO.

MoJ (2013) *Government response to the Justice Committee's Seventh report of Session 2012-13: Youth justice*, London: HMSO.

MoJ (2014) *Transforming youth custody: Government response to the consultation*, London: HMSO.

MoJ (2015) *Statistics on race and the criminal justice system 2014*, London: HMSO.

MoJ (2016a) *Statistics on women and the criminal justice system 2015 – A Ministry of Justice publication under Section 95 of the Criminal Justice Act 1991*, London: HMSO.

MoJ (2016b) *What works in managing young people who offend? A summary of the international evidence*, Ministry of Justice Analytical Series, London: HMSO.

MoJ and NOMS (National Offender Management Service) (2008) *Working with the third sector to reduce re-offending: Securing effective partnerships (2008-2011)*, London: MoJ.

MPS (Metropolitan Police Service) Authority (2007) *MPS response to guns, gangs and knives in London* (http://policeauthority.org/metropololitian/committees/x-cop/2007/070503/05/index.htm).

Muncie, J. (2009) *Youth and crime* (3rd edn), London: Sage.

Neuberger, Baroness (2009) *Volunteering across the CJS*, London: Cabinet Office.

NOMS (National Offender Management System) and YJB (Youth Justice Board) (2007) *Believing we can: Promoting the contribution faith-based organisations can make to reducing adult and youth re-offending: A consultative document*, London: NOMS and YJB.

ONS (Office for National Statistics) (2017) 'Young people not in education, employment or training (NEET)', *Statistical Bulletin*, 23 February, London: ONS.

Scarman, the Rt Hon Lord (1981) *The Brixton disorders 10-12 April 1981*, London: HMSO.

Scottish Executive (2005) *Measurement of the extent of youth crime in Scotland*, Edinburgh: DTZ Pieda Consulting.

Scottish Government Social Research (2010a) *Troublesome youth groups, gangs and knife carrying in Scotland*, Edinburgh: Queens Printers of Scotland.

Scottish Government Social Research (2010b) *Gang membership and knife carrying: Findings from the Edinburgh study of youth transitions and crime*, Edinburgh: Queens Printers of Scotland.

Shaw, M. and Hannah-Moffat, K. (2000) 'Gender, diversity and risk assessment in Canadian corrections', *Probation Journal*, 47, 163-72.

Shaw, M. and Hannah-Moffat, K. (2004) 'How cognitive skills forgot about gender and diversity', in G. Mair (ed) *What matters in probation*, Cullompton: Willan, Chapter 5.

Smith, D. and McAra, L. (2004) *Gender and youth offending*, Edinburgh: University of Edinburgh.

Solomos, J. (1988) *Black youth, racism and the state*, Cambridge: Cambridge University Press.

Spalek, B. and Lambert, B. (2008) 'Muslim communities, counter-terrorism and counter-radicalization: A critically reflective approach to engagement', *International Journal of Law, Crime and Justice*, 36, 257-70.

Taylor, C. (2016) *Review of the youth justice system in England and Wales*, London: Ministry of Justice.

Times Online (2009) 'Rise in race crime against non-Whites: Around half the victims of race crimes in Scotland were of Asian origin and 95 percent of the perpetrators Whites', 31 March (www.timesonline.co.uk/tol/news/uk/scotland/article6011657.ece).

Uhrig, N. (2016) *Black, Asian and minority ethnic disproportionality in the criminal justice system in England and Wales*, London: MoJ Analytical Services.

UNHCR (UN Refugee Agency) (2016) *Unaccompanied and separated children in Europe*, Briefing Note, 23 May (www.unhcr.org/uk/partners/partners/57da92de7/background-document-unaccompanied-separated-children-europe.html?query=unaccompanied children).

Wardak, A. (2000) *Social control and deviance: A South Asian community in Scotland*, Aldershot: Ashgate.

Webster, C. (1997) 'The construction of British "Asian" criminality', *International Journal of the Sociology of Law*, 25(1), 65-86.

Wilner, A.S. and Dubouloz, C.-J. (2011) 'Transformative radicalization: Applying learning theory to Islamist radicalization', *Studies in Conflict & Terrorism*, 34, 418-38.

YJB (Youth Justice Board) (2009) *Girls and offending: Patterns, perceptions and interventions*, London: YJB.

YJB (2014) *YJB corporate plan 2014-17 and business plan 2014/15*, London: HMSO.

YJB (2015a) *Reducing reoffending: Furthering our understanding*, London: HMSO.

YJB (2015b) *AID (Assess and Improve Document) reoffending toolkit*, London: HMSO.

YJB/Ministry of Justice (MoJ) (2015) *National analysis of reoffending data, for those aged 10-17 England and Wales*, London: HMSO.

YJB/MoJ (2016) *Youth justice statistics 2014/15 England and Wales*, London: HMSO.

YJB/MoJ (2017) *Youth justice statistics 2015/16 England and Wales*, Statistics Bulletin, Executive Summary. London: MoJ.

Young, J. (1997) 'Left realist criminology: Radical in its analysis, realist in its policy', in M. Maguire, R. Morgan and R. Reiner (eds) *The handbook of criminology* (2nd edn), Oxford: Clarendon Press.

Young, J. (2002) 'Critical criminology in the 21st century: Critique, irony and the always unfinished', in K. Carrington and R. Hogg (eds) *Critical criminology*, Cullompton: Willan, 251-84.

Endnote

Karl Atkin, Sangeeta Chattoo, Gary Craig and Ronny Flynn

When writing the first edition of the book in 2011, we discussed the perceived failure of multiculturalism as a political intervention, a view common among European political leaders. Their priority was to facilitate a collective national identity to which all citizens could subscribe. Such a notion of national identity is constantly threatened in the face of a growing intolerance to difference and the persistence of racism in old and new forms.

The rise of casual racism is a latent though pervasive expression of this phenomenon (Nelson and Walton, 2014), while a significant increase in the number of 'race' crimes, especially since the Brexit vote, is a more obvious manifestation of it (Sharman and Jones, 2017). Equally, as highlighted by several chapters in this volume, securitisation (as a policy rhetoric addressing the perceived threats of extremism and terrorism), and its links with recent immigration and austerity policies, create a public space within which racism is reinvented. The lumping of people from particular minority ethnic (especially Muslim) communities with terrorism has become a common, disgraceful elision (see www.childline.org.uk/info-advice/your-feelings/anxiety-stress-panic/worries-about-the-world/).

One of the reiterative conclusions drawn throughout the book is the continued marginalisation, exclusion and disadvantage of most minority ethnic groups – and women in particular – despite 50 years of welfare policy initiatives. Such marginalisation is often the result of political inaction. Even where legislation is introduced, its effectiveness is undermined by a failure to put it into practice. This includes a failure to monitor ethnicity when delivering services and acting on any identified variations, alongside a more general failure on the part of research and policy to ensure that ethnicity is incorporated as an intrinsic dimension in the collection and use of evidence (see Berghs et al, 2016). Even where evidence points clearly to the need for restorative action as, for example, in the case of the close association between ethnicity and poverty, the response tends to be broad-brush rather than being effectively targeted at those most disadvantaged. Implicit assumptions underpinning much policy-making and service provision are that services are developed, delivered and used on what is effectively a level playing field, where no groups experience particular barriers to access. The evidence presented in this book fundamentally challenges these assumptions, reminding us of the deep structural inequalities that keep minority ethnic groups from achieving their full potential as active citizens. As Kymlicka (2001) argues, to treat people equally, you might need to treat them differently.

While thinking about citizenship in a postmodern, globalised and dynamic world of transnational or diasporic identities, we also need to understand the concept as one that challenges traditional, territorial boundaries of nationhood and state. Similarly, we must acknowledge that multiculturalism as a progressive political project has yet to find an ideal solution to reconciling ethnic and religious difference and diversity within a framework of fundamental universal human rights. For example, gender or intergenerational relationships within some minority groups will appear to be oppressive to others who take a particular secular-liberal or feminist viewpoint. At the same time, the issues of racialisation and essentialisation of these religious or cultural groups, as well as socioeconomic inequalities and forms of discrimination in the labour market, highlight the double standards within the liberal democratic tradition of Western European polities. The inclusion of Muslims and the recognition of religious identities within the public space in a secular state, as symbolised in the different responses to the controversy over wearing the headscarf in Britain and France, remains an important challenge for the liberal and egalitarian agenda of a redefined multiculturalism, as an ongoing project of inclusion and political justice (rather than assimilation in the past).

This book provides, we believe, an excellent (if necessarily incomplete) overview of the likely challenges facing those committed to ensuring that social policy can meaningfully engage with ethnicity and 'race' at an intersection with other forms of disadvantage and discrimination. Several chapters in the book emphasised the importance of conceptual engagement with the complexities of defining 'race', ethnicity and different forms of racism, exclusion and discrimination that result in the socioeconomic and political marginalisation of particular minority ethnic groups. This includes questioning definitions of the 'other' and how we perceive cultural and religious difference, while simultaneously developing policies that acknowledge the need to challenge discrimination, lack of appropriate access and inequities in service provision at various levels.

In taking a (sometimes long) historical view of the various sectors of welfare, this book reminds us that there is a lot to learn from the past. As is clear from the chapters, longstanding problems of discrimination and inequity, although now relatively clearly identified, often remain unresolved or reinvented. Essentialism, which has long been discredited in most academic circles, has re-emerged, as research, policy and practice respond to the multi-ethnic nature of British society. This is ironic, since our understanding of ethnicity has become increasingly sophisticated and the well-understood processes of disadvantage and discrimination, alongside a new-found interest in cultural identity, can sometimes delude us into thinking that there is little else to be done. Our growing awareness, however, has not always equated with a more responsive welfare provision, and indeed there is a widespread fear that the modest gains of the past few years are being rolled back. Witness, for example, elements within public bodies such as the police arguing that 'race' relations legislation is becoming a burden, while businesses have been encouraged to think that the Equality Act is creating unnecessary bureaucratic burdens.

It is worth mentioning that 'community cohesion' is a return to the language of assimilation rather than a move forward to a culture of respect for diversity and difference. The new focus on cohesion is quite clearly a way of reframing the 'race' equality discourse to deflect attention away from the growth of racism in British society. Surprisingly, many of those active in policy and research appear to have accepted this reframing without challenging its underlying assumptions. Indeed, it is important to ponder the social and political consequences of the loss of a focus on 'race' in policy-making and legislation, such as in the Black housing sector, which tried to tackle racism and discrimination more directly.

As Charles Taylor (1994) and others have reminded us, focusing on the needs of minority ethnic populations is not the same as responding to those needs. Despite a willingness on the part of liberal welfare states to tackle discrimination, public organisations not only struggle to reconcile key ideas – such as institutional racism and community cohesion – within a policy framework, but often lack a political strategy or commitment to initiate change or confront unhelpful developments such as the growth of racist behaviour or the rise of far-right political groups. On the one hand, the idea of super-diversity is finding both academic and policy acceptance, as the multifaceted nature of identity politics, intersectionality and discrimination find discursive expression within public debates. On the other hand, our ideas about discrimination and disadvantage do not easily map on to previously familiar scenes associated with ethnicity (and 'race'), gender, social class, disability, sexuality, faith and age. Nonetheless, accommodating diversity within larger meta–narratives associated with social justice and social inclusion remains, we would suggest, a continued and ever-important goal for social policy. The change in legislation towards a single equalities framework captured in the Single Equalities Act 2010 symbolises this cross-cutting of themes, although its impact on tackling racism remains unclear. Some of us are clearly deeply concerned by this move since – as is clear from this volume – racism remains a deeply divisive political issue that affects the life chances of millions of British citizens rather than being a slightly troubling but marginal issue, which most politicians and policy-makers simply want to wish away.

As Parekh, Modood and others argue, the fact that the UK is a multicultural (multi-ethnic) state cannot be denied, and that the political project of multiculturalism (as a policy), rather than being dead, has hardly yet started. This brings us face to face with the promise and limitations of multiculturalism as a political theory or perspective, as outlined by Parekh (2000, p 338). Parekh defines a multicultural perspective as composed of three interrelated principles:

that human beings are culturally embedded; the inevitability and desirability of cultural diversity and intercultural dialogue; and the internal plurality within each culture. Here we have a notion of different cultural, religious and other social groups being in dialogue with each other in which difference is respected, rather than living in segregated 'ghettos'. The sense of belonging and togetherness is derived from membership of a common political community, with mutual interests and rights as citizens, and sharing fundamental moral principles that uphold social justice and democracy (Parekh, 2000, p 341). Diversity, however, does not necessarily mean fragmentation, but rather, an interconnected society that can accommodate difference in different forms. This challenge is ever more salient today, as new minority ethnic groups arrive within the UK and settle here.

In editing this volume, we aim to challenge the concepts, processes and social policies that have sustained the economic, political and cultural marginalisation of people of minority ethnic origins. In providing a historical view of welfare provision and policies related to 'race' and ethnicity over time, we highlighted the conceptual shifts that have led to positive and, at times, retrograde policy moves. Some of the chapters representing particular sectors of welfare might, however, read more like a description of how far the achievements of these historical shifts have fallen short of the goals of equal opportunity and anti-racism, highlighting gaps between policy and practice. To that extent, the (at times) uneven nature of this collection represents the internal developments within a particular sector, its own history and its culture of representation and critique. Reading across these chapters allows the reader to see how far we have come in some sectors (and it is important to acknowledge this), and how far we lag behind in others, and perhaps to make use of the gains in some areas to accelerate progress elsewhere. Equally, since the terms of a particular discourse constitute a field and its subject (see Foucault, 1983), it is hard to provide a self-critique from within. We are aware, for example, that even though we tried to challenge the ascription of ethnicity to only people of minority ethnic groups, most of the chapters in the book do not deal with White majority populations. We hope that the volume as a whole inspires new ways of approaching welfare and social policy, and of destabilising old power dynamics between the majority and the minority or 'host' and 'immigrant' groups, in anticipation of a society that is equal, inclusive, fair and just for all.

References

Berghs, M., Atkin, K., Graham, H., Hatton, C. and Thomas, C. (2016) 'Implications for public health research of models and theories of disability: A scoping study and evidence synthesis', *Public Health Research*, 4(8).

Foucault, M. (1983) *The order of things: An archaeology of the human sciences*, London: Routledge.

Kymlicka, W. (2001) *Politics in the vernacular: Nationalism, multiculturalism and citizenship*, Oxford: Oxford University Press.

Nelson, J. and Walton, J. (2014) 'Explainer: What is casual racism?', The Conversation, 1 September (https://theconversation.com/explainer-what-is-casual-racism-30464).

Parekh, B. (2000) *The future of multi-racial Britain: The Parekh report*, London: Runnymede Trust.

Sharman, J. and Jones, I. (2017) 'Hate crimes rise by up to 100 per cent across England and Wales, figures reveal', *The Independent*, 15 February (www.independent.co.uk/news/uk/home-news/brexit-vote-hate-crime-rise-100-per-cent-england-wales-police-figures-new-racism-eu-a7580516.html).

Taylor, C. (1994) *Multiculturalism: Examining the politics of recognition*, Princeton, NJ: Princeton University Press.

Postscript

Samara Linton

Lost tongues

For those who are nostalgic for a land they can barely remember, purely because it was a place they could call their own. For those who embraced the growing pains of acculturation, because with them came the promise of opportunity and advance. For those who craft new identities, blending memories and stories, songs and tongues as they learn to redefine home.

I sampled these new tongues but my melody
Could not create harmony with theirs.
Our cries clashed and our laughs collided. Try, they insisted.
I went to their homes and ate their food and danced with their friends.
But they were not mine.
It was not them that I longed for.

You asked me to return to you but how could I?
I had been ensnared by the master's tongue.
It had tempted me with its eloquence, wooed me
With its power.
Its fame had me in awe and I learnt to bow.
My image of you was broken.
You were nothing but a fragmented, inferior replica. You were a slang, a fling.
I was bewitched by the master's tongue.
It made real my aspirations and limitless my ambitions.
But it was not mine.
And how can I master that which is not mine?
How can I pay homage to that which chained me?
How can I love that which did not birth me?

When I dream, I dream of you.
I hear your song and I am comforted,
My head is caressed by your lullaby,
And in your laugh I slumber.
Oh sweet tongue, how could I forget you?
You will always be my home.

Index